Shojo Beat

# Shuriken and Pleats 2

STORY & ART BY

**Matsuri Hino**

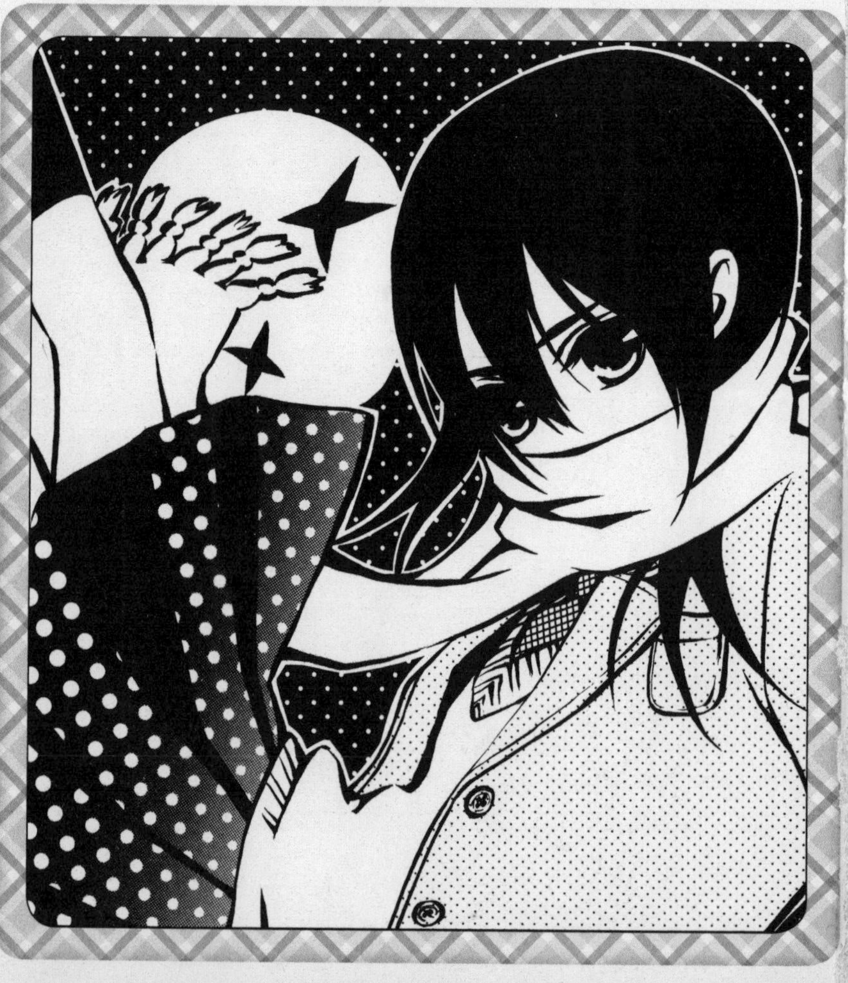

I thought it would be incredible to have a high school girl who puts her own life on the line to protect a stunning older man. I thought some men might have an interest in fiercely loyal and ridiculously serious high school girls. I hope you enjoyed this manga in which I loosened up a bit.

— MATSURI HINO —

**MATSURI HINO** burst onto the manga scene with her title *Kono Yume ga Sametara* (When This Dream Is Over), which was published in *LaLa DX* magazine. Hino was a manga artist a mere nine months after she decided to become one. With the success of her popular series *Captive Hearts*, *MeruPuri*, and *Vampire Knight*, Hino has established herself as a major player in the world of shojo manga.

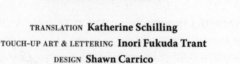

# Shuriken and Pleats ②

## SHOJO BEAT EDITION

### STORY & ART BY
## Matsuri Hino

TRANSLATION **Katherine Schilling**
TOUCH-UP ART & LETTERING **Inori Fukuda Trant**
DESIGN **Shawn Carrico**
EDITOR **Nancy Thistlethwaite**

Shuriken to Pleats by Matsuri Hino
© Matsuri Hino 2015
All rights reserved.
First published in Japan in 2015 by HAKUSENSHA, Inc., Tokyo.
English language translation rights arranged with HAKUSENSHA, Inc., Tokyo.

Printed in the U.S.A.

Published by VIZ Media, LLC
P.O. Box 77010
San Francisco, CA 94107

10 9 8 7 6 5 4 3 2 1
First printing, November 2016

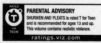
www.shojobeat.com    www.viz.com

# Shuriken and Pleats

vol. 2

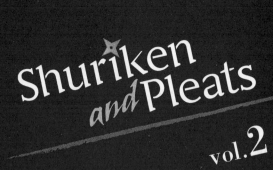

## Contents

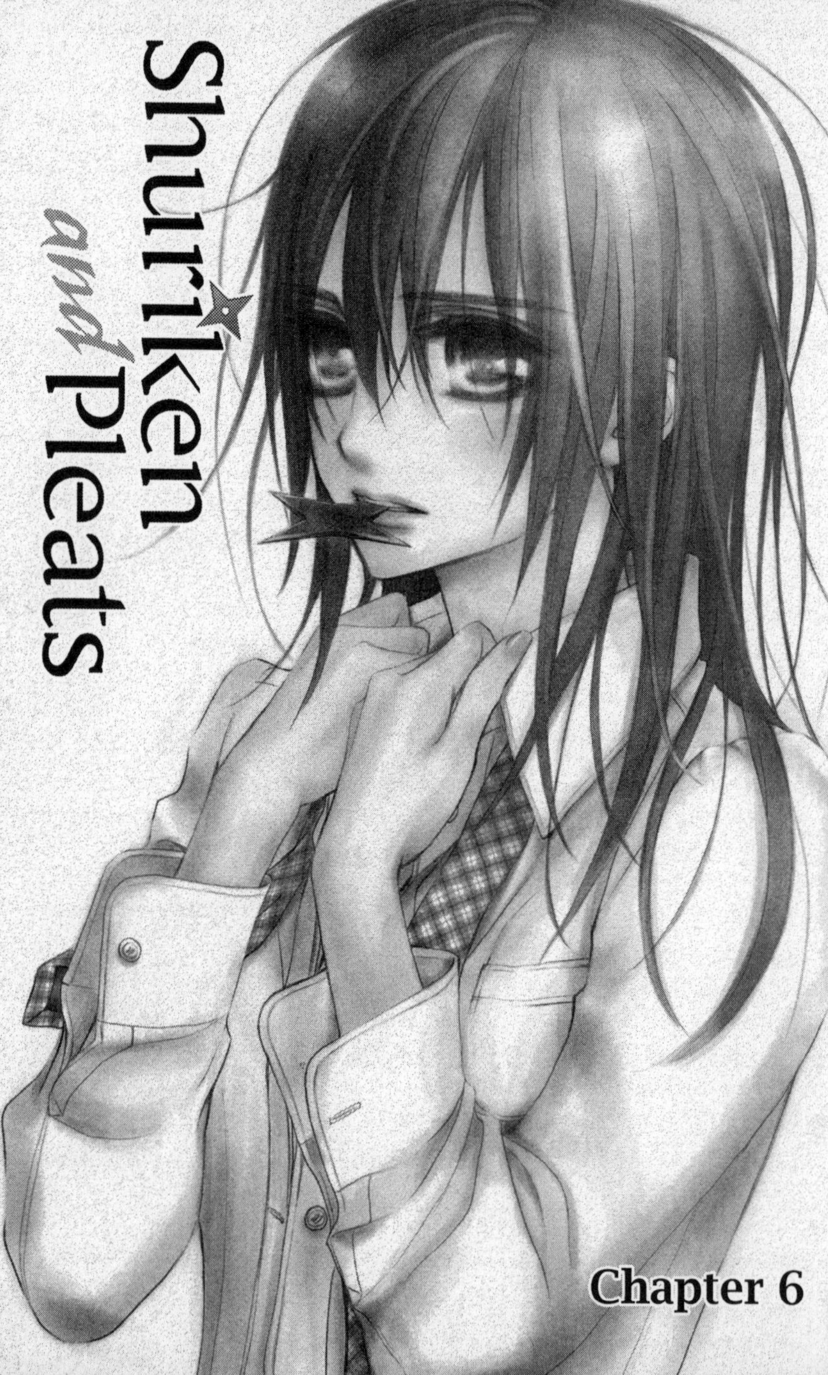
Shuriken and Pleats
Chapter 6

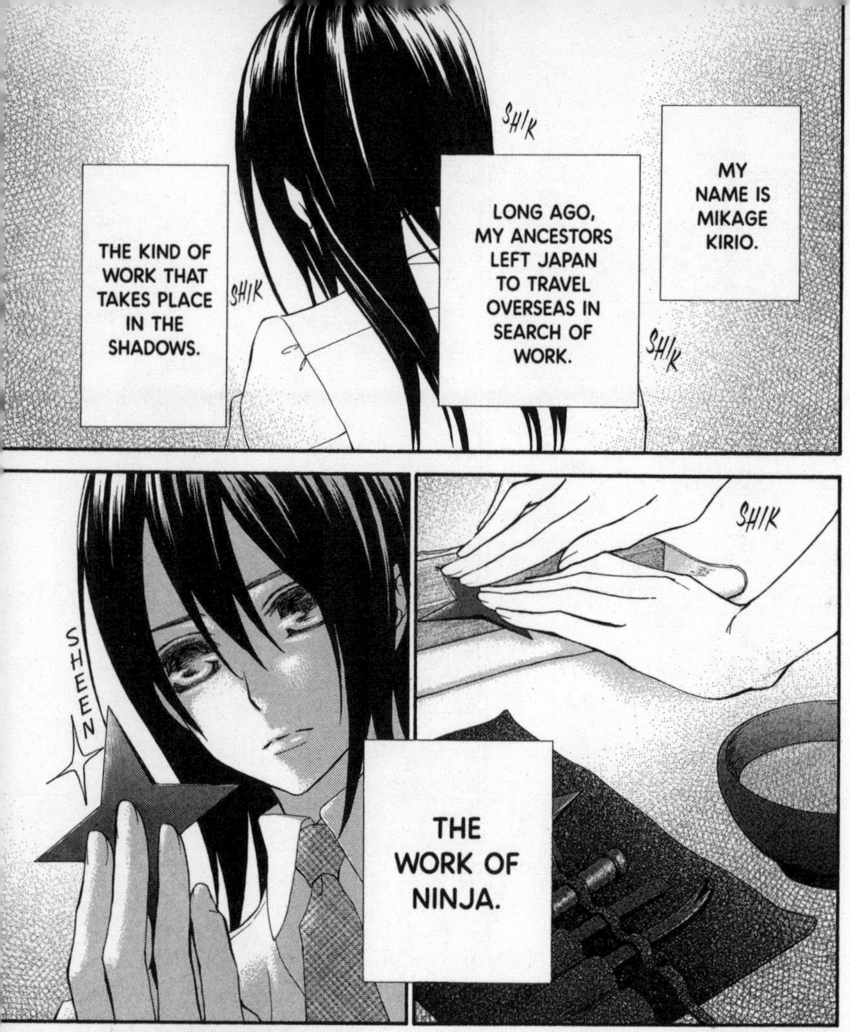
MY NAME IS MIKAGE KIRIO.
SHIK
LONG AGO, MY ANCESTORS LEFT JAPAN TO TRAVEL OVERSEAS IN SEARCH OF WORK.
SHIK
SHIK
THE KIND OF WORK THAT TAKES PLACE IN THE SHADOWS.
SHIK
THE WORK OF NINJA.
SHEEN

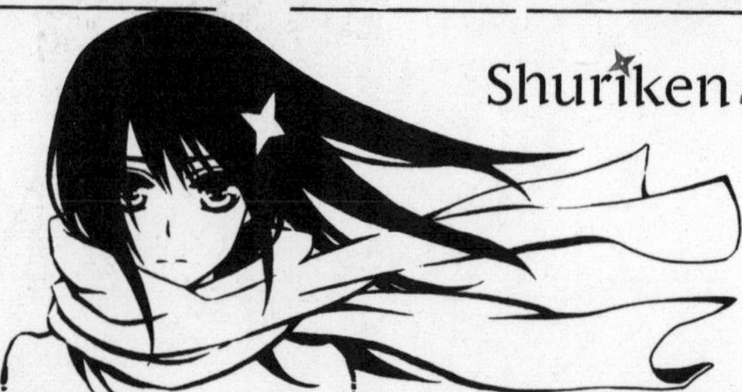

# Shuriken and Pleats

MATSURI HINO

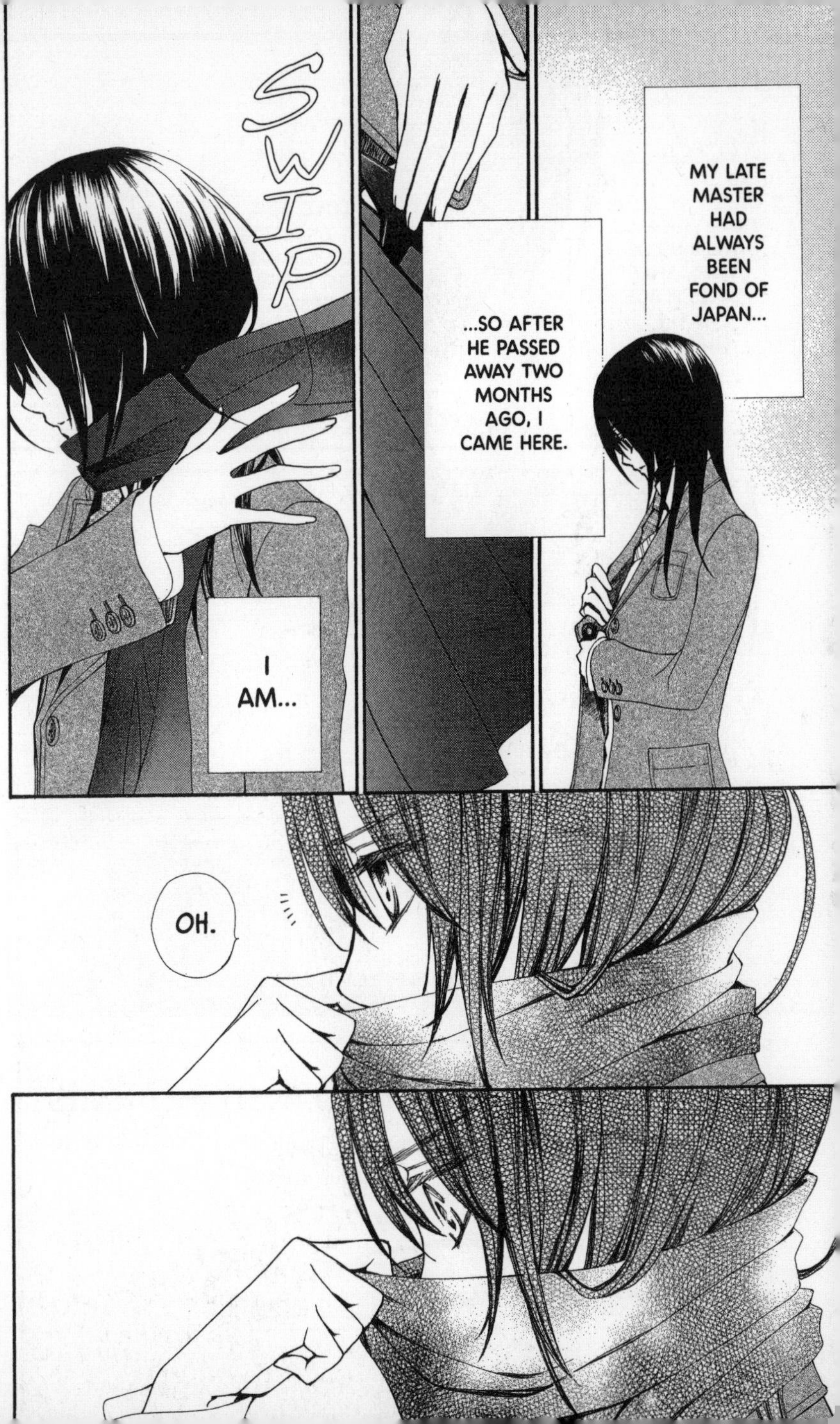
MY LATE MASTER HAD ALWAYS BEEN FOND OF JAPAN...
...SO AFTER HE PASSED AWAY TWO MONTHS AGO, I CAME HERE.
SWIP
I AM...
OH.

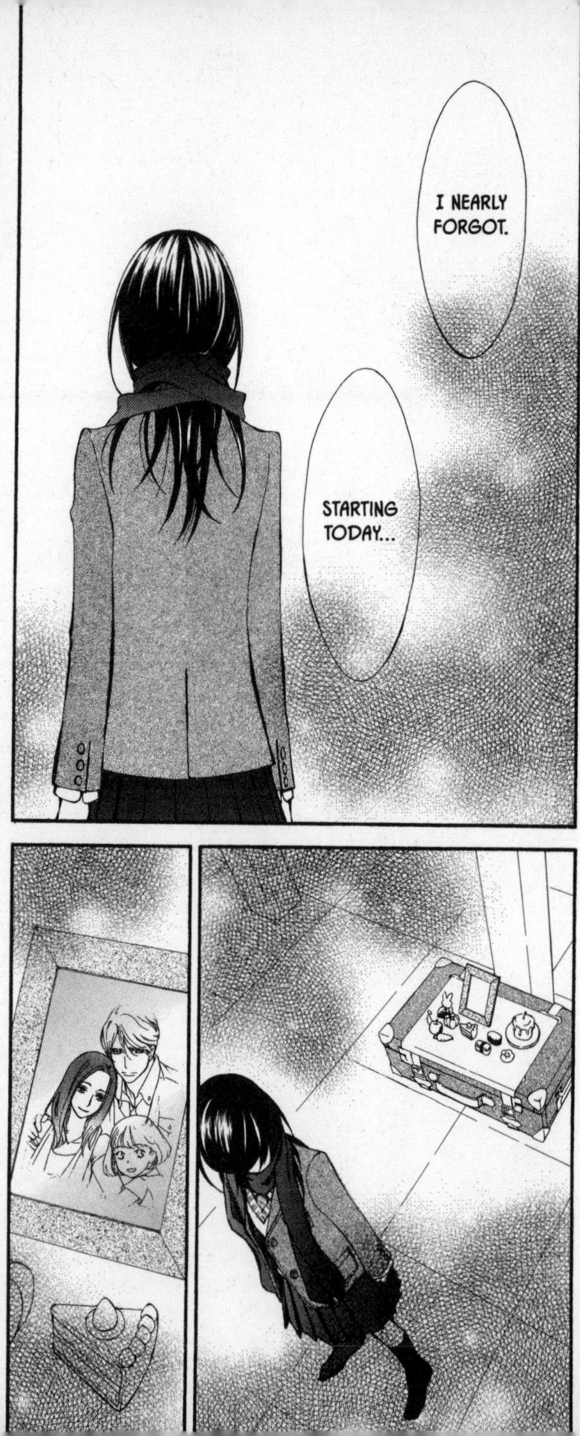
I NEARLY FORGOT.
STARTING TODAY...

Thank you for picking up this book. This is the second and final volume of *Shuriken and Pleats*! I always admired ninja and guards when I was a kid (and I love period pieces), so I always looked for books about ninja and imagined what it would be like to be one. As I was writing this, I tapped into the same childlike wonder I once had. This story started as an excuse to write about a stunning man who is protected by a super-cool high school girl, but it also contains that same nostalgia from my childhood. Despite its simple premise, this series now occupies a special place in my heart.

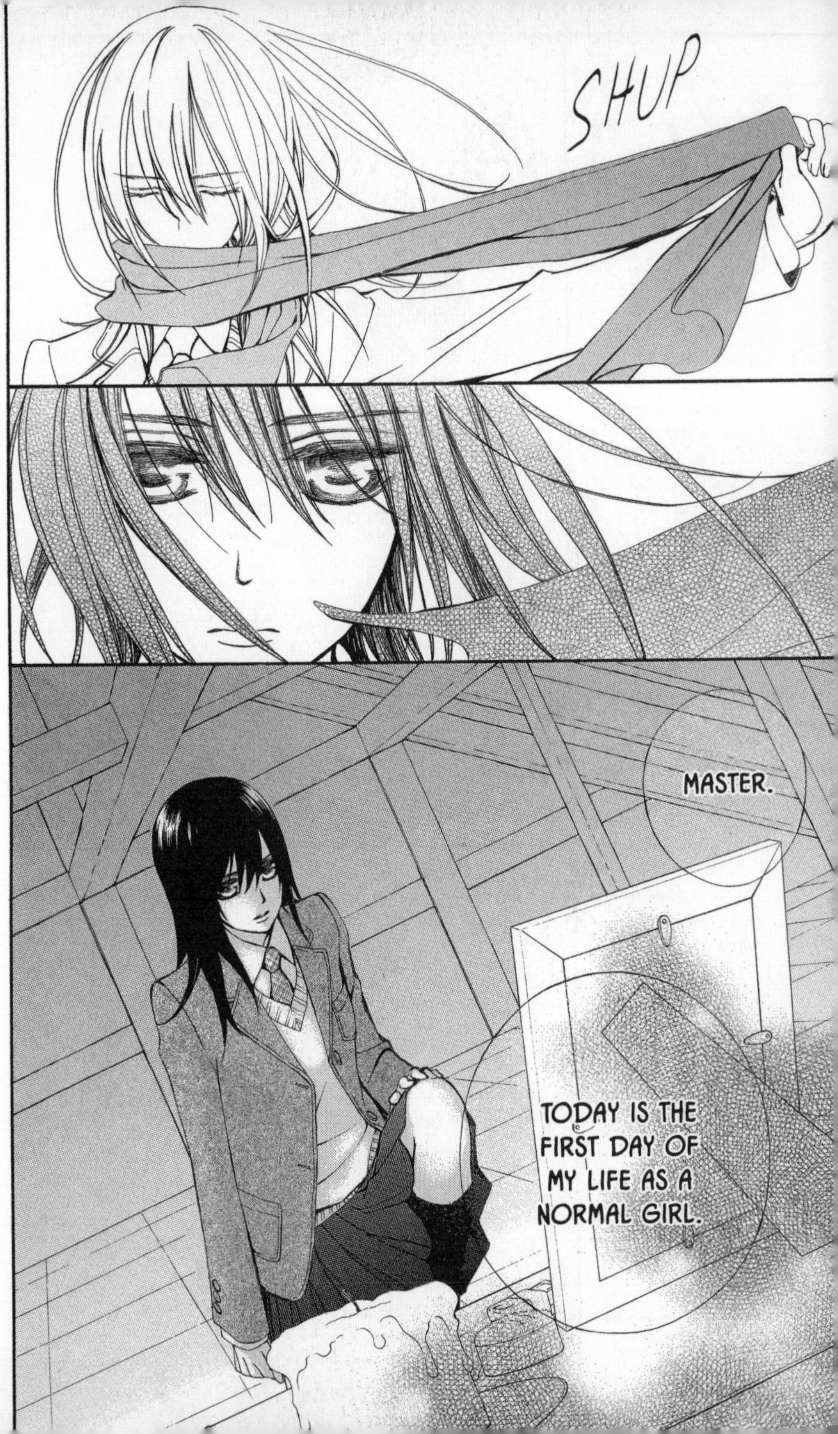
SHUP
MASTER.
TODAY IS THE FIRST DAY OF MY LIFE AS A NORMAL GIRL.

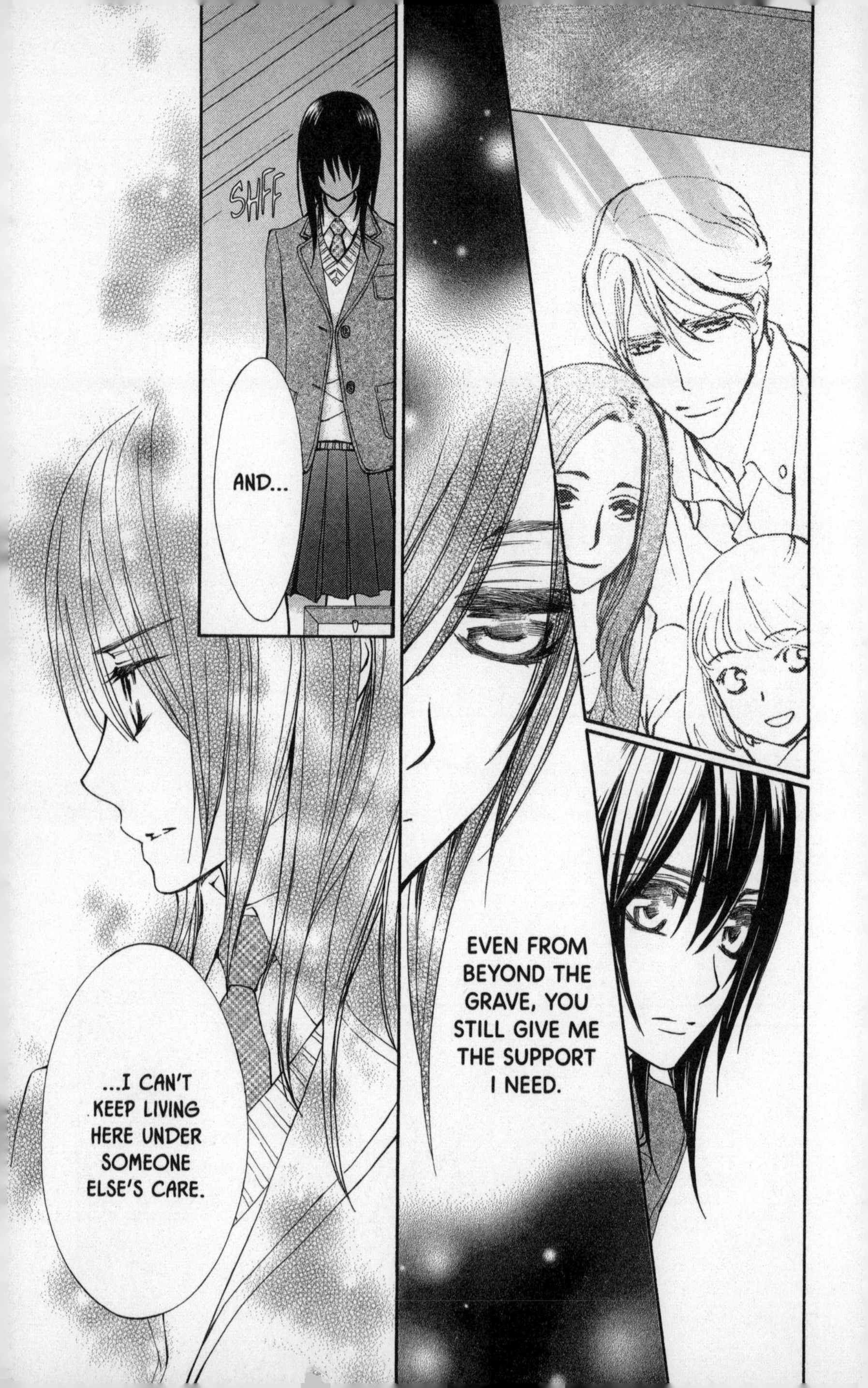
EVEN FROM BEYOND THE GRAVE, YOU STILL GIVE ME THE SUPPORT I NEED.
SHFF
AND...
...I CAN'T KEEP LIVING HERE UNDER SOMEONE ELSE'S CARE.

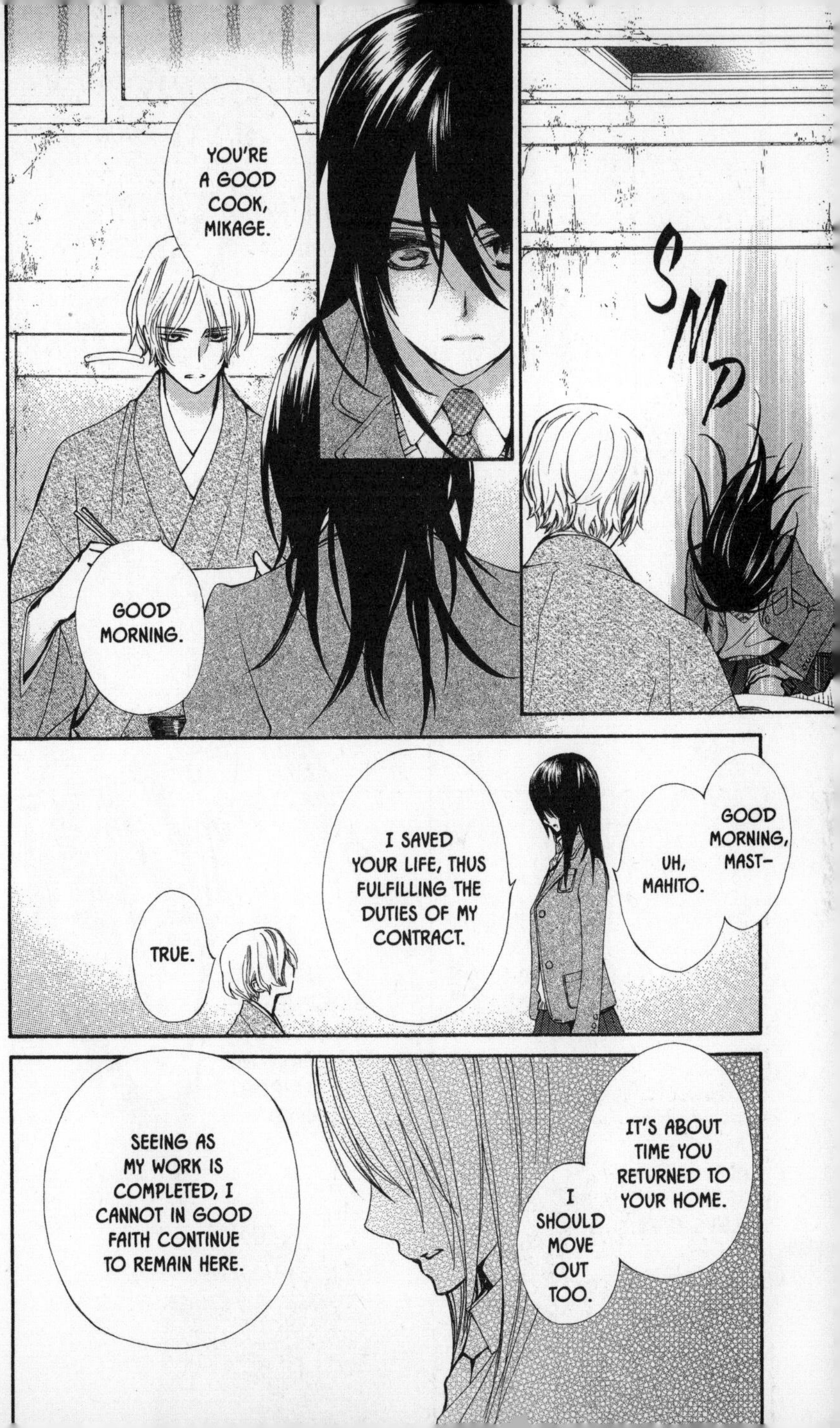
SMP
YOU'RE A GOOD COOK, MIKAGE.
GOOD MORNING.
GOOD MORNING, MAST—
UH, MAHITO.
I SAVED YOUR LIFE, THUS FULFILLING THE DUTIES OF MY CONTRACT.
TRUE.
IT'S ABOUT TIME YOU RETURNED TO YOUR HOME.
I SHOULD MOVE OUT TOO.
SEEING AS MY WORK IS COMPLETED, I CANNOT IN GOOD FAITH CONTINUE TO REMAIN HERE.

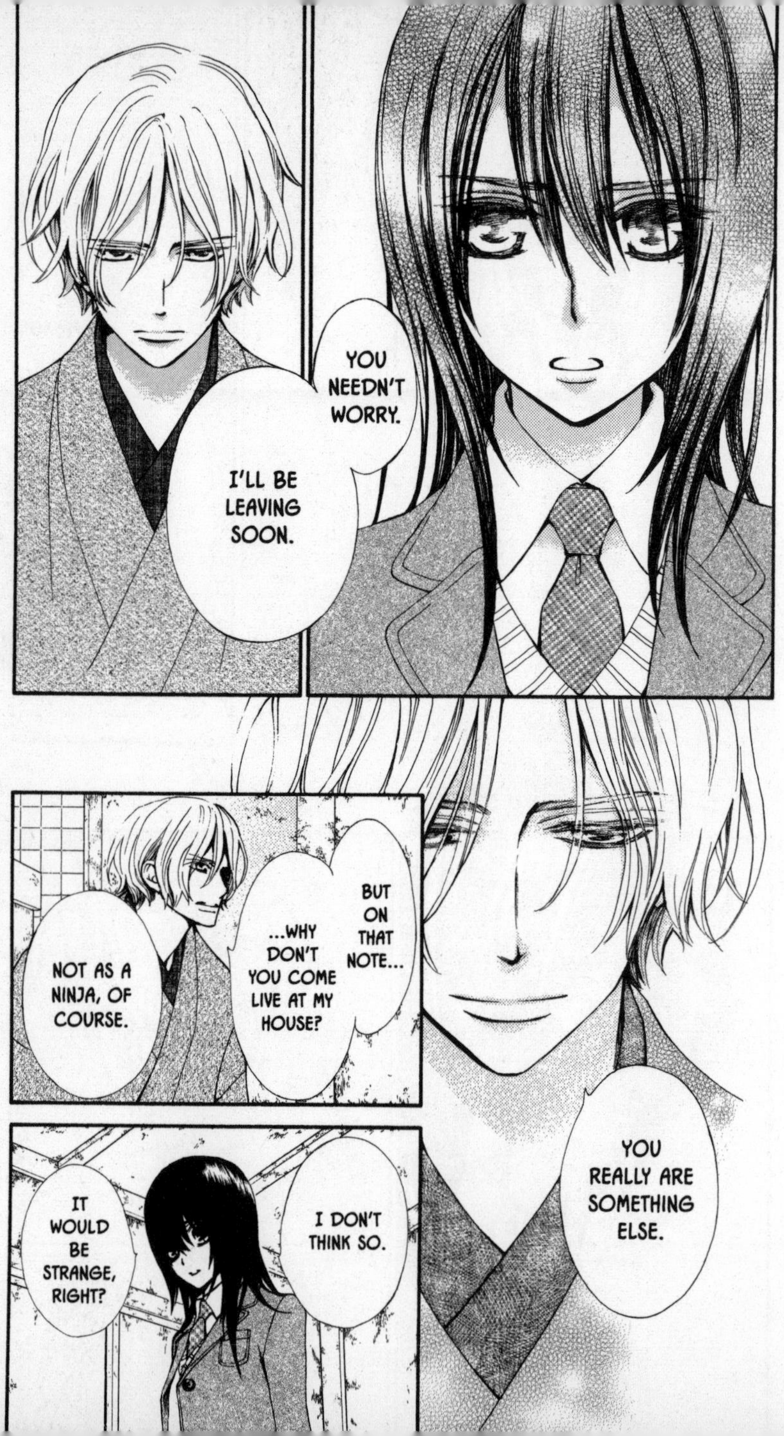
YOU NEEDN'T WORRY.
I'LL BE LEAVING SOON.
YOU REALLY ARE SOMETHING ELSE.
BUT ON THAT NOTE...
...WHY DON'T YOU COME LIVE AT MY HOUSE?
NOT AS A NINJA, OF COURSE.
I DON'T THINK SO.
IT WOULD BE STRANGE, RIGHT?

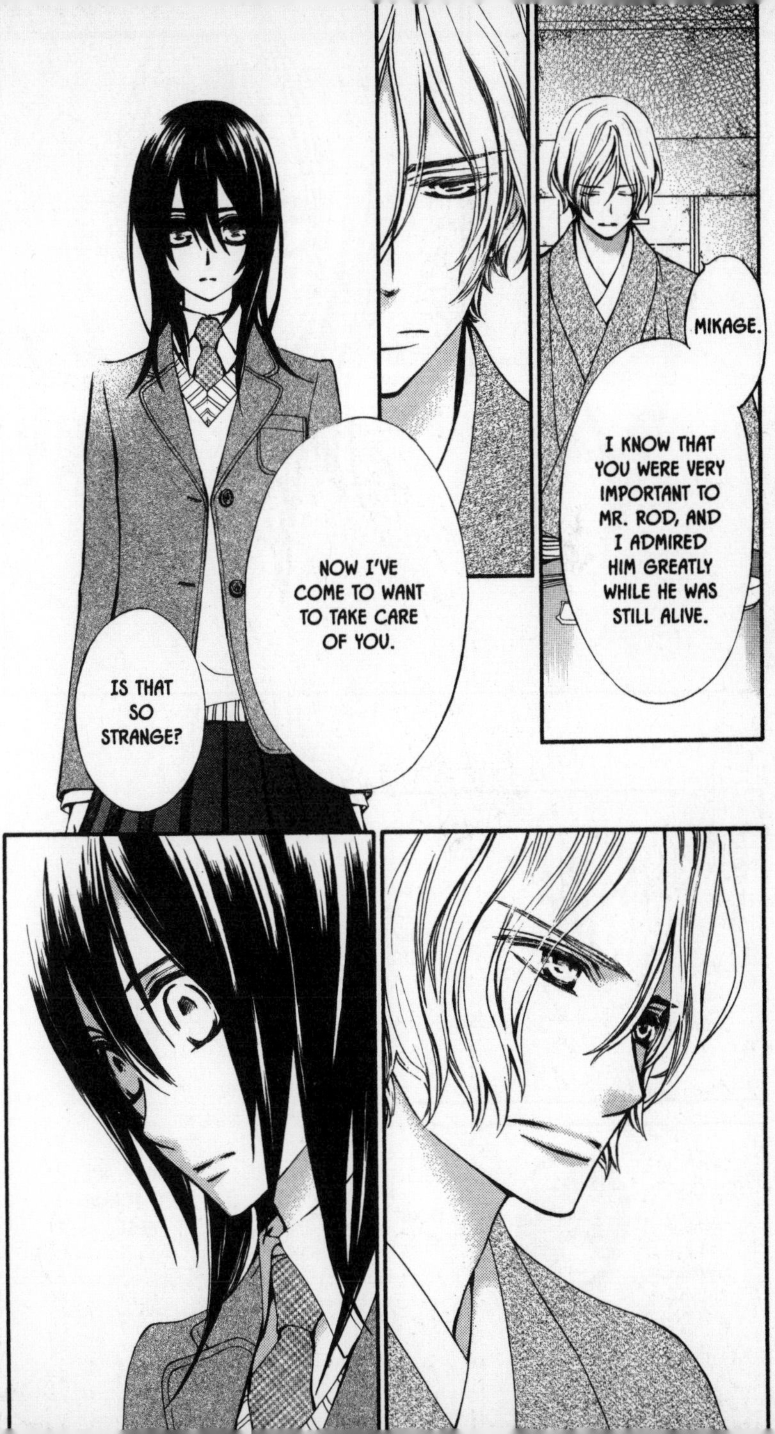
MIKAGE.
I KNOW THAT YOU WERE VERY IMPORTANT TO MR. ROD, AND I ADMIRED HIM GREATLY WHILE HE WAS STILL ALIVE.
NOW I'VE COME TO WANT TO TAKE CARE OF YOU.
IS THAT SO STRANGE?

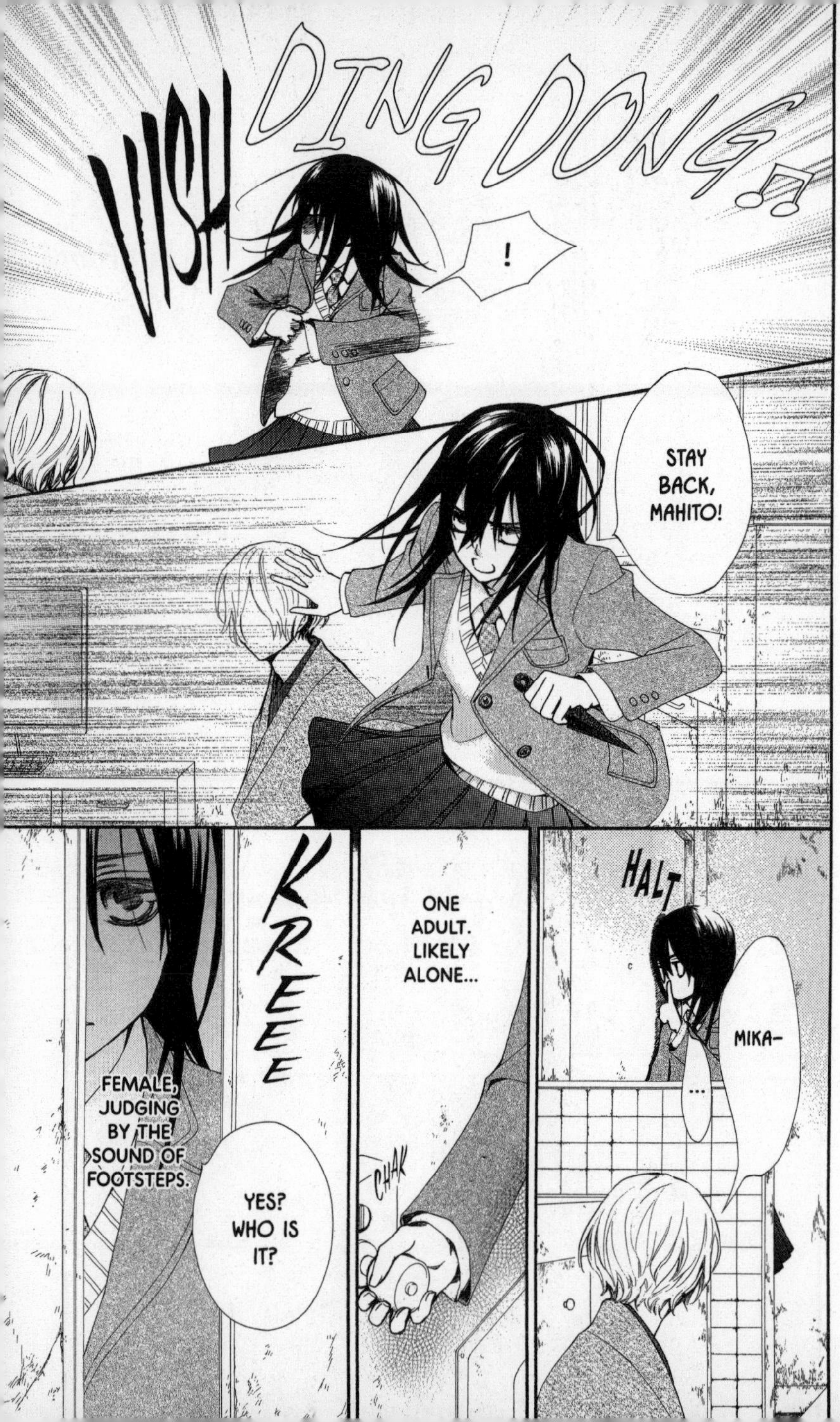
DING DONG
VISH
!
STAY BACK, MAHITO!
HALT
MIKA-
...
ONE ADULT. LIKELY ALONE...
CHAK
KREEE
FEMALE, JUDGING BY THE SOUND OF FOOTSTEPS.
YES? WHO IS IT?

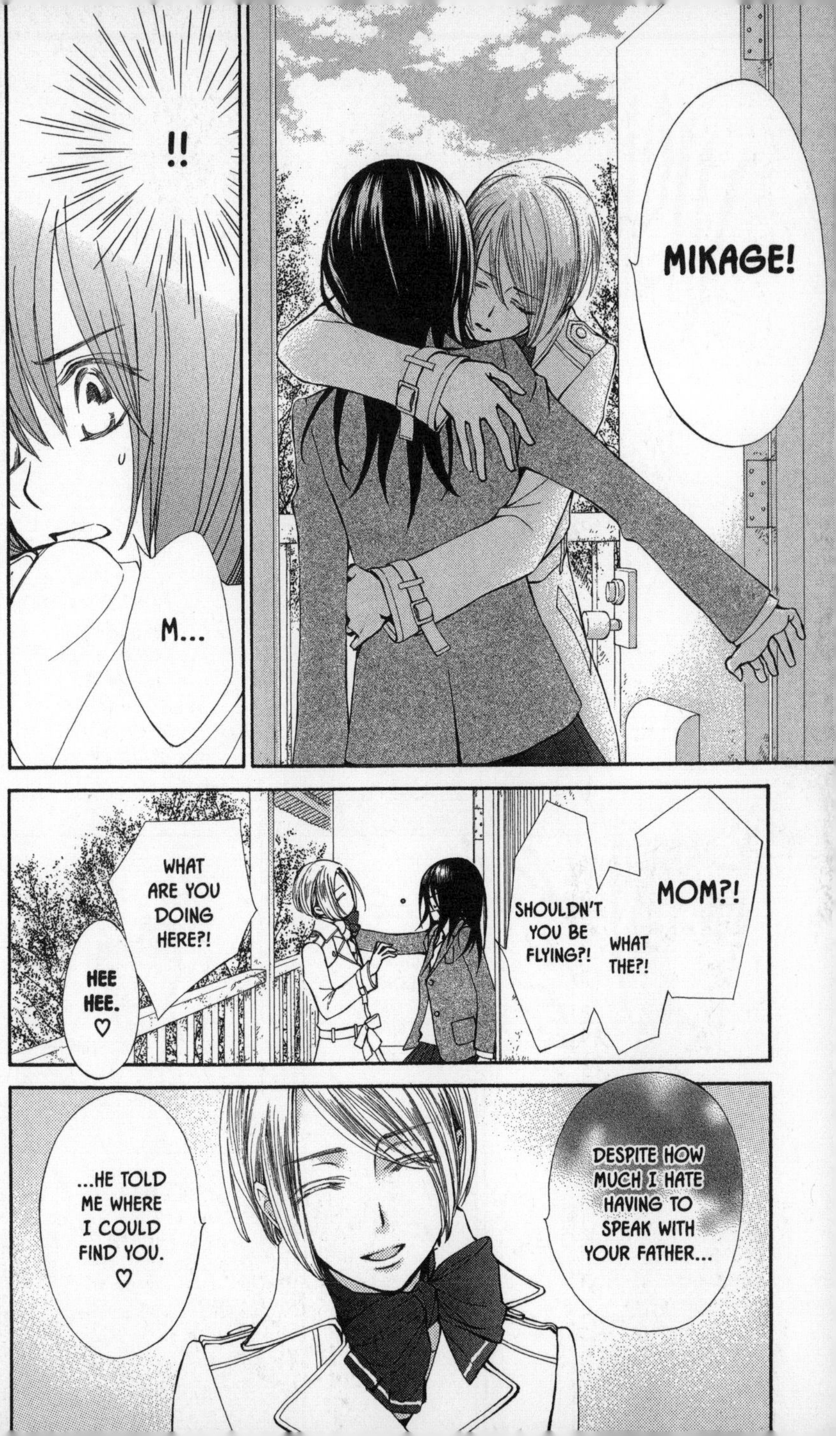
MIKAGE!
!!
M...
MOM?!
WHAT THE?!
SHOULDN'T YOU BE FLYING?!
WHAT ARE YOU DOING HERE?!
HEE HEE. ♡
DESPITE HOW MUCH I HATE HAVING TO SPEAK WITH YOUR FATHER...
...HE TOLD ME WHERE I COULD FIND YOU. ♡

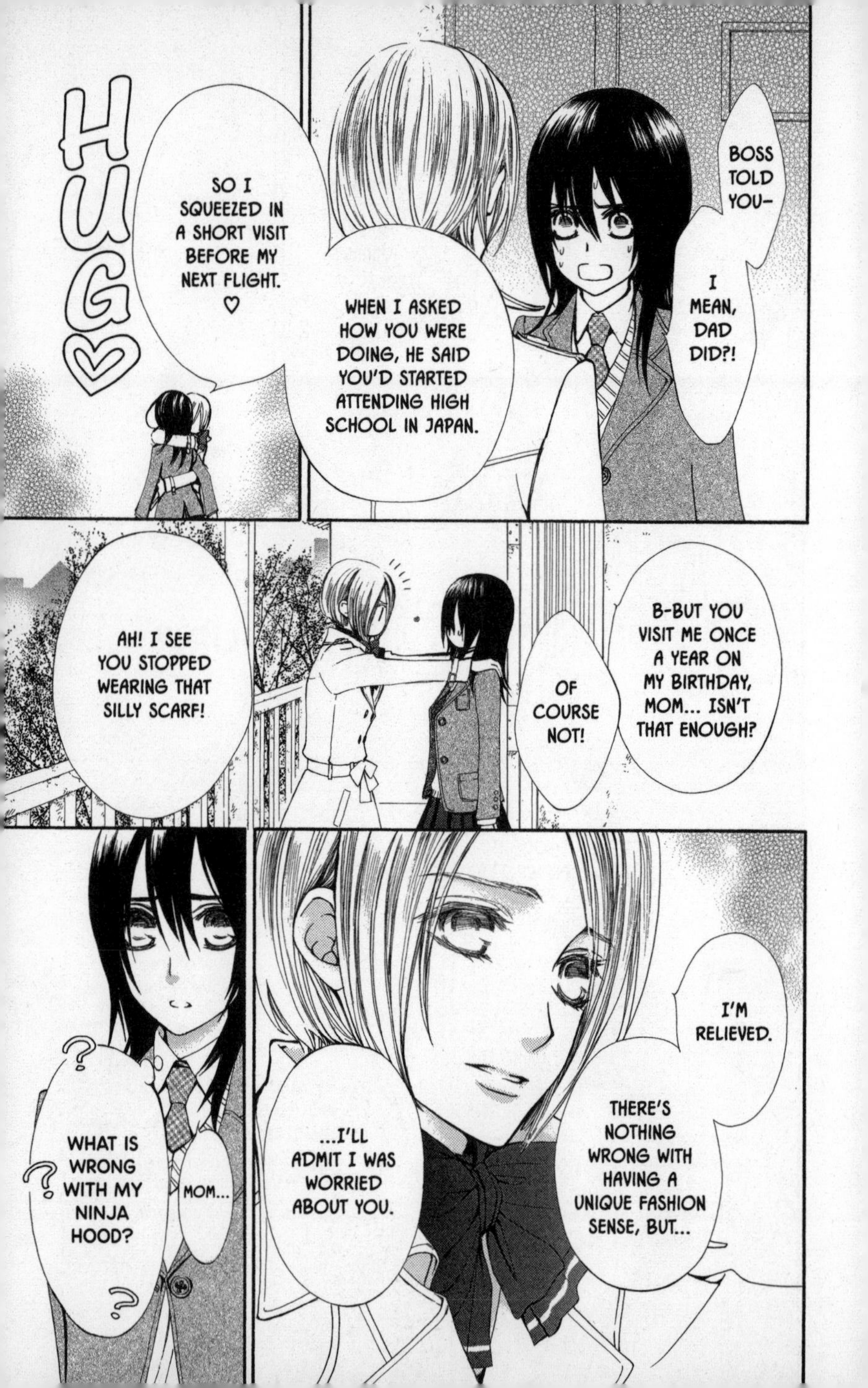
BOSS TOLD YOU-
I MEAN, DAD DID?!
WHEN I ASKED HOW YOU WERE DOING, HE SAID YOU'D STARTED ATTENDING HIGH SCHOOL IN JAPAN.
SO I SQUEEZED IN A SHORT VISIT BEFORE MY NEXT FLIGHT. ♡
HUG ♡
B-BUT YOU VISIT ME ONCE A YEAR ON MY BIRTHDAY, MOM... ISN'T THAT ENOUGH?
OF COURSE NOT!
AH! I SEE YOU STOPPED WEARING THAT SILLY SCARF!
I'M RELIEVED.
THERE'S NOTHING WRONG WITH HAVING A UNIQUE FASHION SENSE, BUT...
...I'LL ADMIT I WAS WORRIED ABOUT YOU.
MOM...
WHAT IS WRONG WITH MY NINJA HOOD?

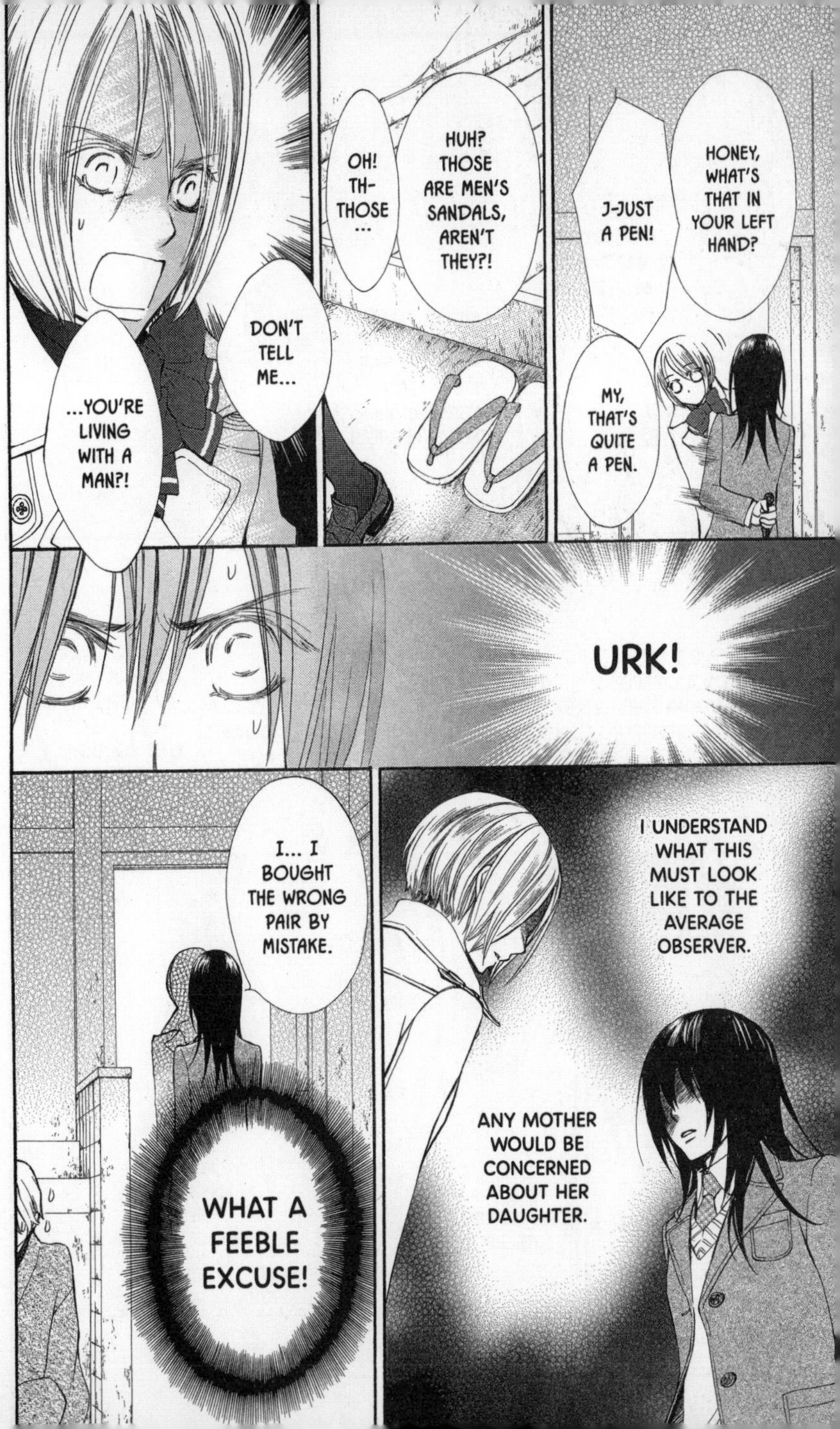
HONEY, WHAT'S THAT IN YOUR LEFT HAND?
J-JUST A PEN!
MY, THAT'S QUITE A PEN.
HUH? THOSE ARE MEN'S SANDALS, AREN'T THEY?!
OH! TH-THOSE...
DON'T TELL ME...
...YOU'RE LIVING WITH A MAN?!
URK!
I UNDERSTAND WHAT THIS MUST LOOK LIKE TO THE AVERAGE OBSERVER.
ANY MOTHER WOULD BE CONCERNED ABOUT HER DAUGHTER.
I... I BOUGHT THE WRONG PAIR BY MISTAKE.
WHAT A FEEBLE EXCUSE!

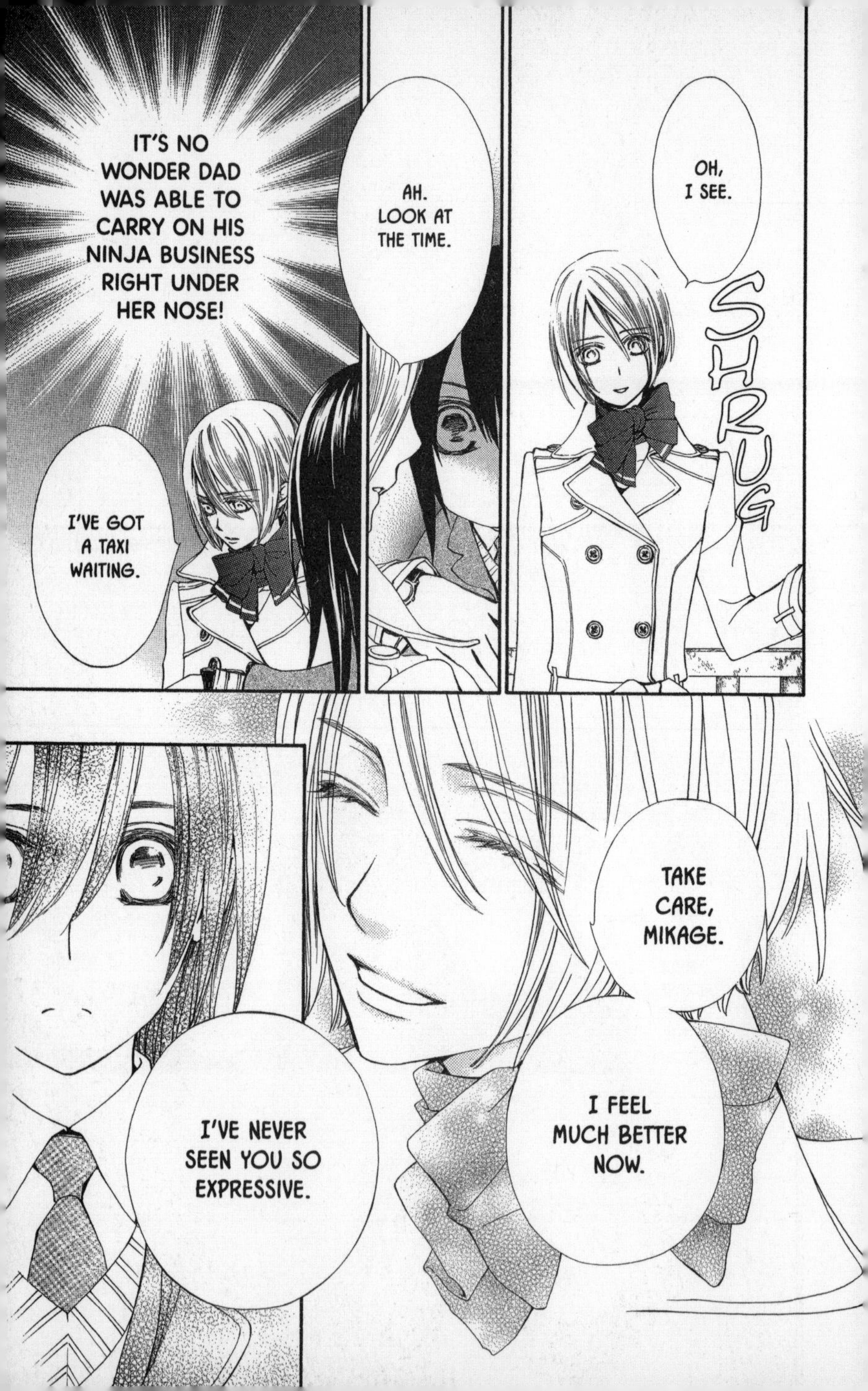
OH, I SEE.
SHRUG
AH. LOOK AT THE TIME.
IT'S NO WONDER DAD WAS ABLE TO CARRY ON HIS NINJA BUSINESS RIGHT UNDER HER NOSE!
I'VE GOT A TAXI WAITING.
TAKE CARE, MIKAGE.
I FEEL MUCH BETTER NOW.
I'VE NEVER SEEN YOU SO EXPRESSIVE.

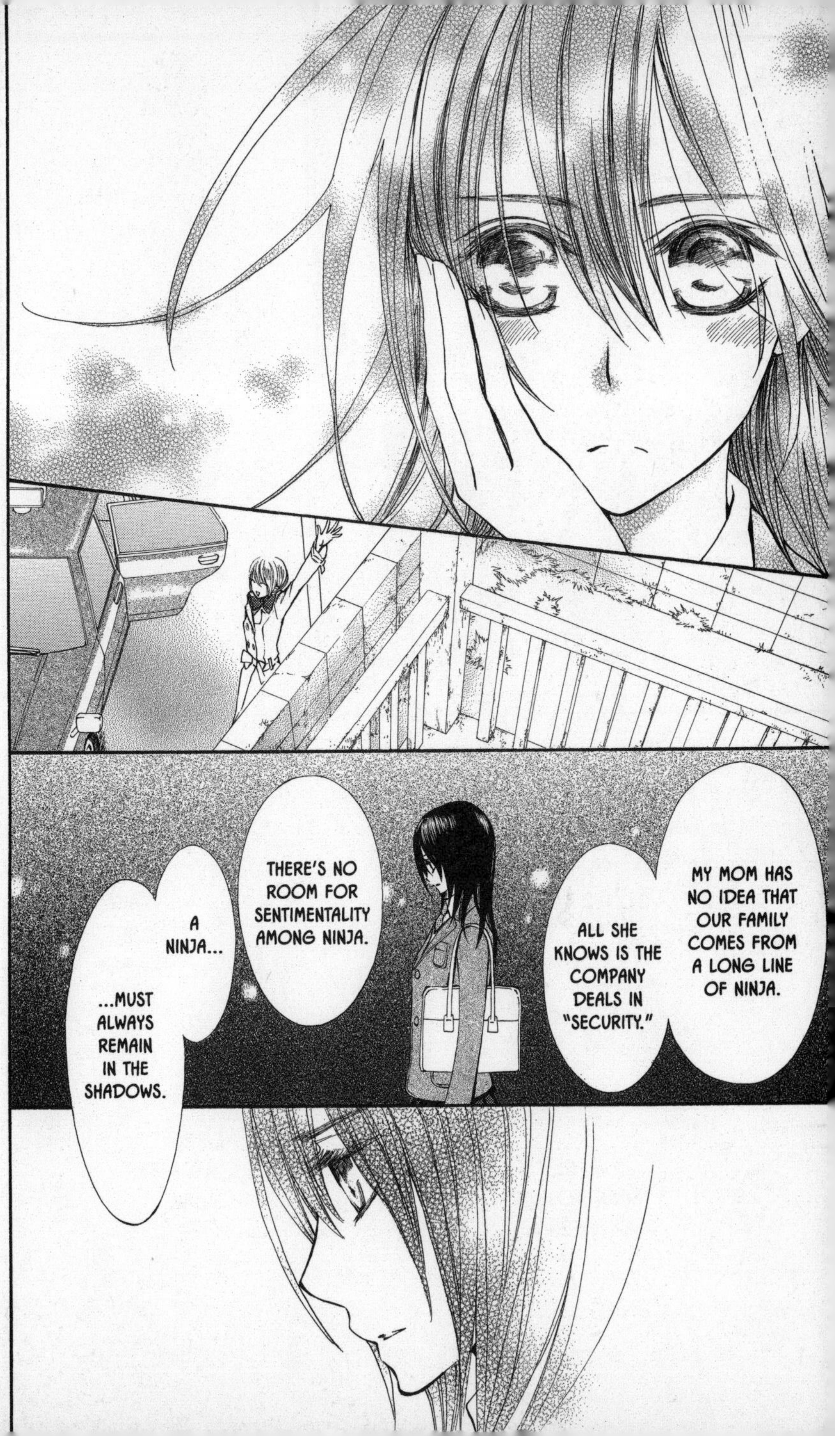
MY MOM HAS NO IDEA THAT OUR FAMILY COMES FROM A LONG LINE OF NINJA.
ALL SHE KNOWS IS THE COMPANY DEALS IN "SECURITY."
THERE'S NO ROOM FOR SENTIMENTALITY AMONG NINJA.
A NINJA...
...MUST ALWAYS REMAIN IN THE SHADOWS.

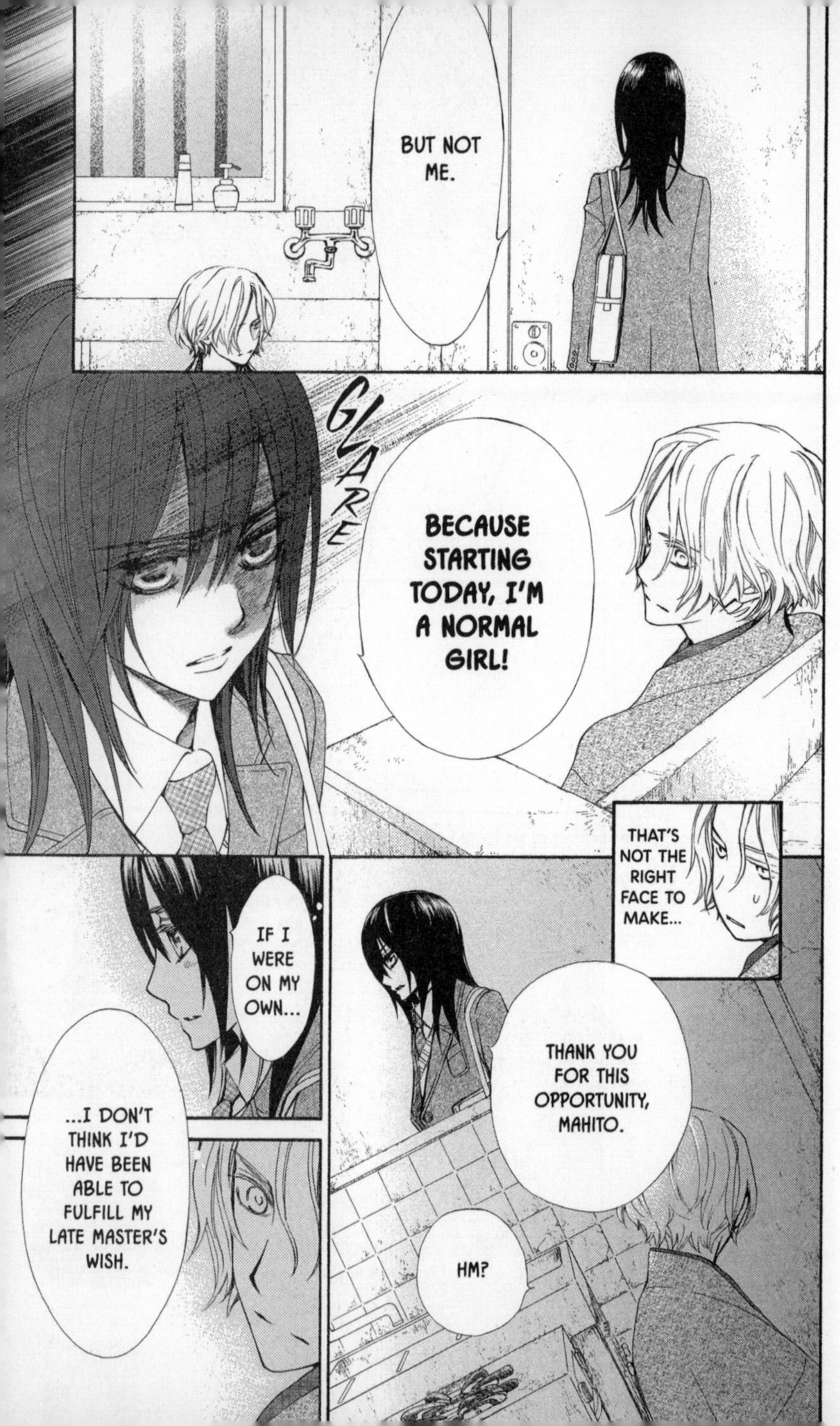
BUT NOT ME.
GLARE
BECAUSE STARTING TODAY, I'M A NORMAL GIRL!
THAT'S NOT THE RIGHT FACE TO MAKE...
THANK YOU FOR THIS OPPORTUNITY, MAHITO.
HM?
IF I WERE ON MY OWN...
...I DON'T THINK I'D HAVE BEEN ABLE TO FULFILL MY LATE MASTER'S WISH.

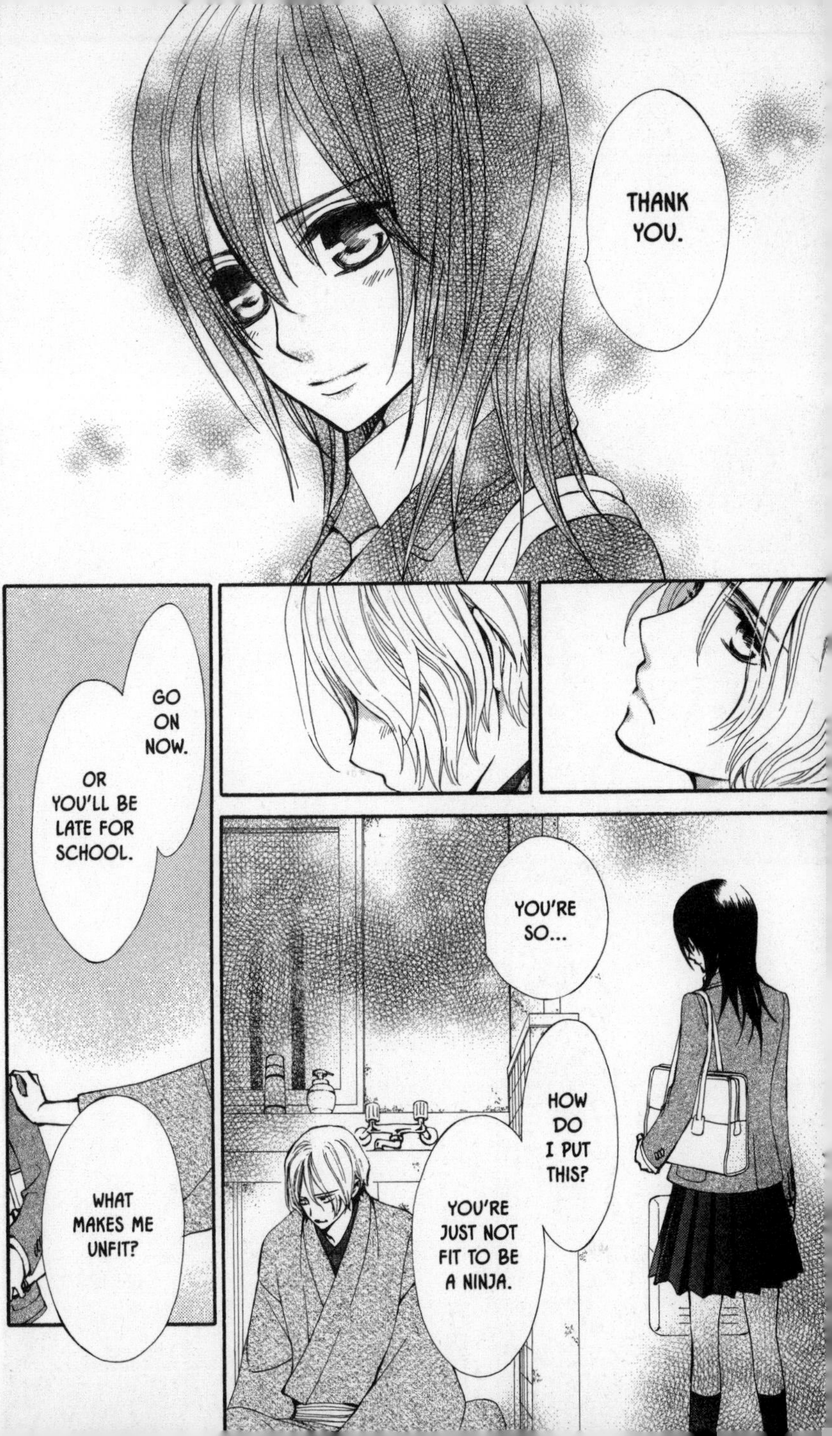
THANK YOU.
YOU'RE SO...
HOW DO I PUT THIS?
YOU'RE JUST NOT FIT TO BE A NINJA.
GO ON NOW.
OR YOU'LL BE LATE FOR SCHOOL.
WHAT MAKES ME UNFIT?

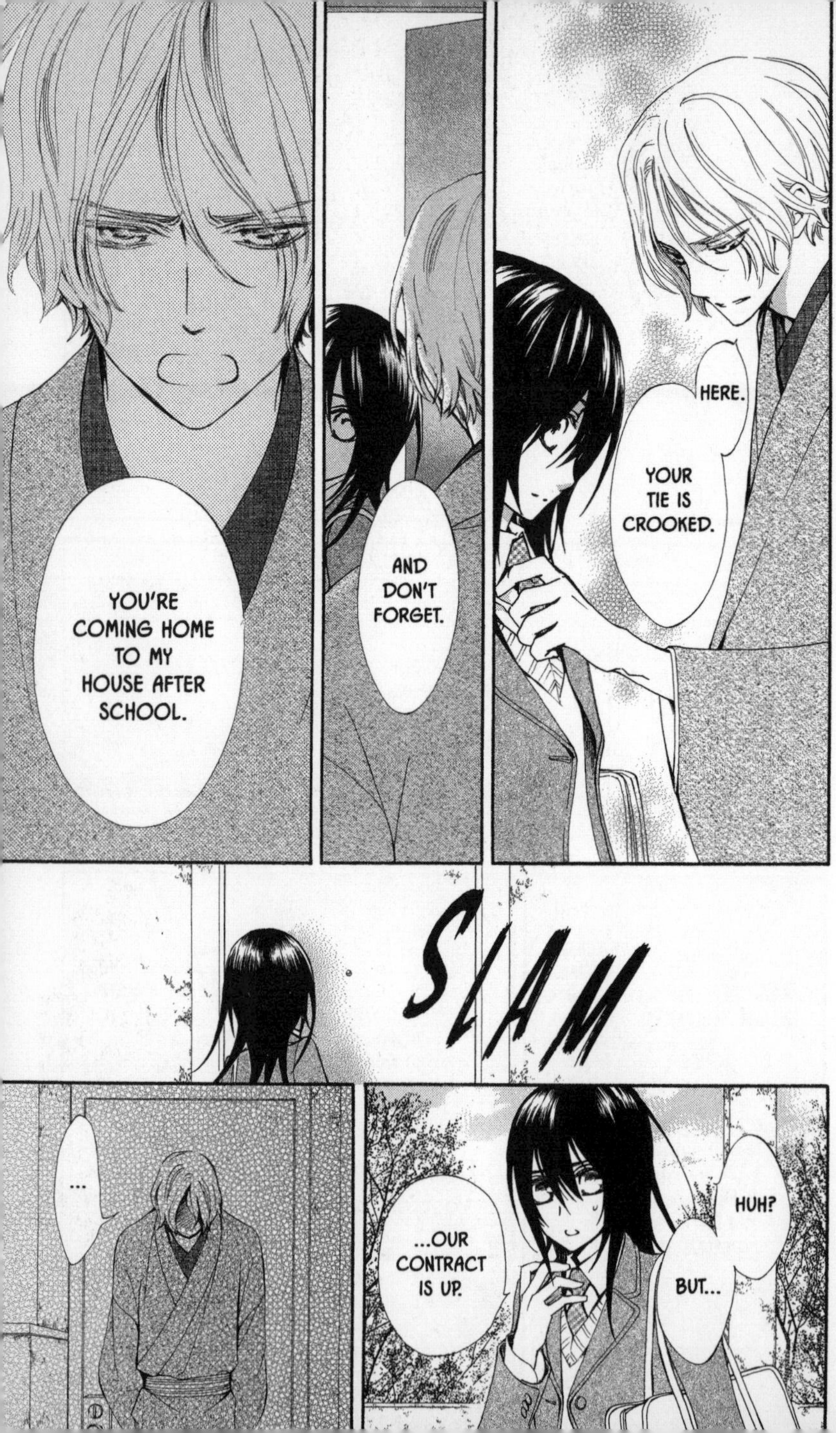
HERE.
YOUR TIE IS CROOKED.
AND DON'T FORGET.
YOU'RE COMING HOME TO MY HOUSE AFTER SCHOOL.
SLAM
HUH?
BUT...
...OUR CONTRACT IS UP.
...

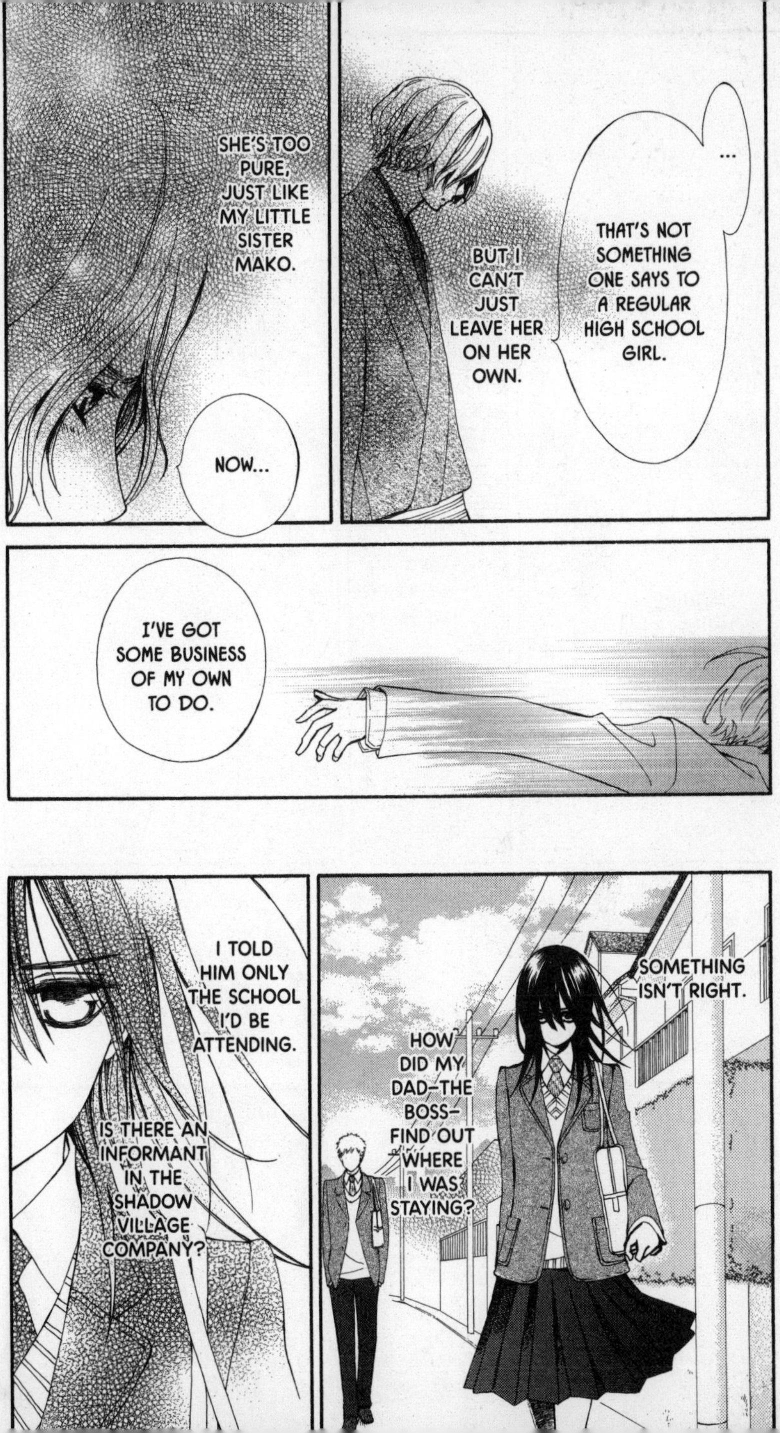
...
THAT'S NOT SOMETHING ONE SAYS TO A REGULAR HIGH SCHOOL GIRL.
BUT I CAN'T JUST LEAVE HER ON HER OWN.
SHE'S TOO PURE, JUST LIKE MY LITTLE SISTER MAKO.
NOW...
I'VE GOT SOME BUSINESS OF MY OWN TO DO.
SOMETHING ISN'T RIGHT.
HOW DID MY DAD—THE BOSS—FIND OUT WHERE I WAS STAYING?
I TOLD HIM ONLY THE SCHOOL I'D BE ATTENDING.
IS THERE AN INFORMANT IN THE SHADOW VILLAGE COMPANY?

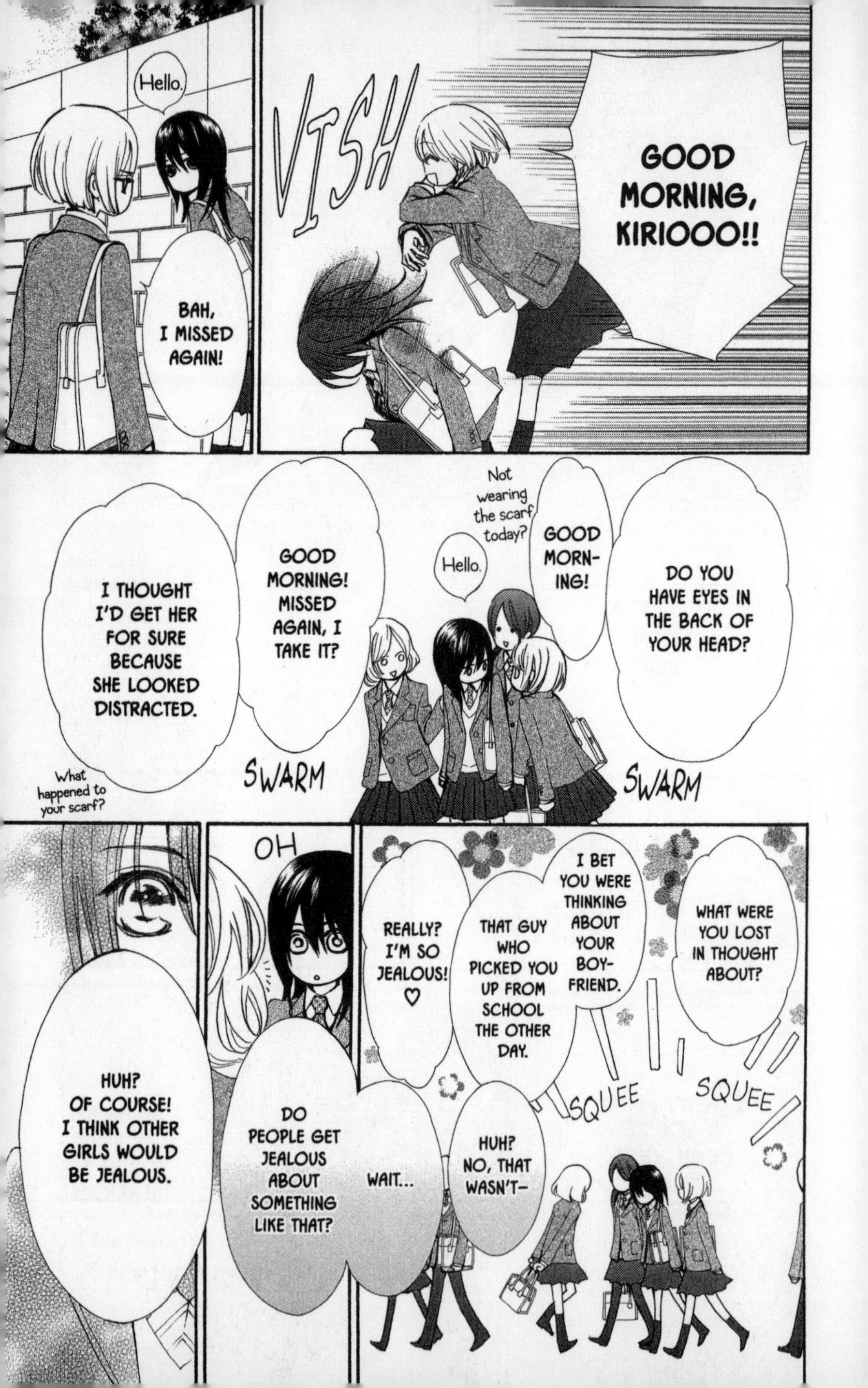
GOOD MORNING, KIRIOOO!!
VISH
Hello.
BAH, I MISSED AGAIN!
DO YOU HAVE EYES IN THE BACK OF YOUR HEAD?
GOOD MORN-ING!
Not wearing the scarf today?
Hello.
GOOD MORNING! MISSED AGAIN, I TAKE IT?
I THOUGHT I'D GET HER FOR SURE BECAUSE SHE LOOKED DISTRACTED.
SWARM
SWARM
What happened to your scarf?
WHAT WERE YOU LOST IN THOUGHT ABOUT?
I BET YOU WERE THINKING ABOUT YOUR BOY-FRIEND.
THAT GUY WHO PICKED YOU UP FROM SCHOOL THE OTHER DAY.
REALLY? I'M SO JEALOUS! ♡
SQUEE
SQUEE
HUH? NO, THAT WASN'T-
WAIT...
OH
DO PEOPLE GET JEALOUS ABOUT SOMETHING LIKE THAT?
HUH? OF COURSE! I THINK OTHER GIRLS WOULD BE JEALOUS.

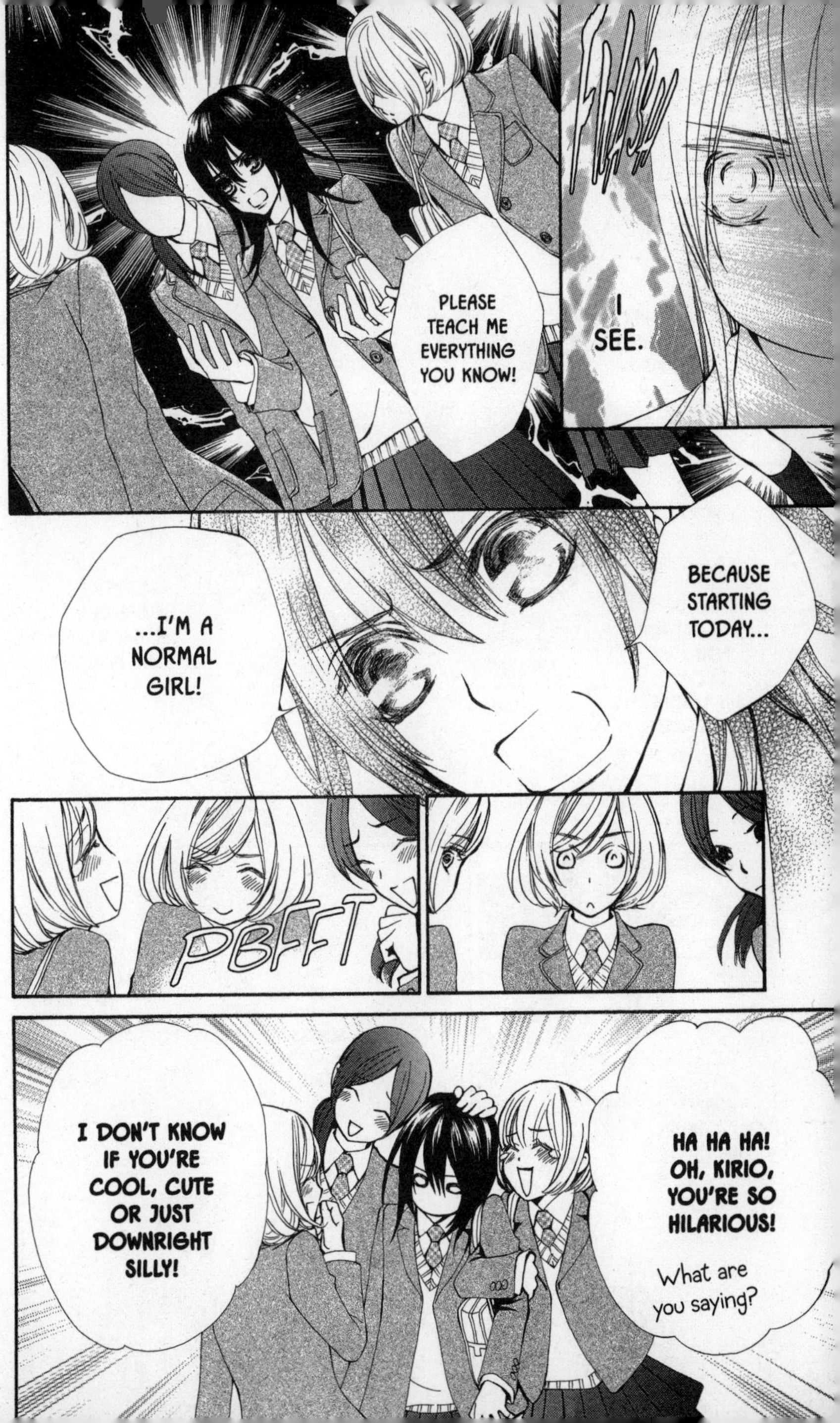
I SEE.
PLEASE TEACH ME EVERYTHING YOU KNOW!
BECAUSE STARTING TODAY...
...I'M A NORMAL GIRL!
PBFFT
HA HA HA! OH, KIRIO, YOU'RE SO HILARIOUS!
What are you saying?
I DON'T KNOW IF YOU'RE COOL, CUTE OR JUST DOWNRIGHT SILLY!

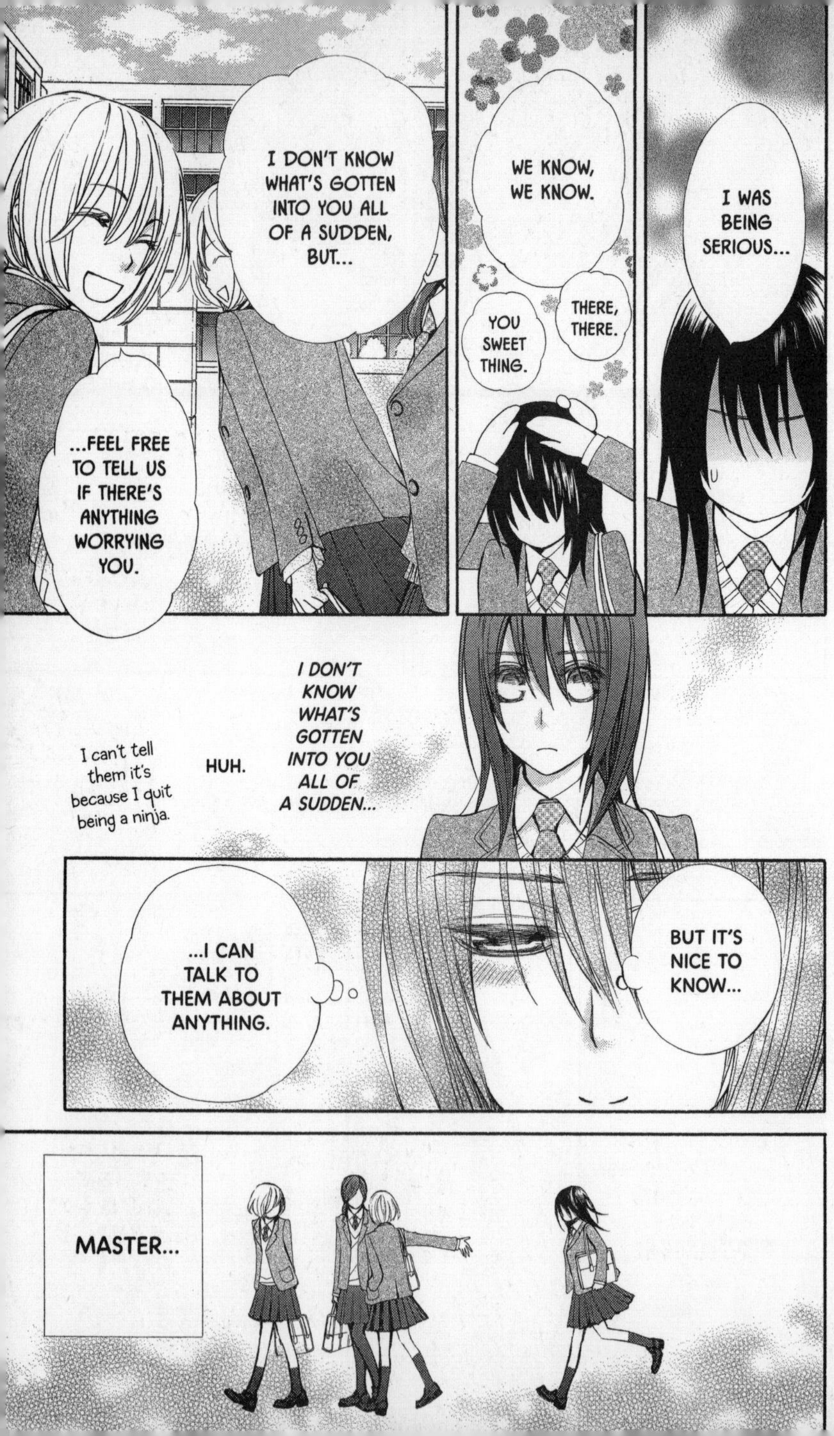
I WAS BEING SERIOUS...
WE KNOW, WE KNOW.
THERE, THERE.
YOU SWEET THING.
I DON'T KNOW WHAT'S GOTTEN INTO YOU ALL OF A SUDDEN, BUT...
...FEEL FREE TO TELL US IF THERE'S ANYTHING WORRYING YOU.
I DON'T KNOW WHAT'S GOTTEN INTO YOU ALL OF A SUDDEN...
HUH.
I can't tell them it's because I quit being a ninja.
BUT IT'S NICE TO KNOW...
...I CAN TALK TO THEM ABOUT ANYTHING.
MASTER...

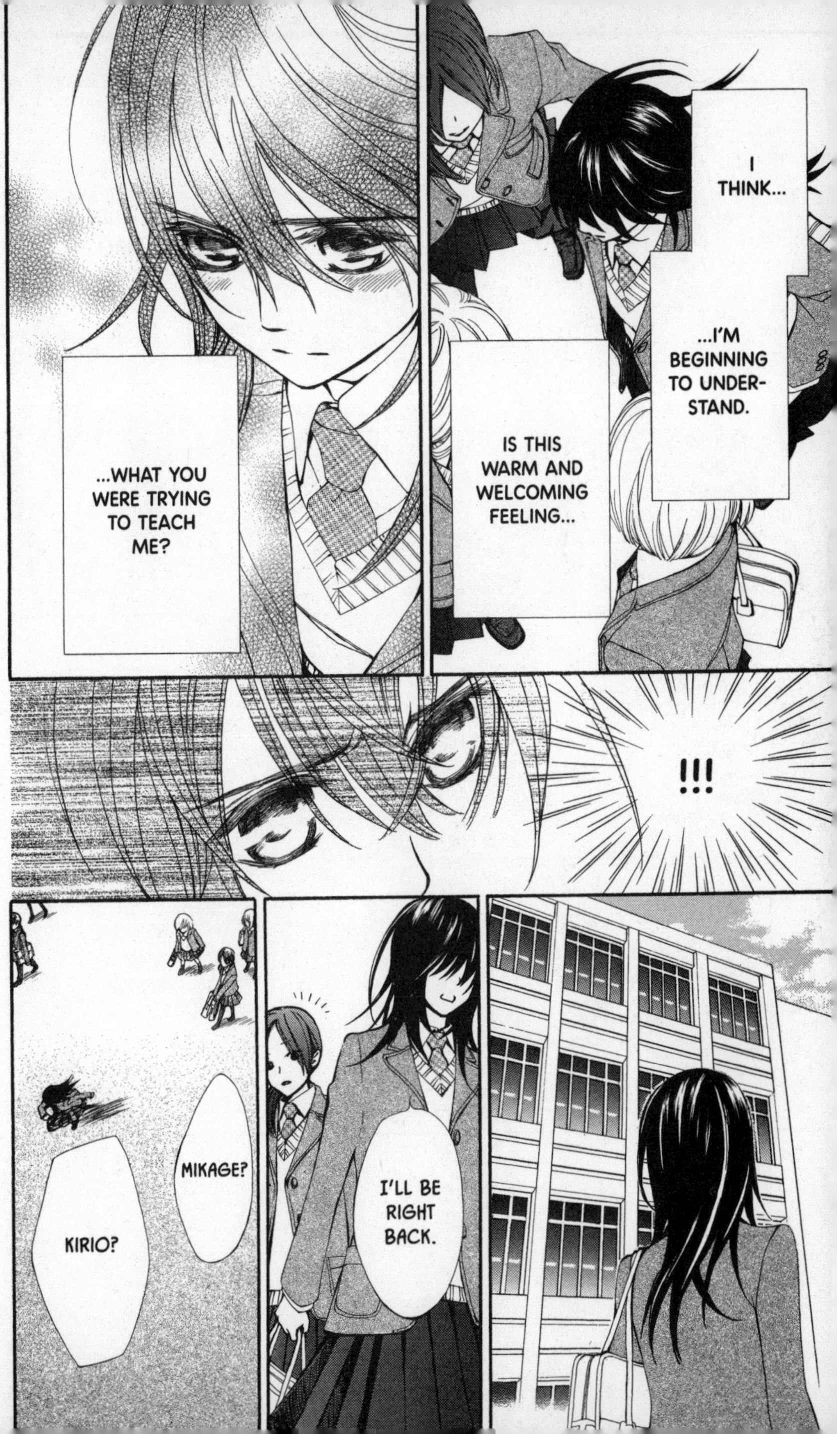
I THINK...
...I'M BEGINNING TO UNDER-STAND.
IS THIS WARM AND WELCOMING FEELING...
...WHAT YOU WERE TRYING TO TEACH ME?
!!!
I'LL BE RIGHT BACK.
MIKAGE?
KIRIO?

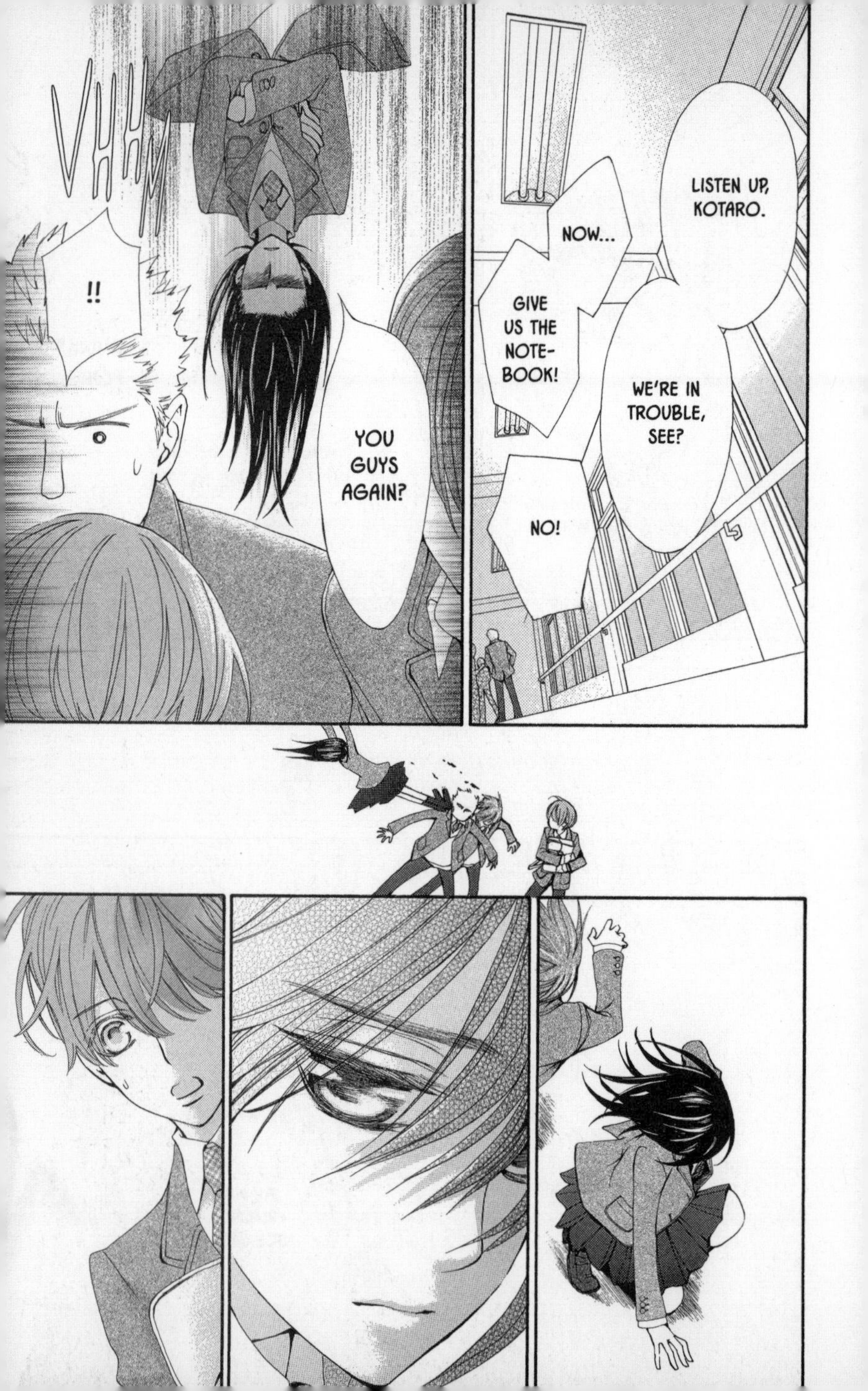
LISTEN UP, KOTARO.
NOW...
WE'RE IN TROUBLE, SEE?
GIVE US THE NOTE-BOOK!
NO!
YOU GUYS AGAIN?
VHHM
!!

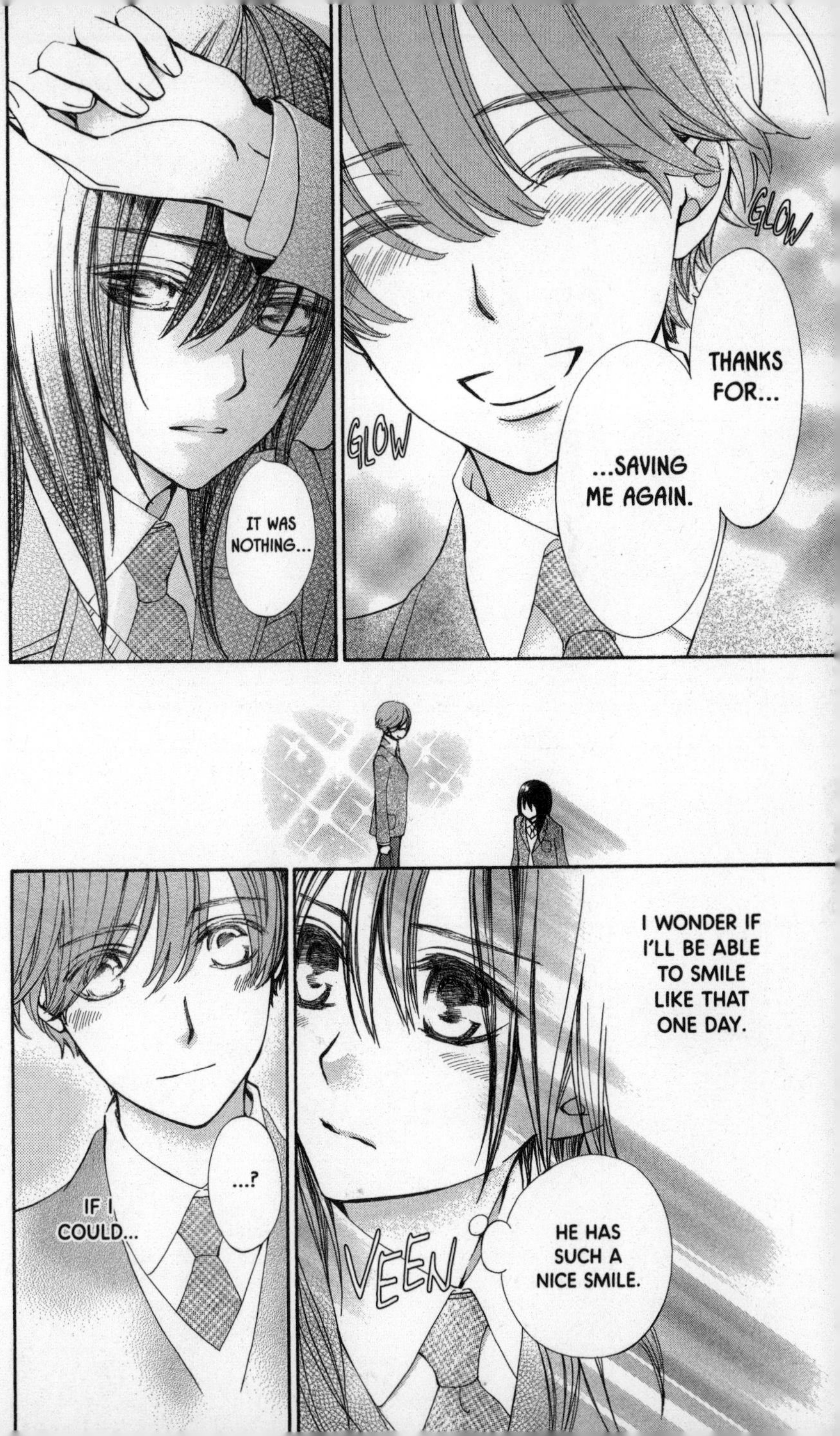
GLOW
THANKS FOR...
GLOW
...SAVING ME AGAIN.
IT WAS NOTHING...
I WONDER IF I'LL BE ABLE TO SMILE LIKE THAT ONE DAY.
HE HAS SUCH A NICE SMILE.
VEEN
...?
IF I COULD...

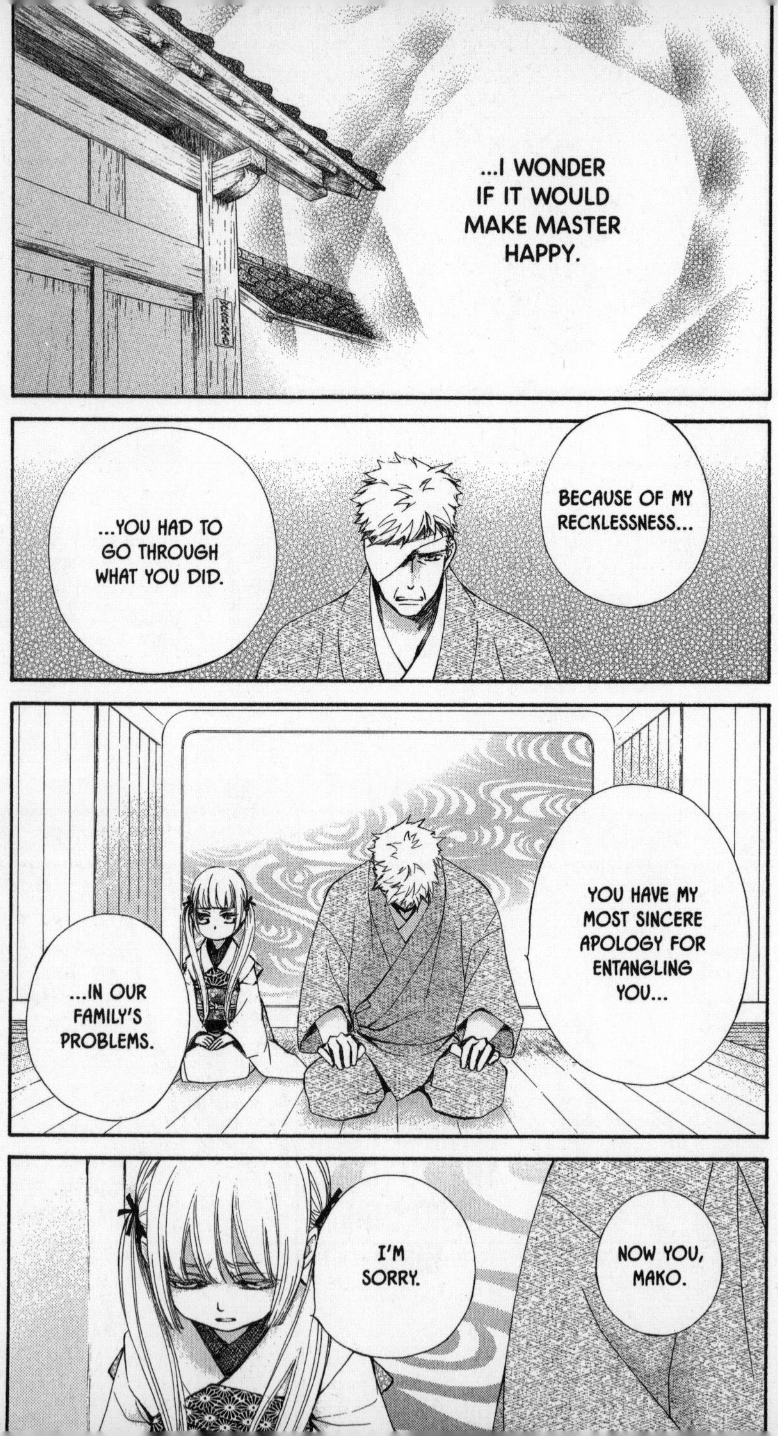
...I WONDER IF IT WOULD MAKE MASTER HAPPY.
BECAUSE OF MY RECKLESSNESS...
...YOU HAD TO GO THROUGH WHAT YOU DID.
YOU HAVE MY MOST SINCERE APOLOGY FOR ENTANGLING YOU...
...IN OUR FAMILY'S PROBLEMS.
NOW YOU, MAKO.
I'M SORRY.

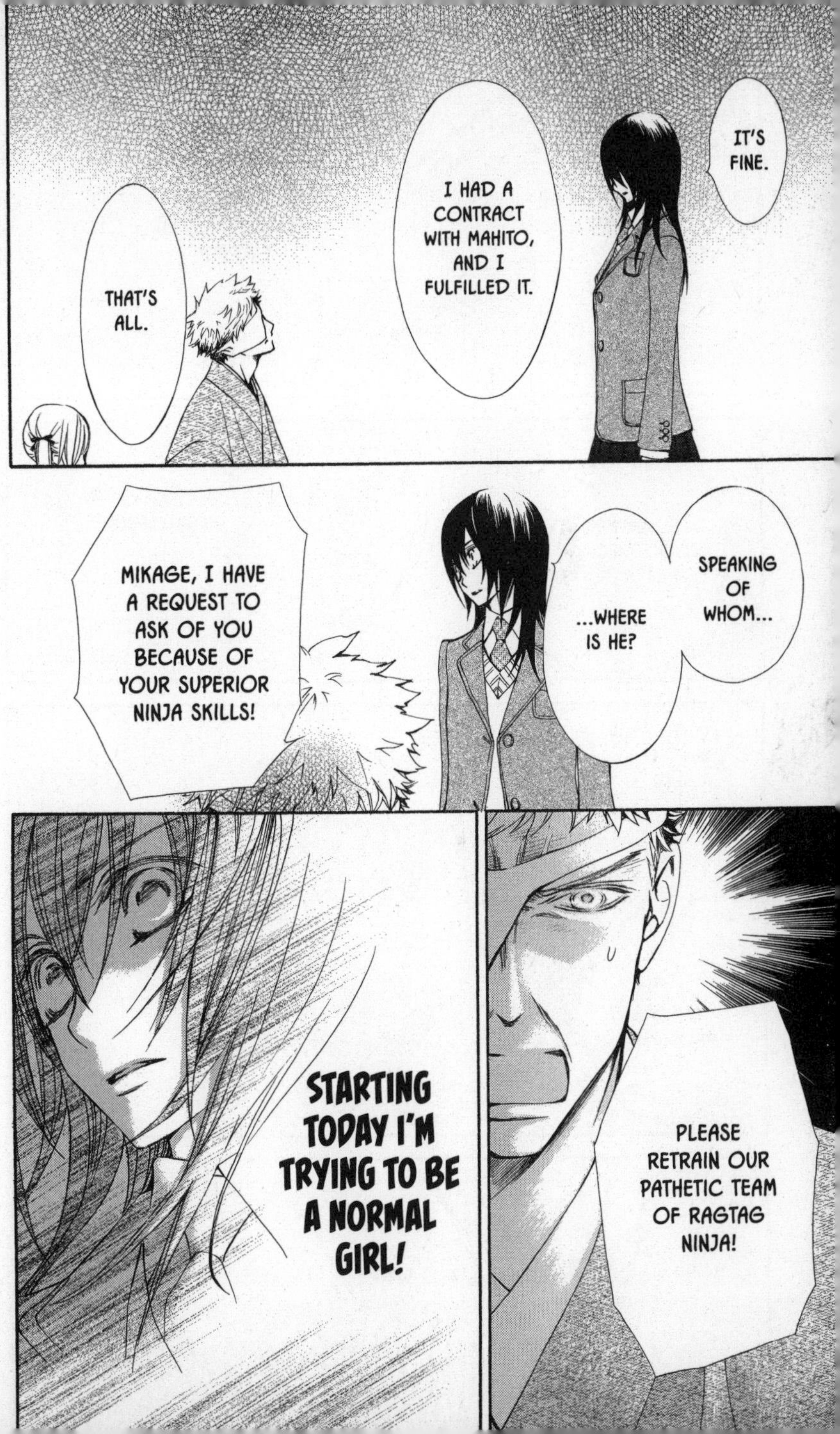
IT'S FINE.
I HAD A CONTRACT WITH MAHITO, AND I FULFILLED IT.
THAT'S ALL.
SPEAKING OF WHOM...
...WHERE IS HE?
MIKAGE, I HAVE A REQUEST TO ASK OF YOU BECAUSE OF YOUR SUPERIOR NINJA SKILLS!
PLEASE RETRAIN OUR PATHETIC TEAM OF RAGTAG NINJA!
STARTING TODAY I'M TRYING TO BE A NORMAL GIRL!

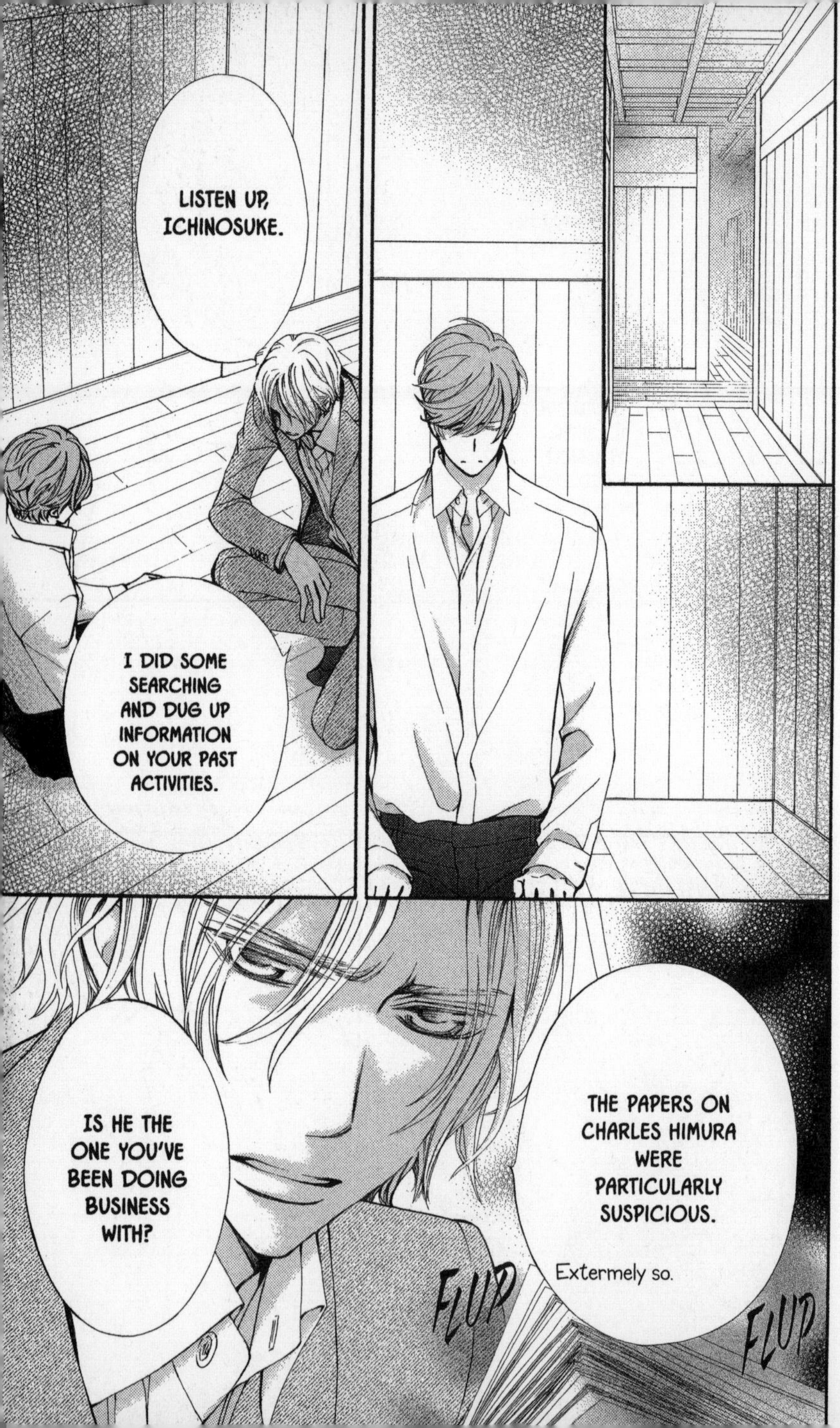
LISTEN UP, ICHINOSUKE.
I DID SOME SEARCHING AND DUG UP INFORMATION ON YOUR PAST ACTIVITIES.
THE PAPERS ON CHARLES HIMURA WERE PARTICULARLY SUSPICIOUS.
Extermely so.
FLUP
FLUP
IS HE THE ONE YOU'VE BEEN DOING BUSINESS WITH?

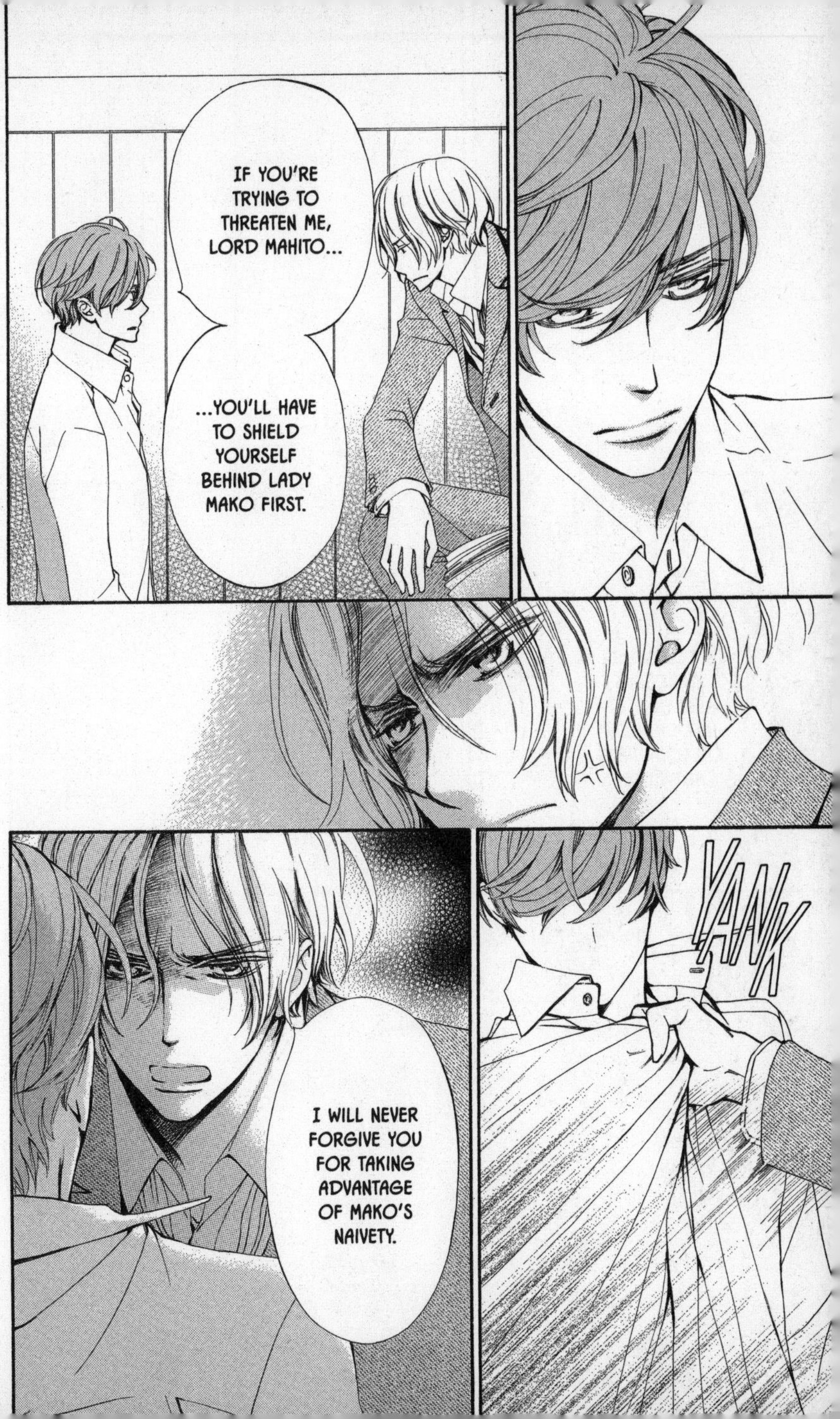
IF YOU'RE TRYING TO THREATEN ME, LORD MAHITO...
...YOU'LL HAVE TO SHIELD YOURSELF BEHIND LADY MAKO FIRST.
YANK
I WILL NEVER FORGIVE YOU FOR TAKING ADVANTAGE OF MAKO'S NAIVETY.

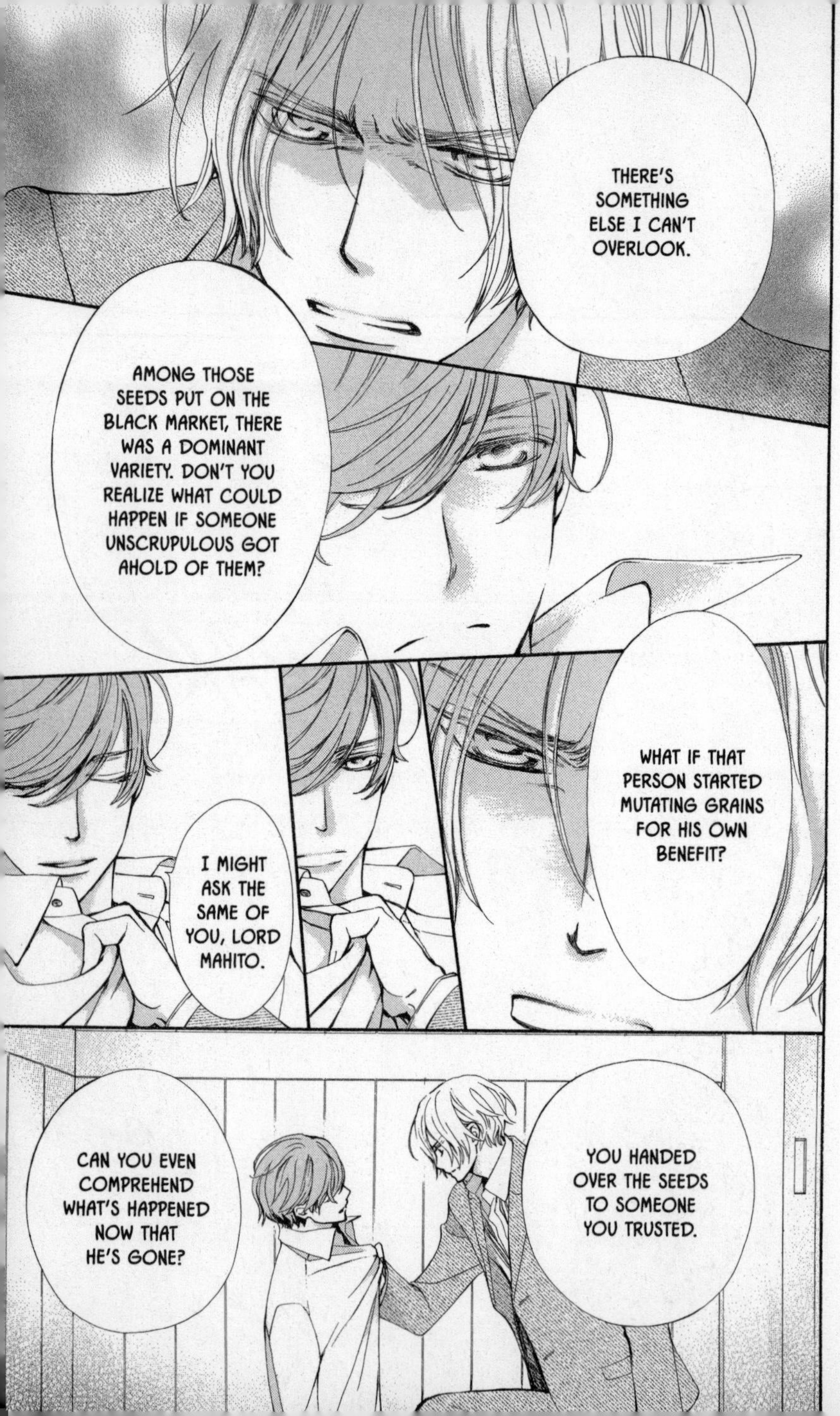
THERE'S SOMETHING ELSE I CAN'T OVERLOOK.
AMONG THOSE SEEDS PUT ON THE BLACK MARKET, THERE WAS A DOMINANT VARIETY. DON'T YOU REALIZE WHAT COULD HAPPEN IF SOMEONE UNSCRUPULOUS GOT AHOLD OF THEM?
WHAT IF THAT PERSON STARTED MUTATING GRAINS FOR HIS OWN BENEFIT?
I MIGHT ASK THE SAME OF YOU, LORD MAHITO.
YOU HANDED OVER THE SEEDS TO SOMEONE YOU TRUSTED.
CAN YOU EVEN COMPREHEND WHAT'S HAPPENED NOW THAT HE'S GONE?

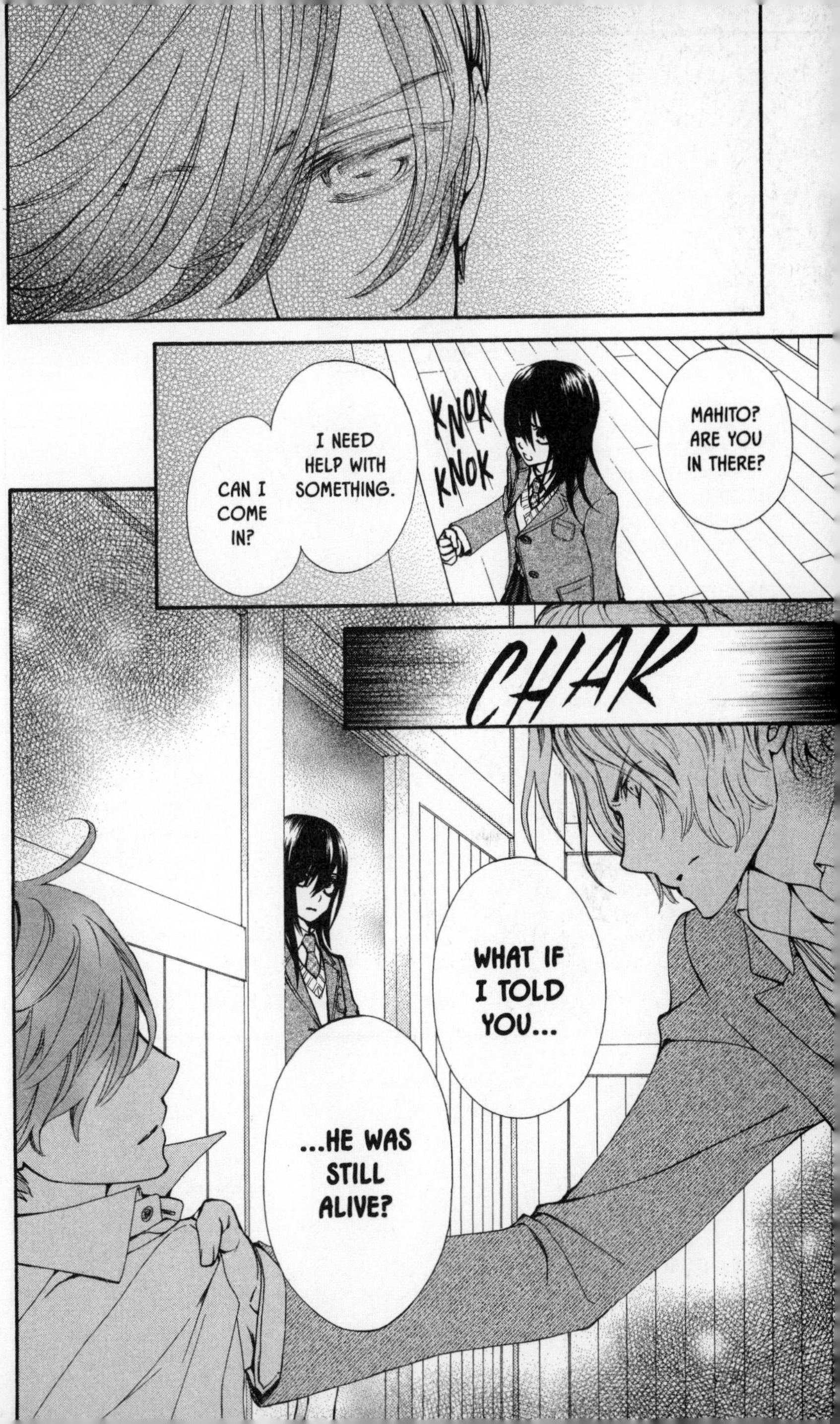
MAHITO? ARE YOU IN THERE?
KNOK KNOK
I NEED HELP WITH SOMETHING.
CAN I COME IN?
CHAK
WHAT IF I TOLD YOU...
...HE WAS STILL ALIVE?

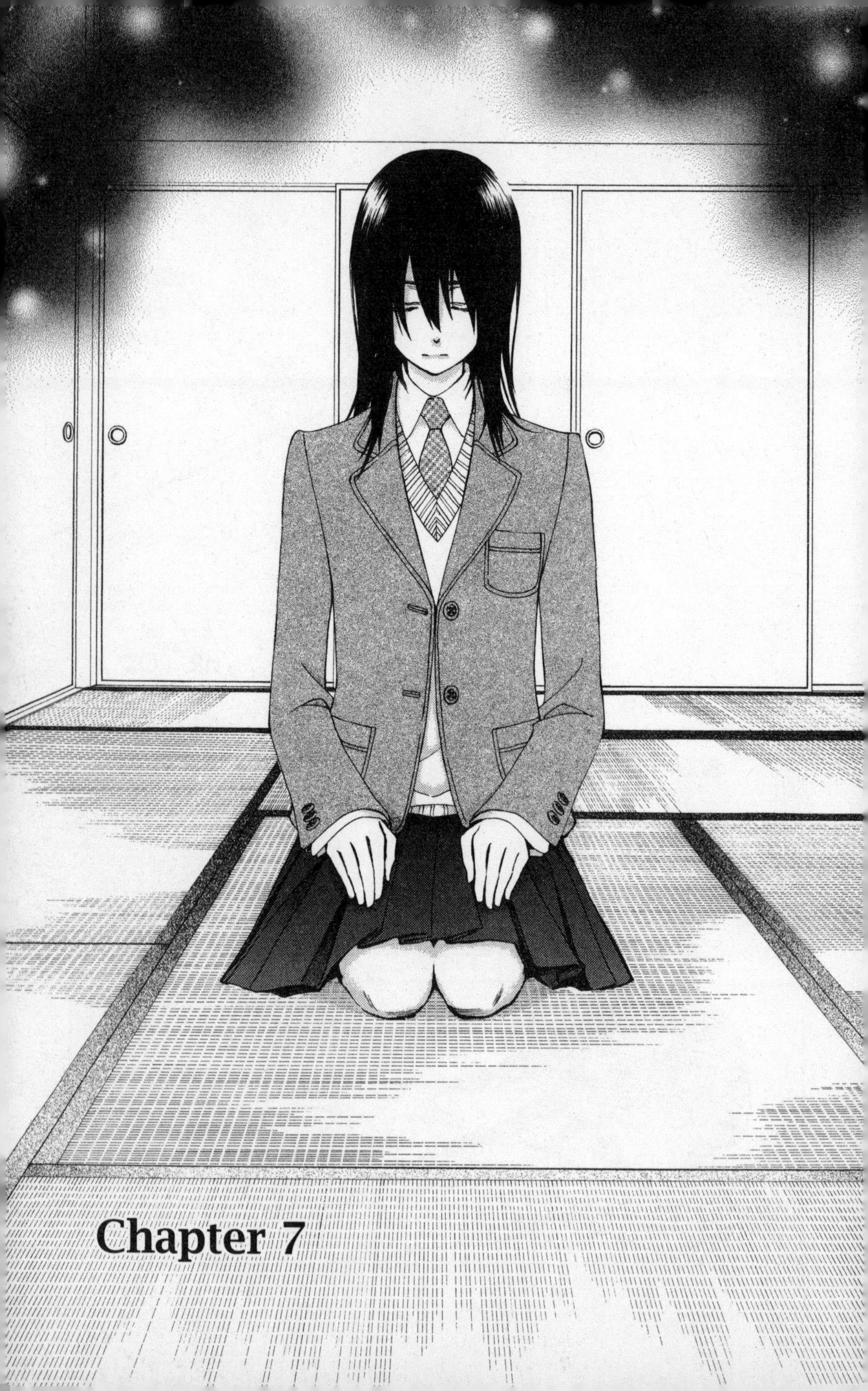
Chapter 7

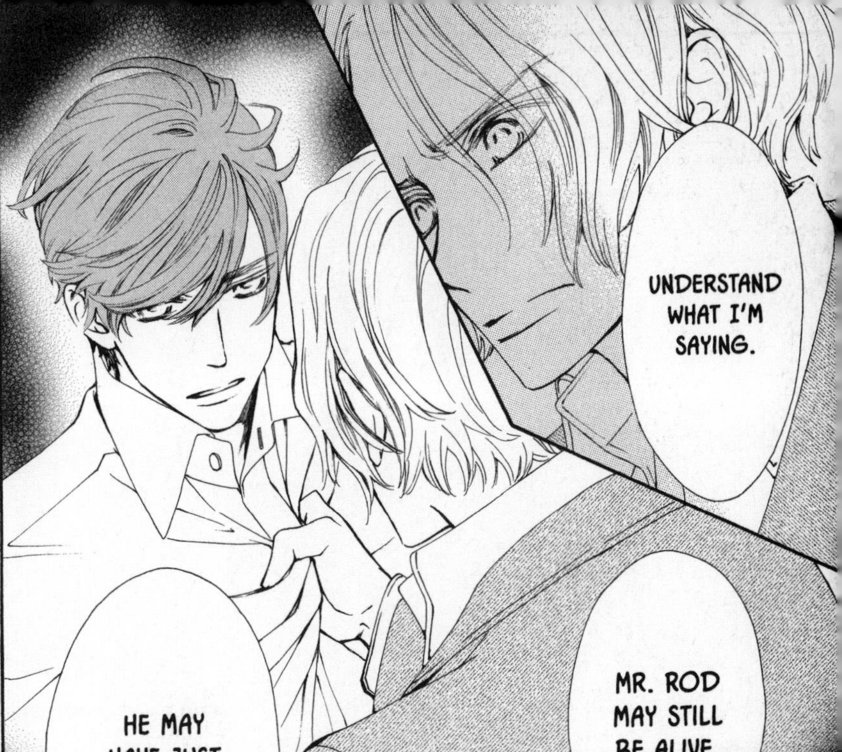
UNDERSTAND WHAT I'M SAYING.
MR. ROD MAY STILL BE ALIVE.
HE MAY HAVE JUST BEEN USING YOU...

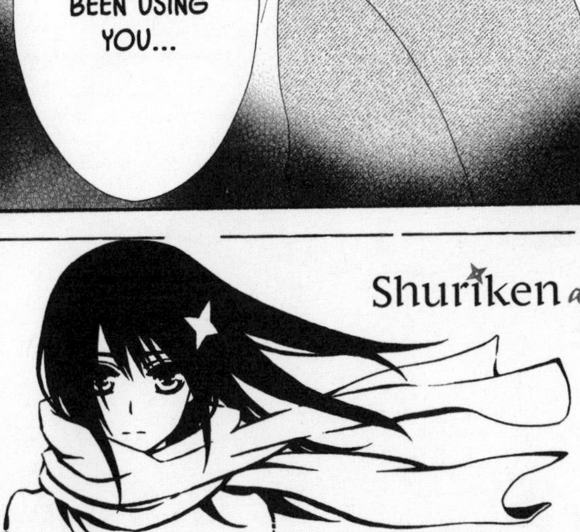

# Shuriken and Pleats

MATSURI HINO

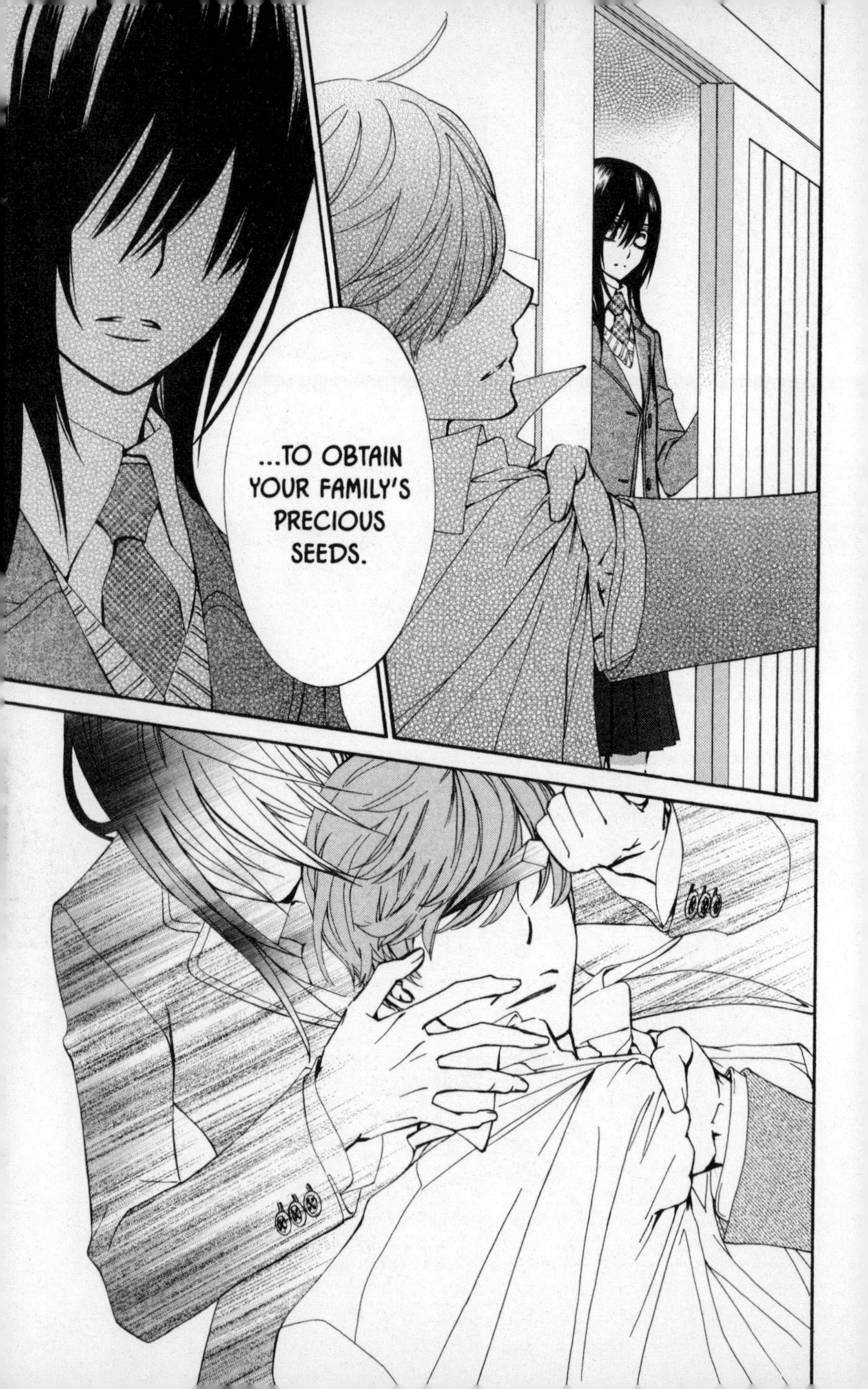
...TO OBTAIN YOUR FAMILY'S PRECIOUS SEEDS.

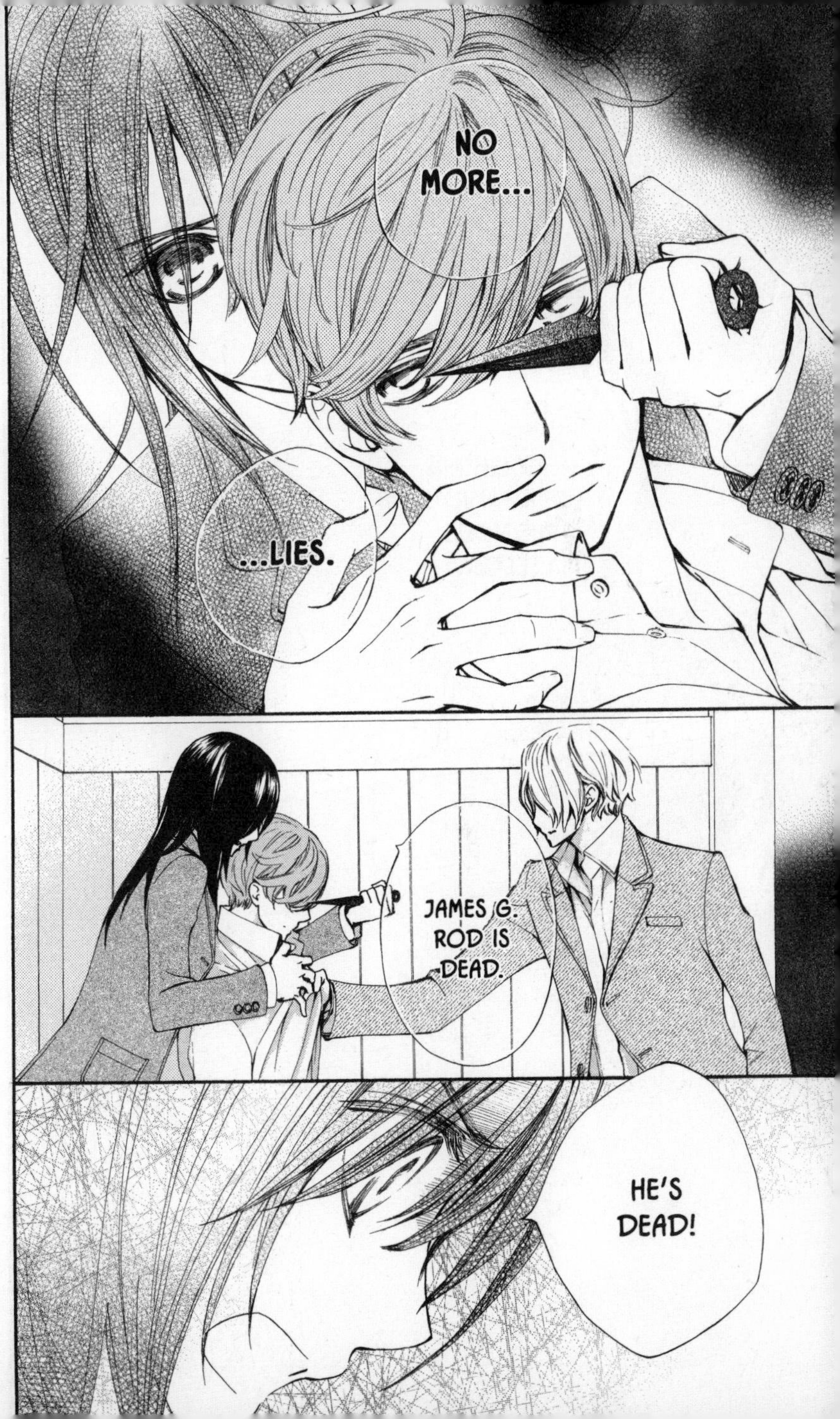
NO MORE...
...LIES.
JAMES G. ROD IS DEAD.
HE'S DEAD!

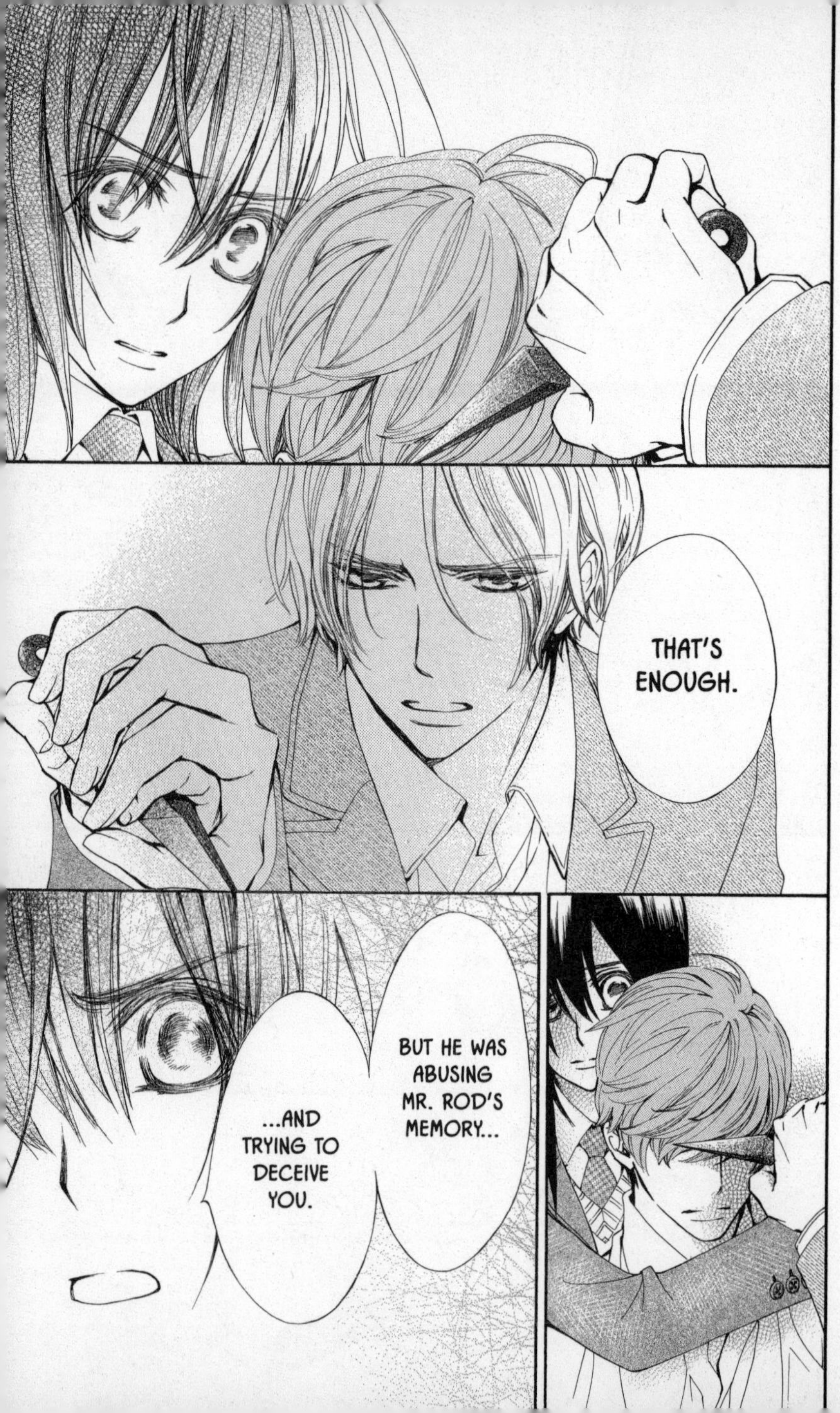
THAT'S ENOUGH.
BUT HE WAS ABUSING MR. ROD'S MEMORY...
...AND TRYING TO DECEIVE YOU.

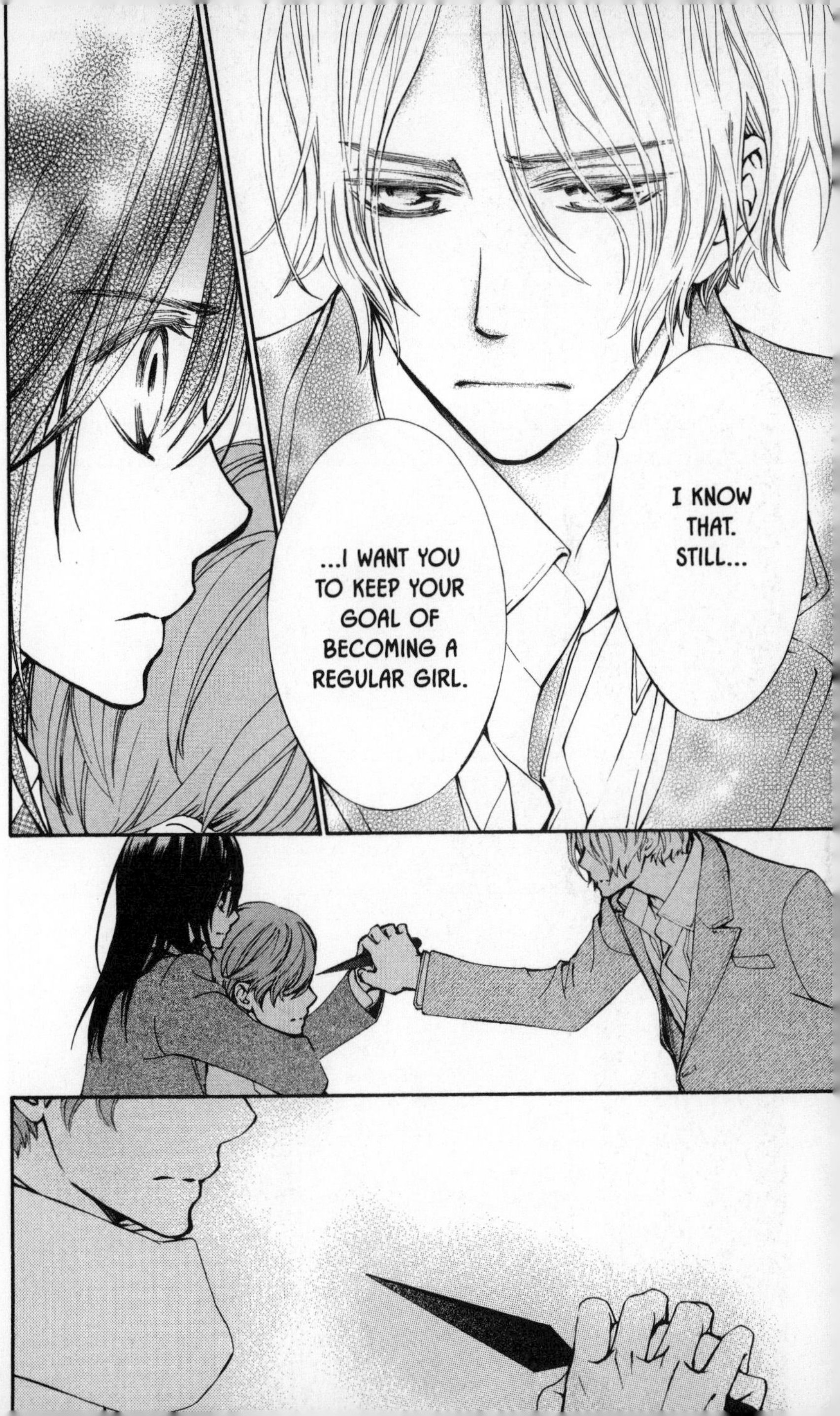
I KNOW THAT. STILL...
...I WANT YOU TO KEEP YOUR GOAL OF BECOMING A REGULAR GIRL.

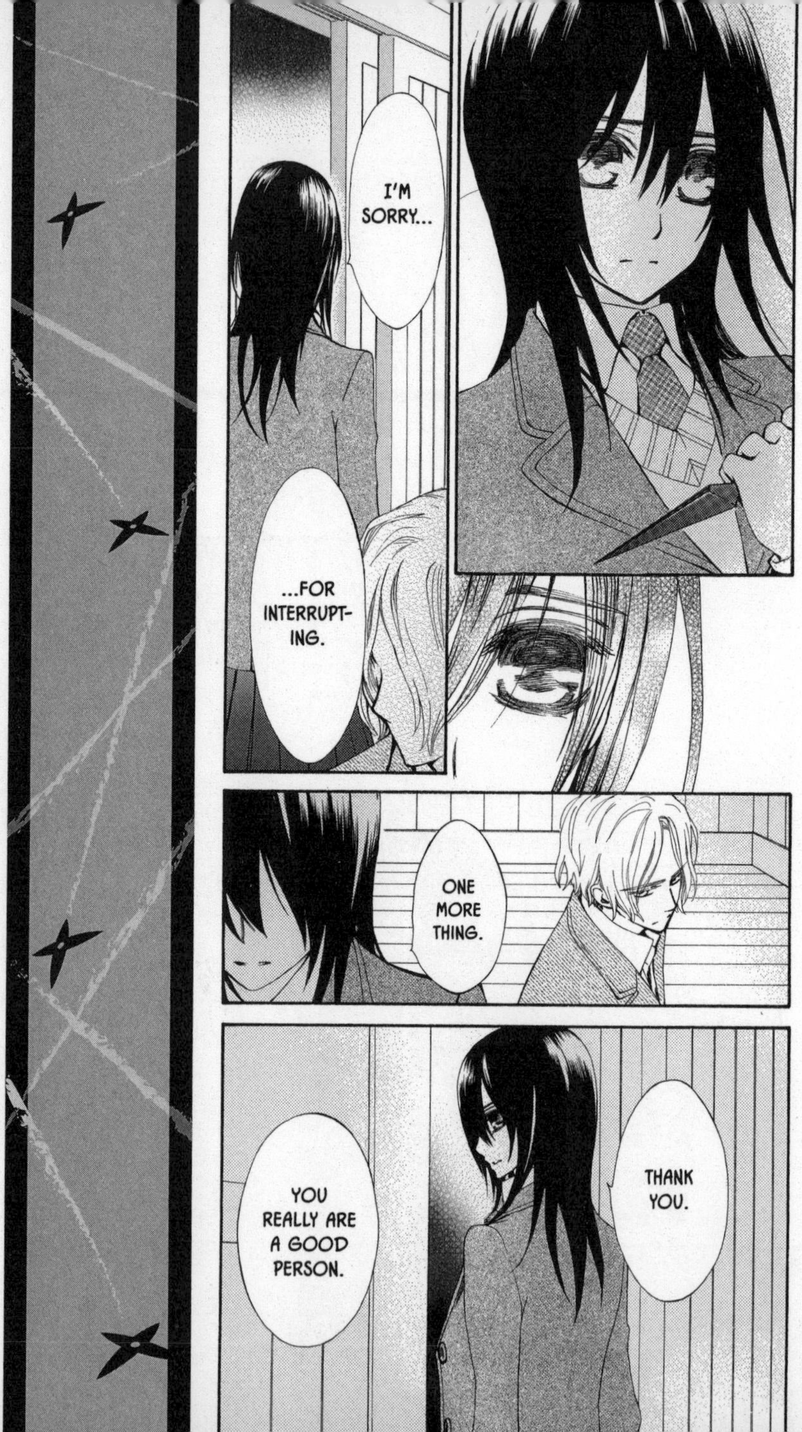
I'M SORRY...
...FOR INTERRUPTING.
ONE MORE THING.
THANK YOU.
YOU REALLY ARE A GOOD PERSON.

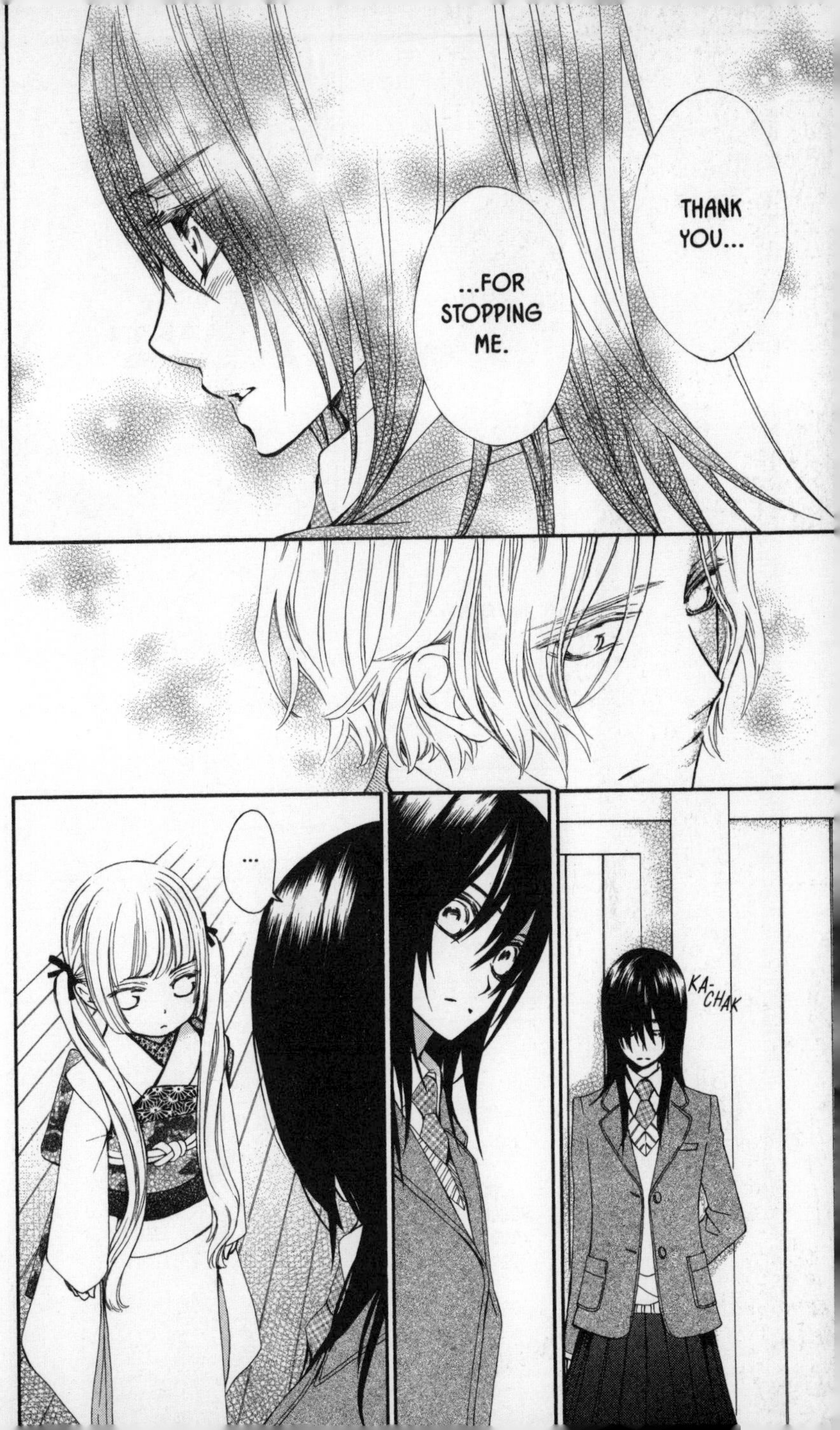
THANK YOU...
...FOR STOPPING ME.
KA-CHAK
...

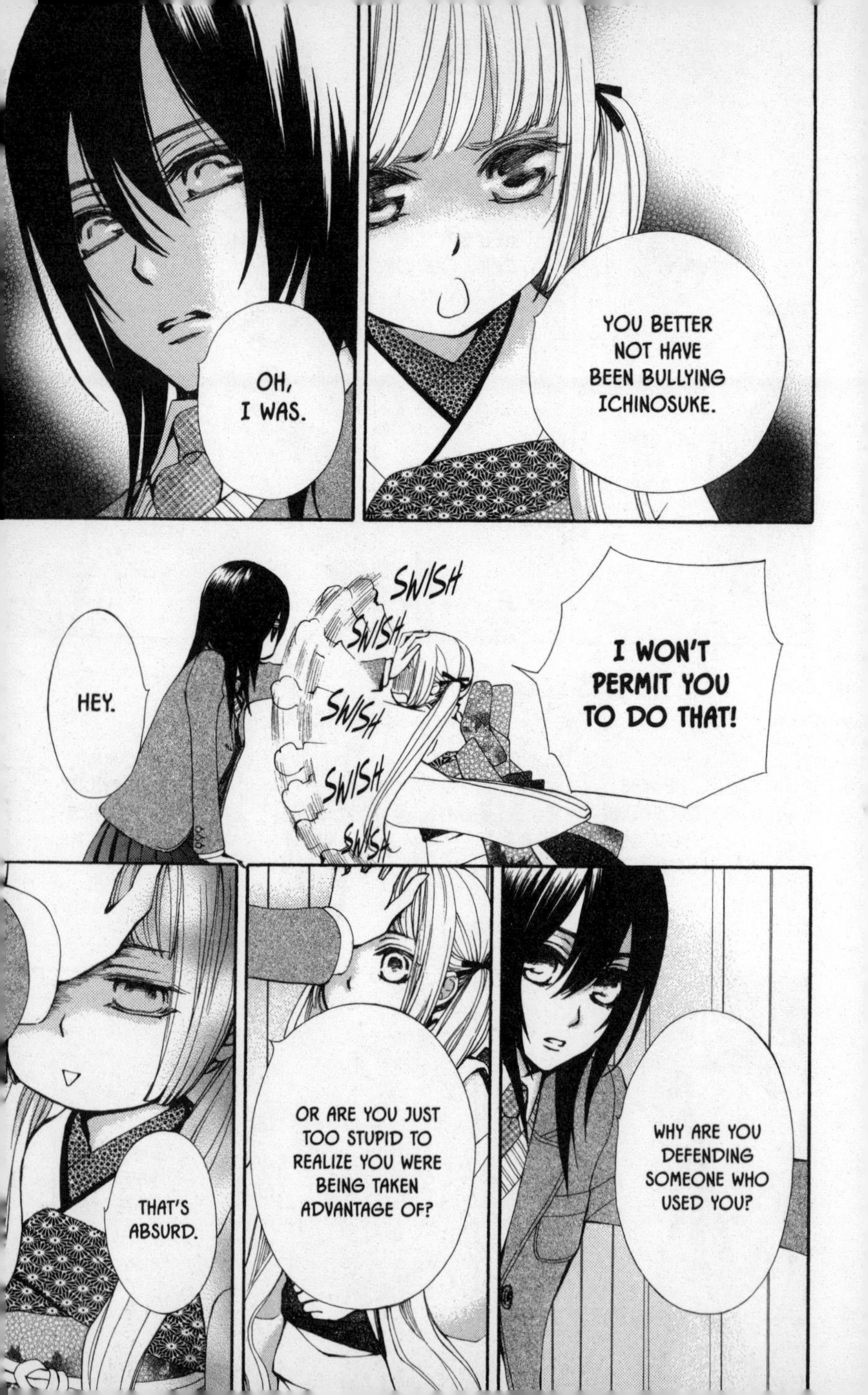
YOU BETTER NOT HAVE BEEN BULLYING ICHINOSUKE.
OH, I WAS.
I WON'T PERMIT YOU TO DO THAT!
SWISH
SWISH
SWISH
SWISH
SWISH
HEY.
WHY ARE YOU DEFENDING SOMEONE WHO USED YOU?
OR ARE YOU JUST TOO STUPID TO REALIZE YOU WERE BEING TAKEN ADVANTAGE OF?
THAT'S ABSURD.

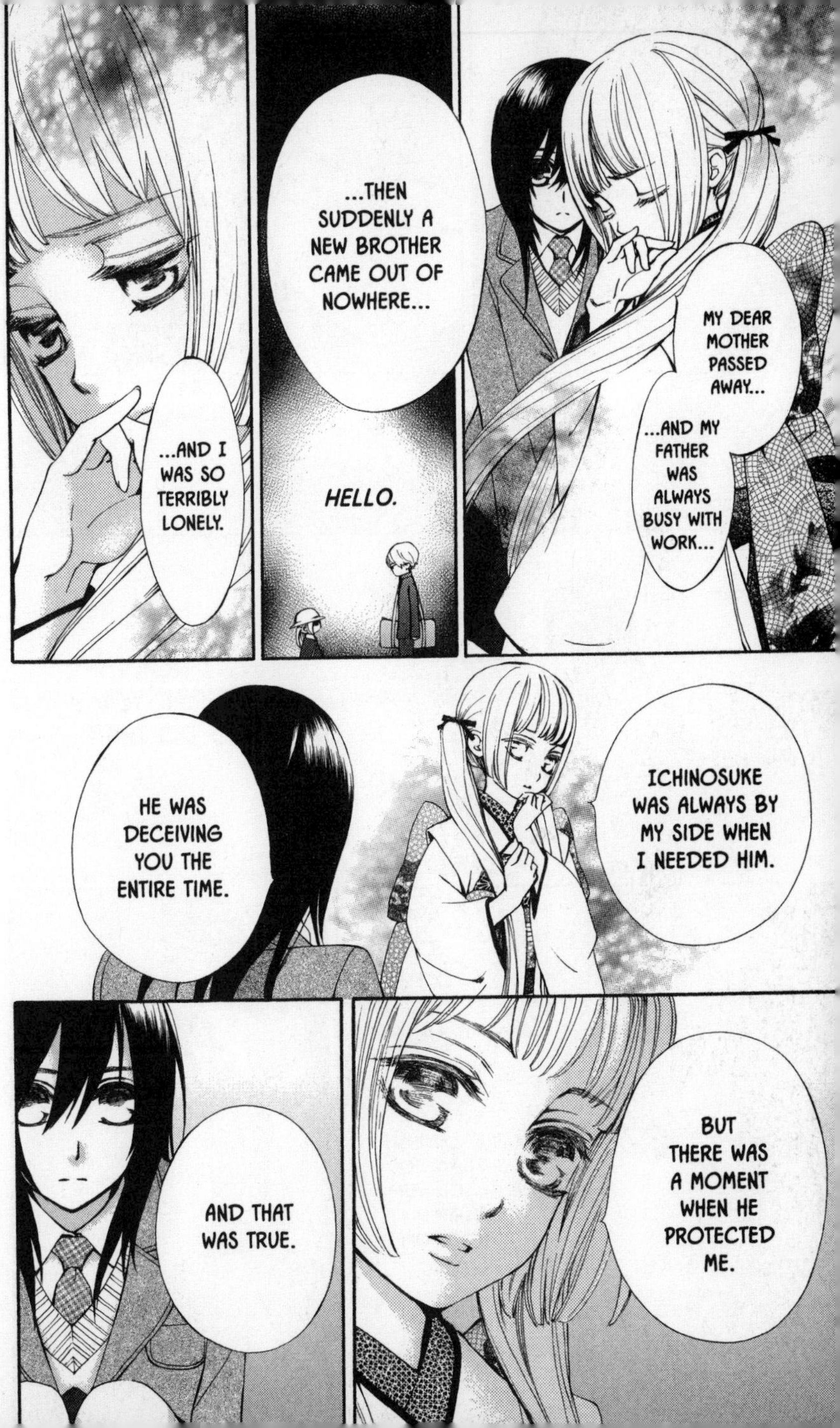
MY DEAR MOTHER PASSED AWAY...
...AND MY FATHER WAS ALWAYS BUSY WITH WORK...
...THEN SUDDENLY A NEW BROTHER CAME OUT OF NOWHERE...
HELLO.
...AND I WAS SO TERRIBLY LONELY.
ICHINOSUKE WAS ALWAYS BY MY SIDE WHEN I NEEDED HIM.
HE WAS DECEIVING YOU THE ENTIRE TIME.
BUT THERE WAS A MOMENT WHEN HE PROTECTED ME.
AND THAT WAS TRUE.

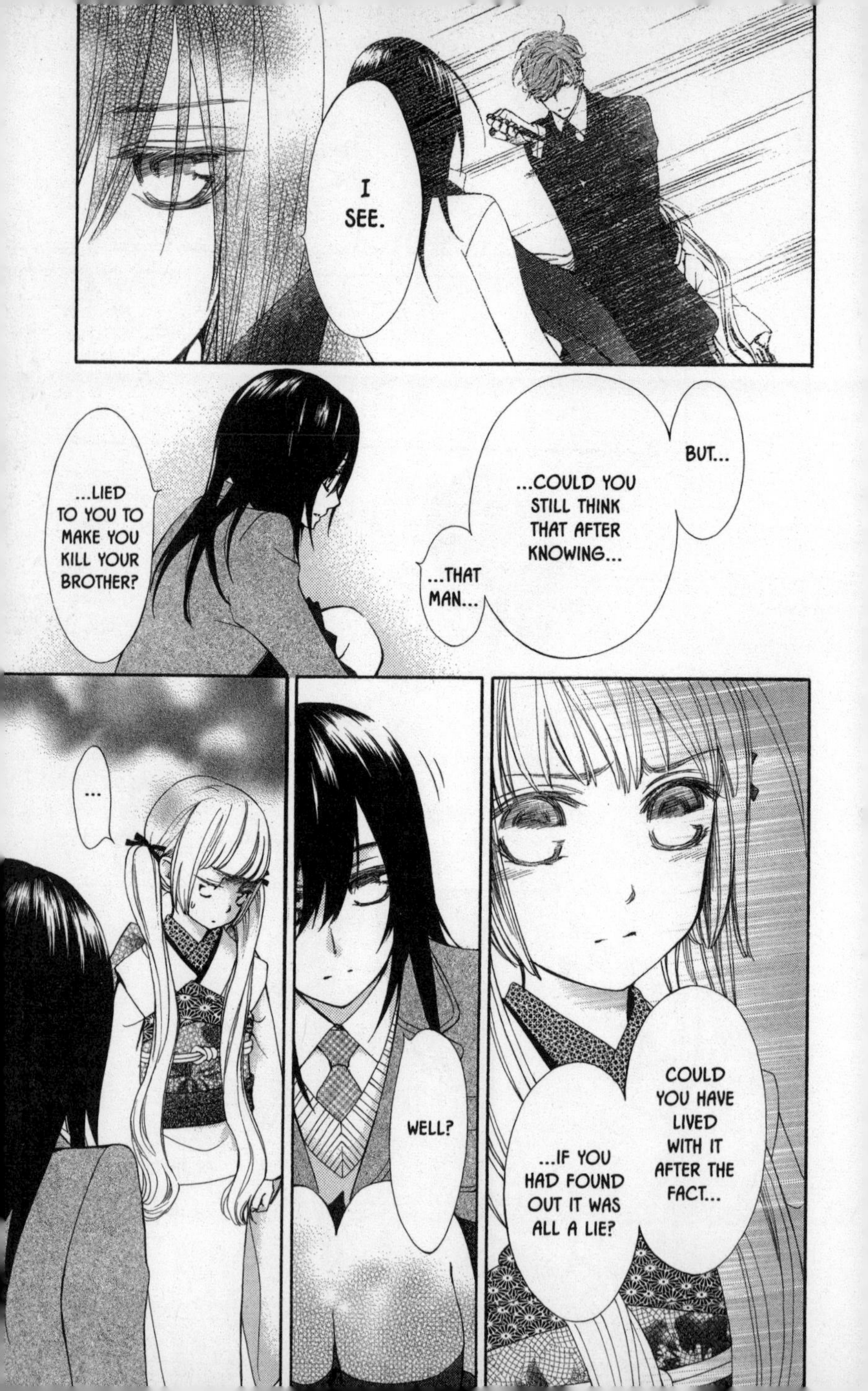
I SEE.
BUT...
...COULD YOU STILL THINK THAT AFTER KNOWING...
...THAT MAN...
...LIED TO YOU TO MAKE YOU KILL YOUR BROTHER?
COULD YOU HAVE LIVED WITH IT AFTER THE FACT...
...IF YOU HAD FOUND OUT IT WAS ALL A LIE?
WELL?
...

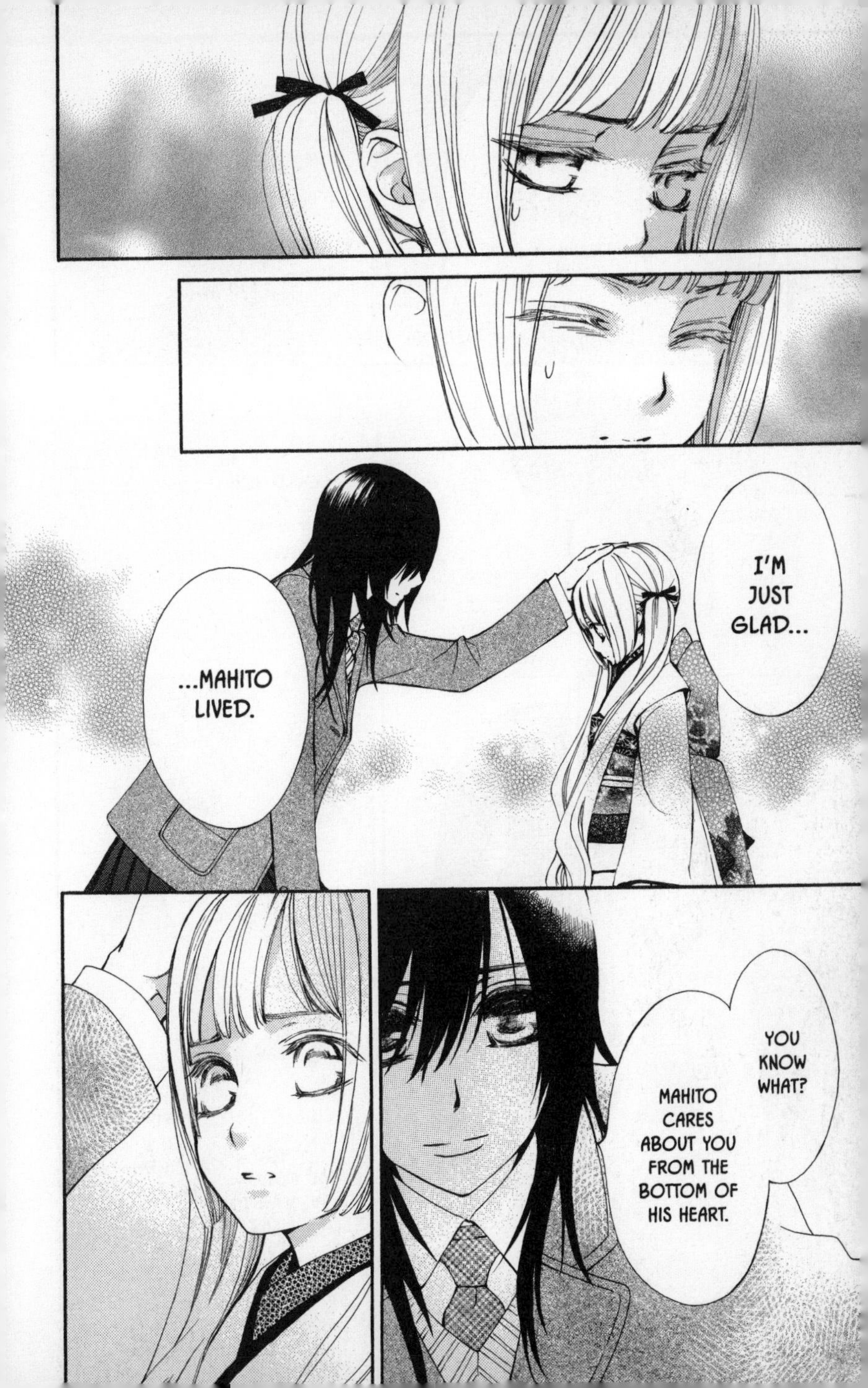
I'M JUST GLAD...
...MAHITO LIVED.
YOU KNOW WHAT? MAHITO CARES ABOUT YOU FROM THE BOTTOM OF HIS HEART.

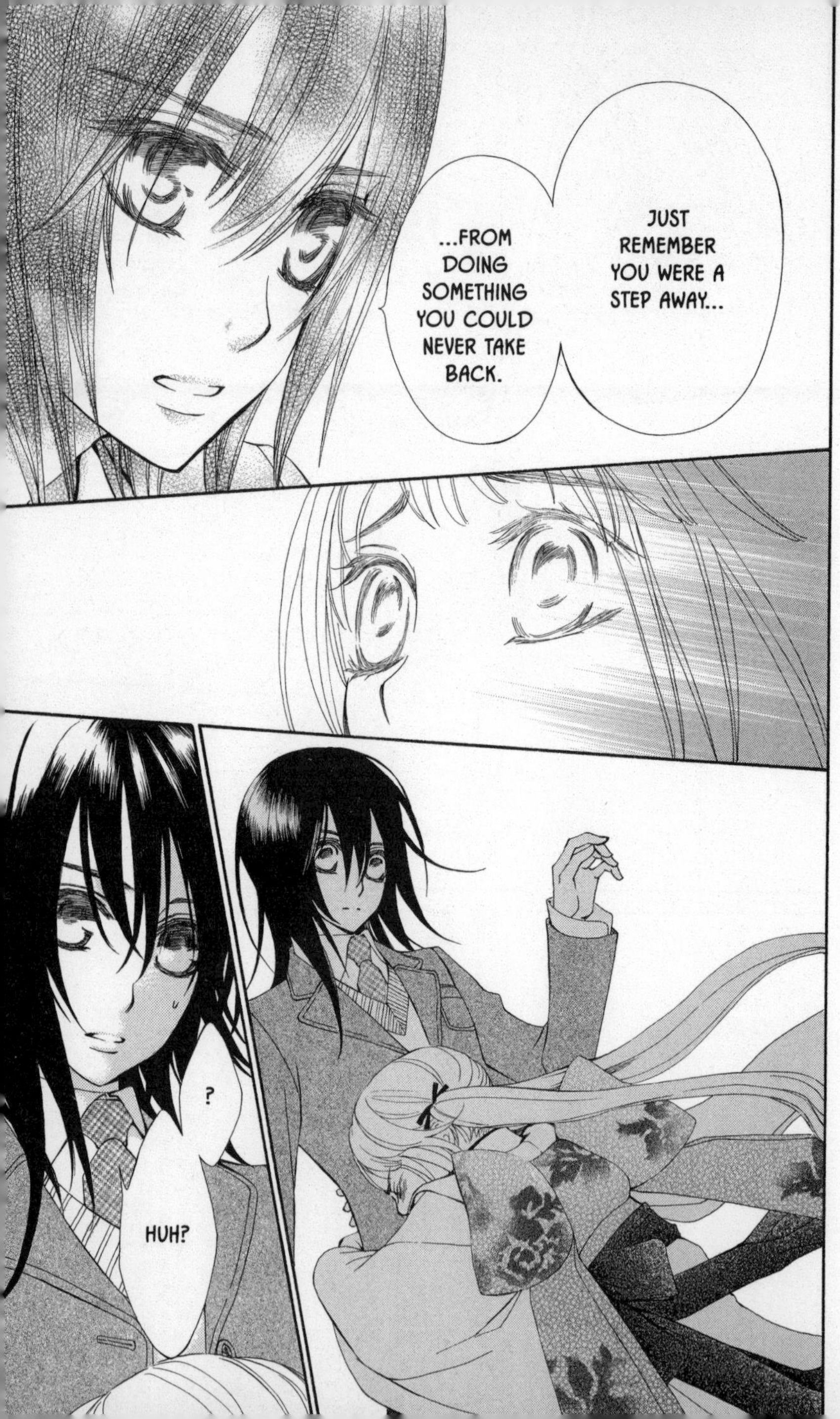
JUST REMEMBER YOU WERE A STEP AWAY...
...FROM DOING SOMETHING YOU COULD NEVER TAKE BACK.
?
HUH?

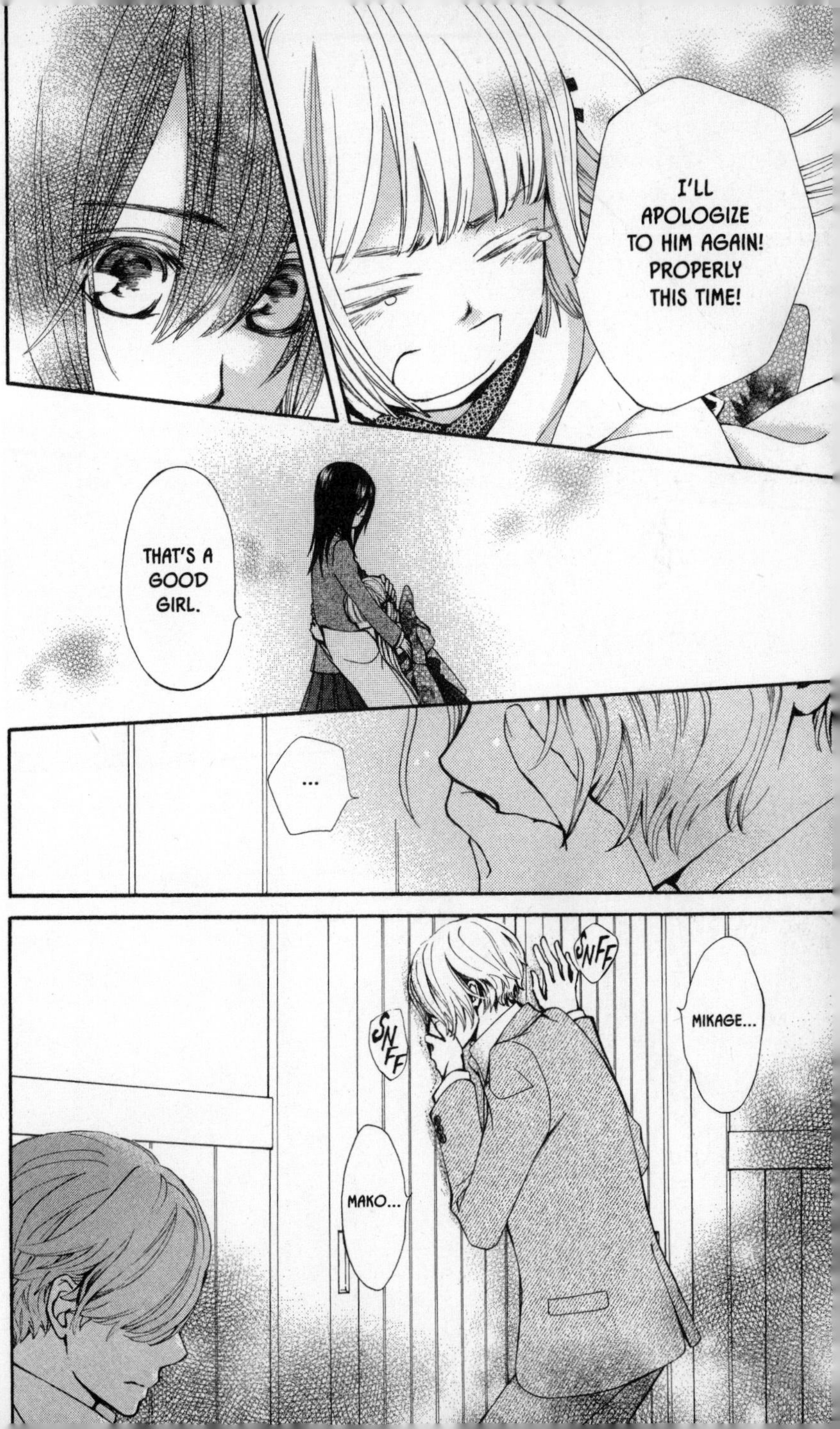
I'LL APOLOGIZE TO HIM AGAIN! PROPERLY THIS TIME!
THAT'S A GOOD GIRL.
...
MIKAGE...
SNFF
SNFF
MAKO...

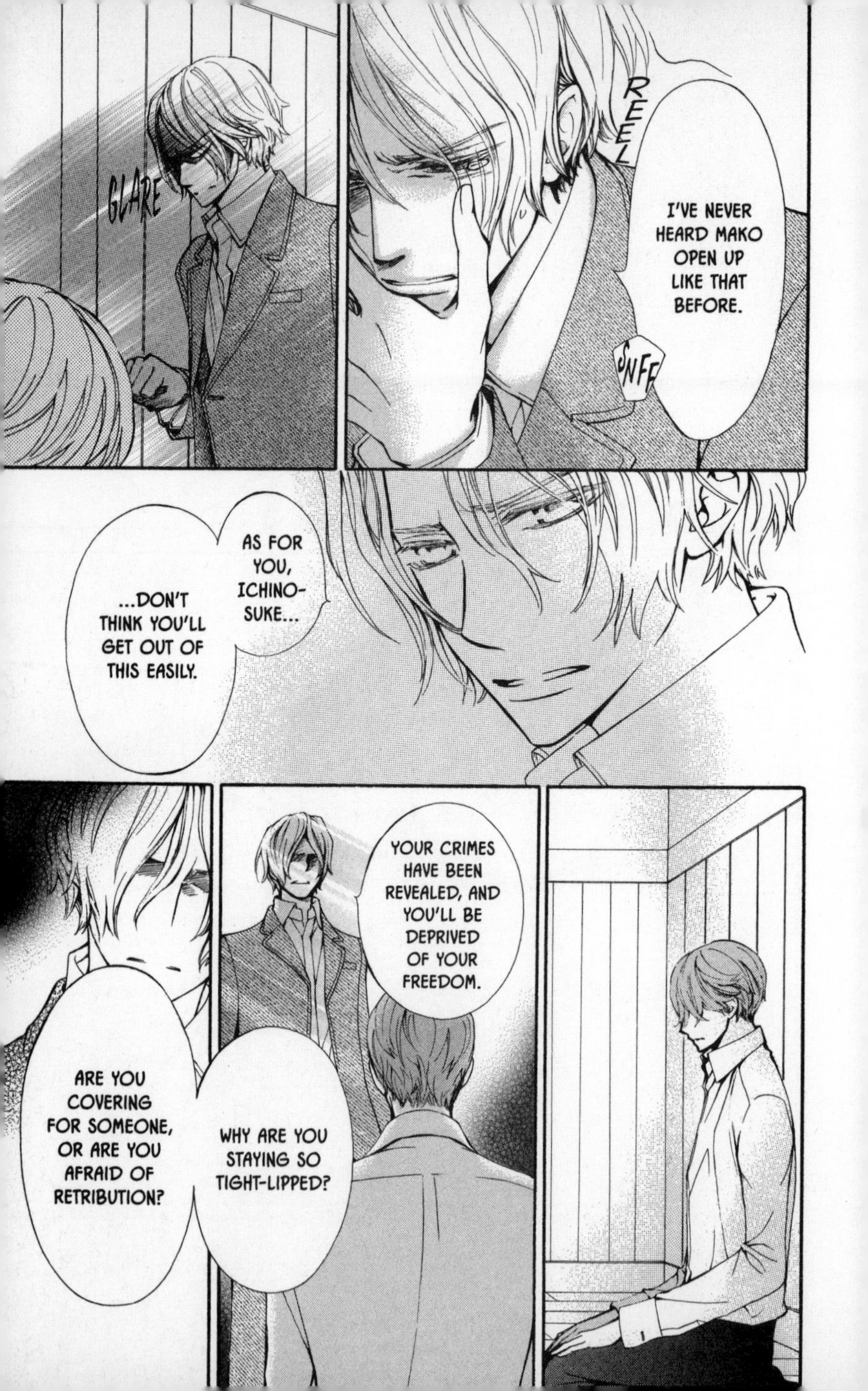
REEL
I'VE NEVER HEARD MAKO OPEN UP LIKE THAT BEFORE.
SNFF
GLARE
AS FOR YOU, ICHINO-SUKE...
...DON'T THINK YOU'LL GET OUT OF THIS EASILY.
YOUR CRIMES HAVE BEEN REVEALED, AND YOU'LL BE DEPRIVED OF YOUR FREEDOM.
WHY ARE YOU STAYING SO TIGHT-LIPPED?
ARE YOU COVERING FOR SOMEONE, OR ARE YOU AFRAID OF RETRIBUTION?

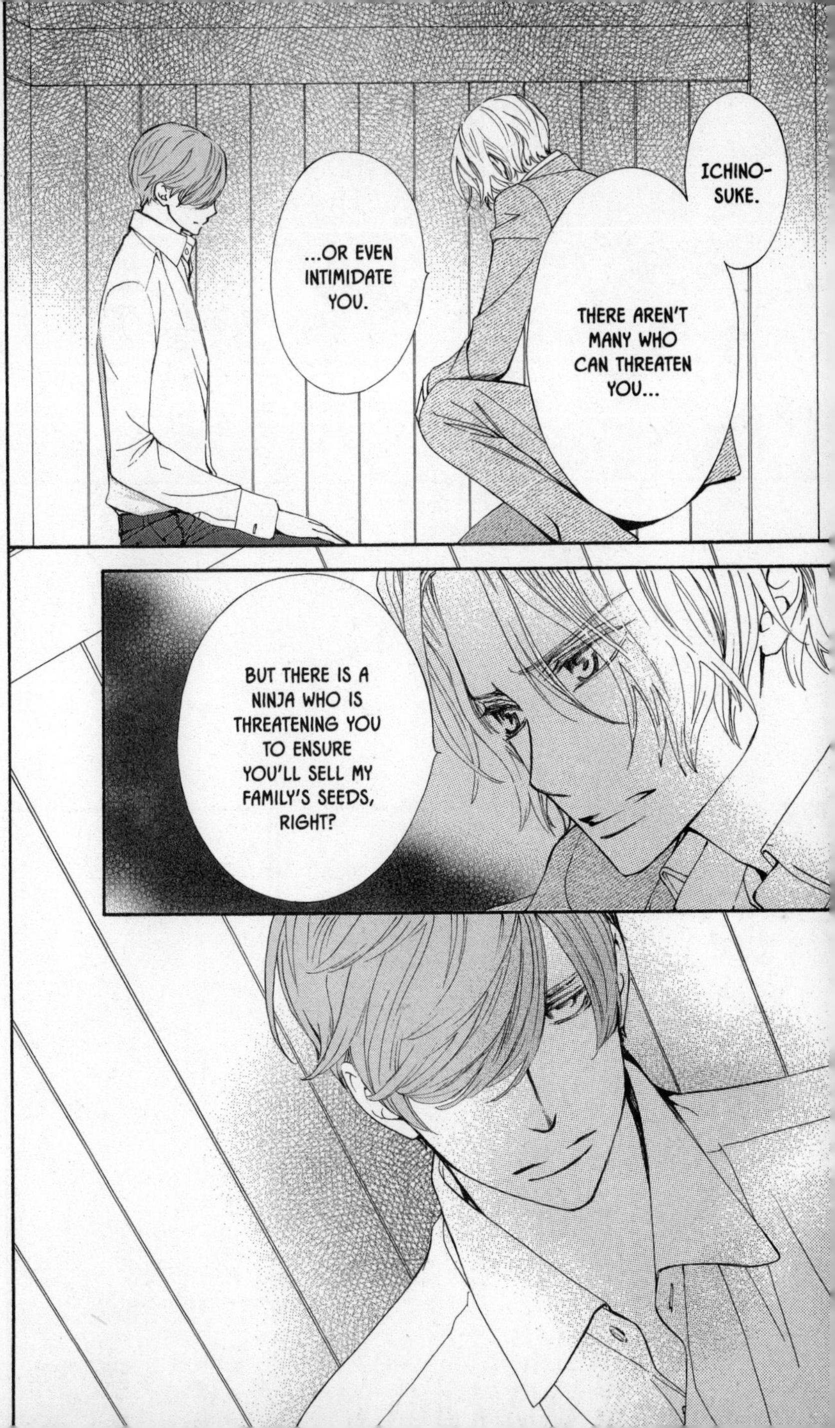
ICHINO-SUKE.
THERE AREN'T MANY WHO CAN THREATEN YOU...
...OR EVEN INTIMIDATE YOU.
BUT THERE IS A NINJA WHO IS THREATENING YOU TO ENSURE YOU'LL SELL MY FAMILY'S SEEDS, RIGHT?

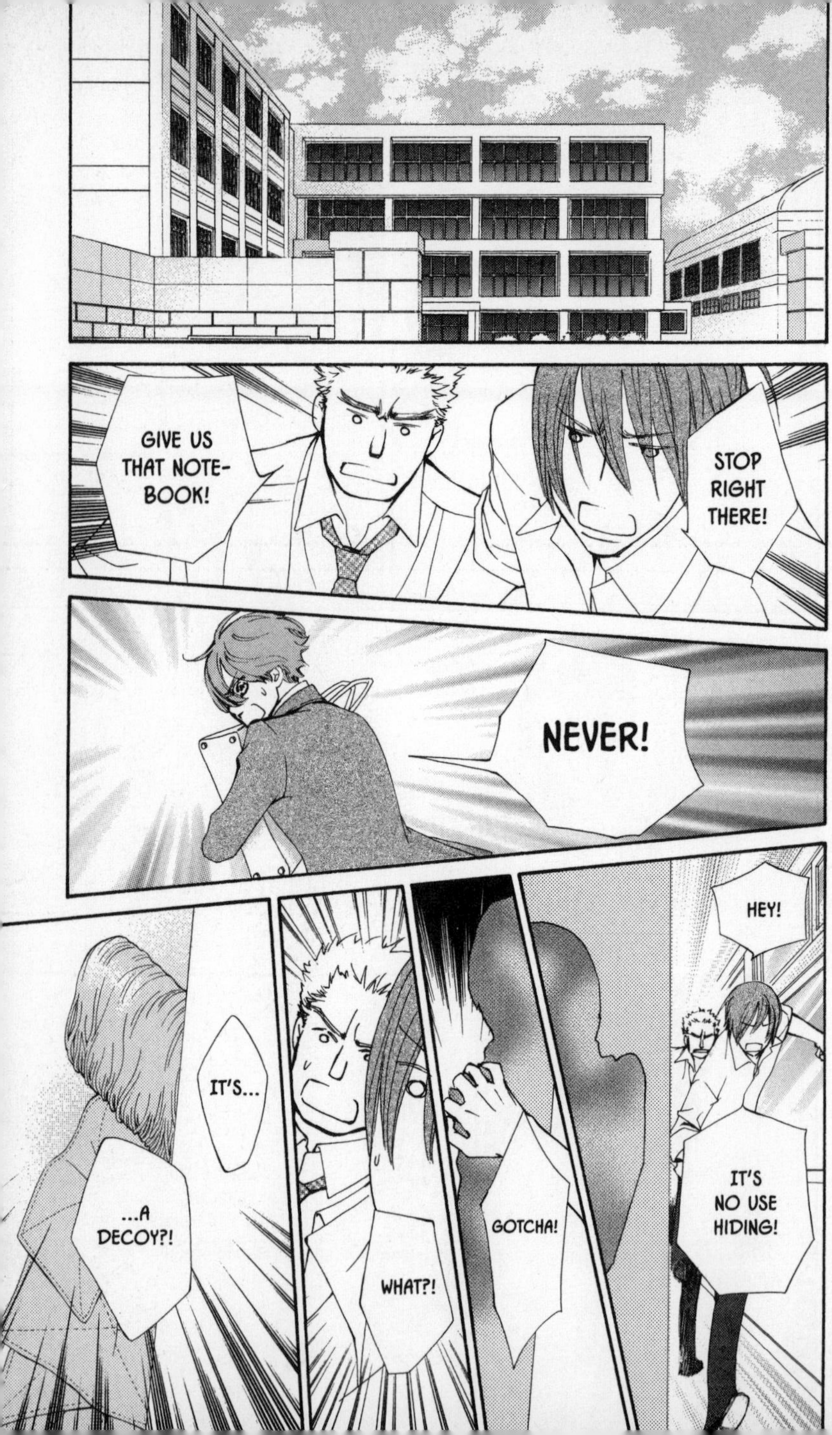
STOP RIGHT THERE!
GIVE US THAT NOTE-BOOK!
NEVER!
HEY!
IT'S NO USE HIDING!
GOTCHA!
WHAT?!
IT'S...
...A DECOY?!

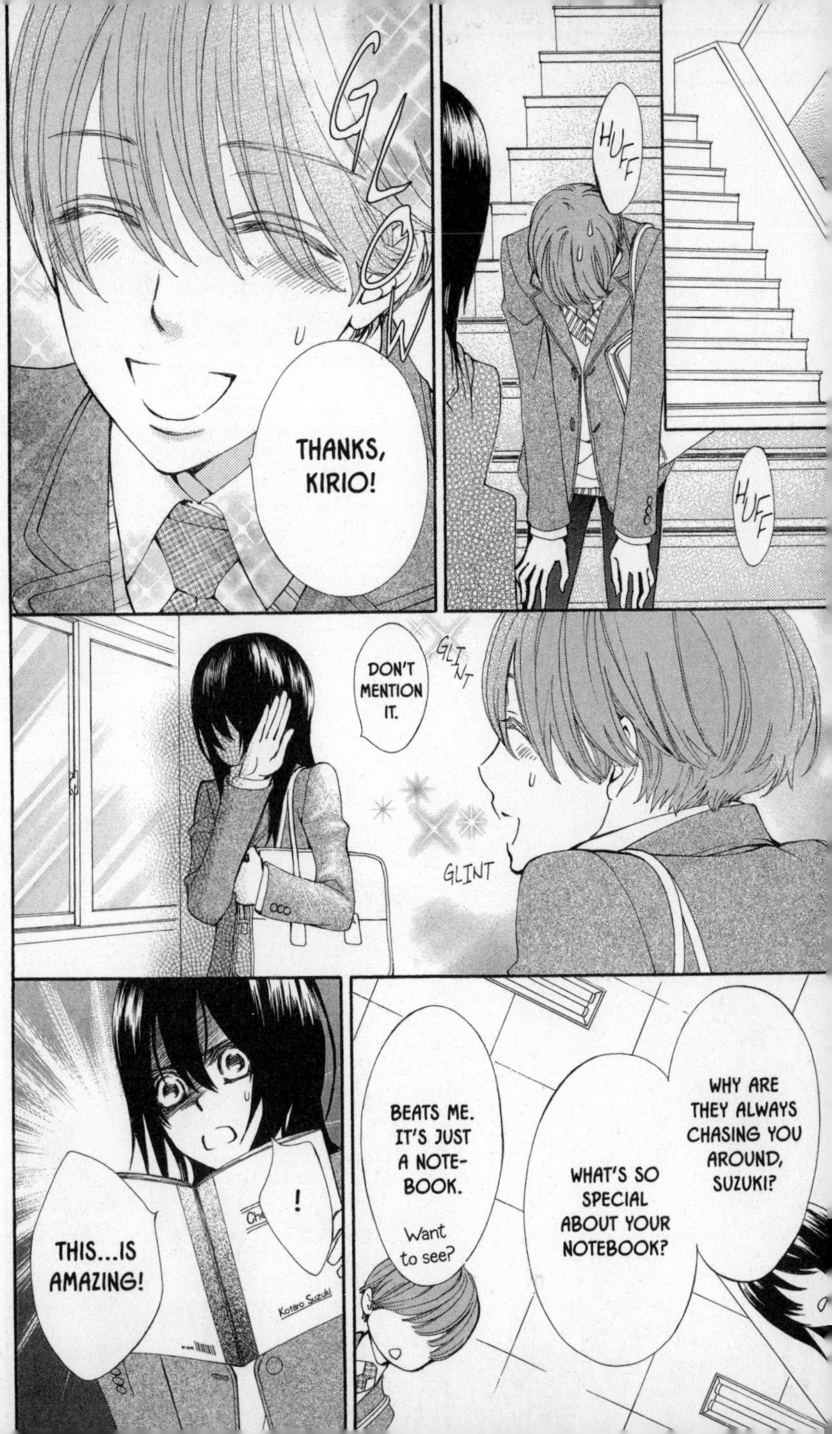
HUFF
HUFF
GLOW
THANKS, KIRIO!
DON'T MENTION IT.
GLINT
GLINT
WHY ARE THEY ALWAYS CHASING YOU AROUND, SUZUKI?
WHAT'S SO SPECIAL ABOUT YOUR NOTEBOOK?
BEATS ME. IT'S JUST A NOTE-BOOK.
Want to see?
!
THIS...IS AMAZING!
Kotaro Suzuki

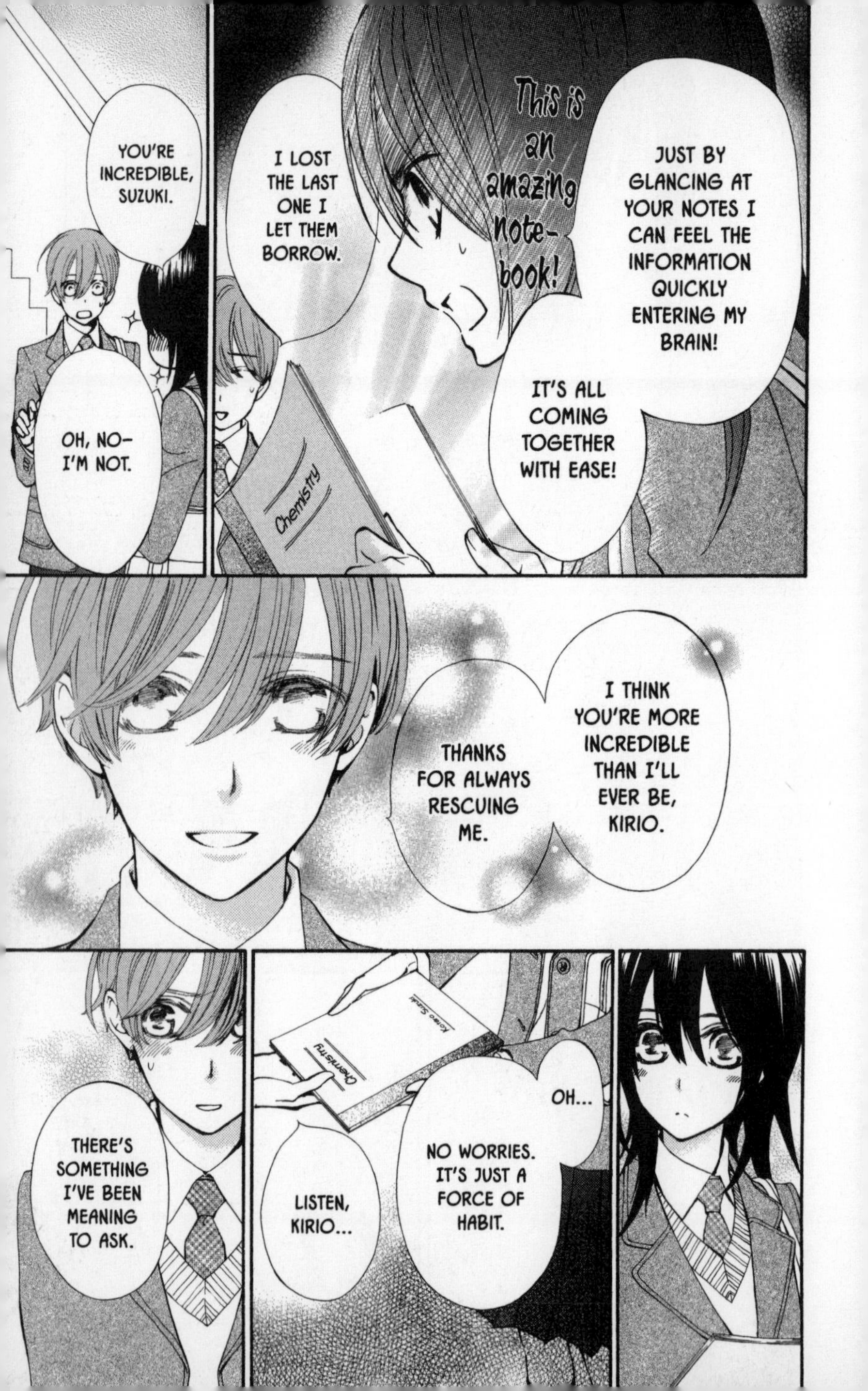
JUST BY GLANCING AT YOUR NOTES I CAN FEEL THE INFORMATION QUICKLY ENTERING MY BRAIN!
This is an amazing note-book!
IT'S ALL COMING TOGETHER WITH EASE!
I LOST THE LAST ONE I LET THEM BORROW.
Chemistry
YOU'RE INCREDIBLE, SUZUKI.
OH, NO— I'M NOT.
I THINK YOU'RE MORE INCREDIBLE THAN I'LL EVER BE, KIRIO.
THANKS FOR ALWAYS RESCUING ME.
OH...
NO WORRIES. IT'S JUST A FORCE OF HABIT.
Chemistry
LISTEN, KIRIO...
THERE'S SOMETHING I'VE BEEN MEANING TO ASK.

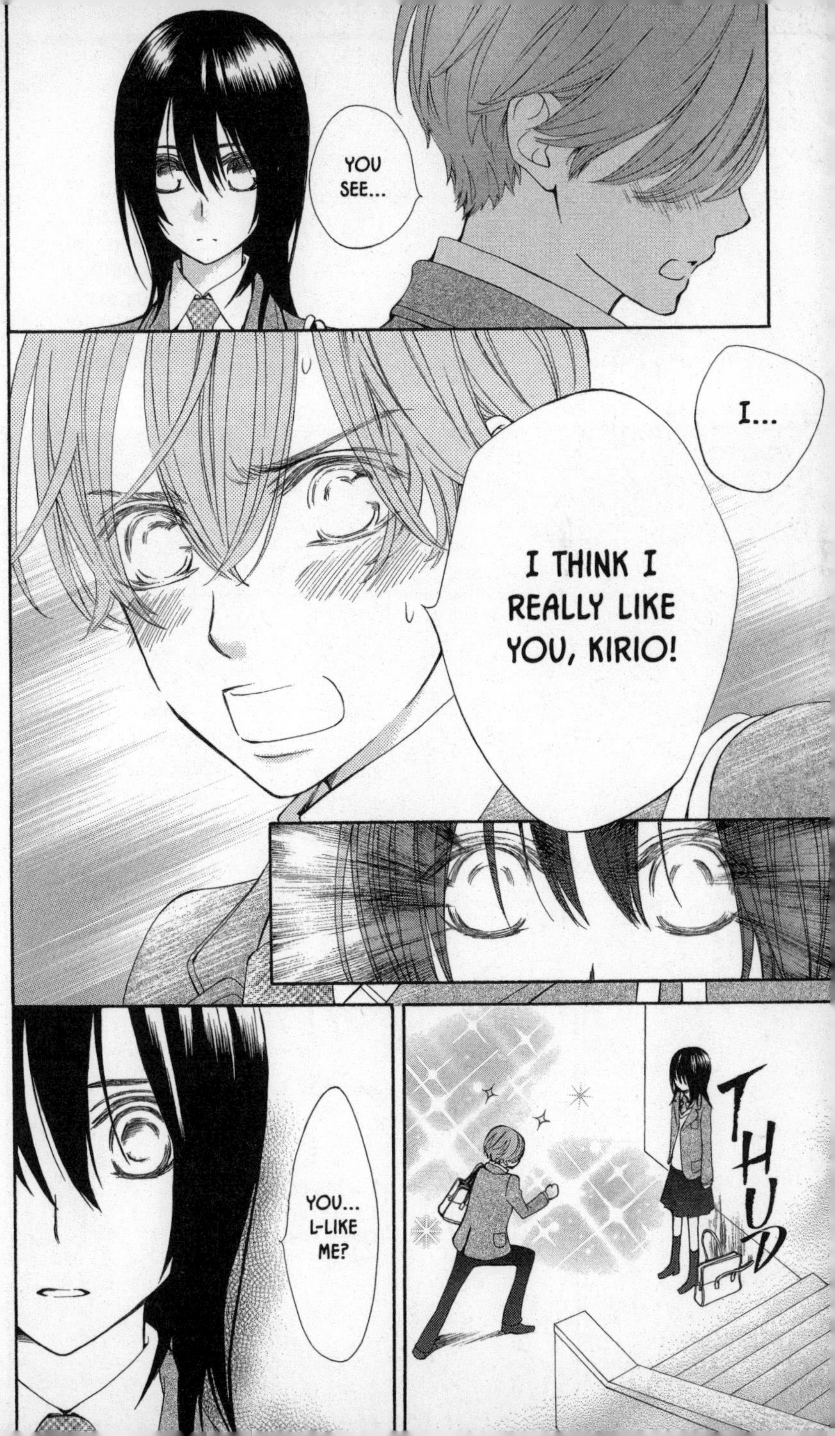
YOU SEE...
I...
I THINK I REALLY LIKE YOU, KIRIO!
THUD
YOU... L-LIKE ME?

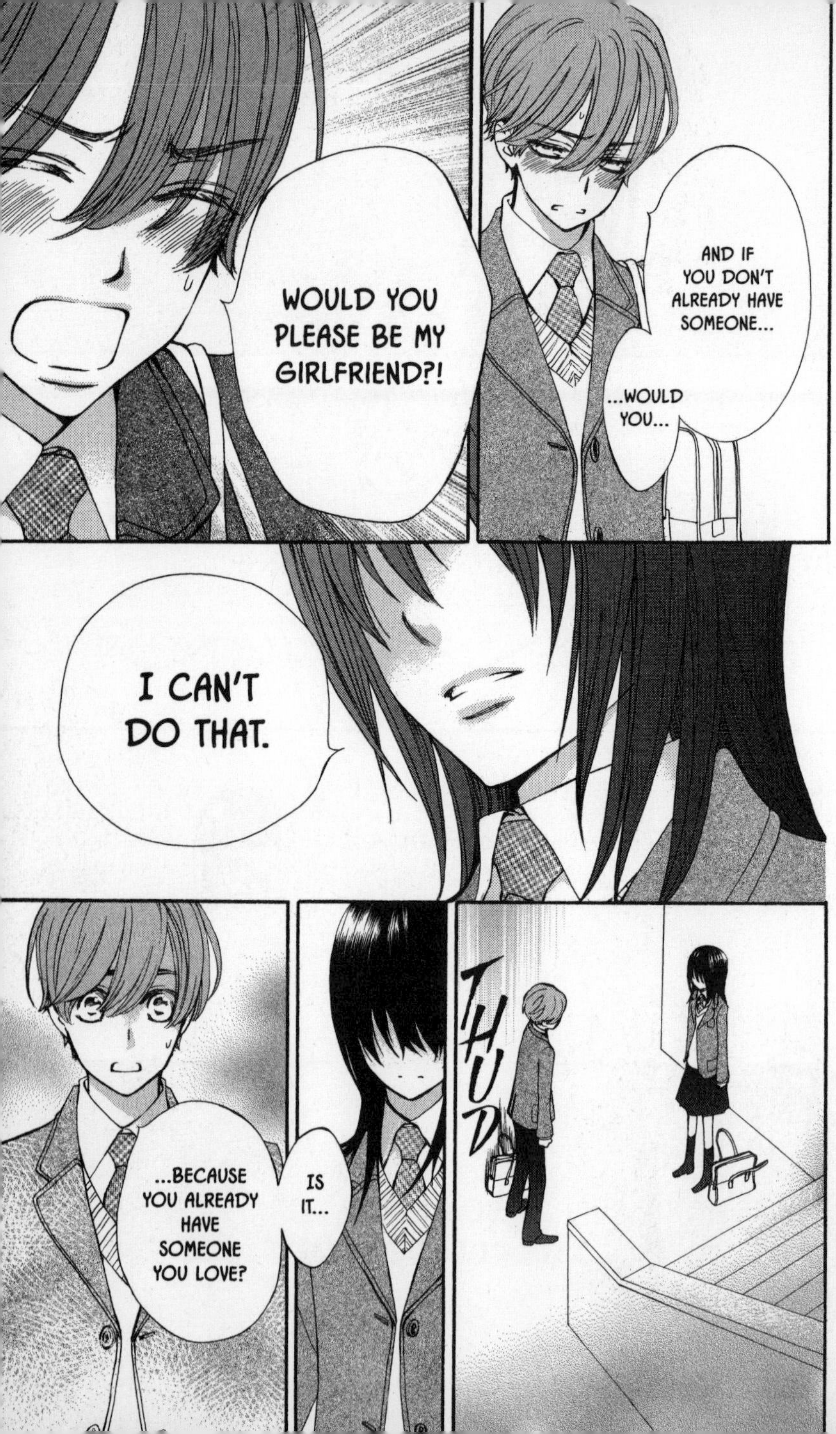
AND IF YOU DON'T ALREADY HAVE SOMEONE...
...WOULD YOU...
WOULD YOU PLEASE BE MY GIRLFRIEND?!
I CAN'T DO THAT.
THUD
IS IT...
...BECAUSE YOU ALREADY HAVE SOMEONE YOU LOVE?

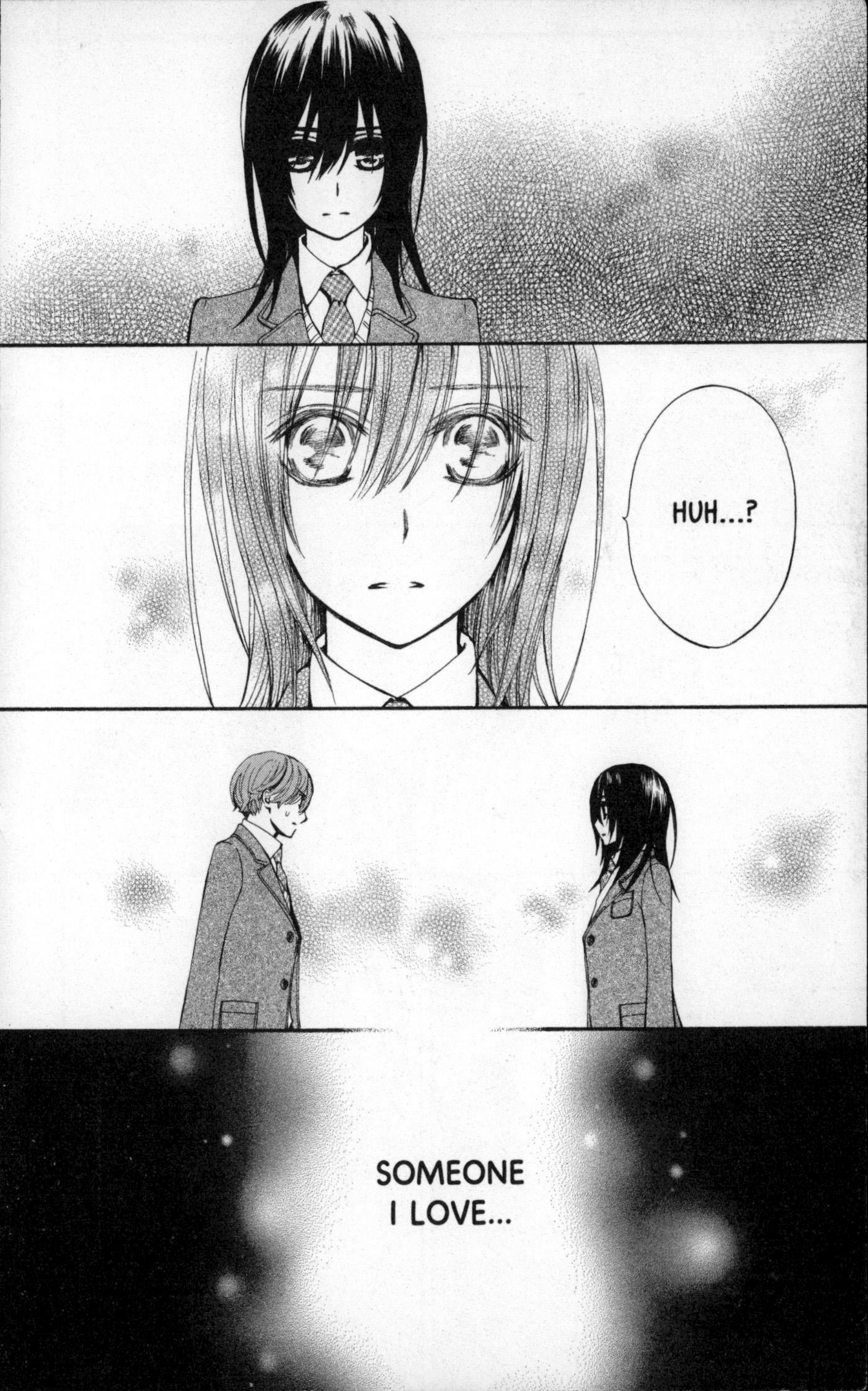
HUH...?
SOMEONE I LOVE...

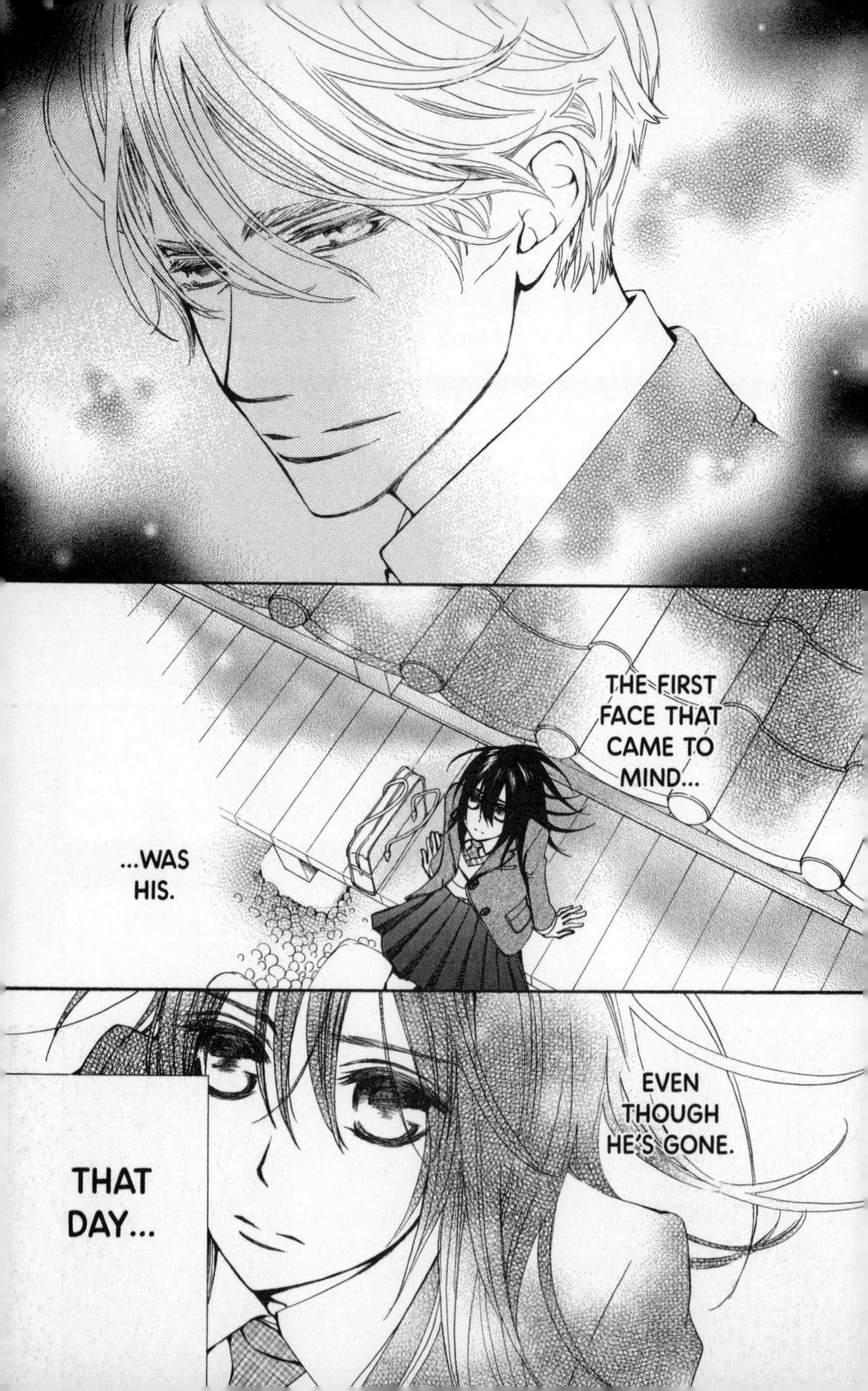
THE FIRST FACE THAT CAME TO MIND...
...WAS HIS.
EVEN THOUGH HE'S GONE.
THAT DAY...

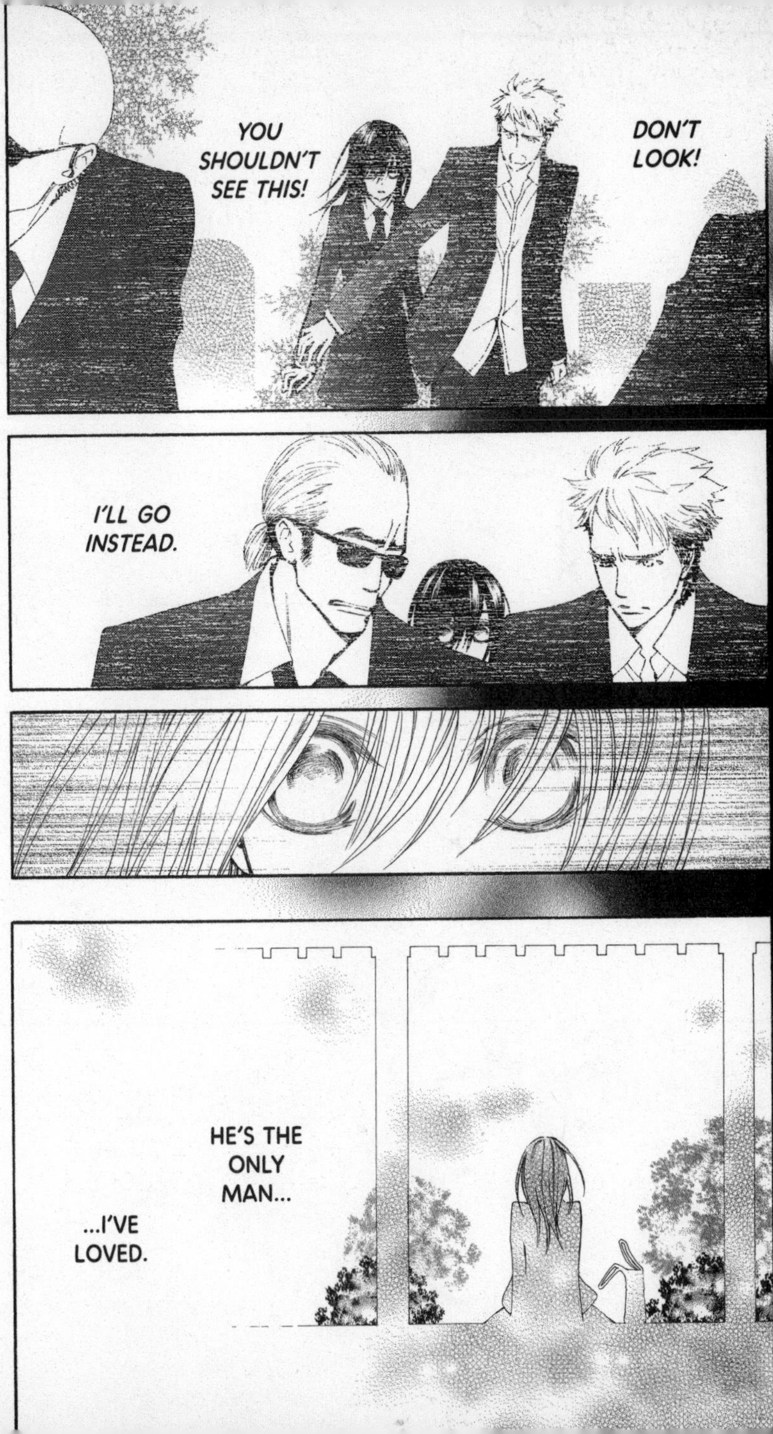
DON'T LOOK!
YOU SHOULDN'T SEE THIS!
I'LL GO INSTEAD.
HE'S THE ONLY MAN...
...I'VE LOVED.

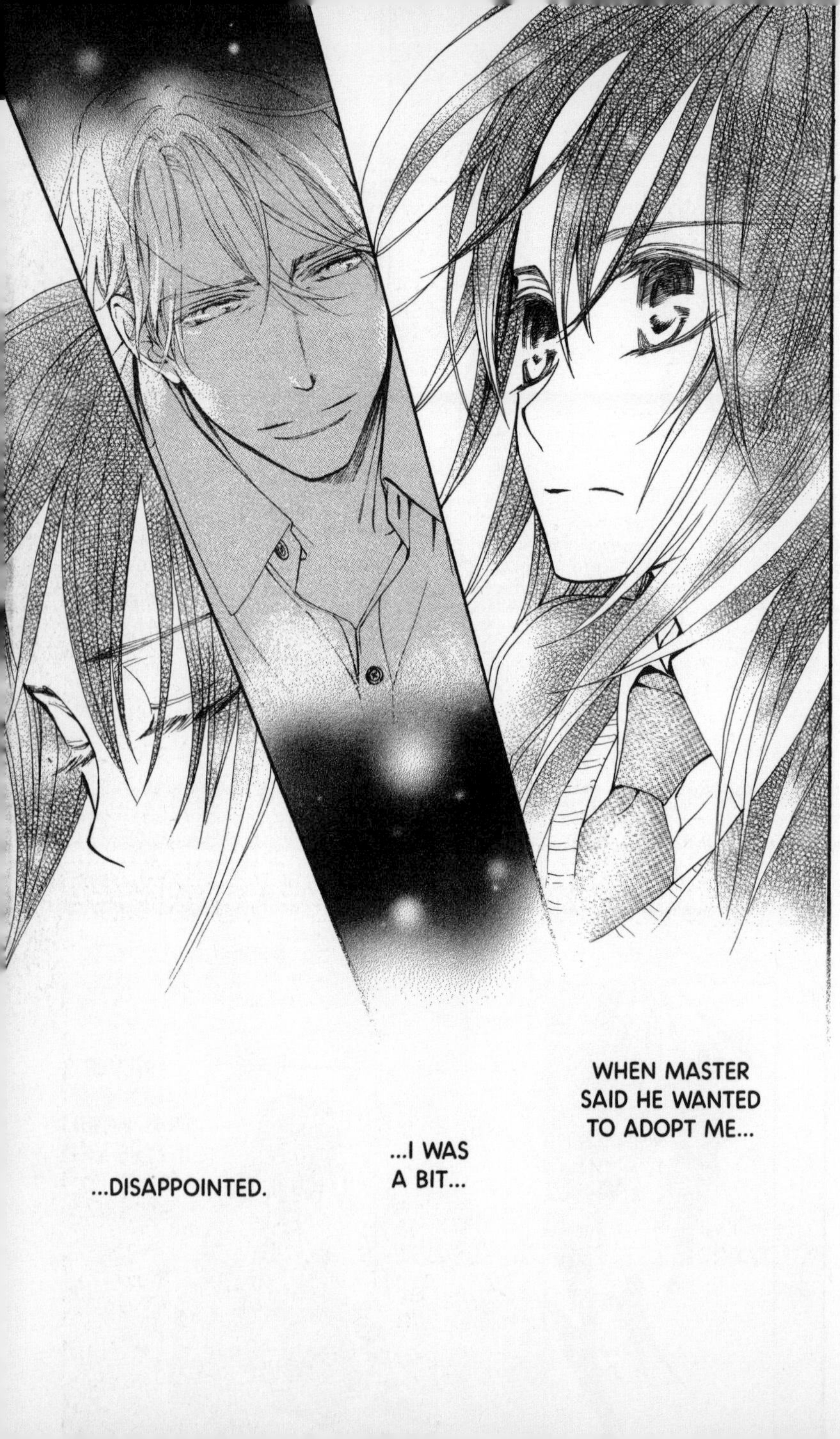
WHEN MASTER SAID HE WANTED TO ADOPT ME...
...I WAS A BIT...
...DISAPPOINTED.

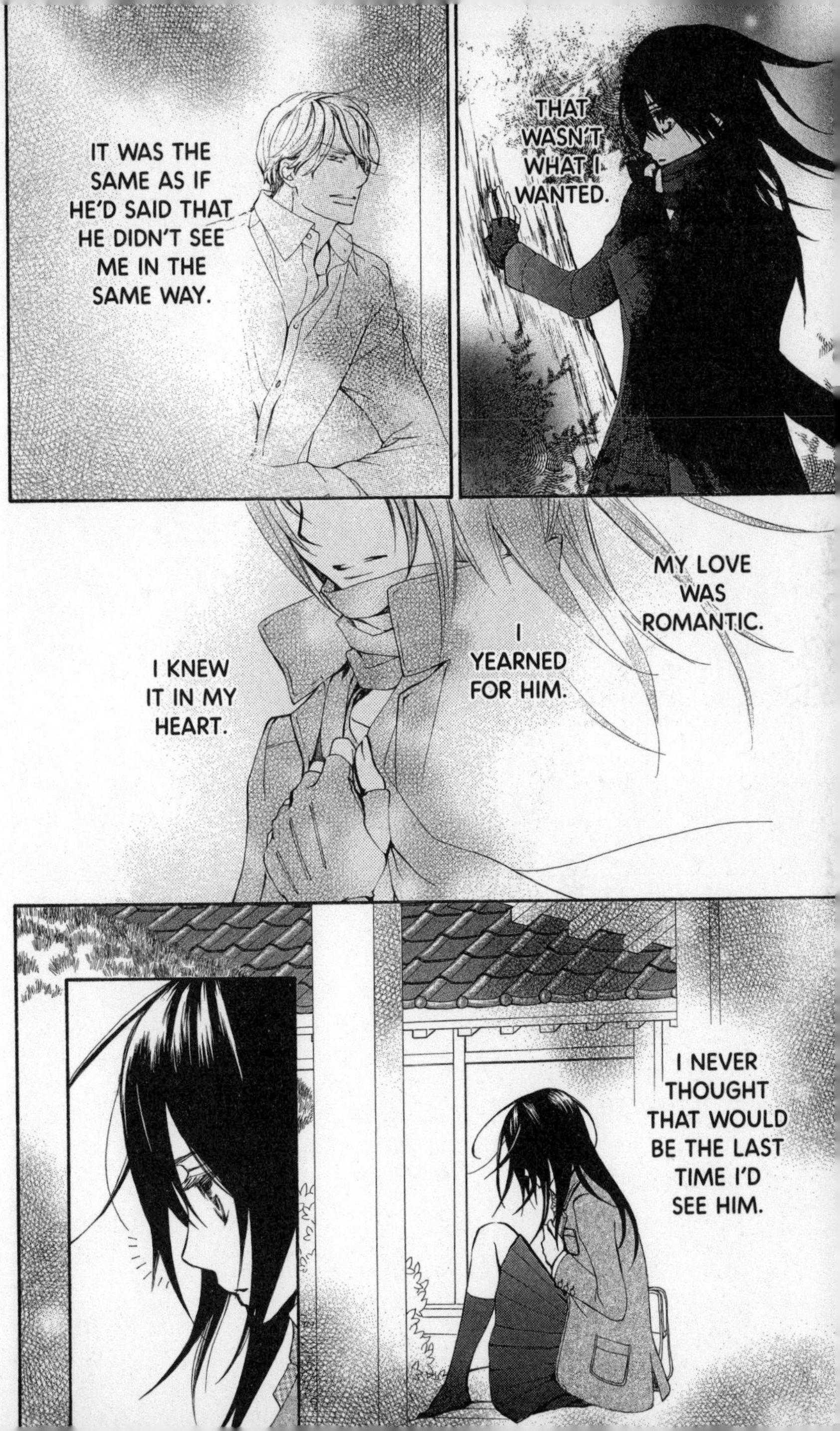
THAT WASN'T WHAT I WANTED.
IT WAS THE SAME AS IF HE'D SAID THAT HE DIDN'T SEE ME IN THE SAME WAY.
MY LOVE WAS ROMANTIC.
I YEARNED FOR HIM.
I KNEW IT IN MY HEART.
I NEVER THOUGHT THAT WOULD BE THE LAST TIME I'D SEE HIM.

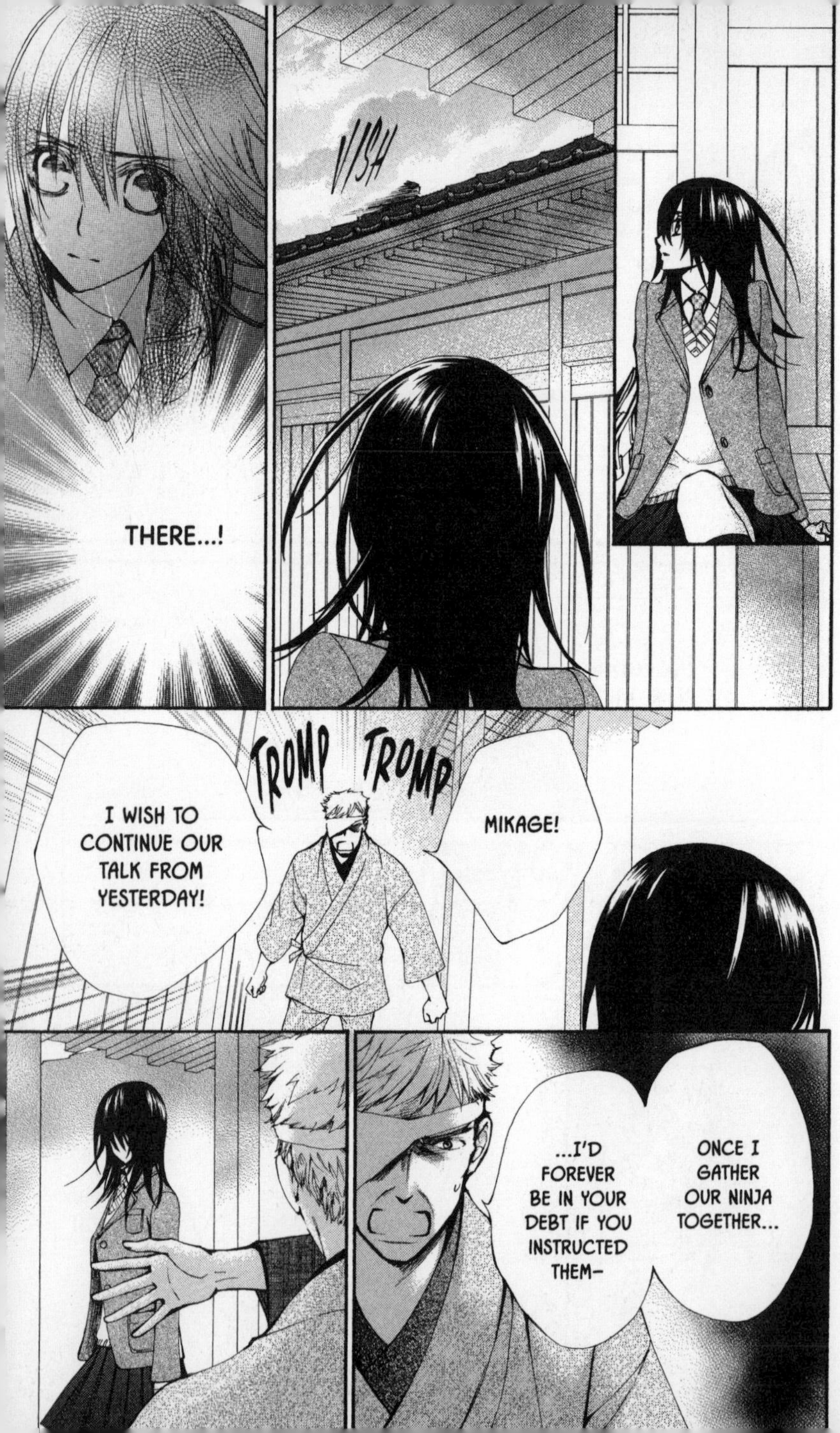
VISH
THERE...!
MIKAGE!
TROMP TROMP
I WISH TO CONTINUE OUR TALK FROM YESTERDAY!
ONCE I GATHER OUR NINJA TOGETHER...
...I'D FOREVER BE IN YOUR DEBT IF YOU INSTRUCTED THEM–

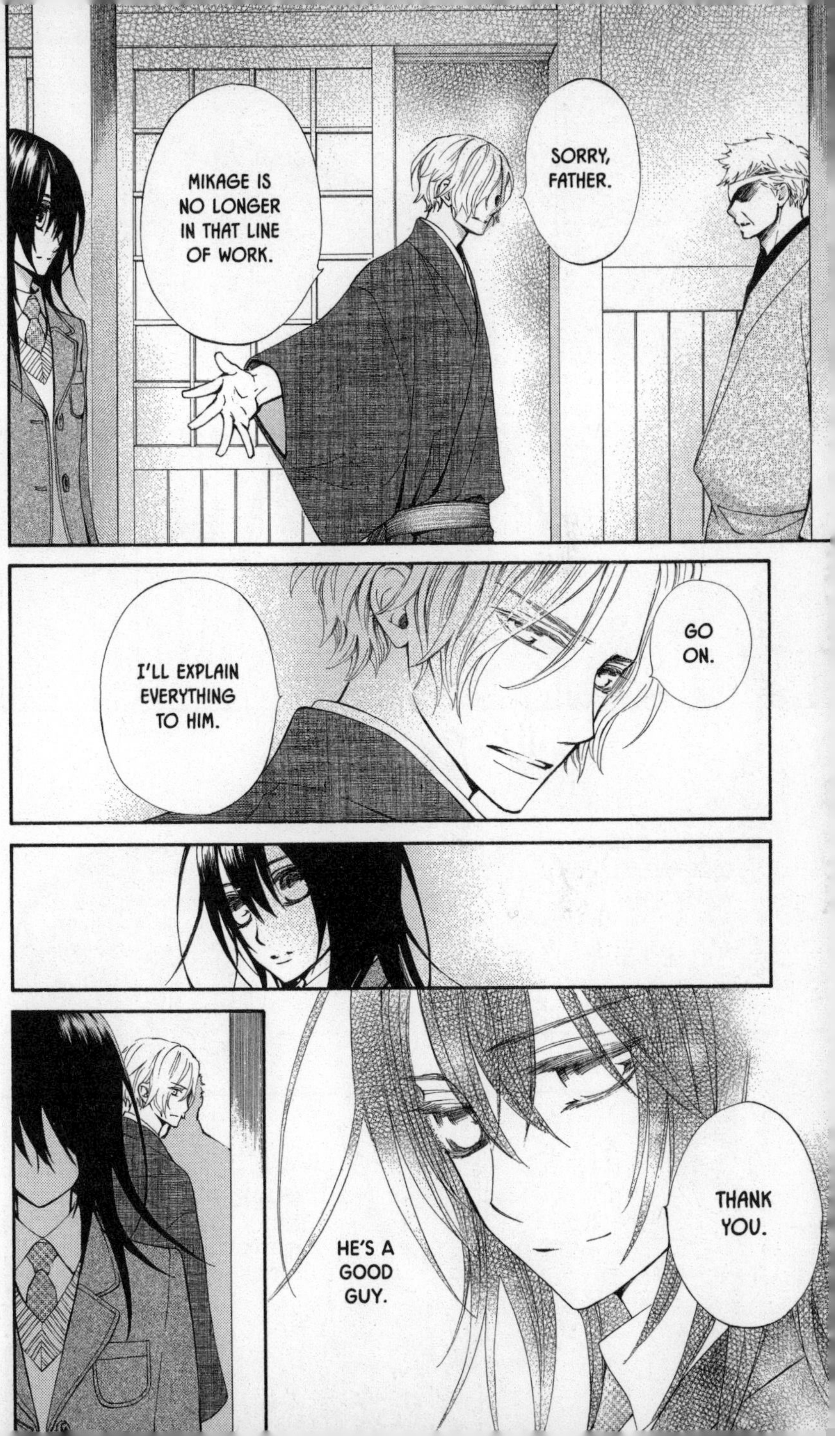
SORRY, FATHER.
MIKAGE IS NO LONGER IN THAT LINE OF WORK.
GO ON.
I'LL EXPLAIN EVERYTHING TO HIM.
THANK YOU.
HE'S A GOOD GUY.

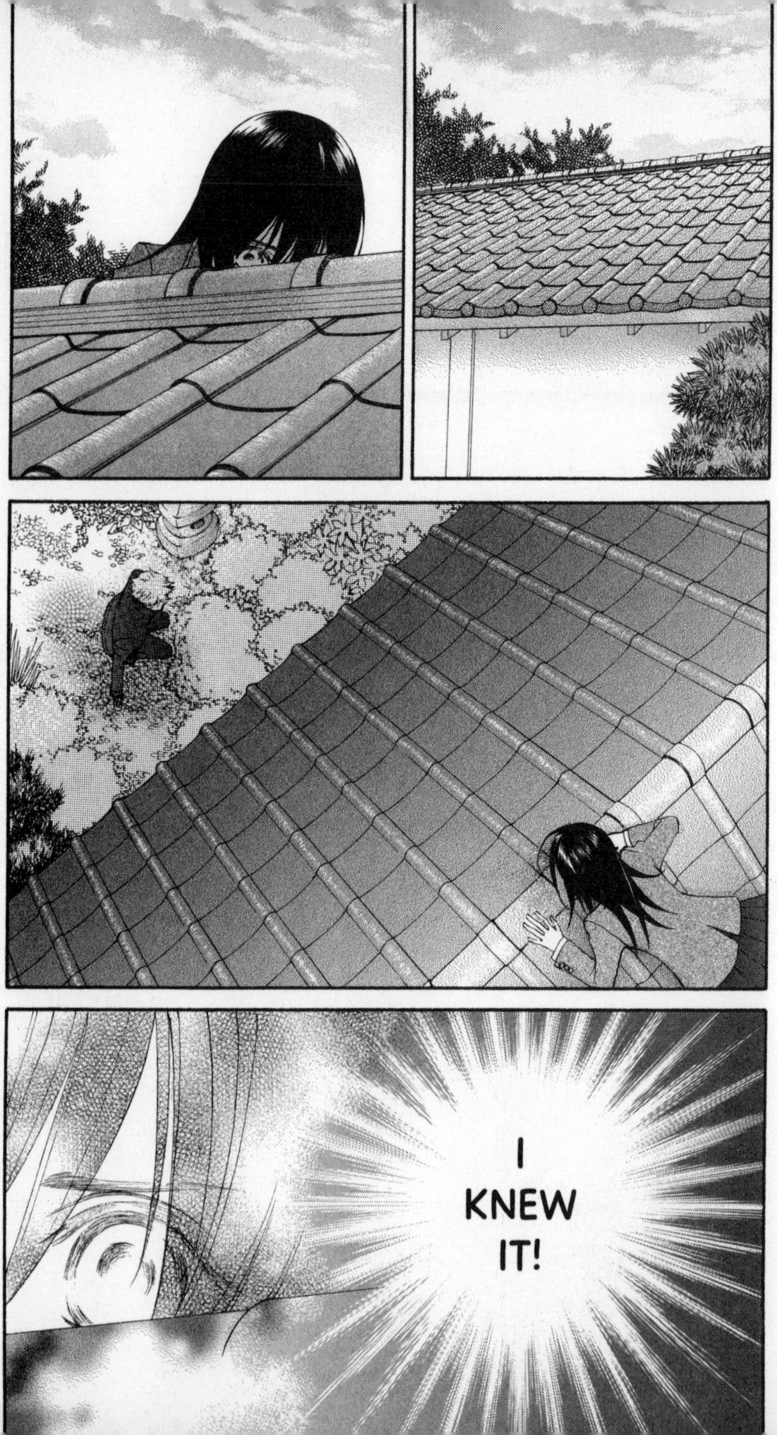
I KNEW IT!

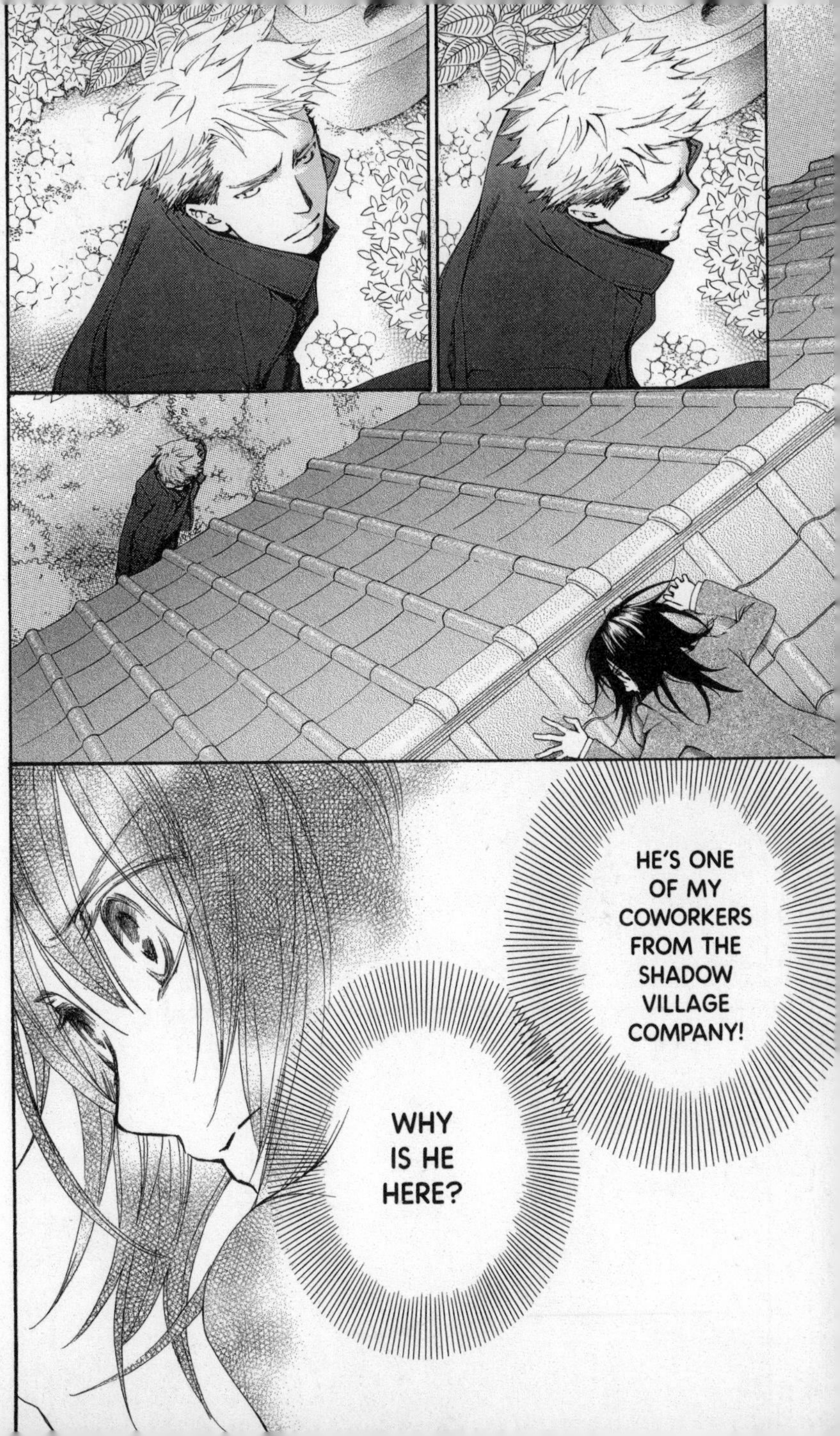
HE'S ONE OF MY COWORKERS FROM THE SHADOW VILLAGE COMPANY!
WHY IS HE HERE?

# Chapter 8

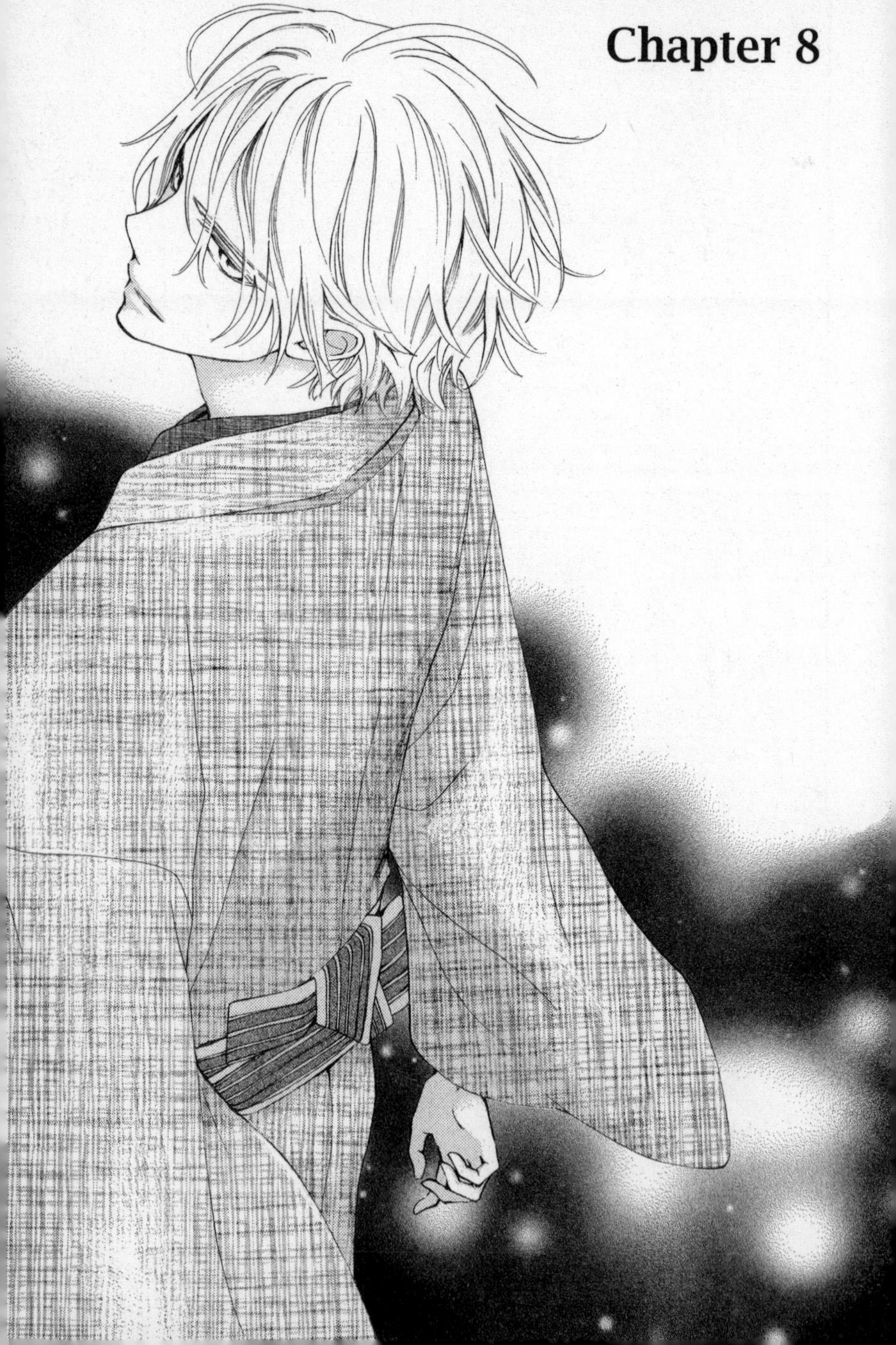

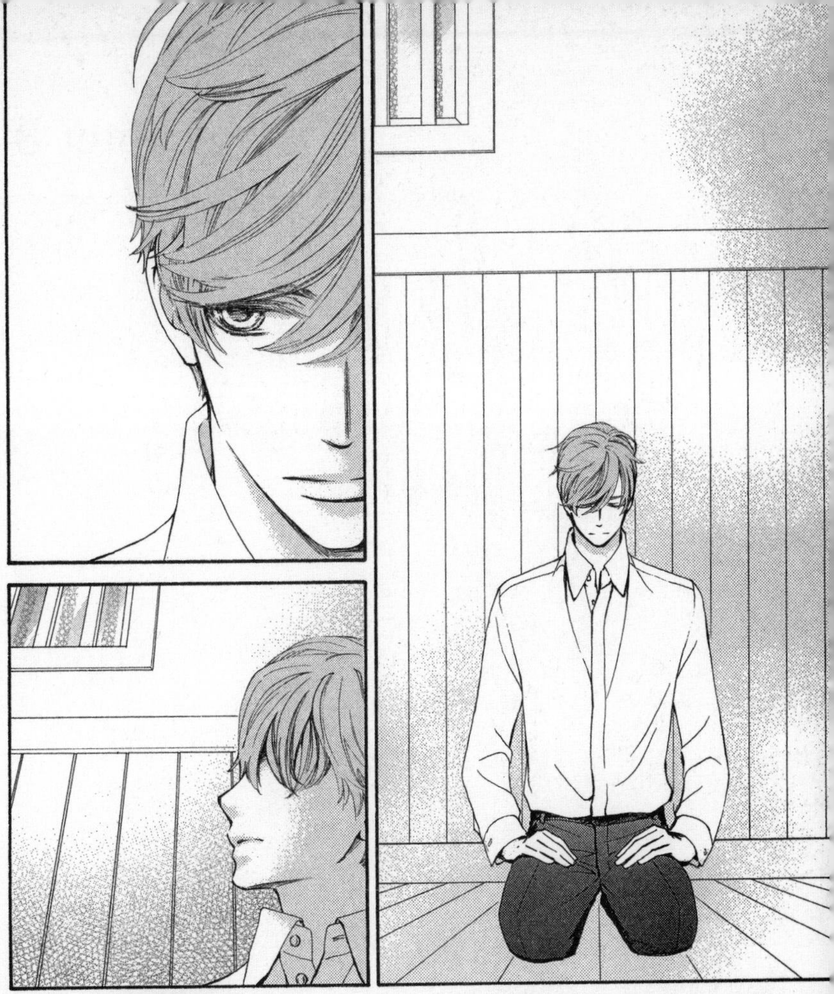

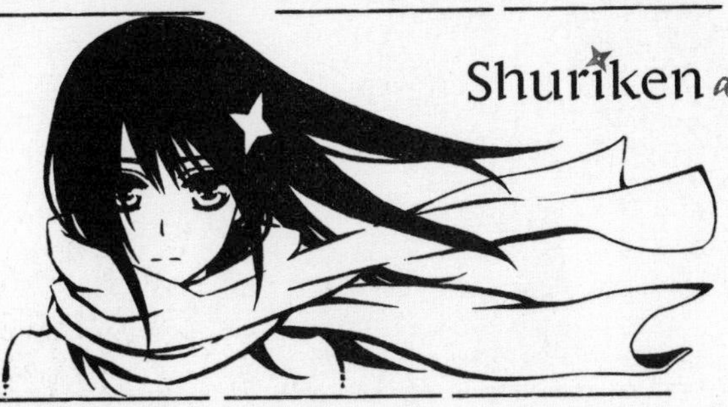

# Shuriken and Pleats

MATSURI HINO

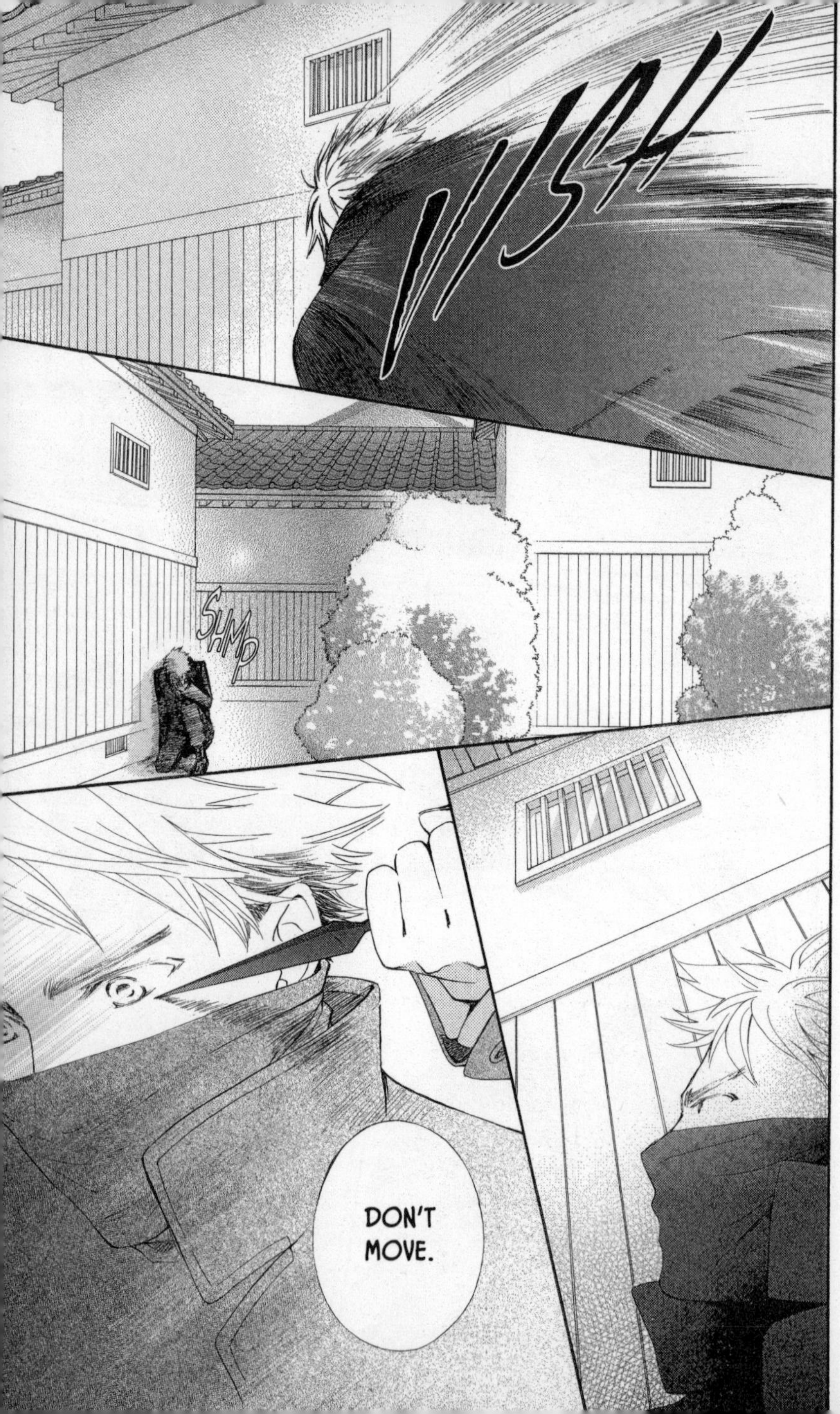
VISH
SHMP
DON'T MOVE.

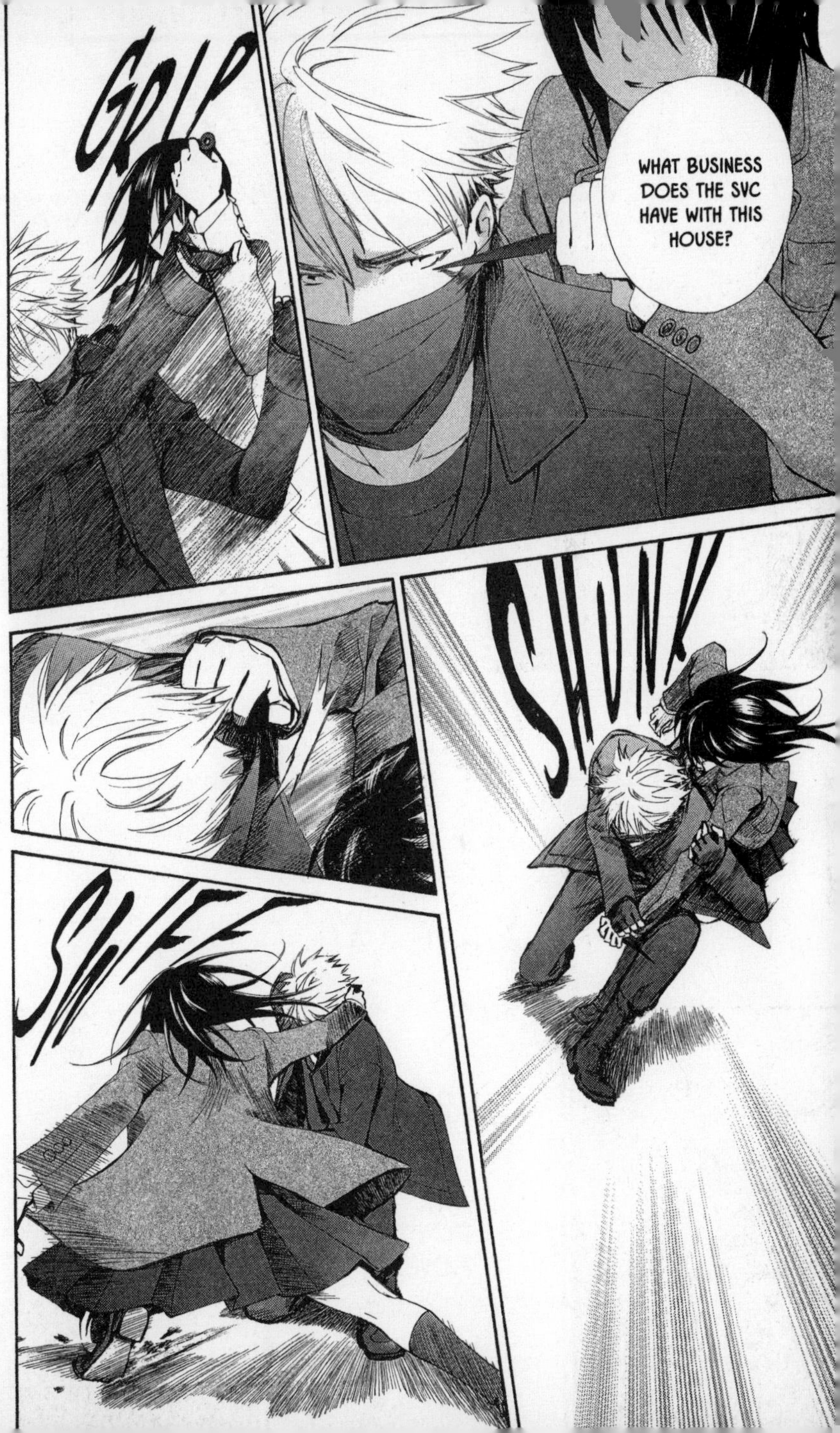
WHAT BUSINESS DOES THE SVC HAVE WITH THIS HOUSE?
GRIP
SHUNK
SHFF

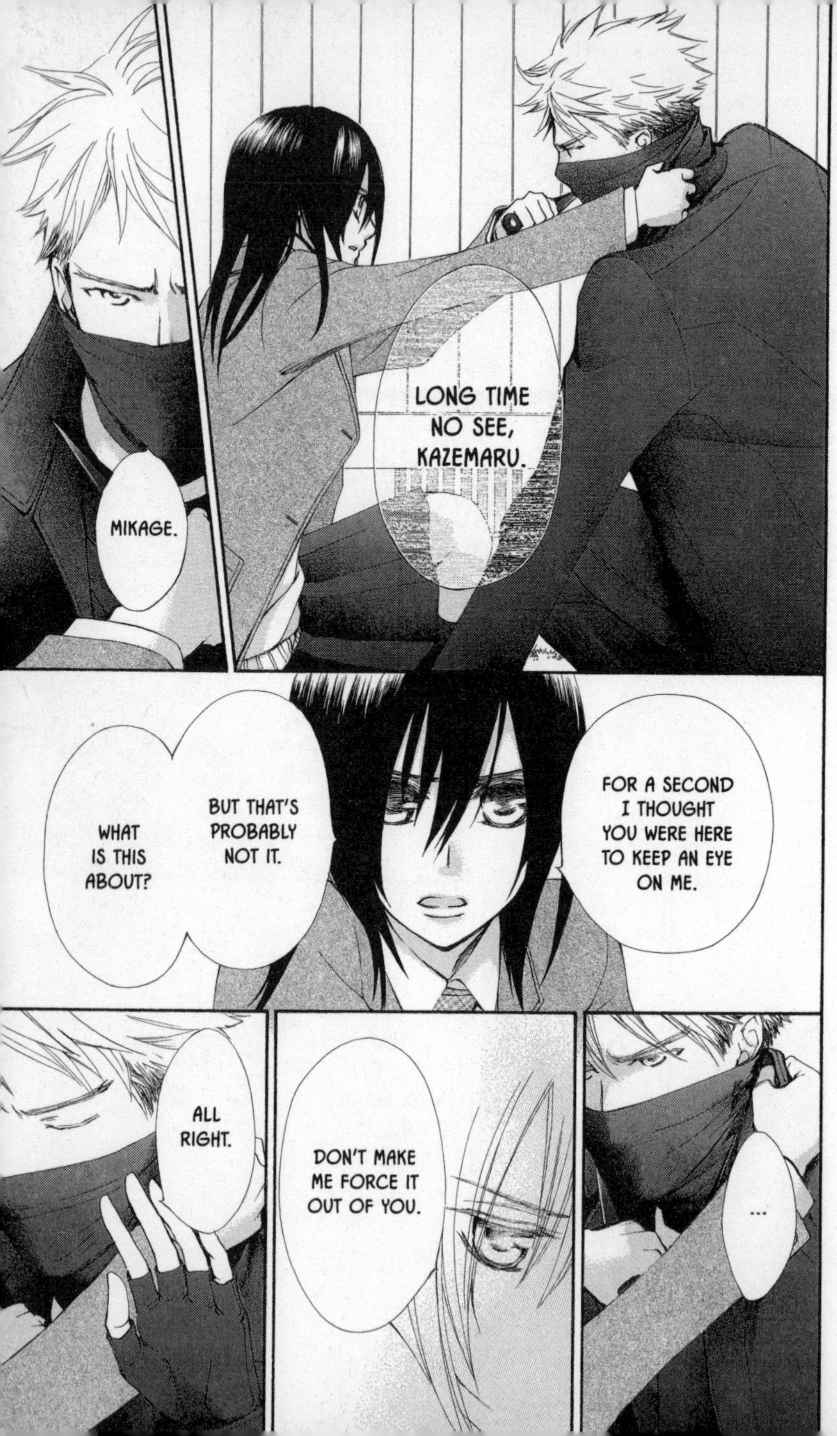
LONG TIME NO SEE, KAZEMARU.
MIKAGE.
FOR A SECOND I THOUGHT YOU WERE HERE TO KEEP AN EYE ON ME.
BUT THAT'S PROBABLY NOT IT.
WHAT IS THIS ABOUT?
...
DON'T MAKE ME FORCE IT OUT OF YOU.
ALL RIGHT.

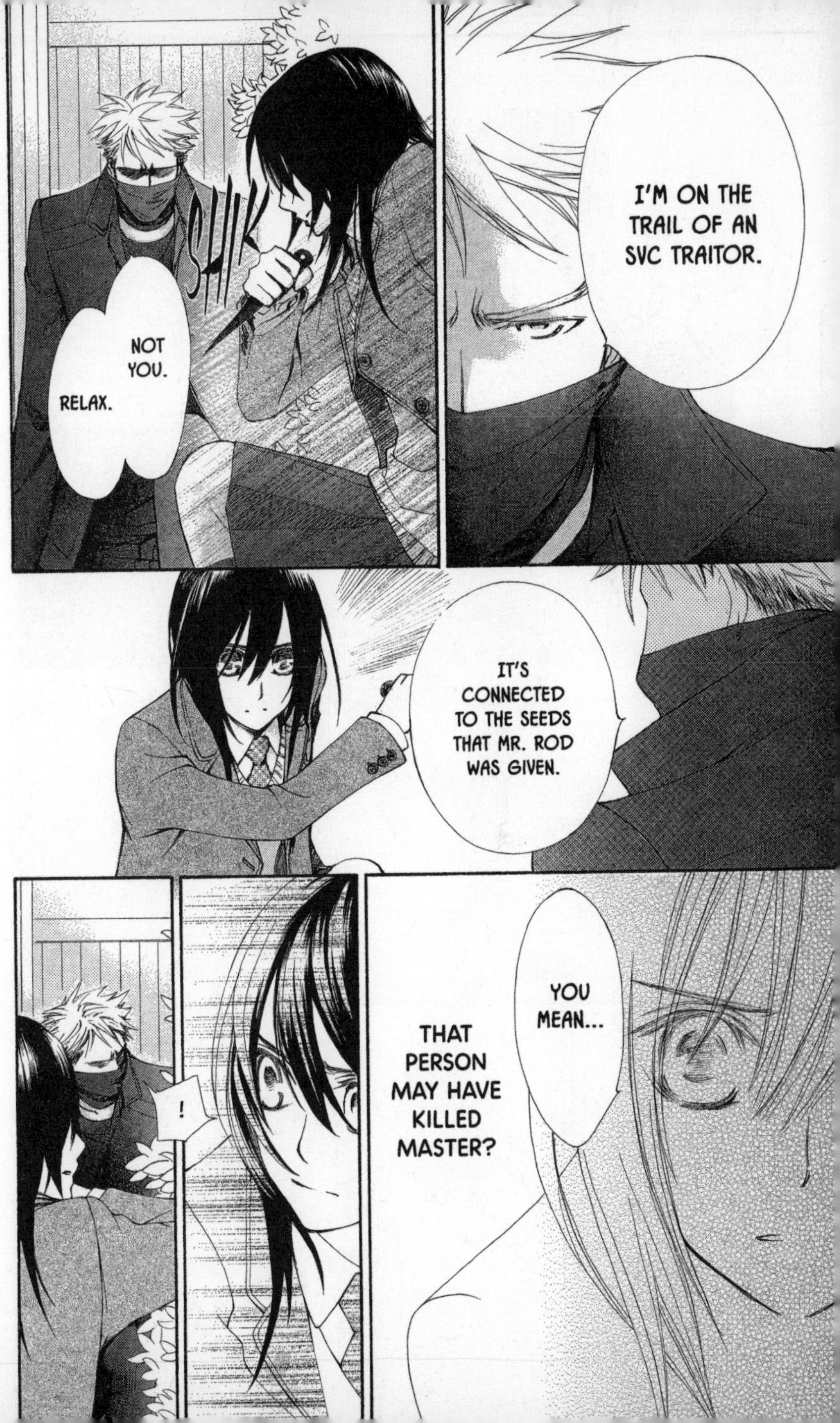
I'M ON THE TRAIL OF AN SVC TRAITOR.
SHIK
NOT YOU.
RELAX.
IT'S CONNECTED TO THE SEEDS THAT MR. ROD WAS GIVEN.
YOU MEAN...
THAT PERSON MAY HAVE KILLED MASTER?
!

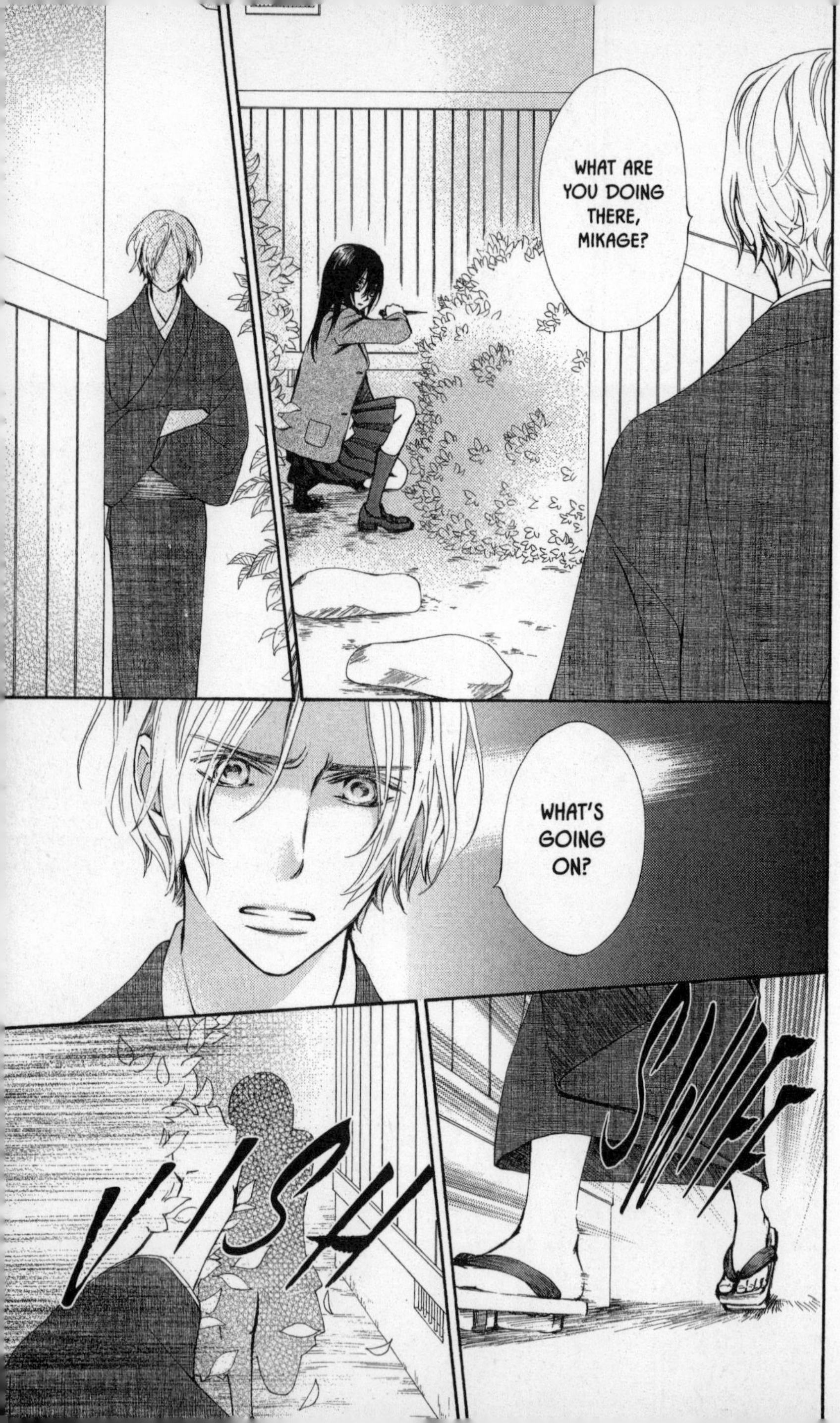
WHAT ARE YOU DOING THERE, MIKAGE?
WHAT'S GOING ON?
SHFF
WISH

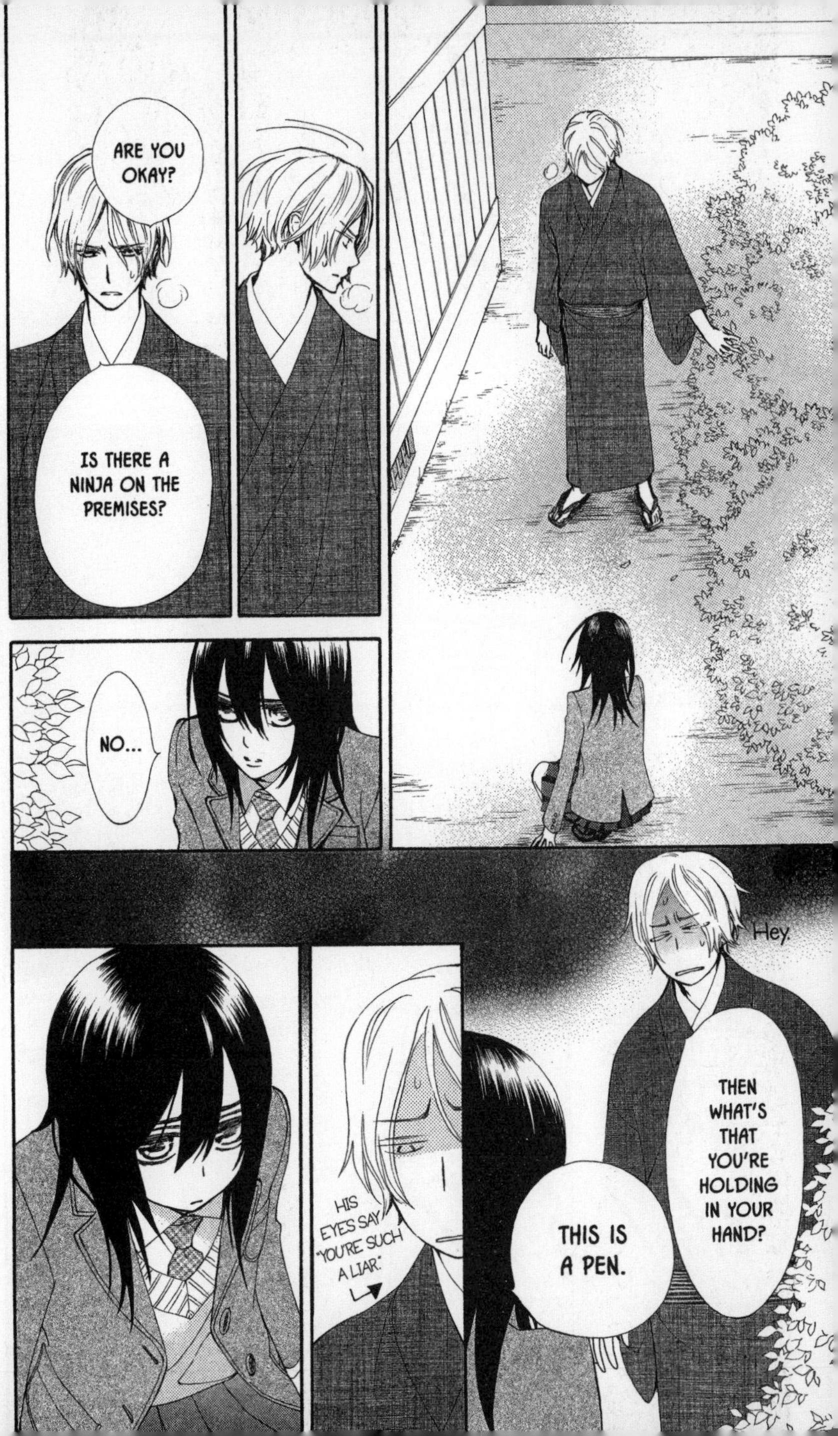
ARE YOU OKAY?
IS THERE A NINJA ON THE PREMISES?
NO...
Hey.
THEN WHAT'S THAT YOU'RE HOLDING IN YOUR HAND?
THIS IS A PEN.
HIS EYES SAY "YOU'RE SUCH A LIAR."

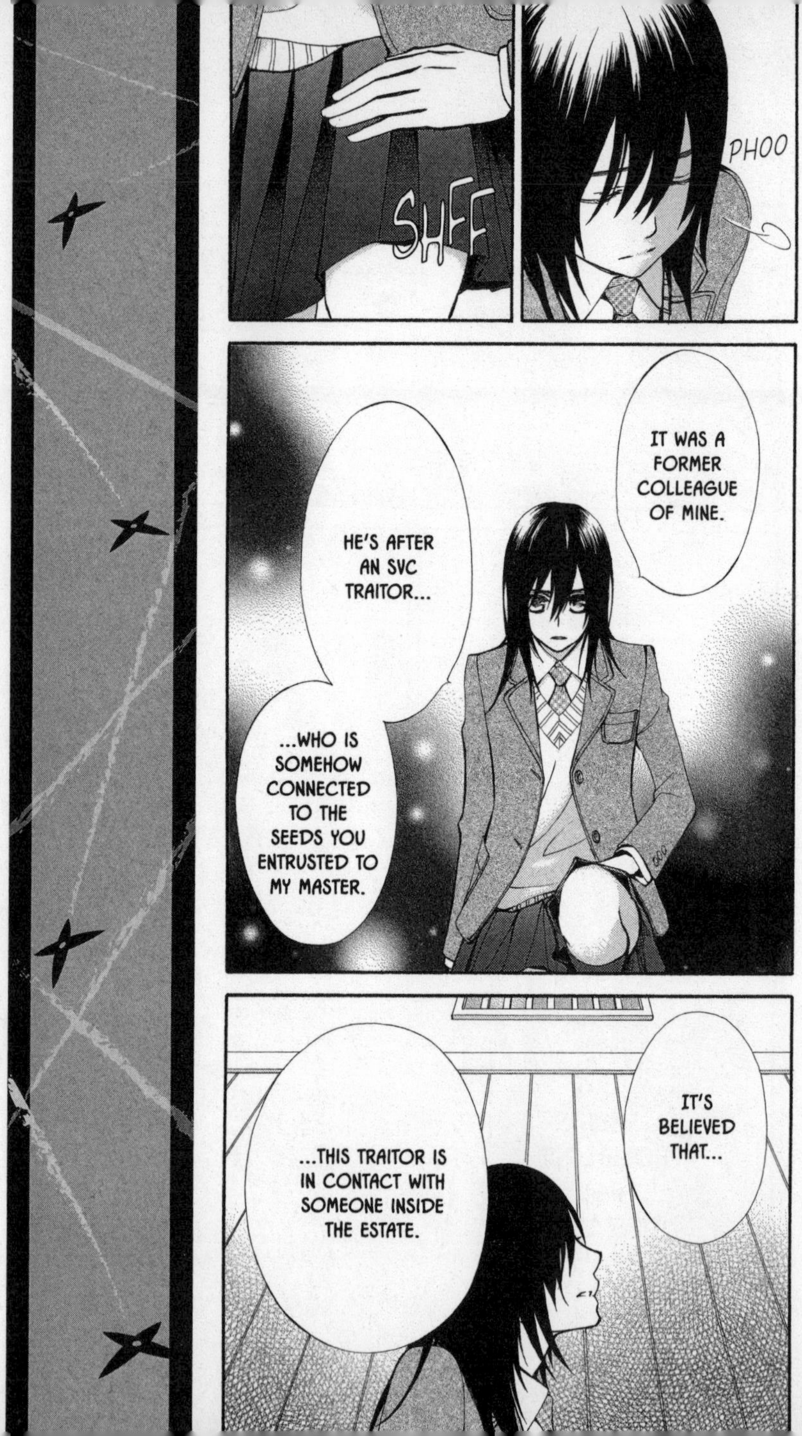
PHOO
SHFF
IT WAS A FORMER COLLEAGUE OF MINE.
HE'S AFTER AN SVC TRAITOR...
...WHO IS SOMEHOW CONNECTED TO THE SEEDS YOU ENTRUSTED TO MY MASTER.
IT'S BELIEVED THAT...
...THIS TRAITOR IS IN CONTACT WITH SOMEONE INSIDE THE ESTATE.

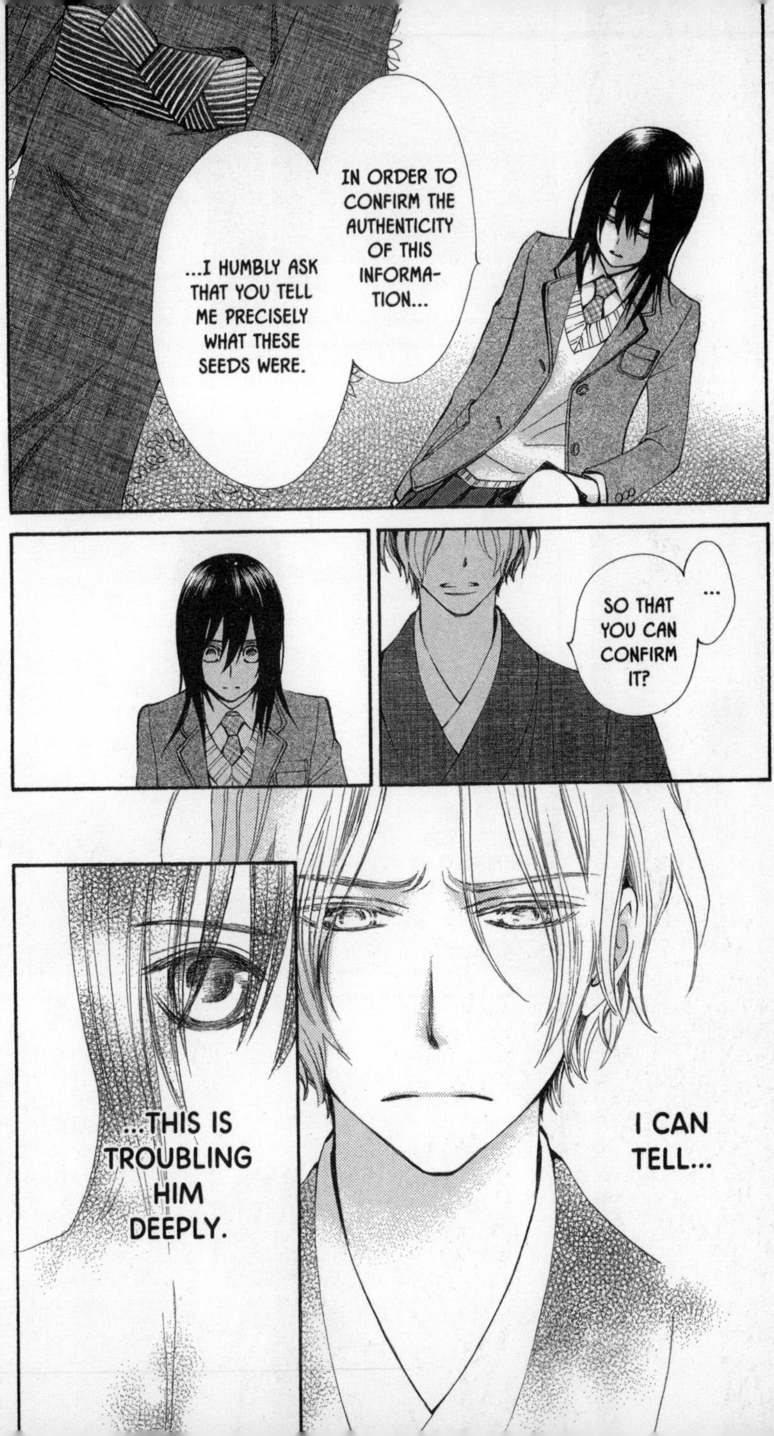
IN ORDER TO CONFIRM THE AUTHENTICITY OF THIS INFORMA-TION...
...I HUMBLY ASK THAT YOU TELL ME PRECISELY WHAT THESE SEEDS WERE.
...
SO THAT YOU CAN CONFIRM IT?
I CAN TELL...
...THIS IS TROUBLING HIM DEEPLY.

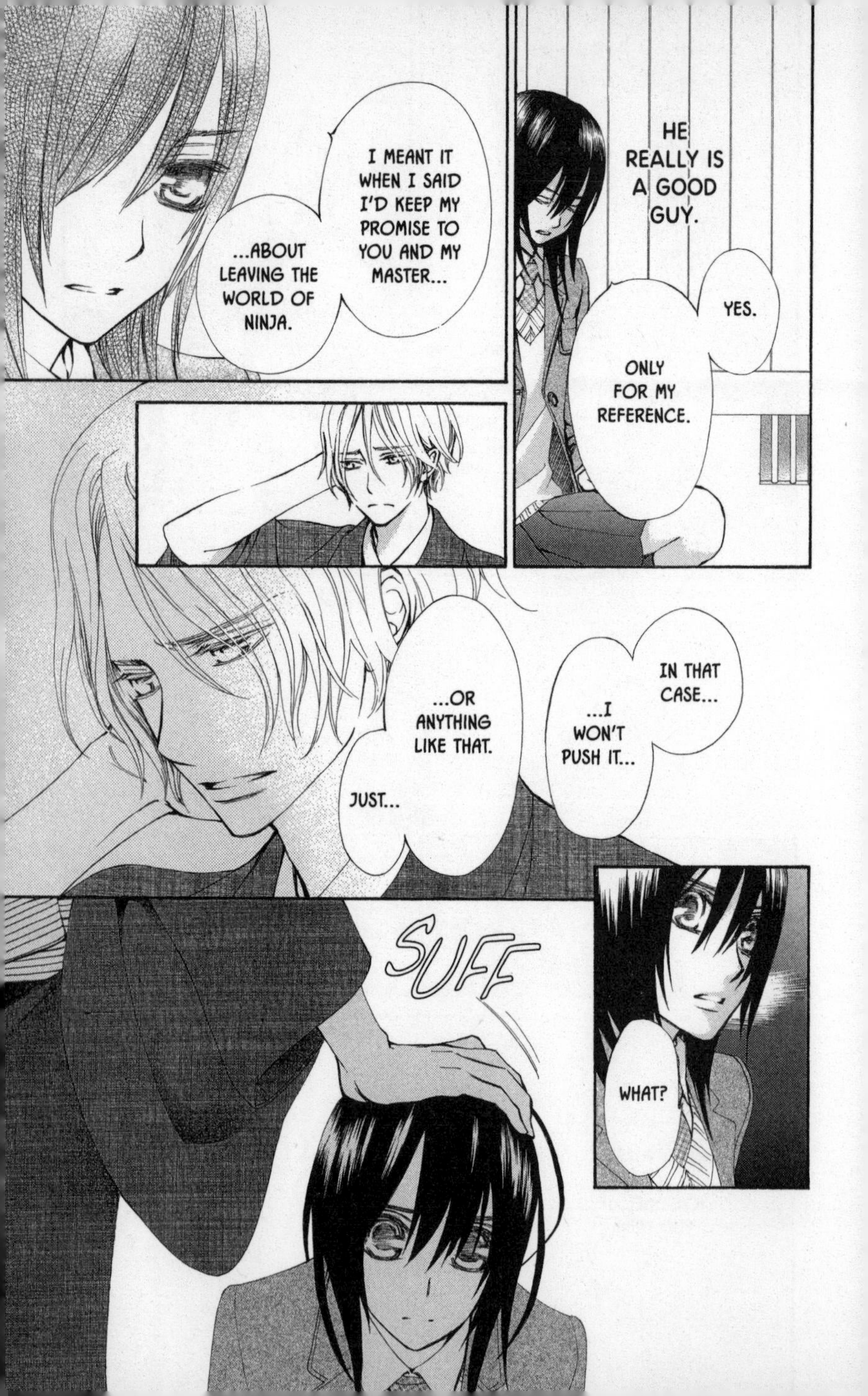
HE REALLY IS A GOOD GUY.
YES.
ONLY FOR MY REFERENCE.
I MEANT IT WHEN I SAID I'D KEEP MY PROMISE TO YOU AND MY MASTER...
...ABOUT LEAVING THE WORLD OF NINJA.
IN THAT CASE...
...I WON'T PUSH IT...
...OR ANYTHING LIKE THAT.
JUST...
WHAT?
SUFF

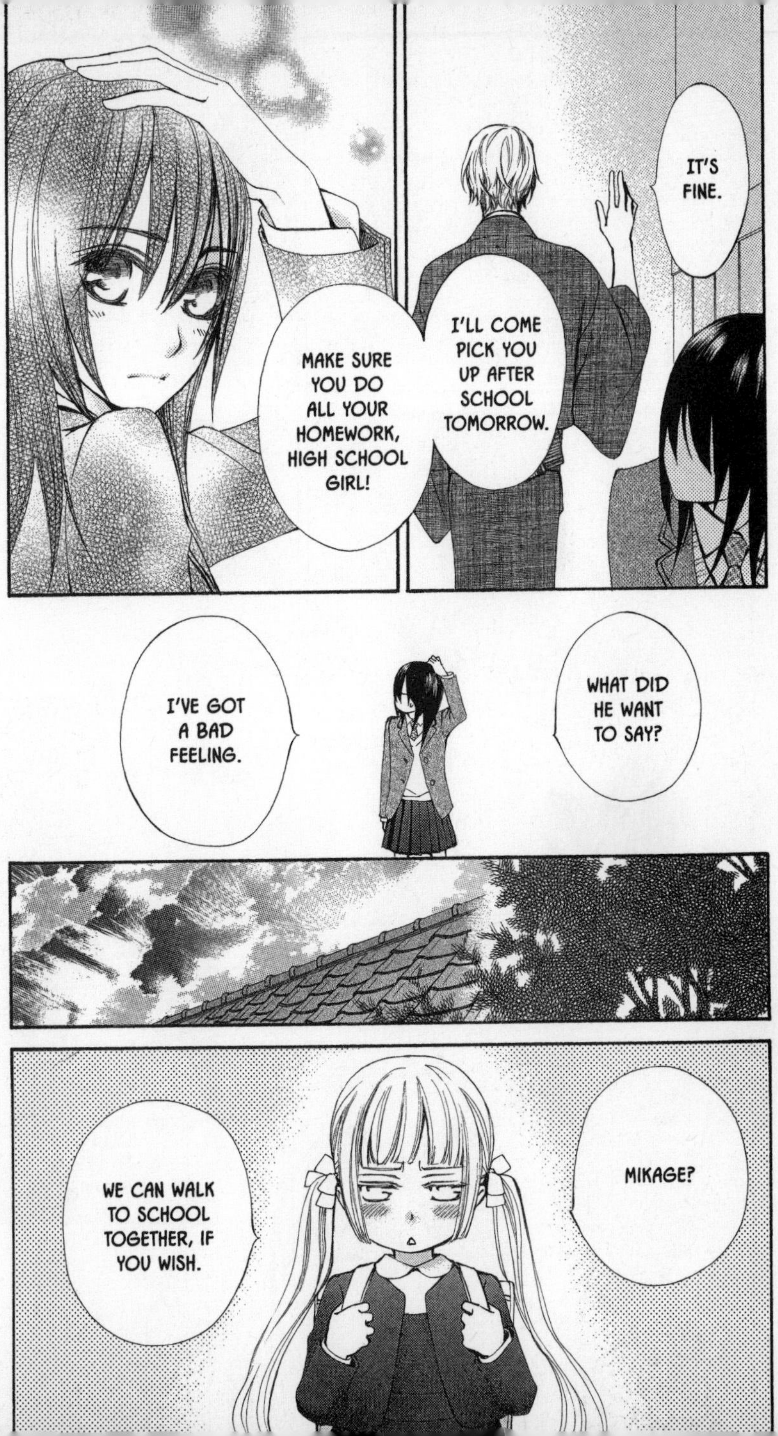
IT'S FINE.
I'LL COME PICK YOU UP AFTER SCHOOL TOMORROW.
MAKE SURE YOU DO ALL YOUR HOMEWORK, HIGH SCHOOL GIRL!
WHAT DID HE WANT TO SAY?
I'VE GOT A BAD FEELING.
MIKAGE?
WE CAN WALK TO SCHOOL TOGETHER, IF YOU WISH.

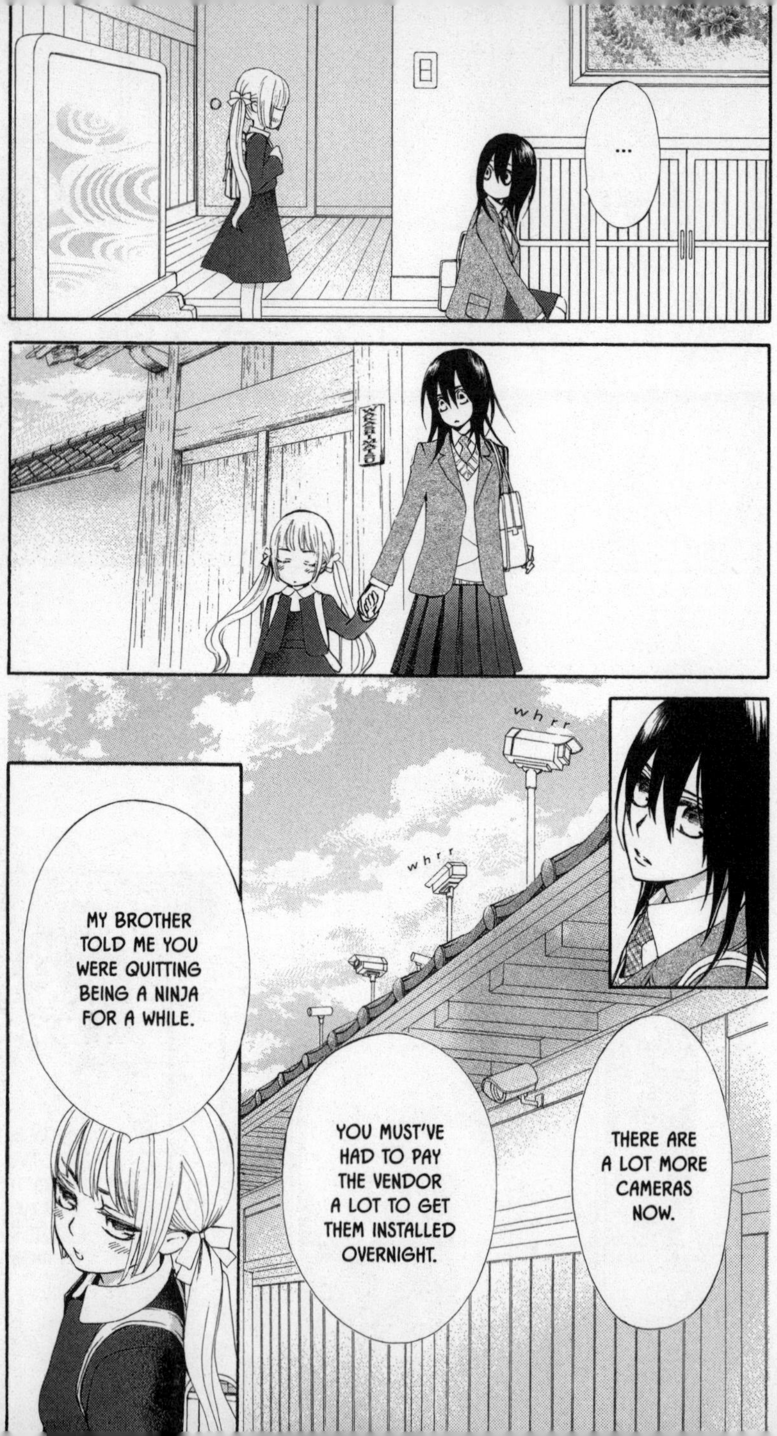
...
whrr
whrr
THERE ARE A LOT MORE CAMERAS NOW.
YOU MUST'VE HAD TO PAY THE VENDOR A LOT TO GET THEM INSTALLED OVERNIGHT.
MY BROTHER TOLD ME YOU WERE QUITTING BEING A NINJA FOR A WHILE.

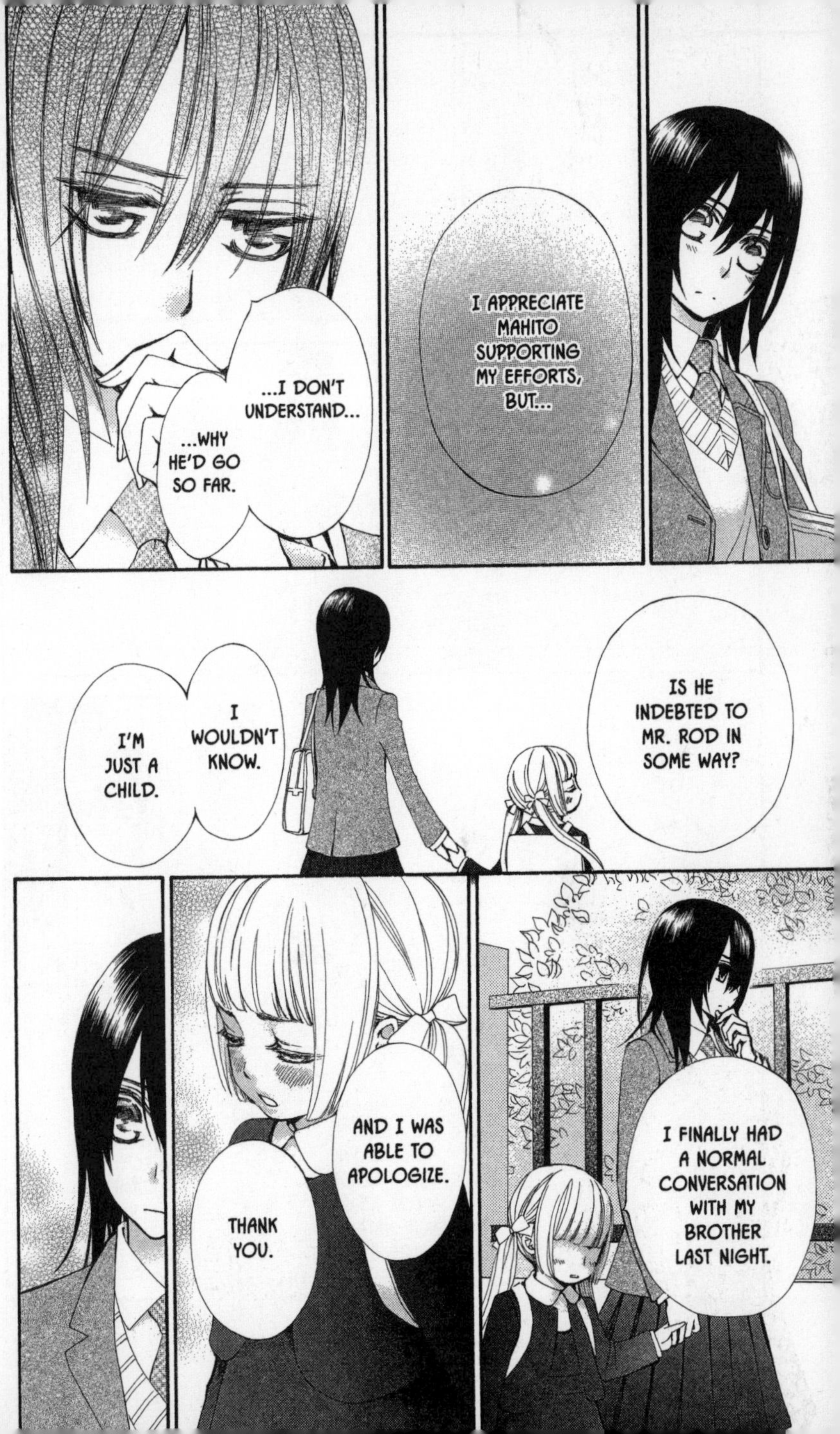
I APPRECIATE MAHITO SUPPORTING MY EFFORTS, BUT...
...I DON'T UNDERSTAND...
...WHY HE'D GO SO FAR.
IS HE INDEBTED TO MR. ROD IN SOME WAY?
I WOULDN'T KNOW.
I'M JUST A CHILD.
I FINALLY HAD A NORMAL CONVERSATION WITH MY BROTHER LAST NIGHT.
AND I WAS ABLE TO APOLOGIZE.
THANK YOU.

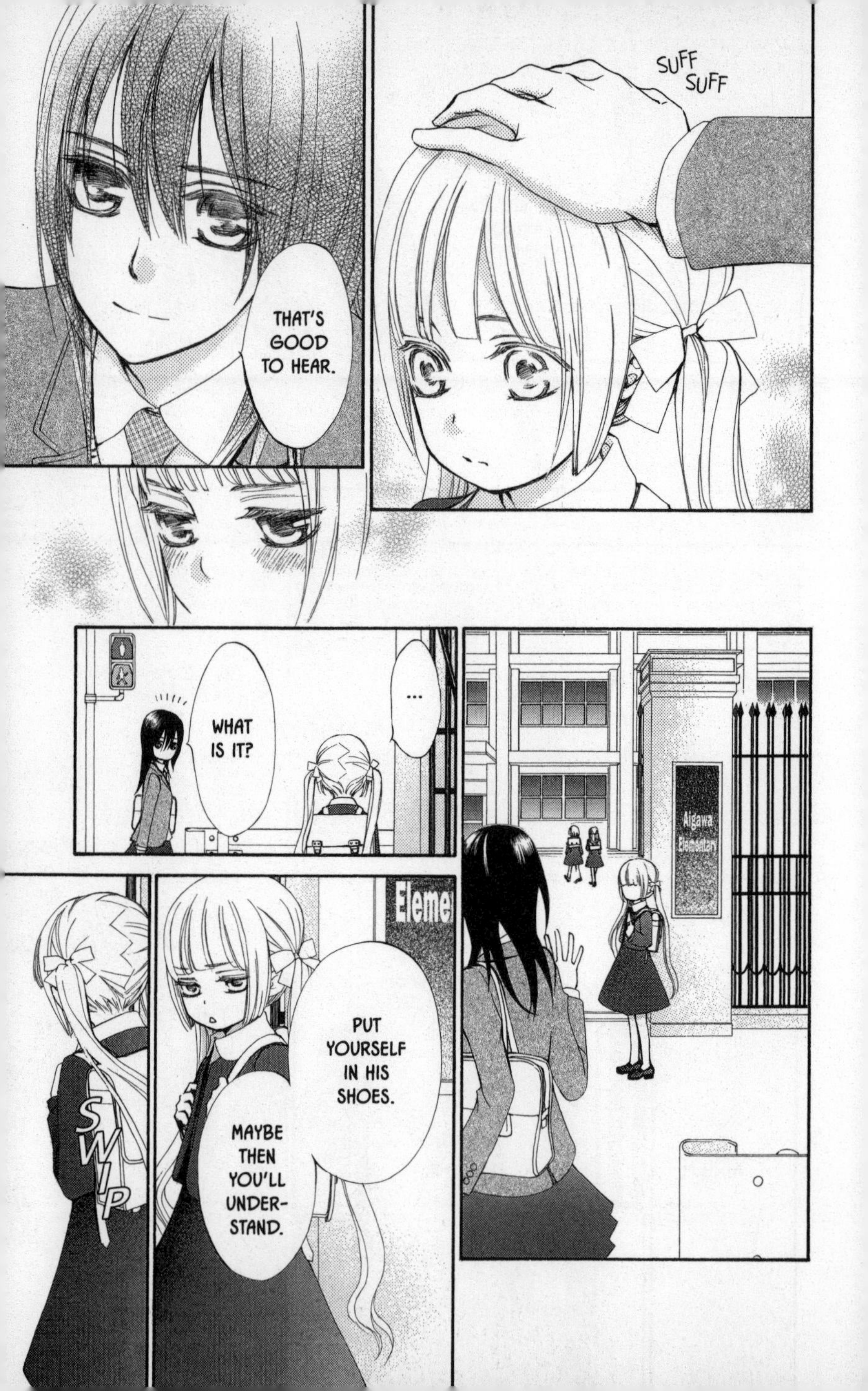
SUFF SUFF
THAT'S GOOD TO HEAR.
...
WHAT IS IT?
Eleme
PUT YOURSELF IN HIS SHOES.
MAYBE THEN YOU'LL UNDER-STAND.
SWIP
Aigawa Elementary

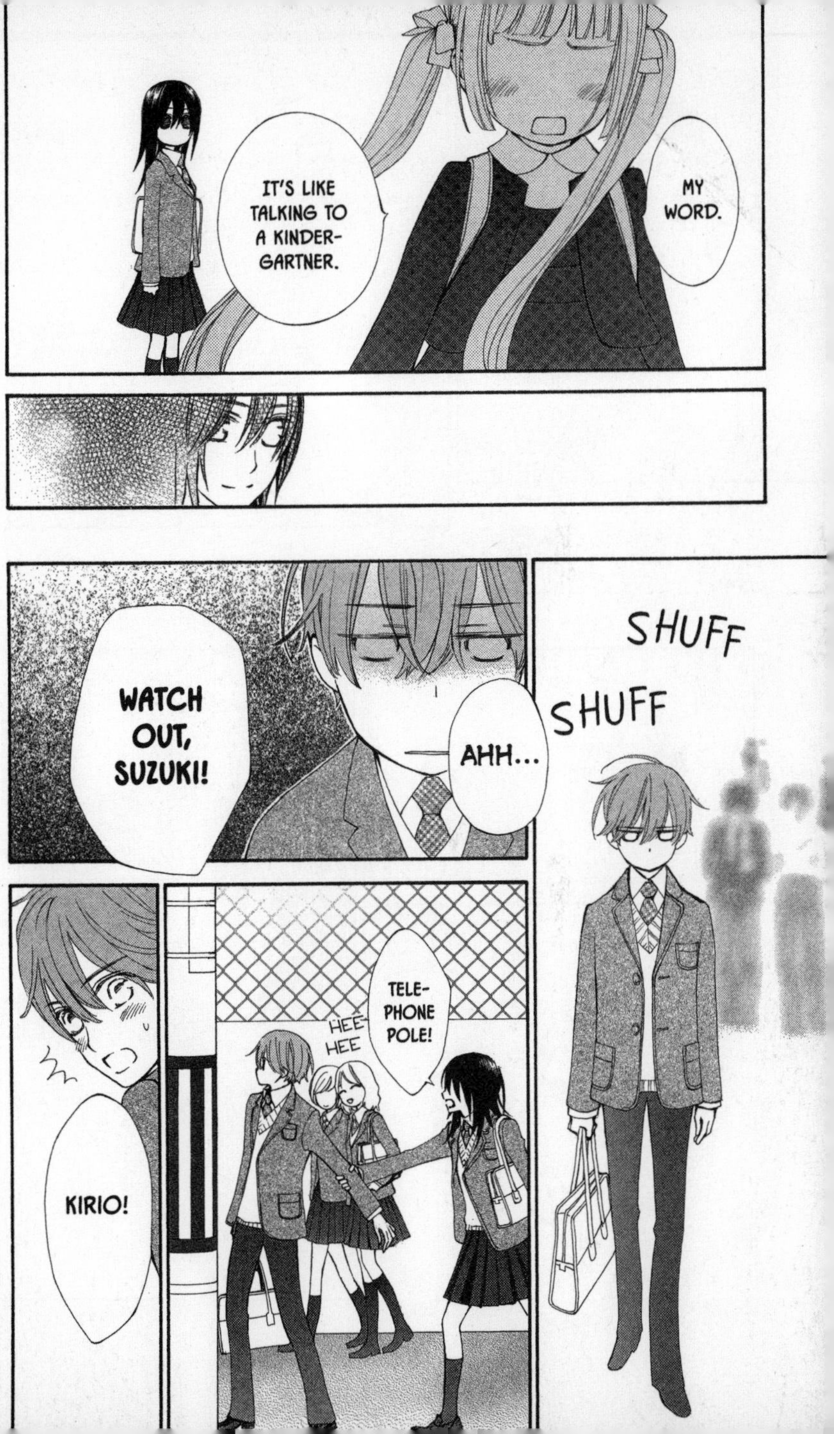
MY WORD.
IT'S LIKE TALKING TO A KINDER-GARTNER.
SHUFF
SHUFF
AHH...
WATCH OUT, SUZUKI!
TELE-PHONE POLE!
HEE HEE
KIRIO!

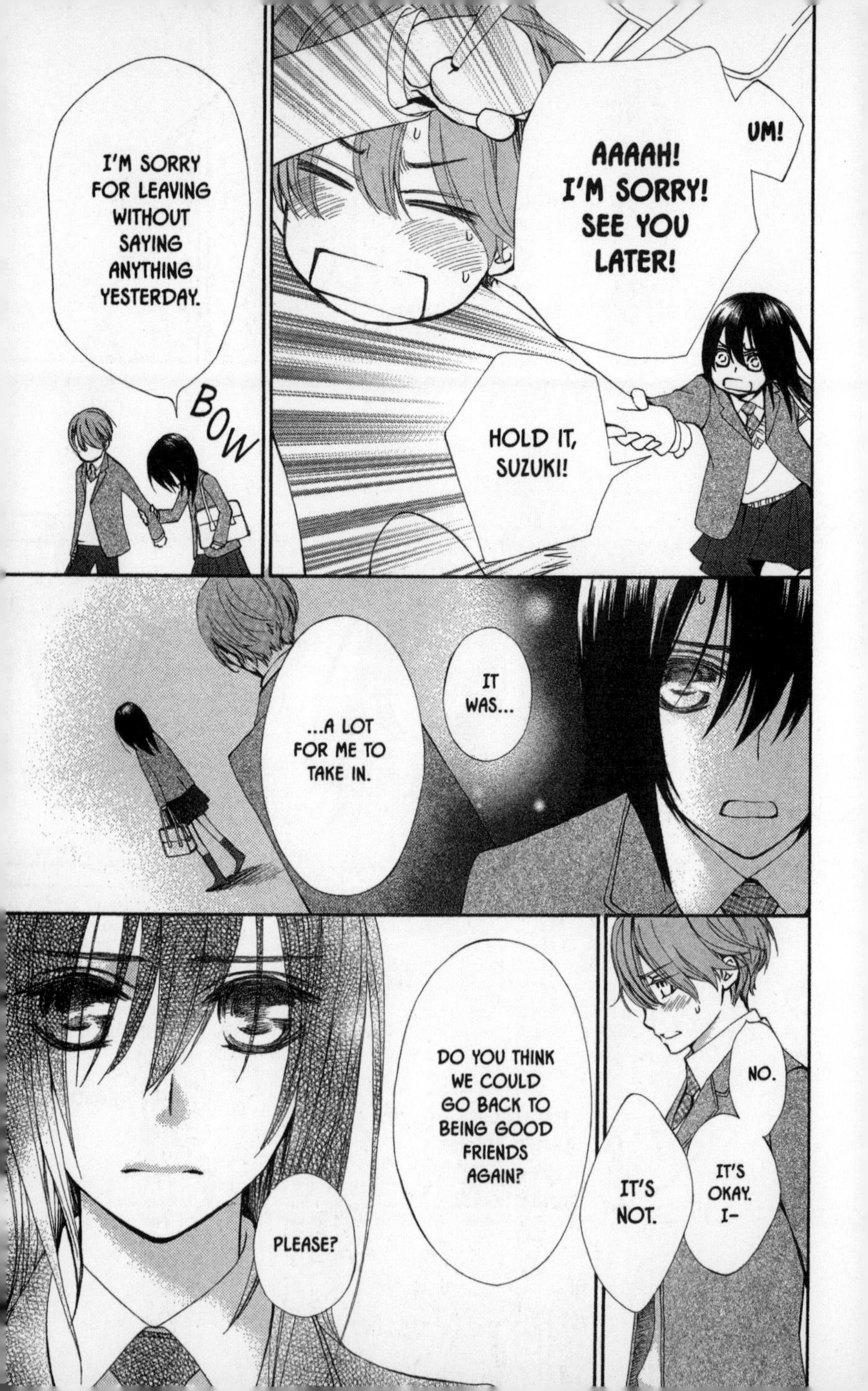
UM!
AAAAH! I'M SORRY! SEE YOU LATER!
HOLD IT, SUZUKI!
I'M SORRY FOR LEAVING WITHOUT SAYING ANYTHING YESTERDAY.
BOW
IT WAS...
...A LOT FOR ME TO TAKE IN.
NO.
IT'S OKAY. I-
IT'S NOT.
DO YOU THINK WE COULD GO BACK TO BEING GOOD FRIENDS AGAIN?
PLEASE?

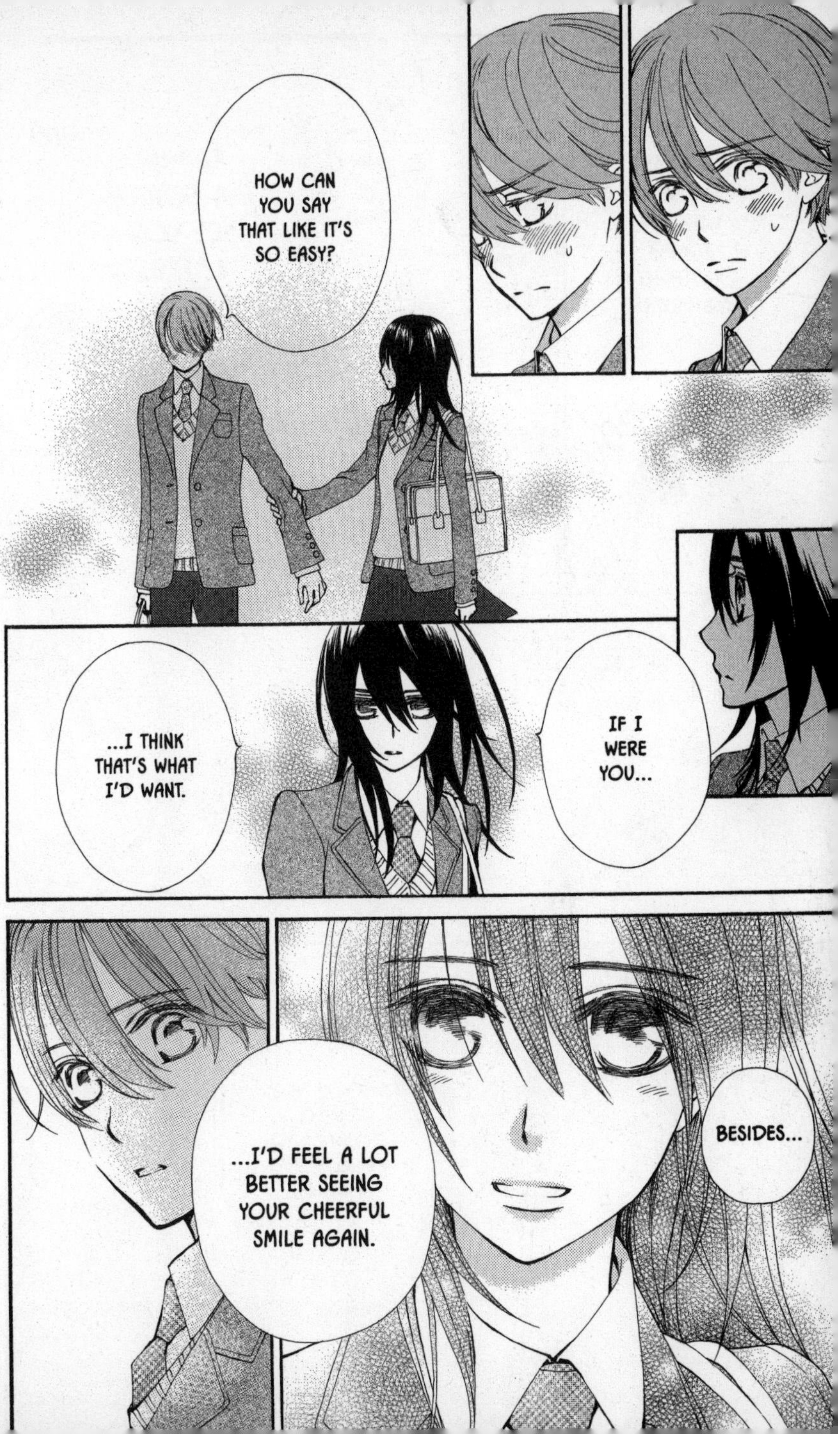
HOW CAN YOU SAY THAT LIKE IT'S SO EASY?
IF I WERE YOU...
...I THINK THAT'S WHAT I'D WANT.
BESIDES...
...I'D FEEL A LOT BETTER SEEING YOUR CHEERFUL SMILE AGAIN.

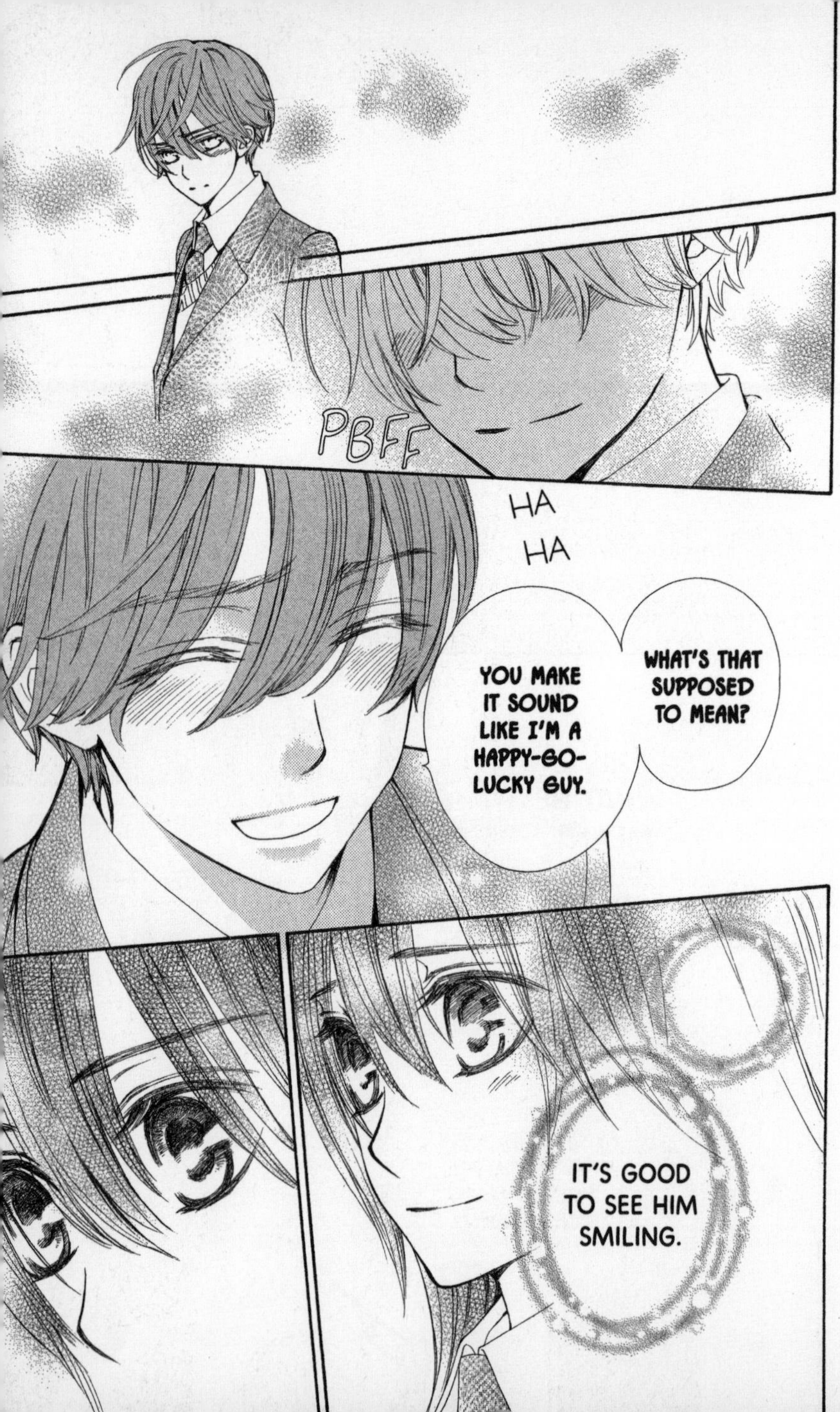
PBFF
HA
HA
WHAT'S THAT SUPPOSED TO MEAN?
YOU MAKE IT SOUND LIKE I'M A HAPPY-GO-LUCKY GUY.
IT'S GOOD TO SEE HIM SMILING.

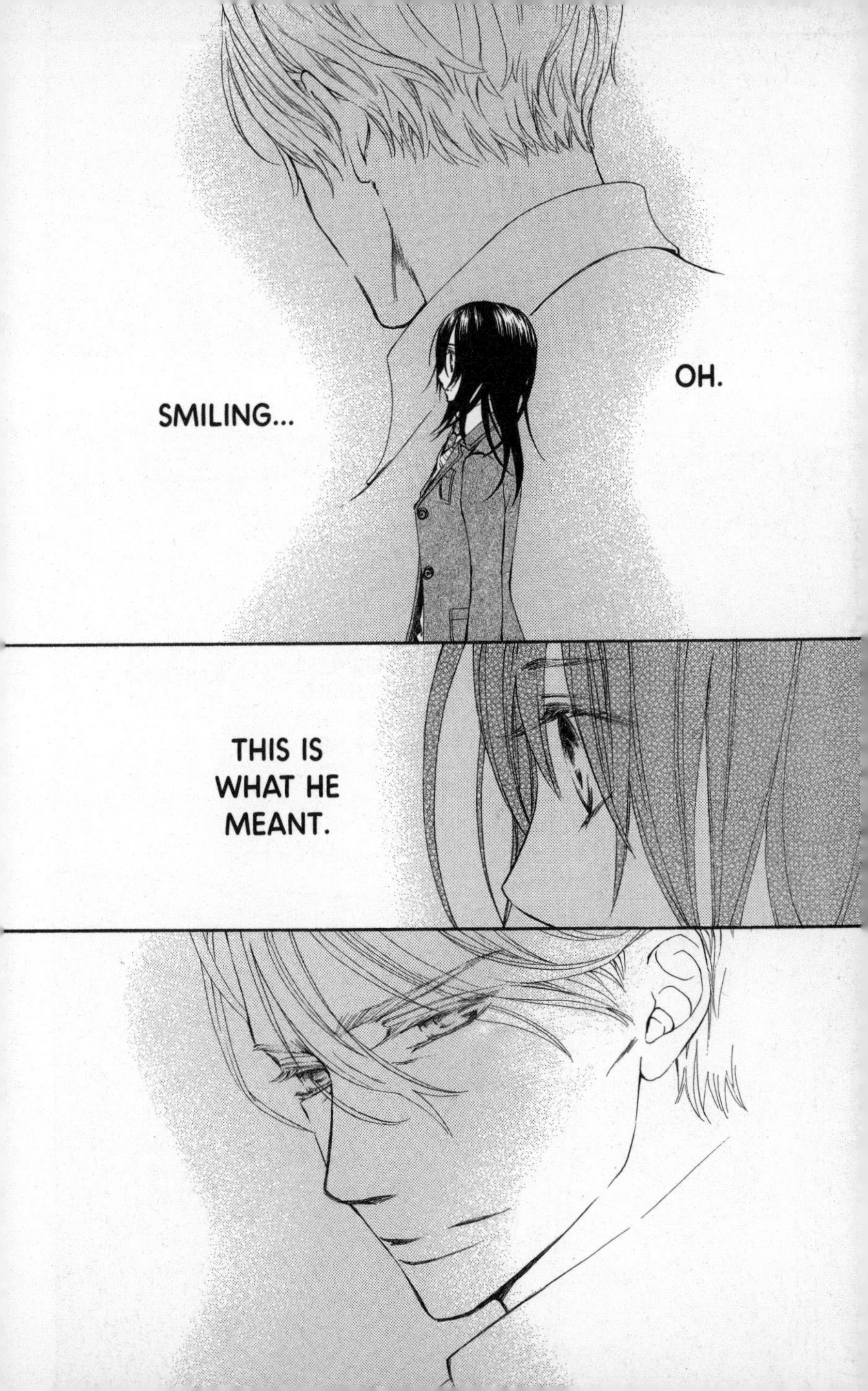
OH.
SMILING...
THIS IS WHAT HE MEANT.

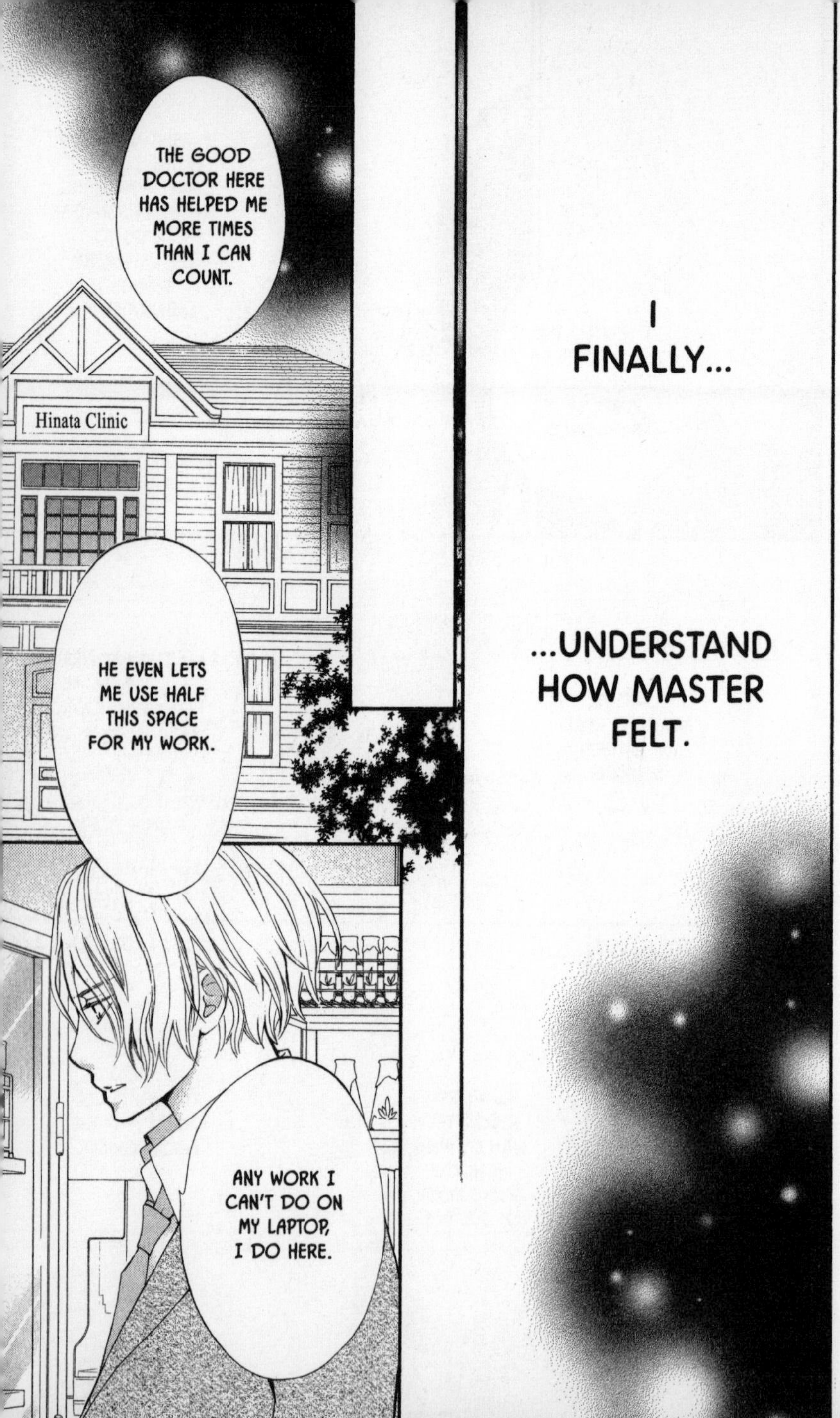
I FINALLY...
...UNDERSTAND HOW MASTER FELT.
THE GOOD DOCTOR HERE HAS HELPED ME MORE TIMES THAN I CAN COUNT.
Hinata Clinic
HE EVEN LETS ME USE HALF THIS SPACE FOR MY WORK.
ANY WORK I CAN'T DO ON MY LAPTOP, I DO HERE.

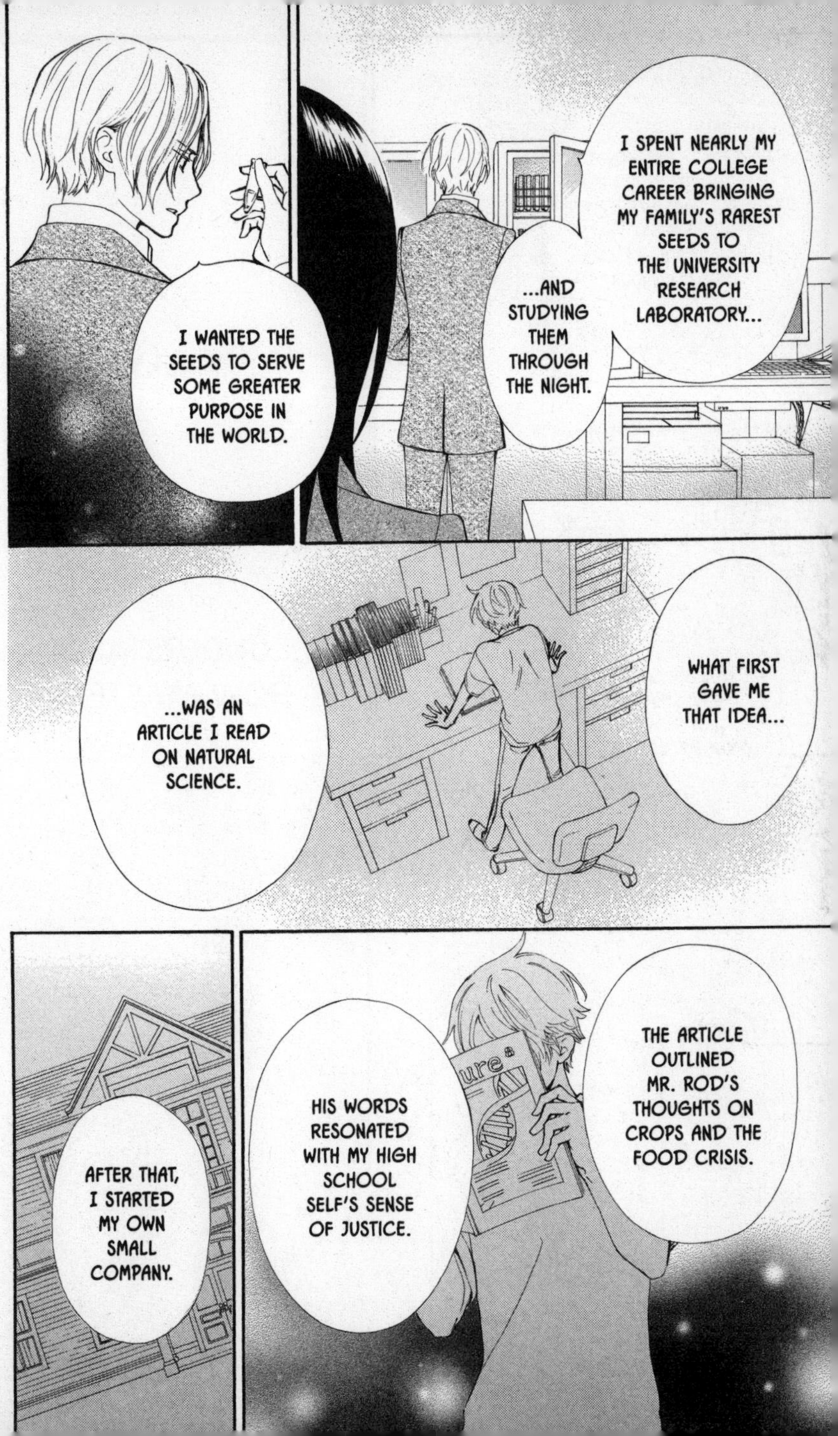
I SPENT NEARLY MY ENTIRE COLLEGE CAREER BRINGING MY FAMILY'S RAREST SEEDS TO THE UNIVERSITY RESEARCH LABORATORY...
...AND STUDYING THEM THROUGH THE NIGHT.
I WANTED THE SEEDS TO SERVE SOME GREATER PURPOSE IN THE WORLD.
WHAT FIRST GAVE ME THAT IDEA...
...WAS AN ARTICLE I READ ON NATURAL SCIENCE.
THE ARTICLE OUTLINED MR. ROD'S THOUGHTS ON CROPS AND THE FOOD CRISIS.
HIS WORDS RESONATED WITH MY HIGH SCHOOL SELF'S SENSE OF JUSTICE.
AFTER THAT, I STARTED MY OWN SMALL COMPANY.

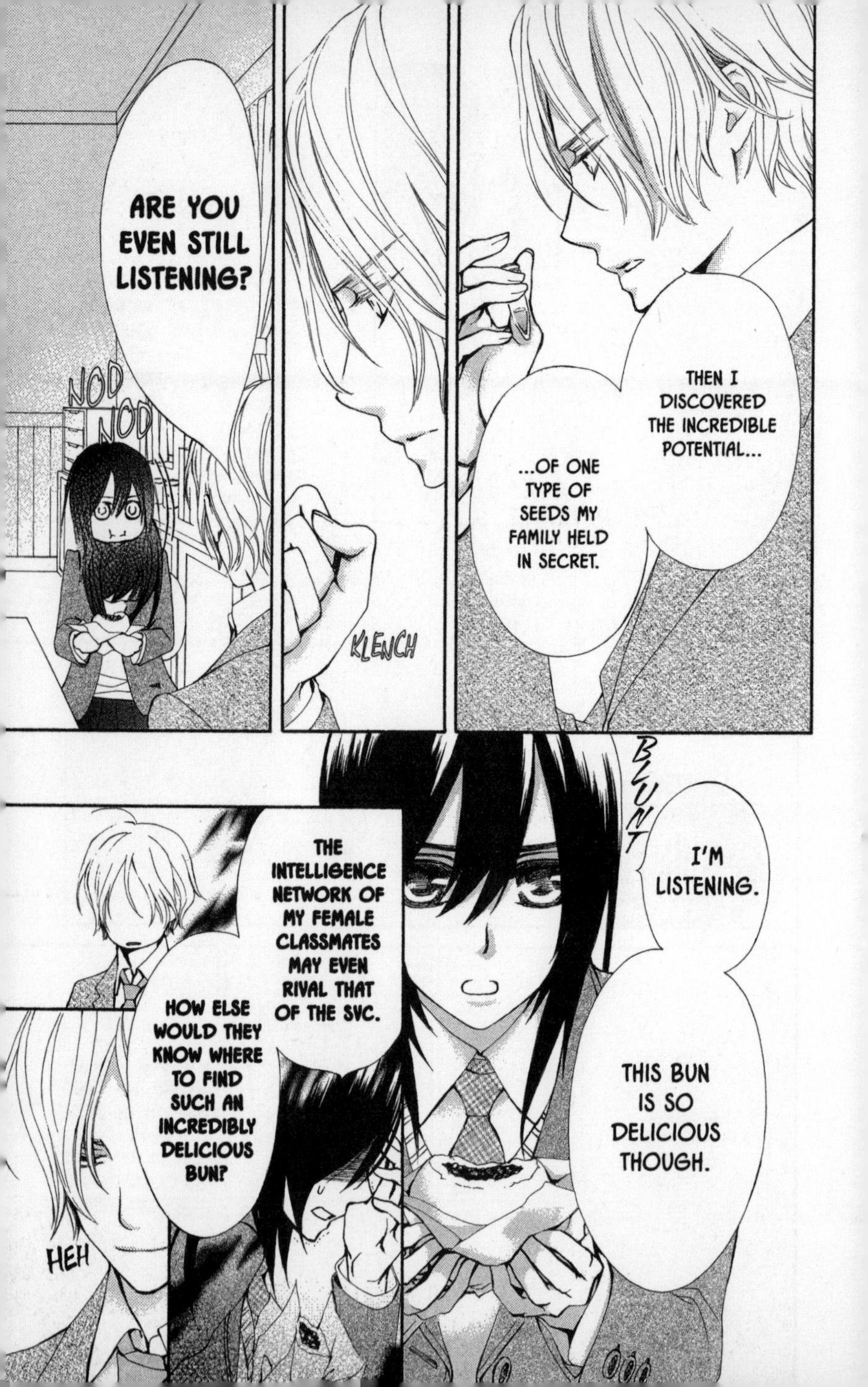
THEN I DISCOVERED THE INCREDIBLE POTENTIAL...
...OF ONE TYPE OF SEEDS MY FAMILY HELD IN SECRET.
KLENCH
ARE YOU EVEN STILL LISTENING?
NOD NOD
BLUNT
I'M LISTENING.
THIS BUN IS SO DELICIOUS THOUGH.
THE INTELLIGENCE NETWORK OF MY FEMALE CLASSMATES MAY EVEN RIVAL THAT OF THE SVC.
HOW ELSE WOULD THEY KNOW WHERE TO FIND SUCH AN INCREDIBLY DELICIOUS BUN?
HEH

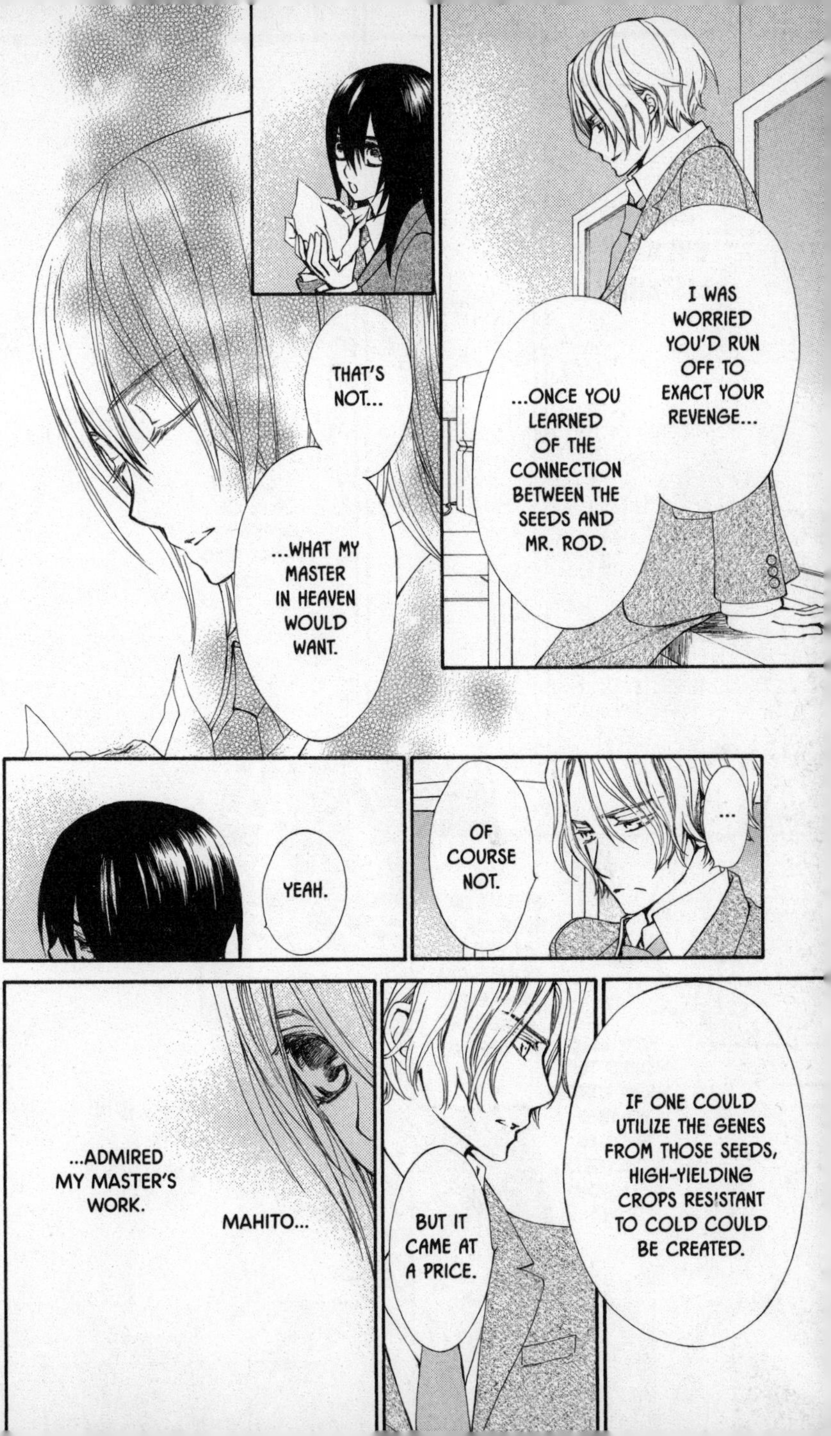
I WAS WORRIED YOU'D RUN OFF TO EXACT YOUR REVENGE...
...ONCE YOU LEARNED OF THE CONNECTION BETWEEN THE SEEDS AND MR. ROD.
THAT'S NOT...
...WHAT MY MASTER IN HEAVEN WOULD WANT.
...
OF COURSE NOT.
YEAH.
IF ONE COULD UTILIZE THE GENES FROM THOSE SEEDS, HIGH-YIELDING CROPS RESISTANT TO COLD COULD BE CREATED.
BUT IT CAME AT A PRICE.
MAHITO...
...ADMIRED MY MASTER'S WORK.

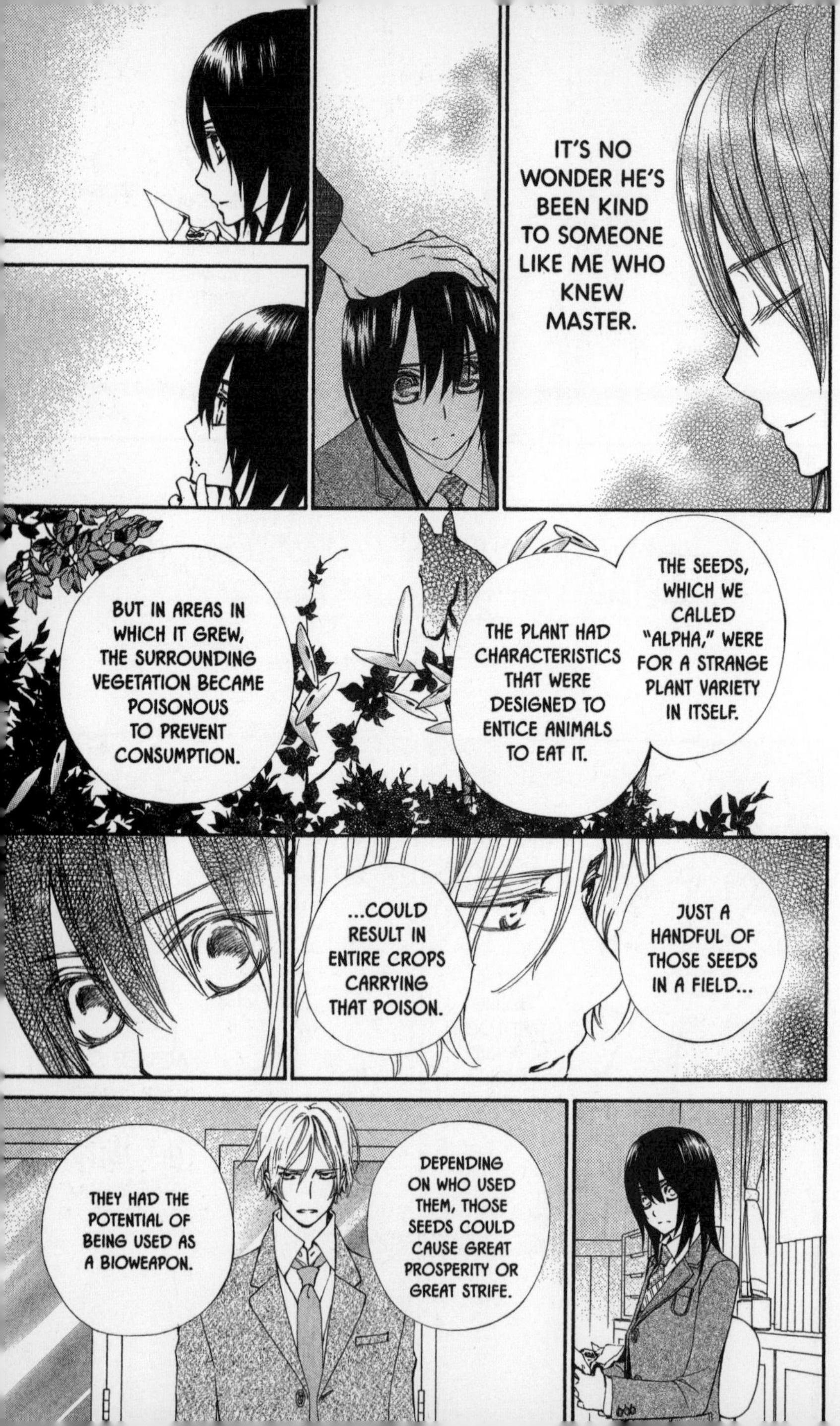
IT'S NO WONDER HE'S BEEN KIND TO SOMEONE LIKE ME WHO KNEW MASTER.
THE SEEDS, WHICH WE CALLED "ALPHA," WERE FOR A STRANGE PLANT VARIETY IN ITSELF.
THE PLANT HAD CHARACTERISTICS THAT WERE DESIGNED TO ENTICE ANIMALS TO EAT IT.
BUT IN AREAS IN WHICH IT GREW, THE SURROUNDING VEGETATION BECAME POISONOUS TO PREVENT CONSUMPTION.
JUST A HANDFUL OF THOSE SEEDS IN A FIELD...
...COULD RESULT IN ENTIRE CROPS CARRYING THAT POISON.
DEPENDING ON WHO USED THEM, THOSE SEEDS COULD CAUSE GREAT PROSPERITY OR GREAT STRIFE.
THEY HAD THE POTENTIAL OF BEING USED AS A BIOWEAPON.

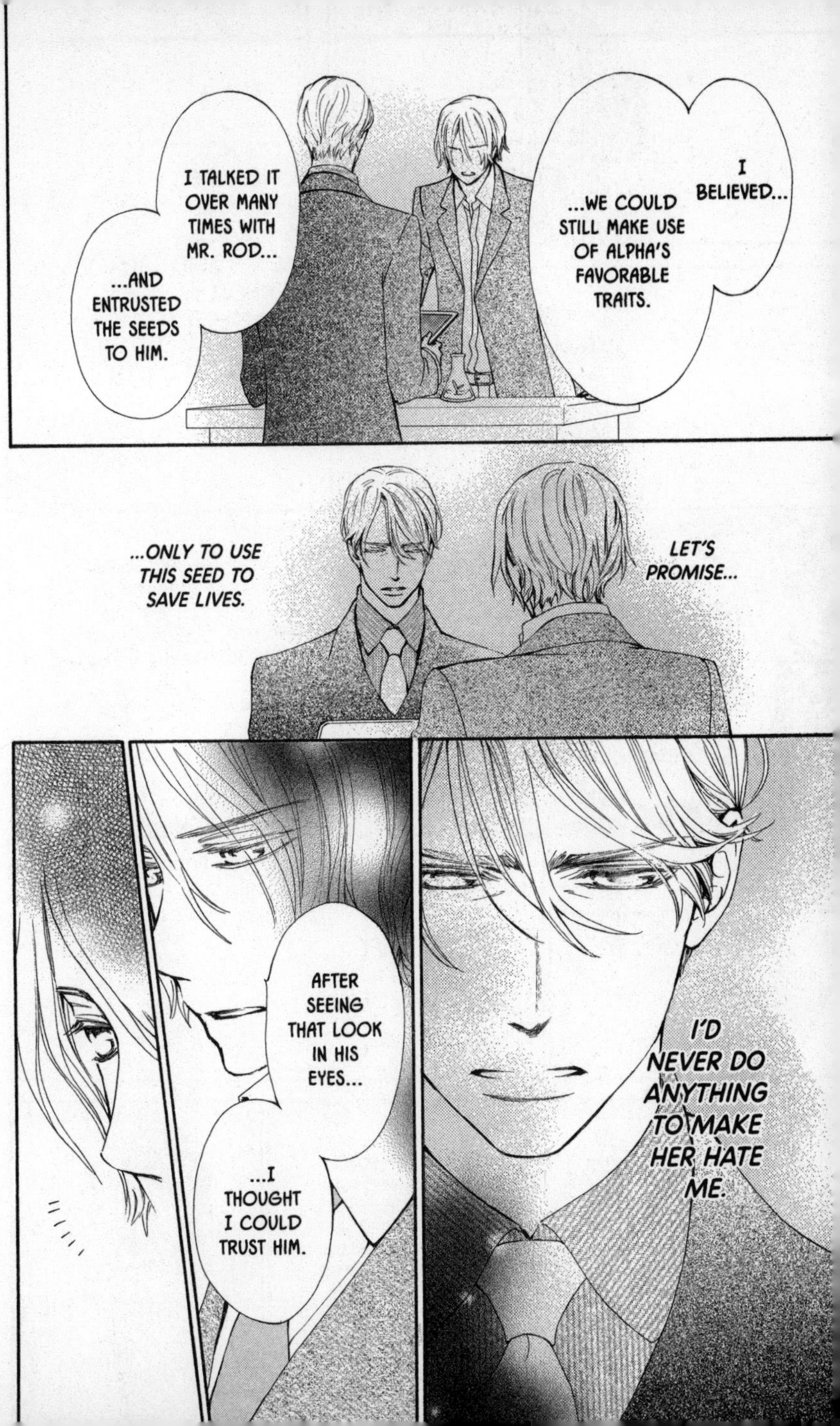
I BELIEVED...
...WE COULD STILL MAKE USE OF ALPHA'S FAVORABLE TRAITS.
I TALKED IT OVER MANY TIMES WITH MR. ROD...
...AND ENTRUSTED THE SEEDS TO HIM.
LET'S PROMISE...
...ONLY TO USE THIS SEED TO SAVE LIVES.
I'D NEVER DO ANYTHING TO MAKE HER HATE ME.
AFTER SEEING THAT LOOK IN HIS EYES...
...I THOUGHT I COULD TRUST HIM.

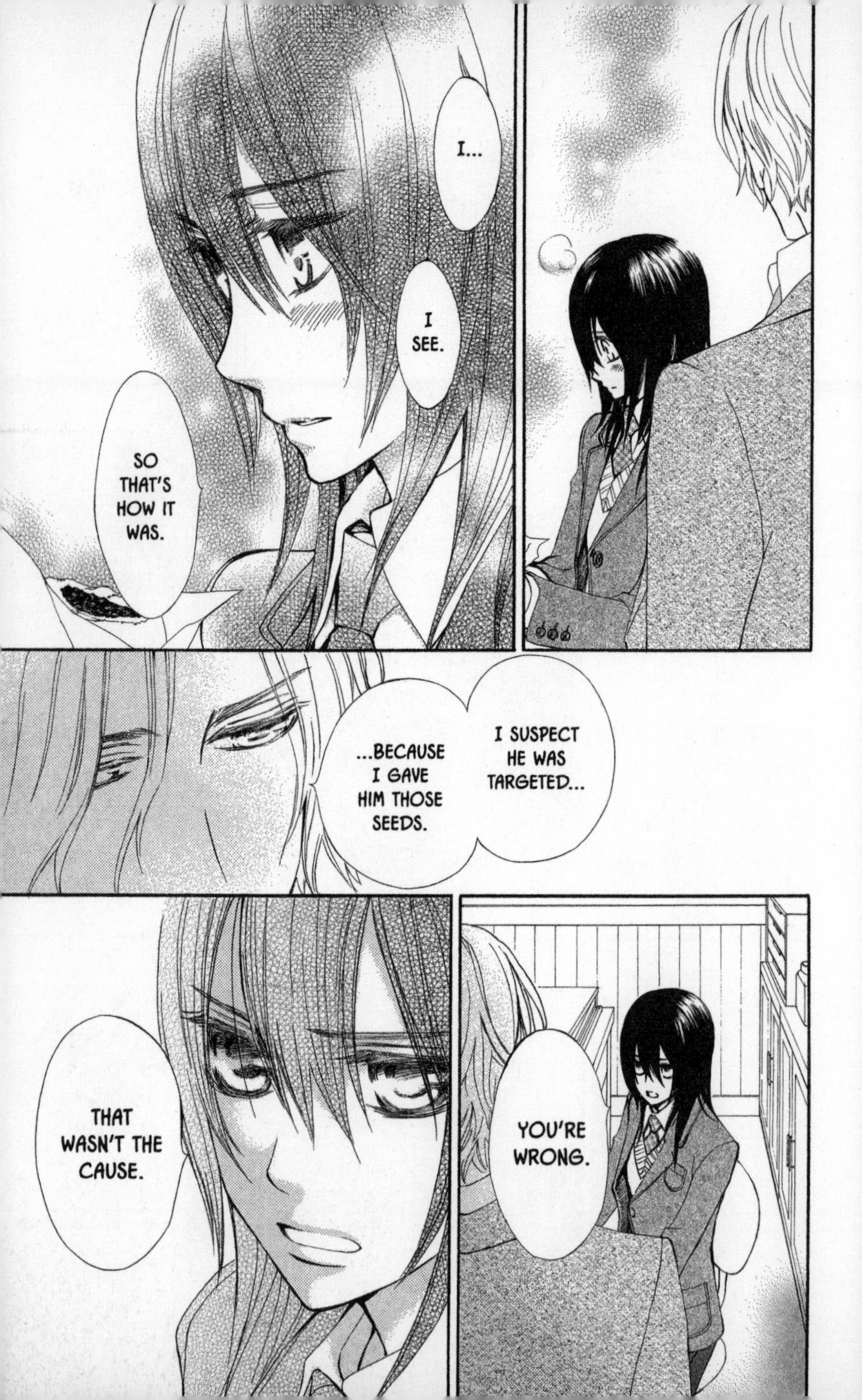
I...
I SEE.
SO THAT'S HOW IT WAS.
I SUSPECT HE WAS TARGETED...
...BECAUSE I GAVE HIM THOSE SEEDS.
YOU'RE WRONG.
THAT WASN'T THE CAUSE.

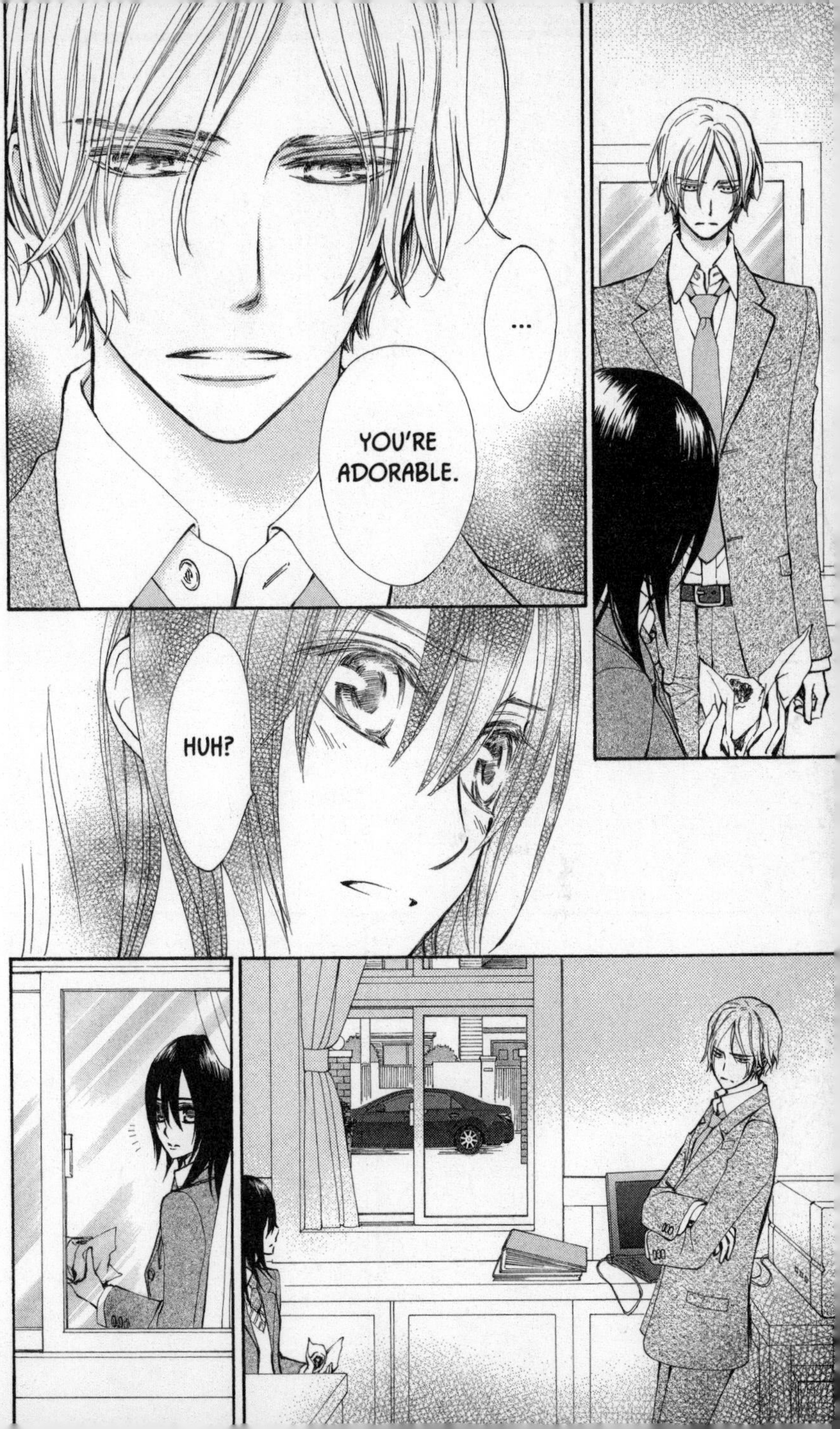
...
YOU'RE ADORABLE.
HUH?

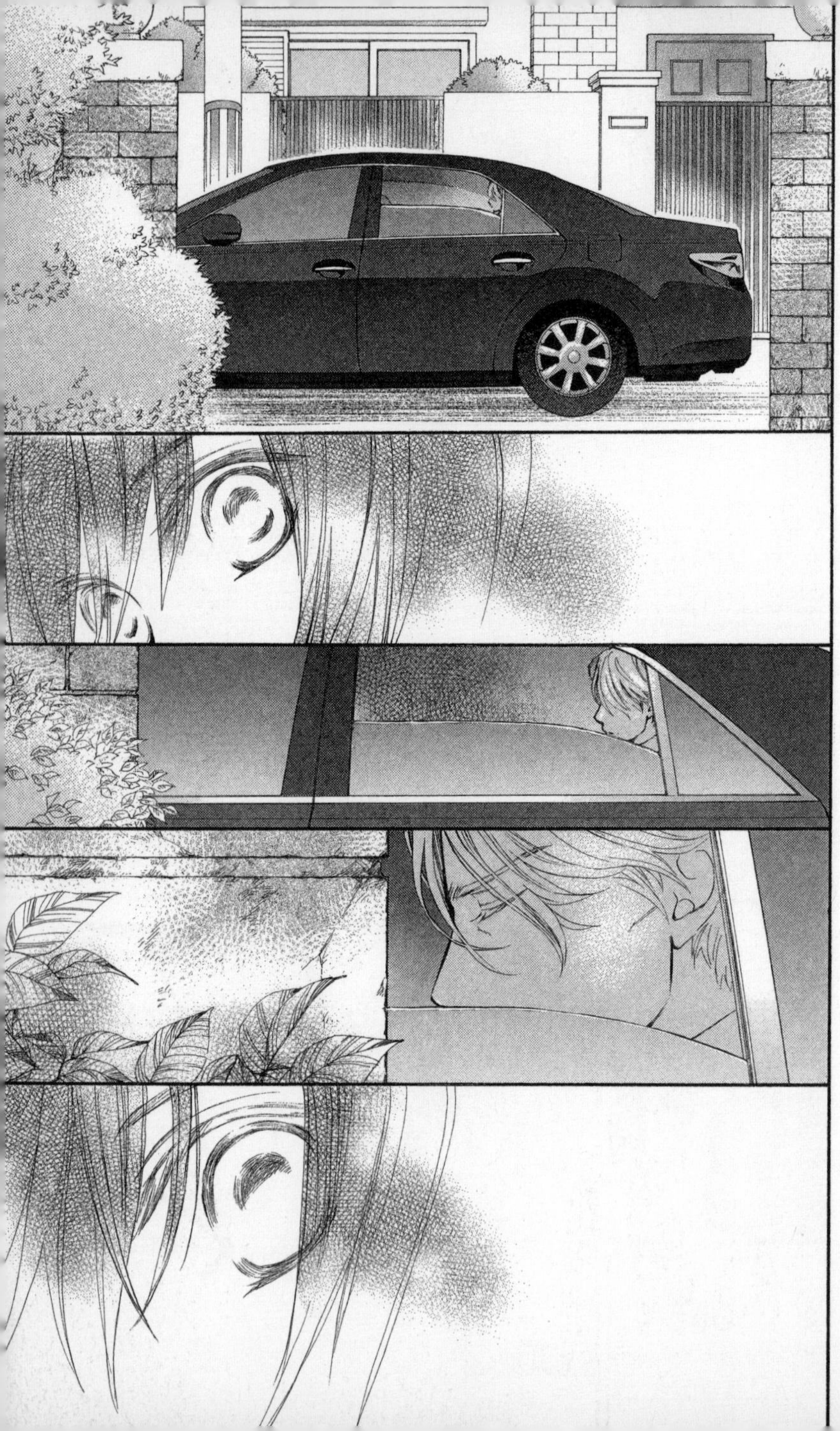

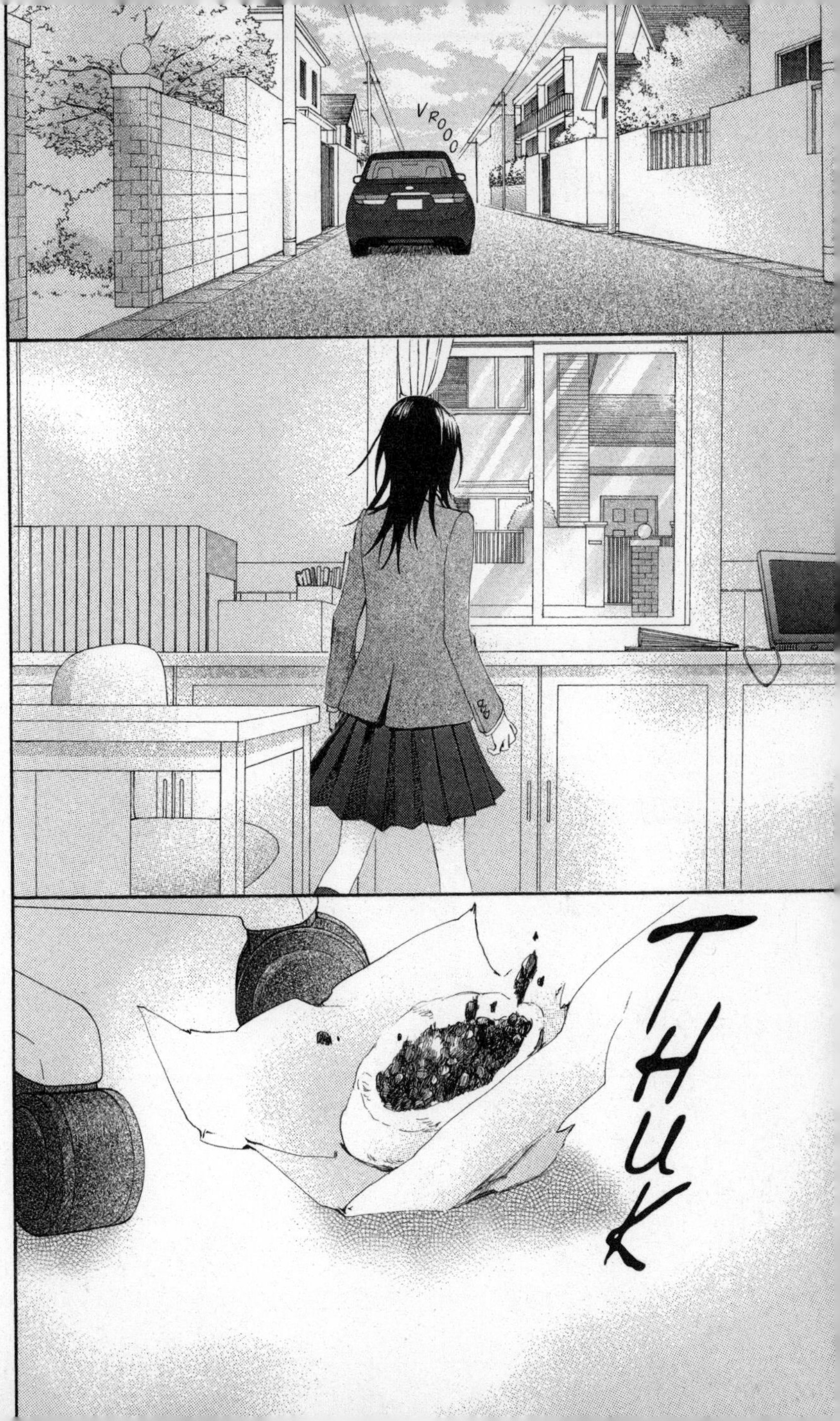
VROOO
THUK

# Chapter 9

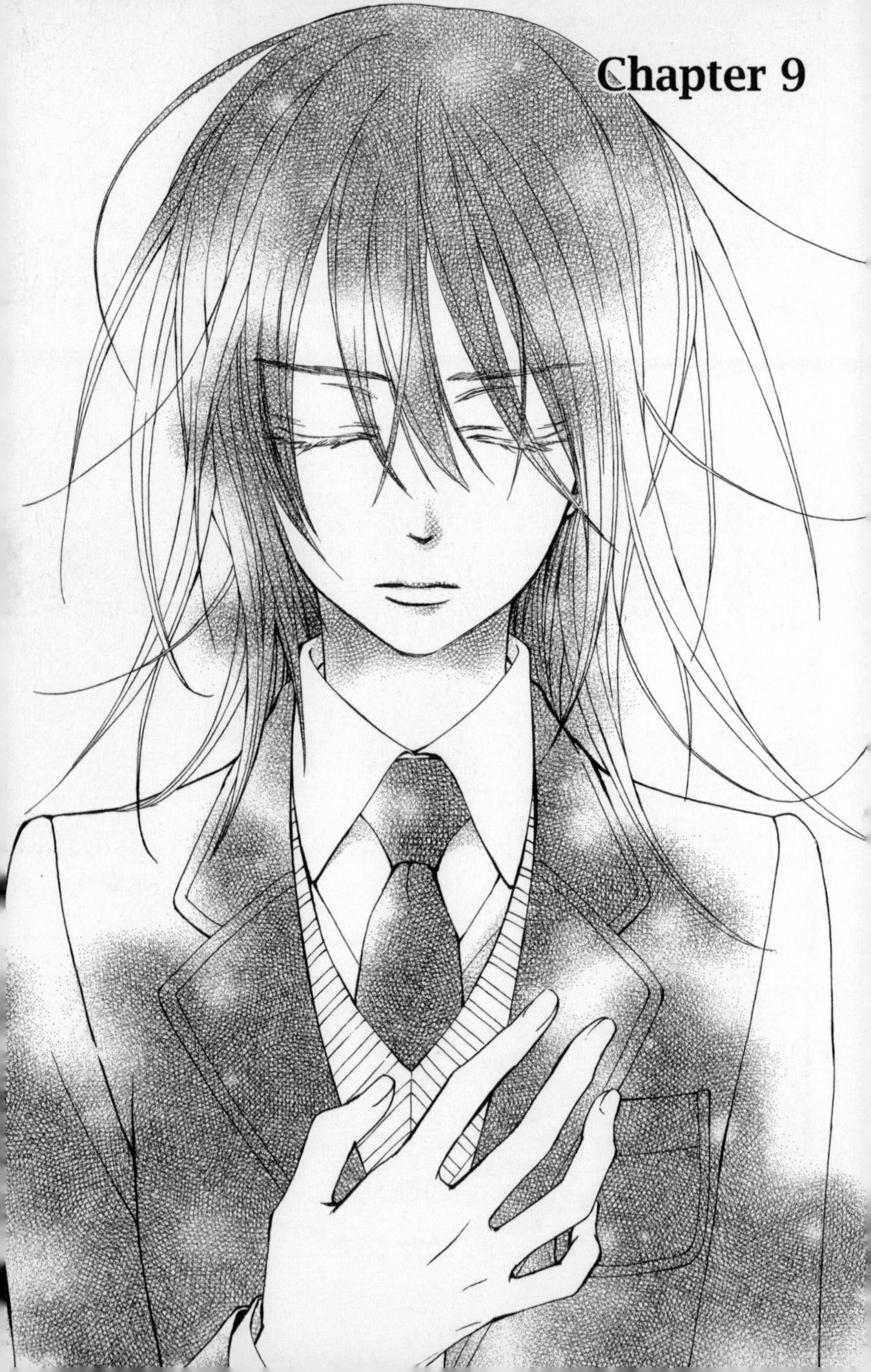

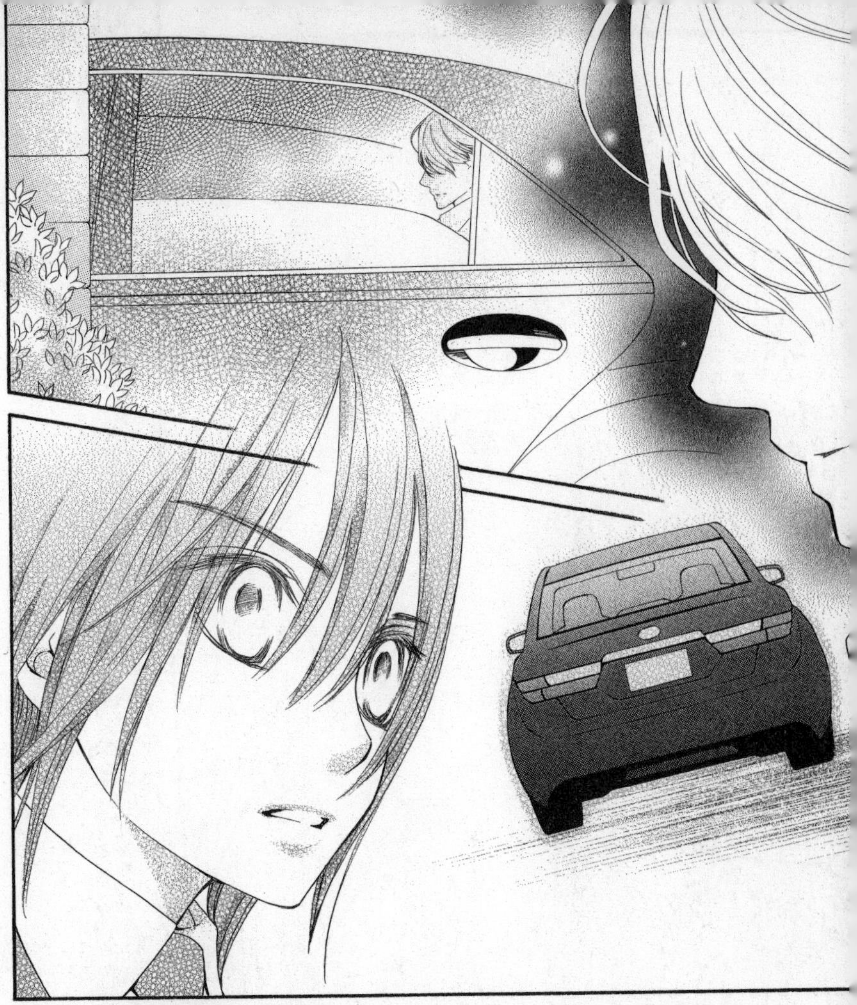

# Shuriken *and* Pleats

MATSURI HINO

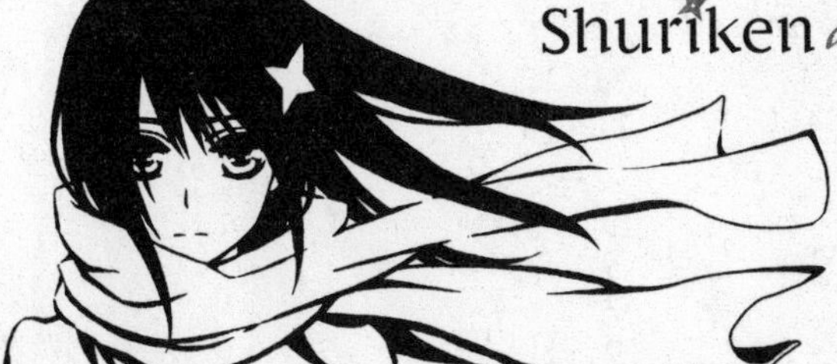

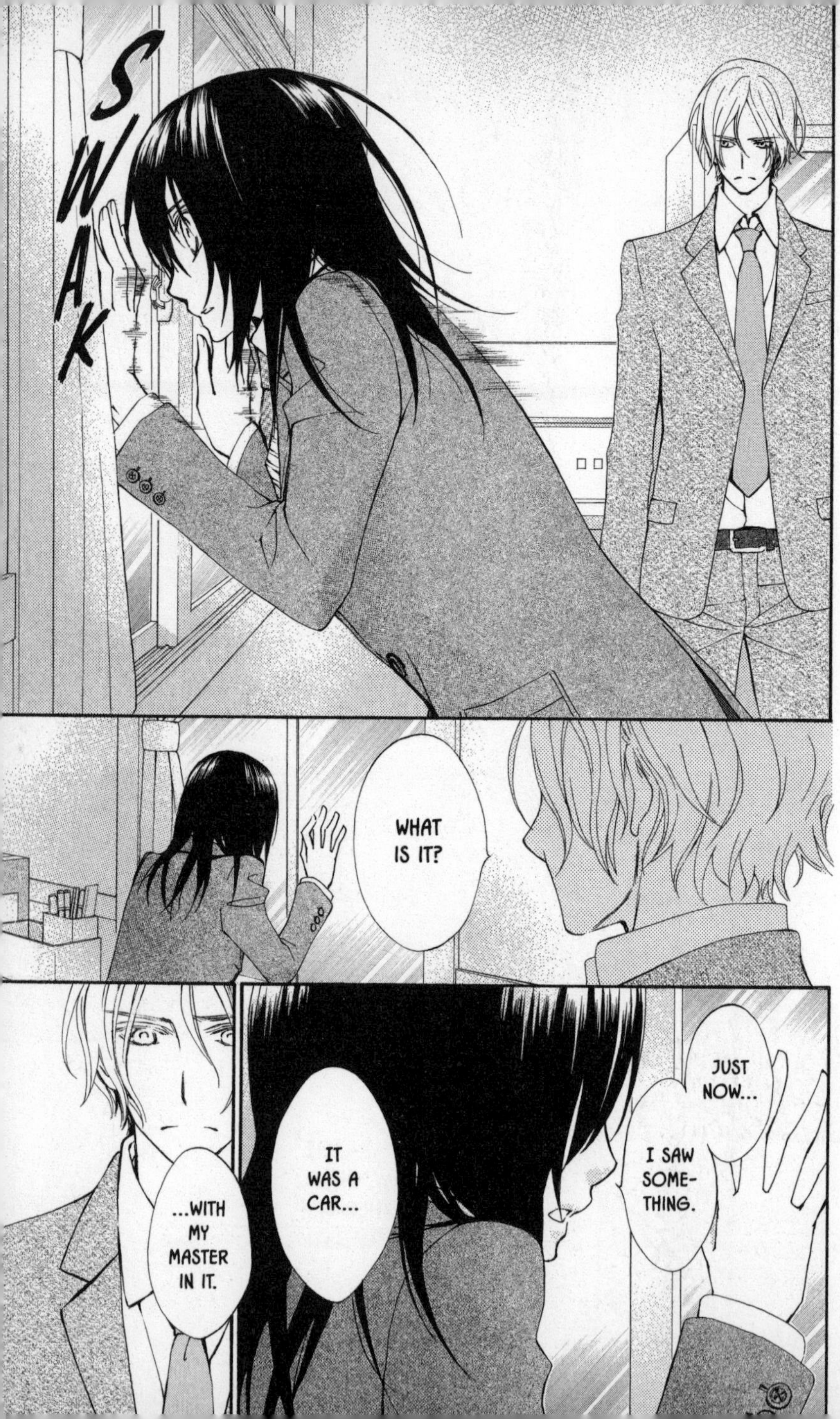
SWAK
WHAT IS IT?
JUST NOW...
I SAW SOMETHING.
IT WAS A CAR...
...WITH MY MASTER IN IT.

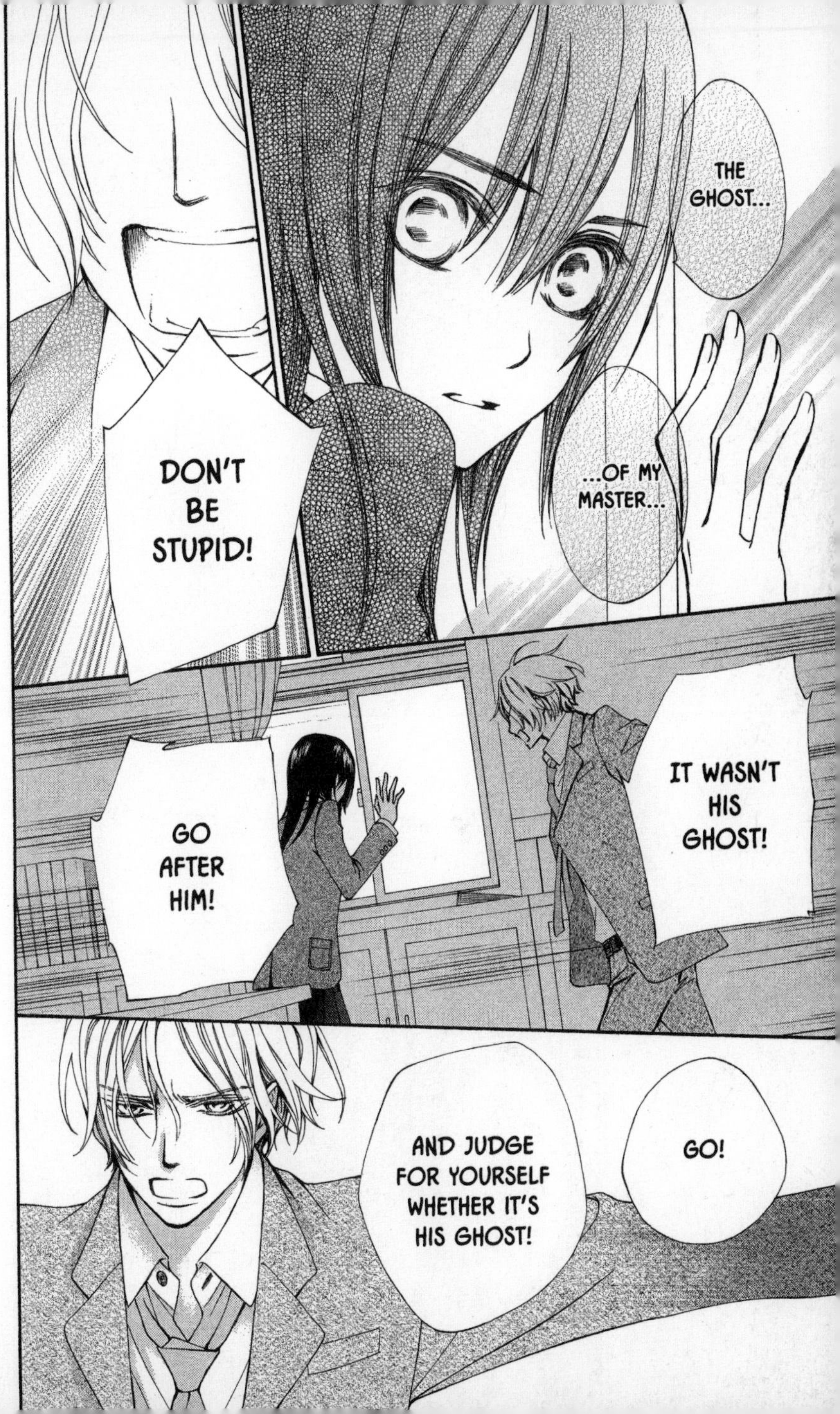
THE GHOST...
...OF MY MASTER...
DON'T BE STUPID!
IT WASN'T HIS GHOST!
GO AFTER HIM!
GO!
AND JUDGE FOR YOURSELF WHETHER IT'S HIS GHOST!

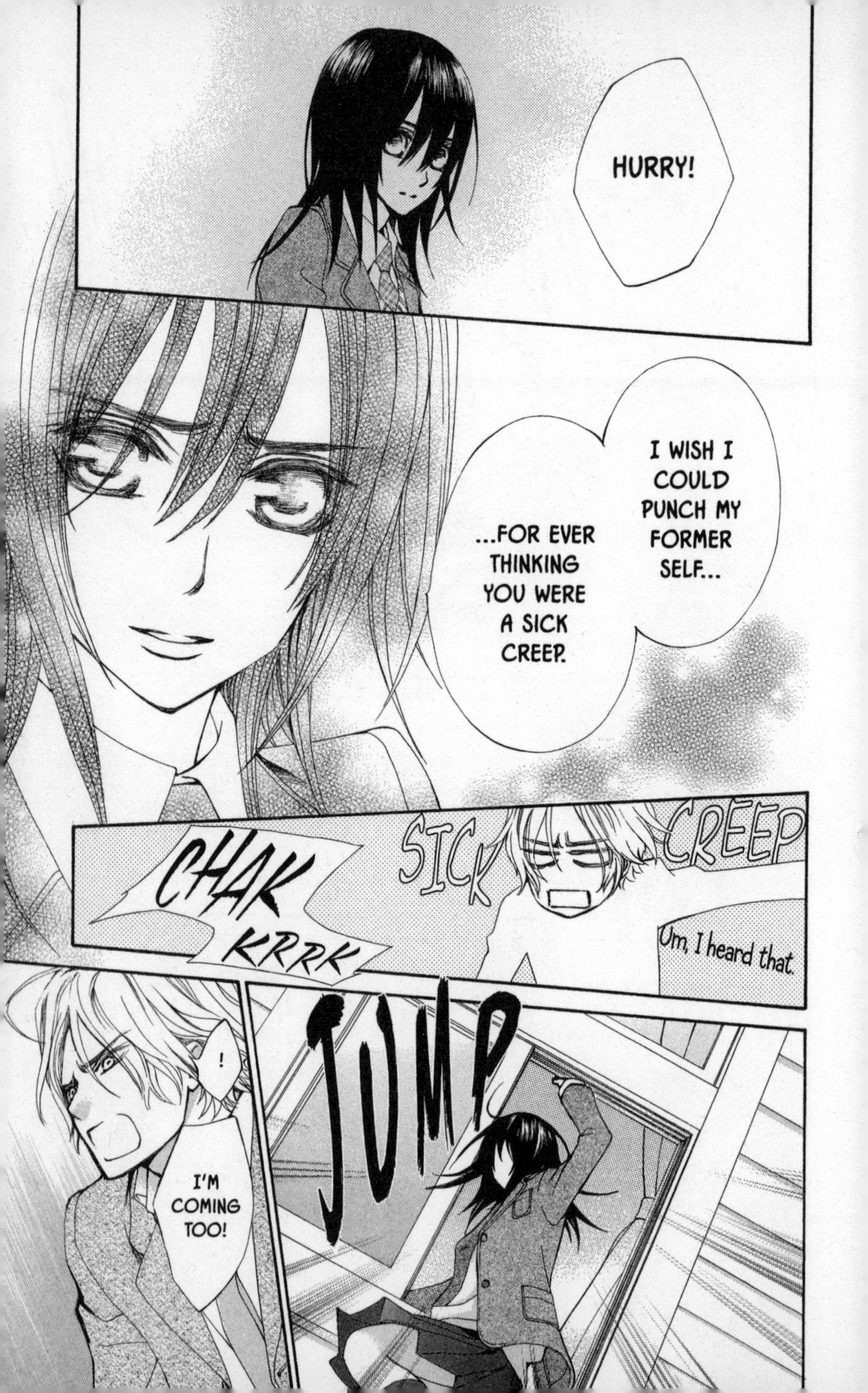
HURRY!
I WISH I COULD PUNCH MY FORMER SELF...
...FOR EVER THINKING YOU WERE A SICK CREEP.
SICK CREEP
Um, I heard that.
CHAK KRRK
JUMP
!
I'M COMING TOO!

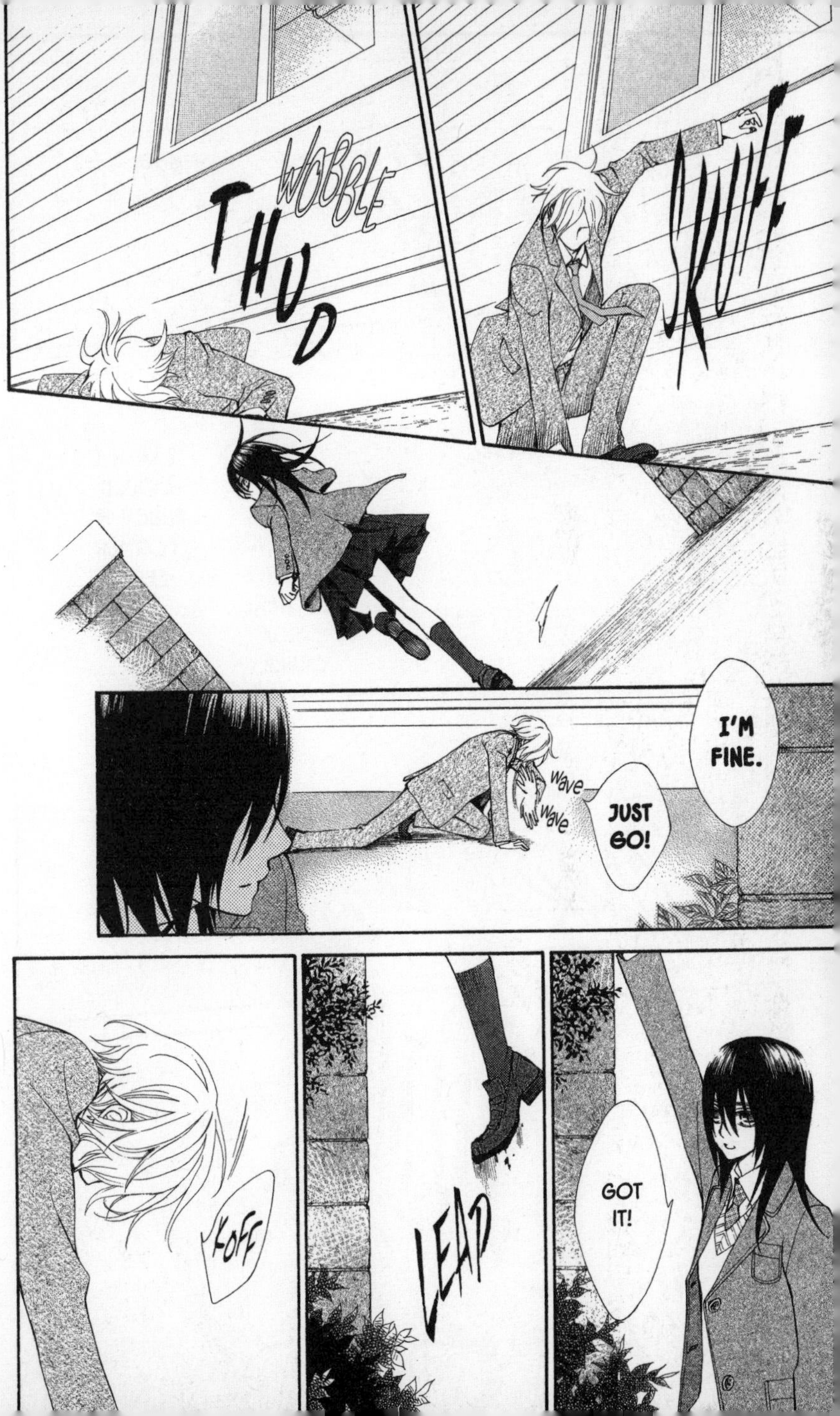
SKUFF
THUD
WOBBLE
I'M FINE.
JUST GO!
wave wave
GOT IT!
LEAP
KOFF

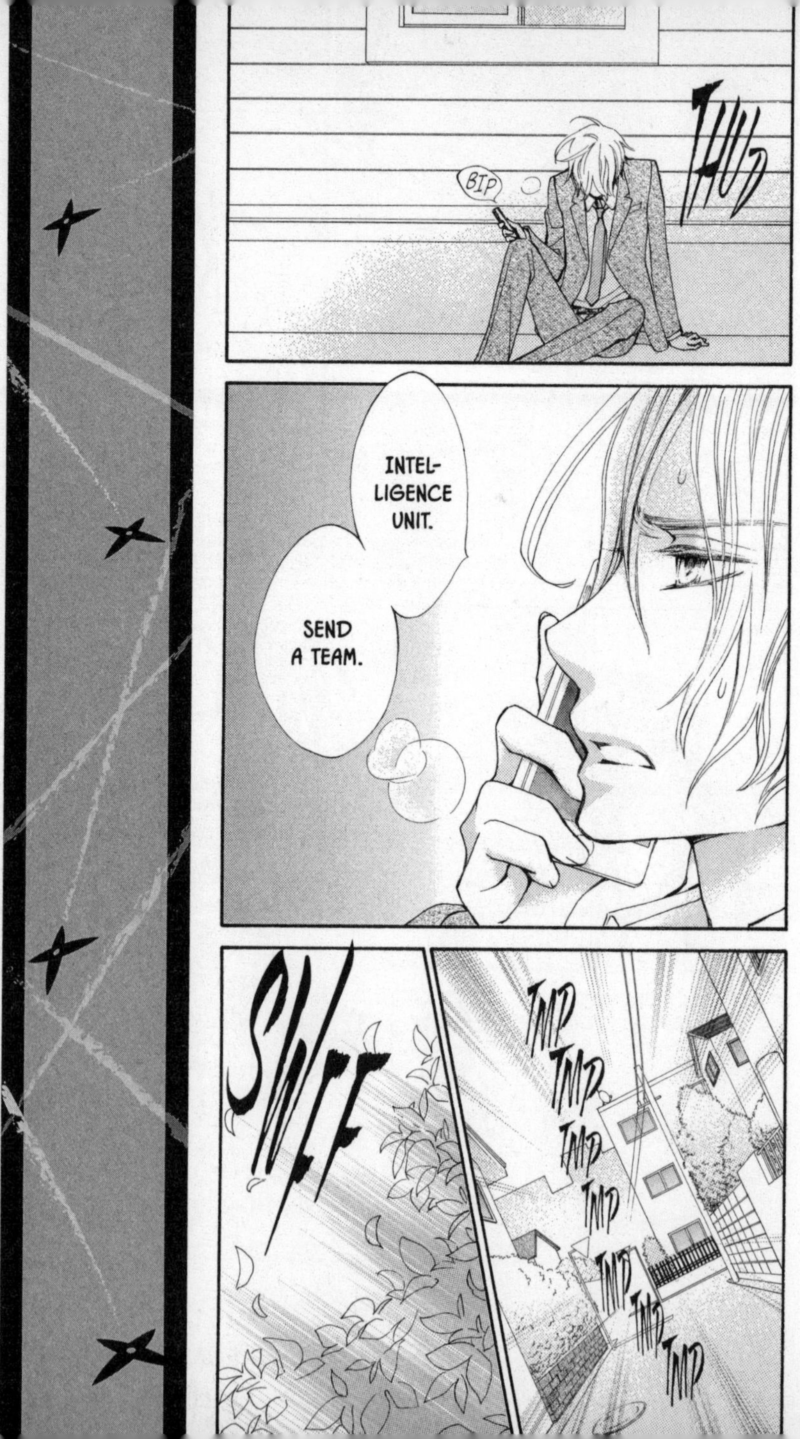
THUD
BIP
INTEL-LIGENCE UNIT.
SEND A TEAM.
TMP TMP TMP TMP TMP TMP TMP TMP
SHFF

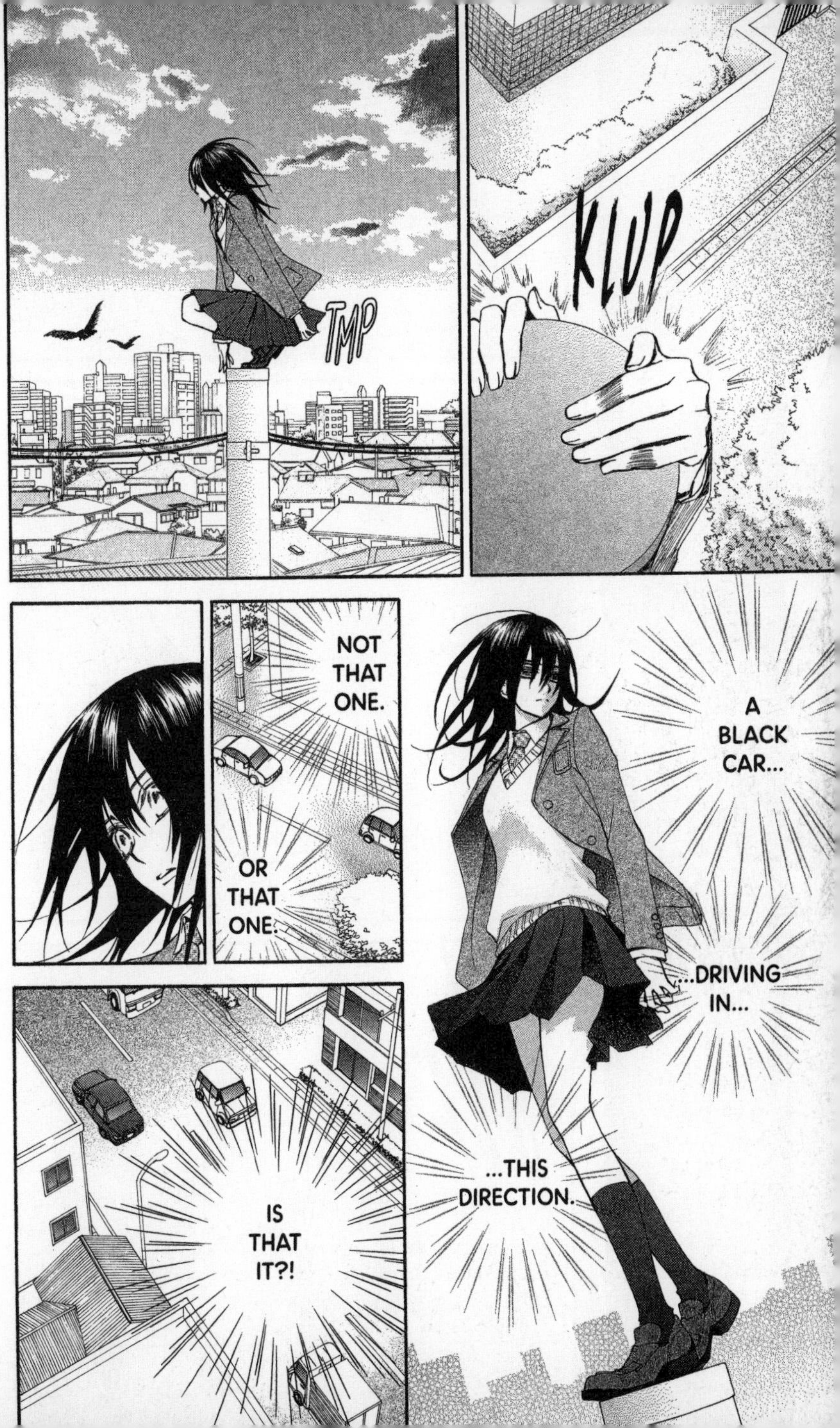
KLUP
TMP
A BLACK CAR...
...DRIVING IN...
...THIS DIRECTION.
NOT THAT ONE.
OR THAT ONE.
IS THAT IT?!

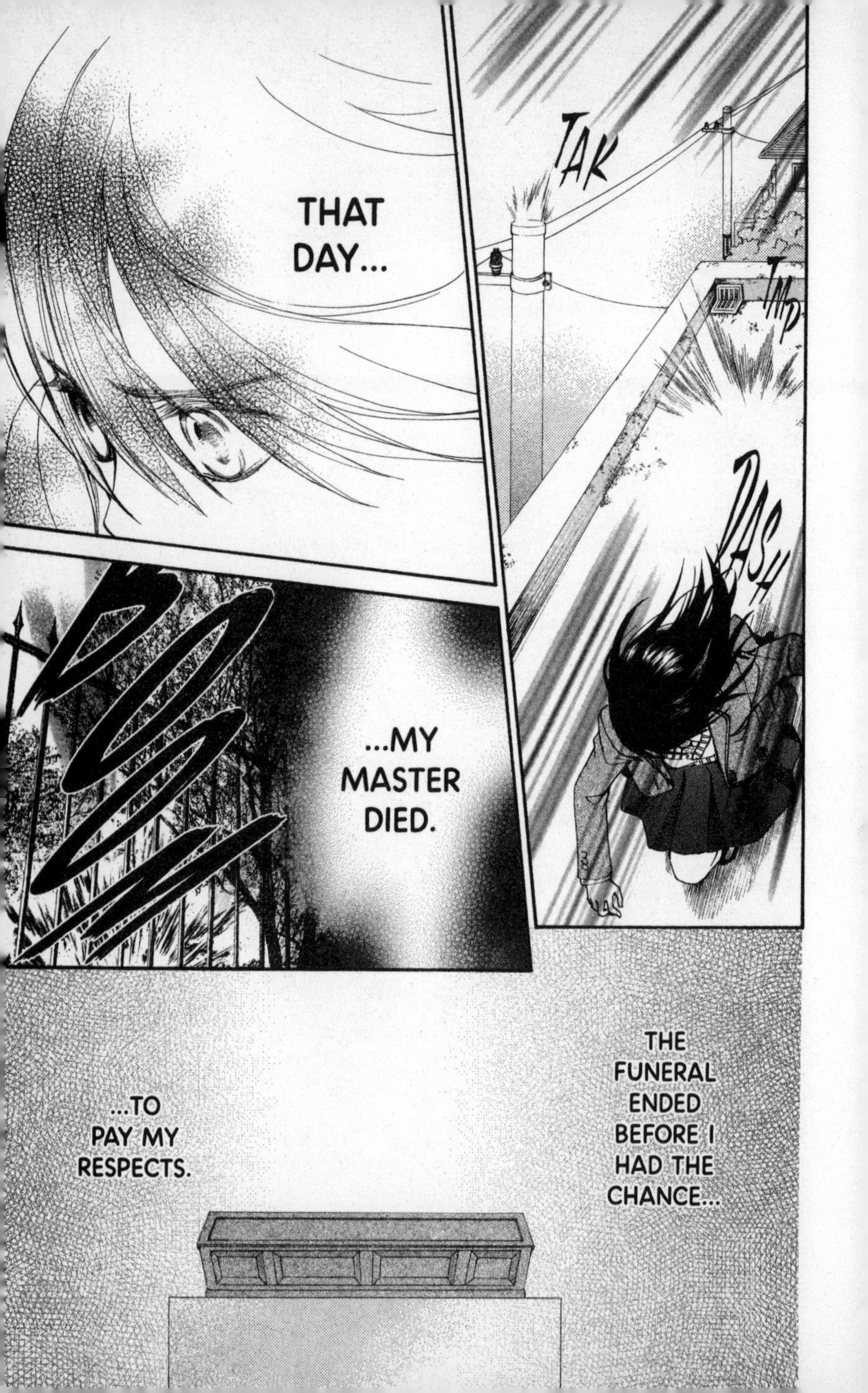
TAK
TMP
DASH
THAT DAY...
...MY MASTER DIED.
THE FUNERAL ENDED BEFORE I HAD THE CHANCE...
...TO PAY MY RESPECTS.

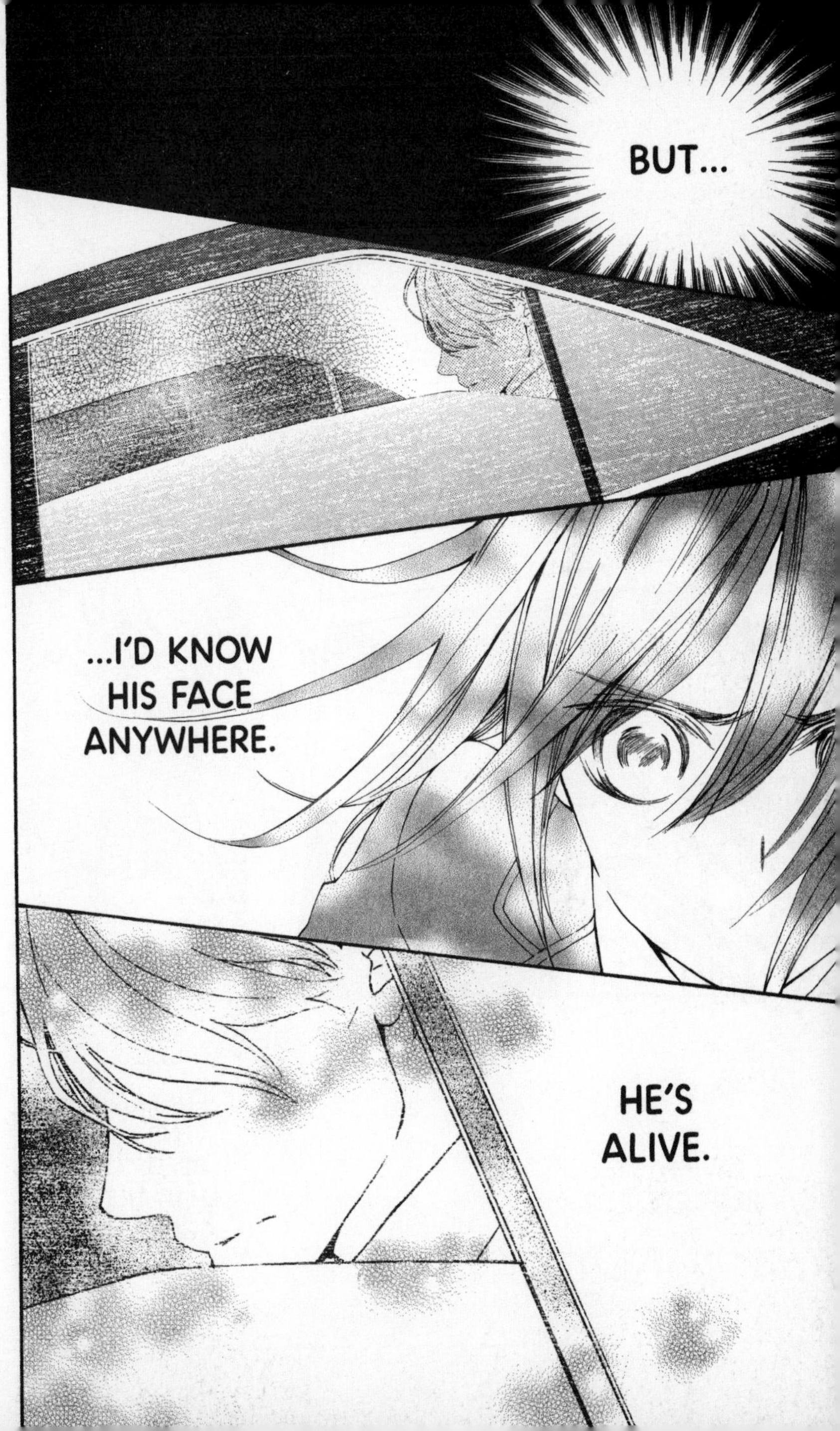
BUT...
...I'D KNOW HIS FACE ANYWHERE.
HE'S ALIVE.

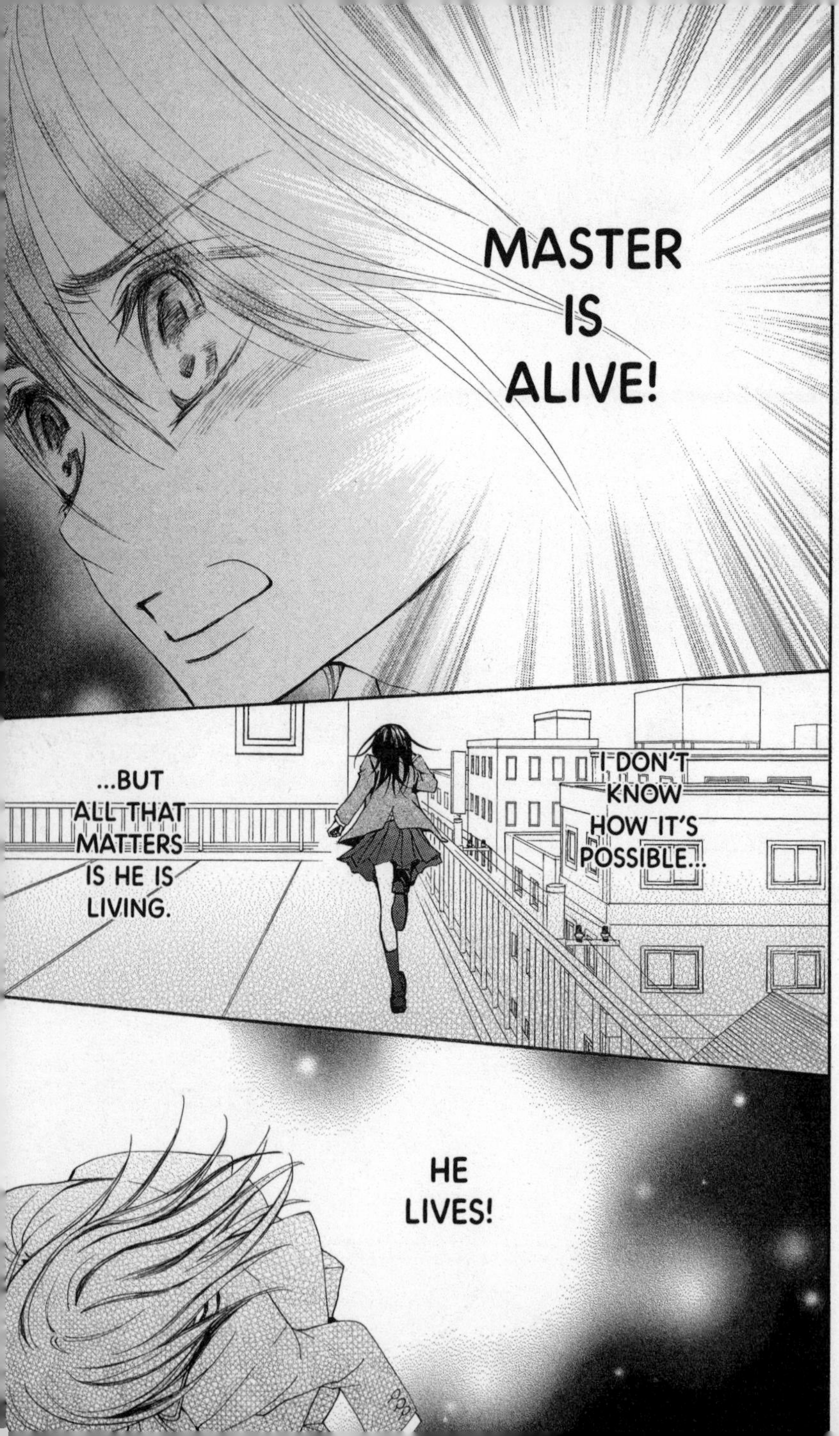
MASTER IS ALIVE!
I DON'T KNOW HOW IT'S POSSIBLE...
...BUT ALL THAT MATTERS IS HE IS LIVING.
HE LIVES!

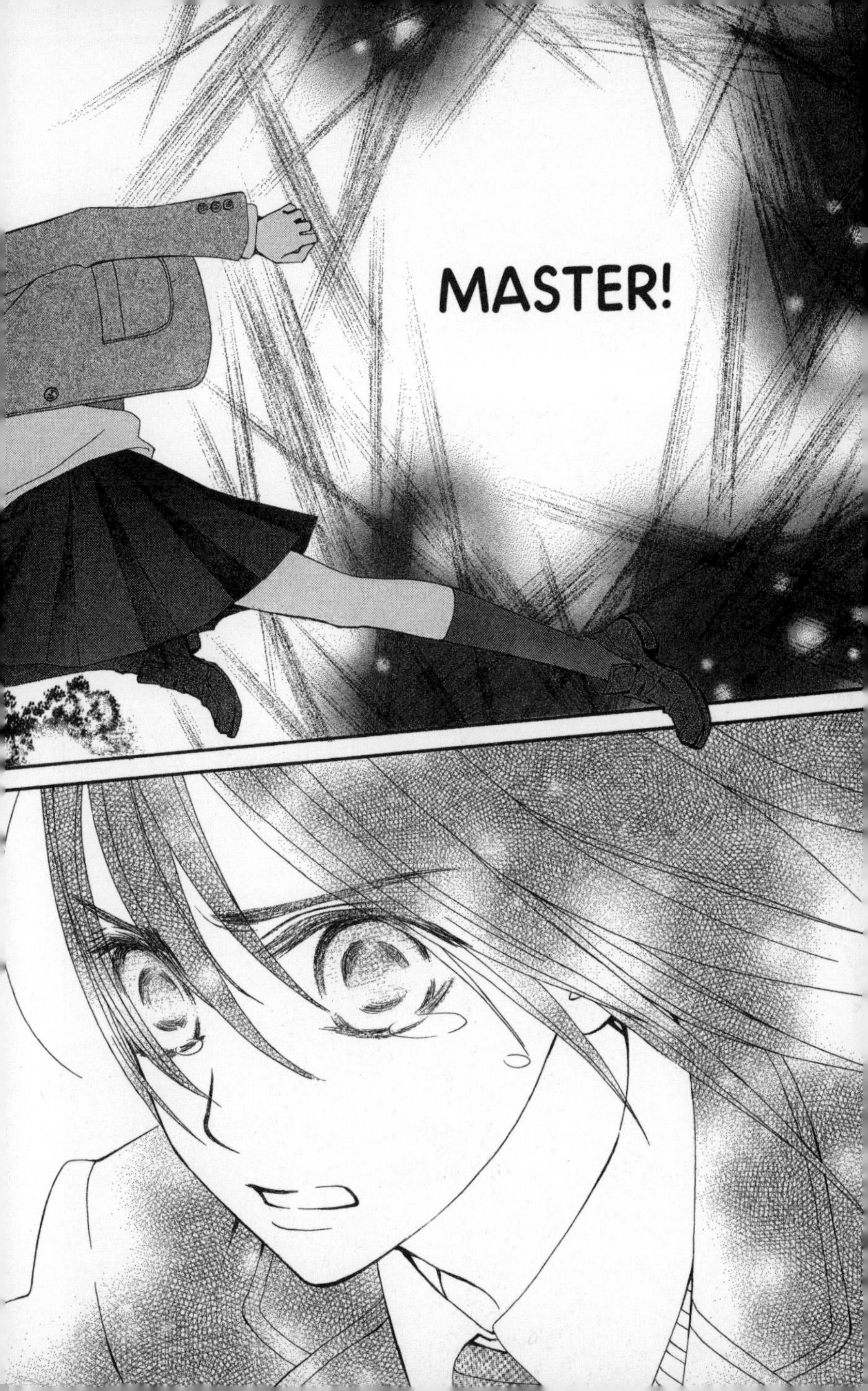
MASTER!

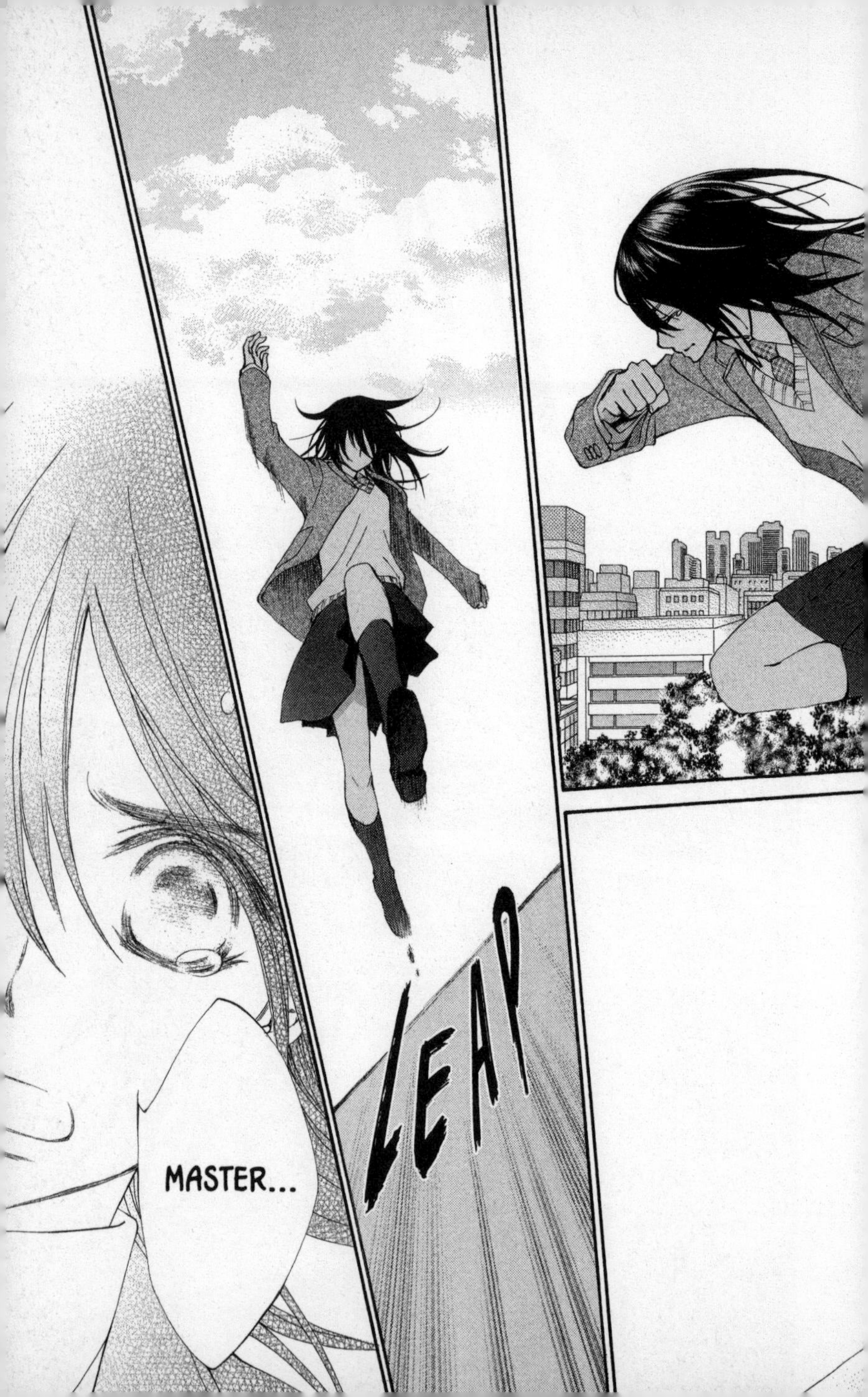
LEAP
MASTER...

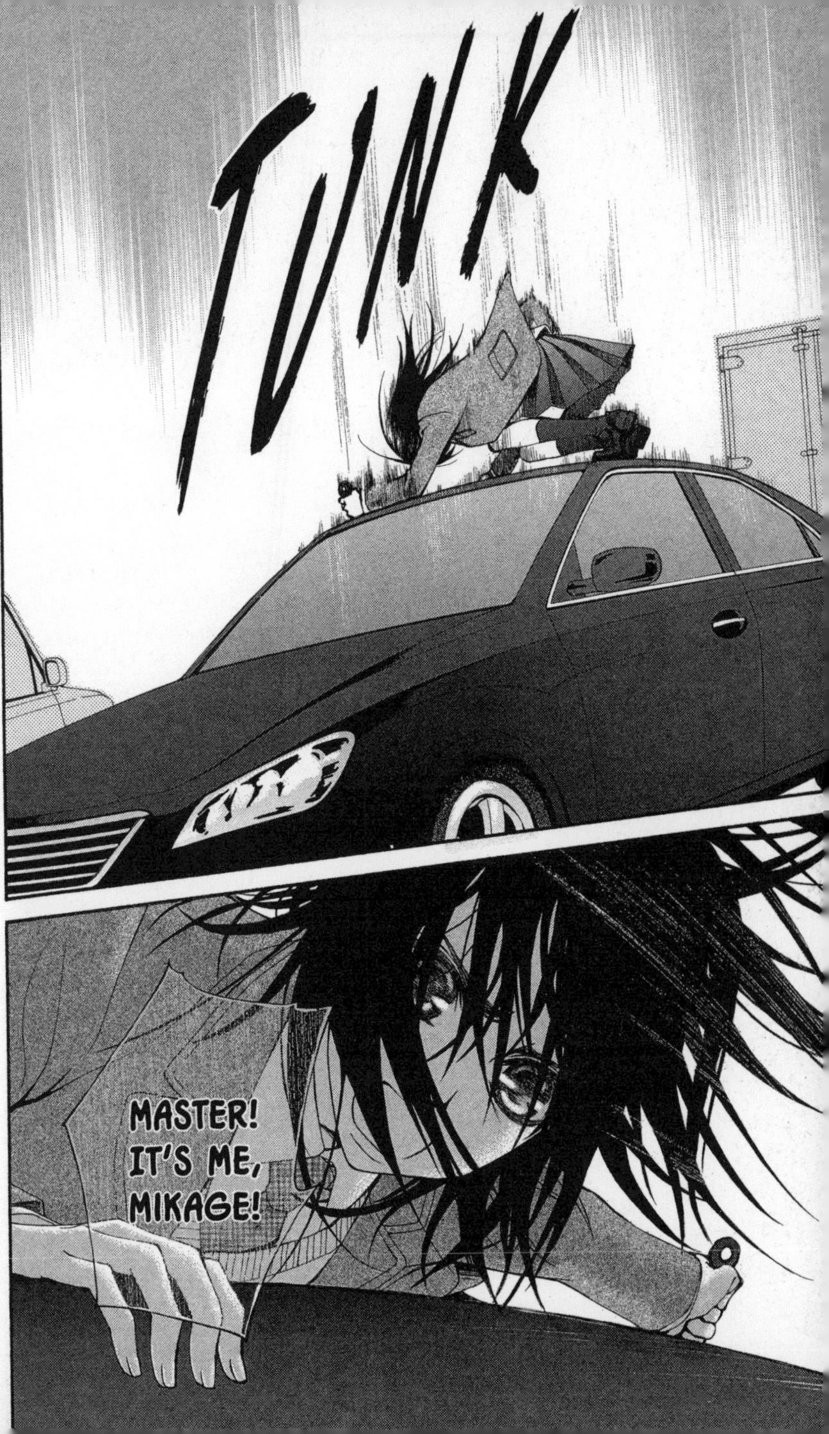
TUNK
MASTER! IT'S ME, MIKAGE!

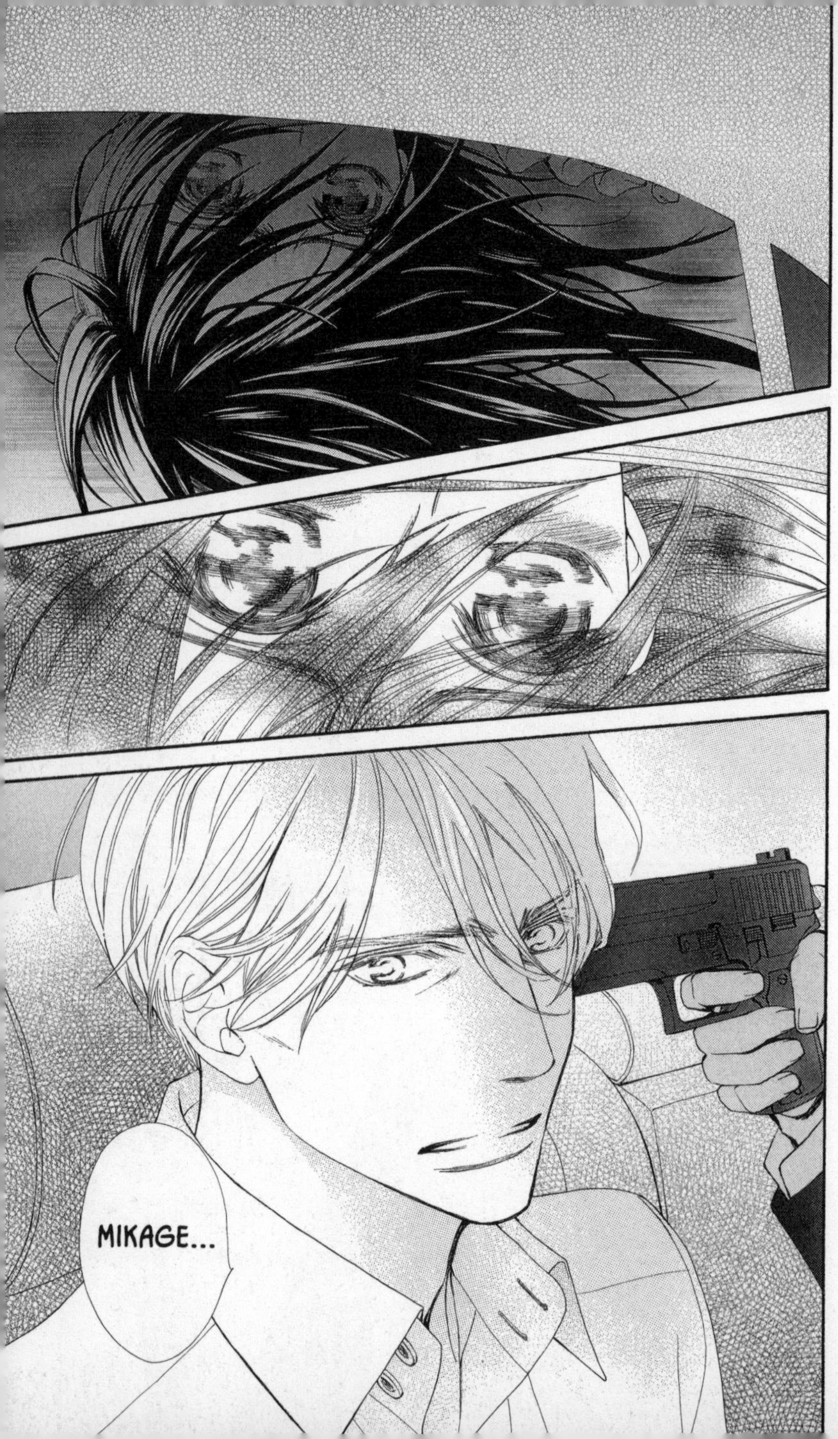
MIKAGE...

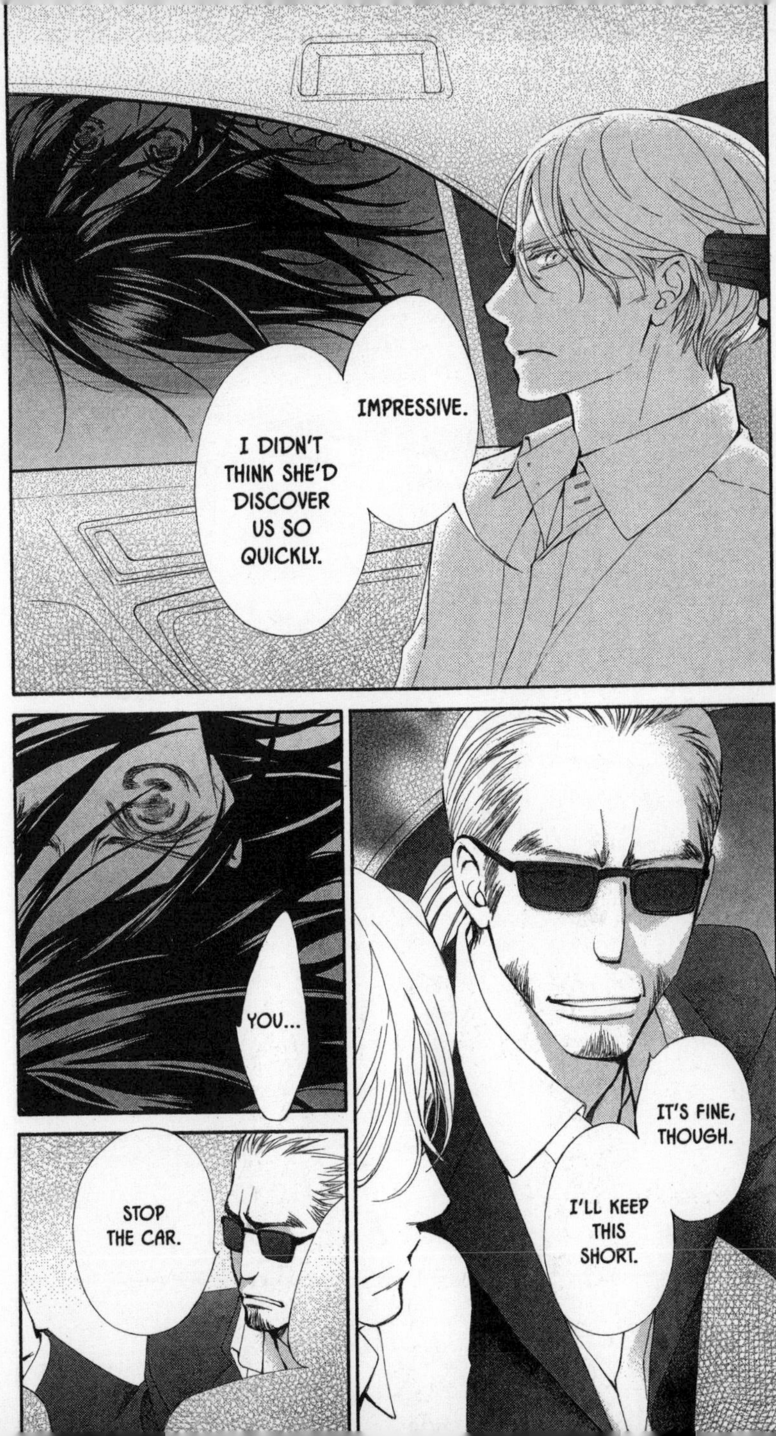
IMPRESSIVE.
I DIDN'T THINK SHE'D DISCOVER US SO QUICKLY.
IT'S FINE, THOUGH.
I'LL KEEP THIS SHORT.
YOU...
STOP THE CAR.

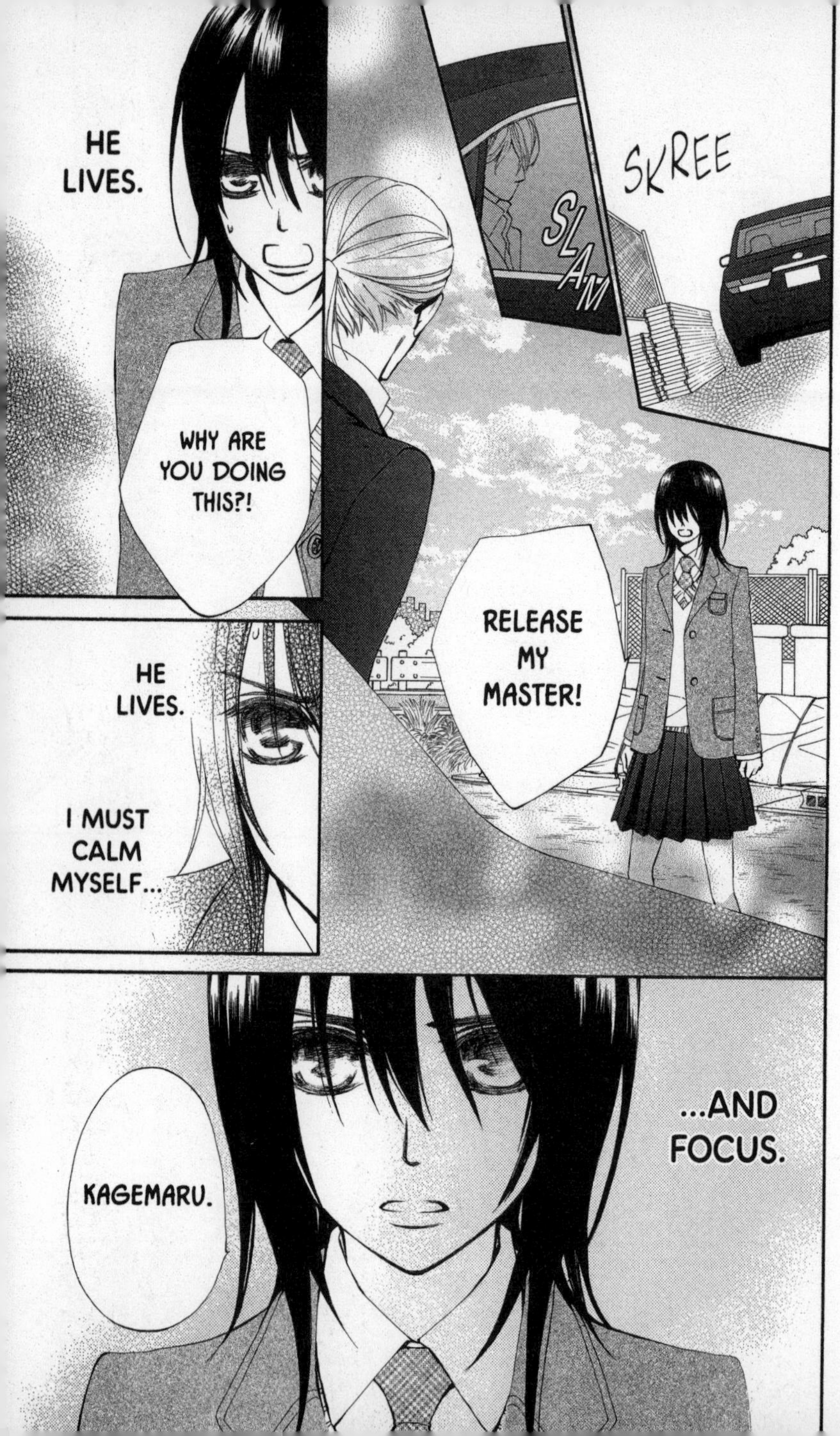
SKREE
SLAM
RELEASE MY MASTER!
HE LIVES.
WHY ARE YOU DOING THIS?!
HE LIVES.
I MUST CALM MYSELF...
...AND FOCUS.
KAGEMARU.

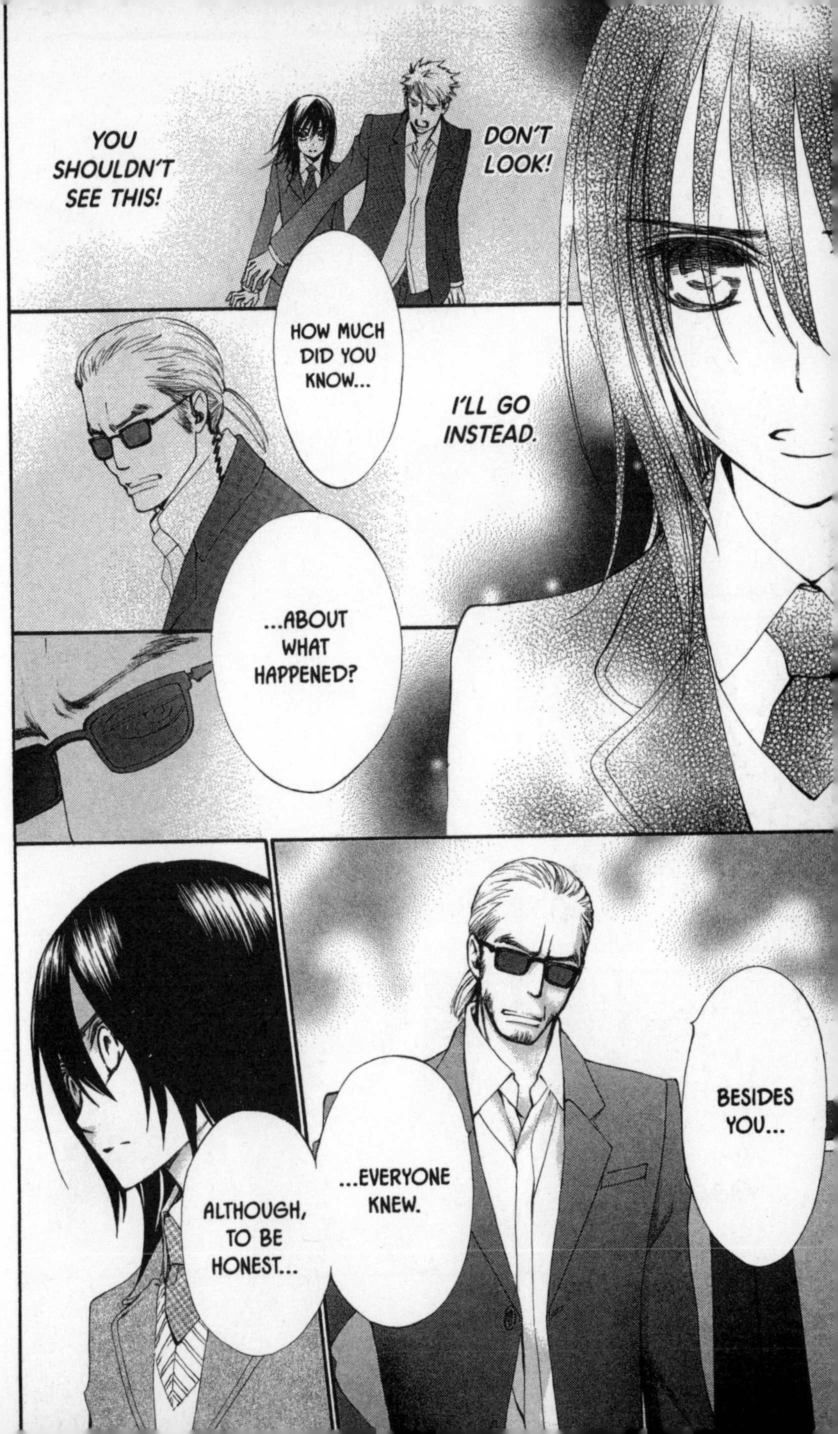
DON'T LOOK!
YOU SHOULDN'T SEE THIS!
I'LL GO INSTEAD.
HOW MUCH DID YOU KNOW...
...ABOUT WHAT HAPPENED?
BESIDES YOU...
...EVERYONE KNEW.
ALTHOUGH, TO BE HONEST...

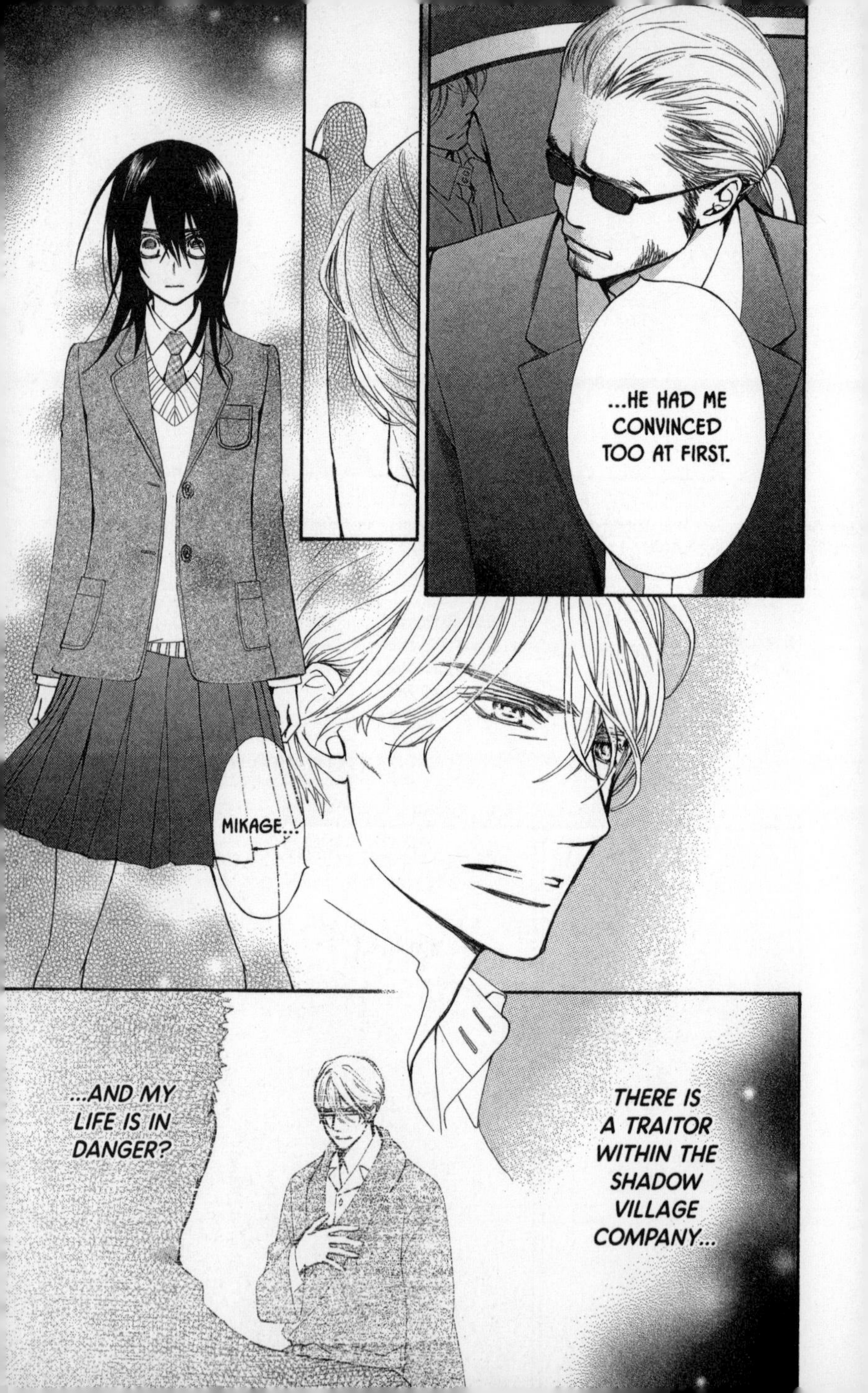
...HE HAD ME CONVINCED TOO AT FIRST.
MIKAGE...
THERE IS A TRAITOR WITHIN THE SHADOW VILLAGE COMPANY...
...AND MY LIFE IS IN DANGER?

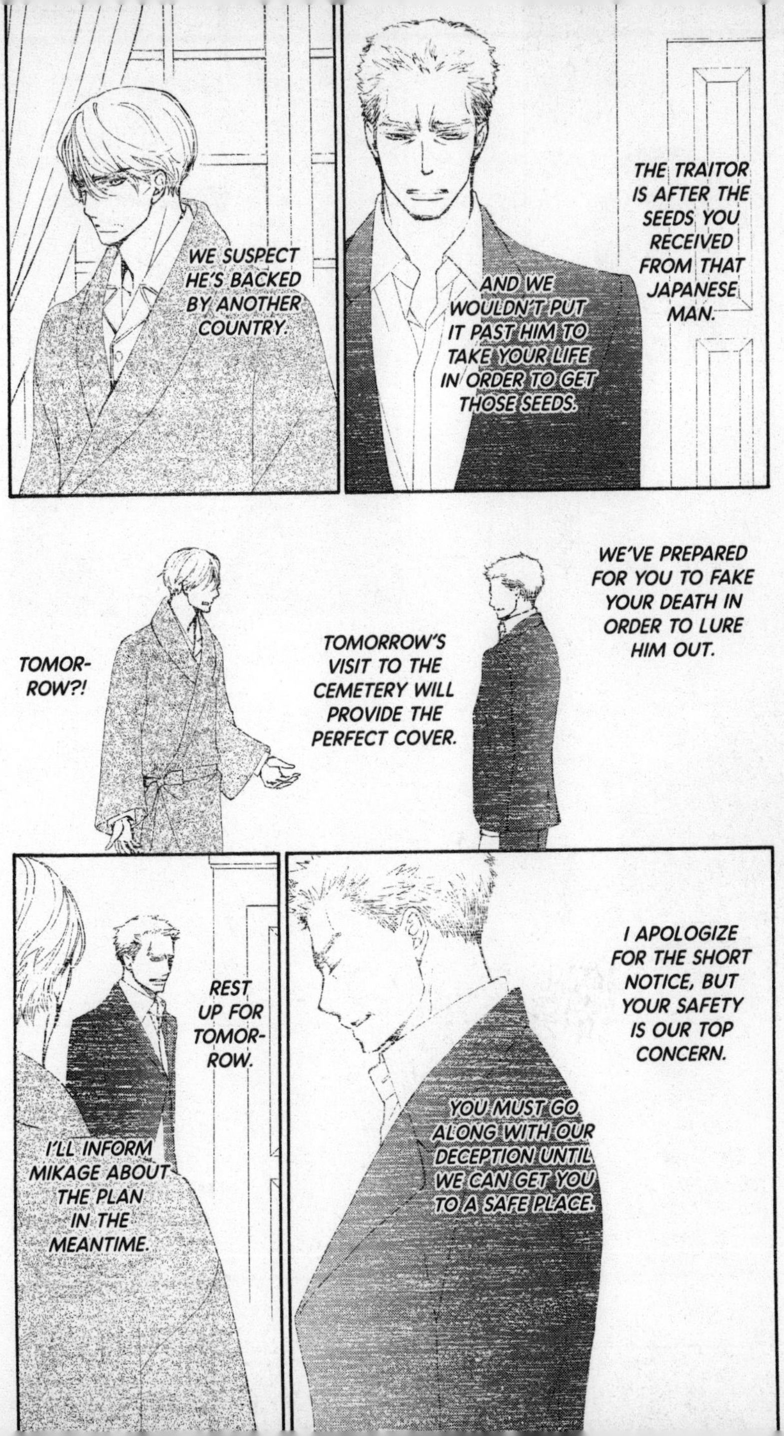
THE TRAITOR IS AFTER THE SEEDS YOU RECEIVED FROM THAT JAPANESE MAN.
AND WE WOULDN'T PUT IT PAST HIM TO TAKE YOUR LIFE IN ORDER TO GET THOSE SEEDS.
WE SUSPECT HE'S BACKED BY ANOTHER COUNTRY.
WE'VE PREPARED FOR YOU TO FAKE YOUR DEATH IN ORDER TO LURE HIM OUT.
TOMORROW'S VISIT TO THE CEMETERY WILL PROVIDE THE PERFECT COVER.
TOMOR-ROW?!
I APOLOGIZE FOR THE SHORT NOTICE, BUT YOUR SAFETY IS OUR TOP CONCERN.
YOU MUST GO ALONG WITH OUR DECEPTION UNTIL WE CAN GET YOU TO A SAFE PLACE.
REST UP FOR TOMOR-ROW.
I'LL INFORM MIKAGE ABOUT THE PLAN IN THE MEANTIME.

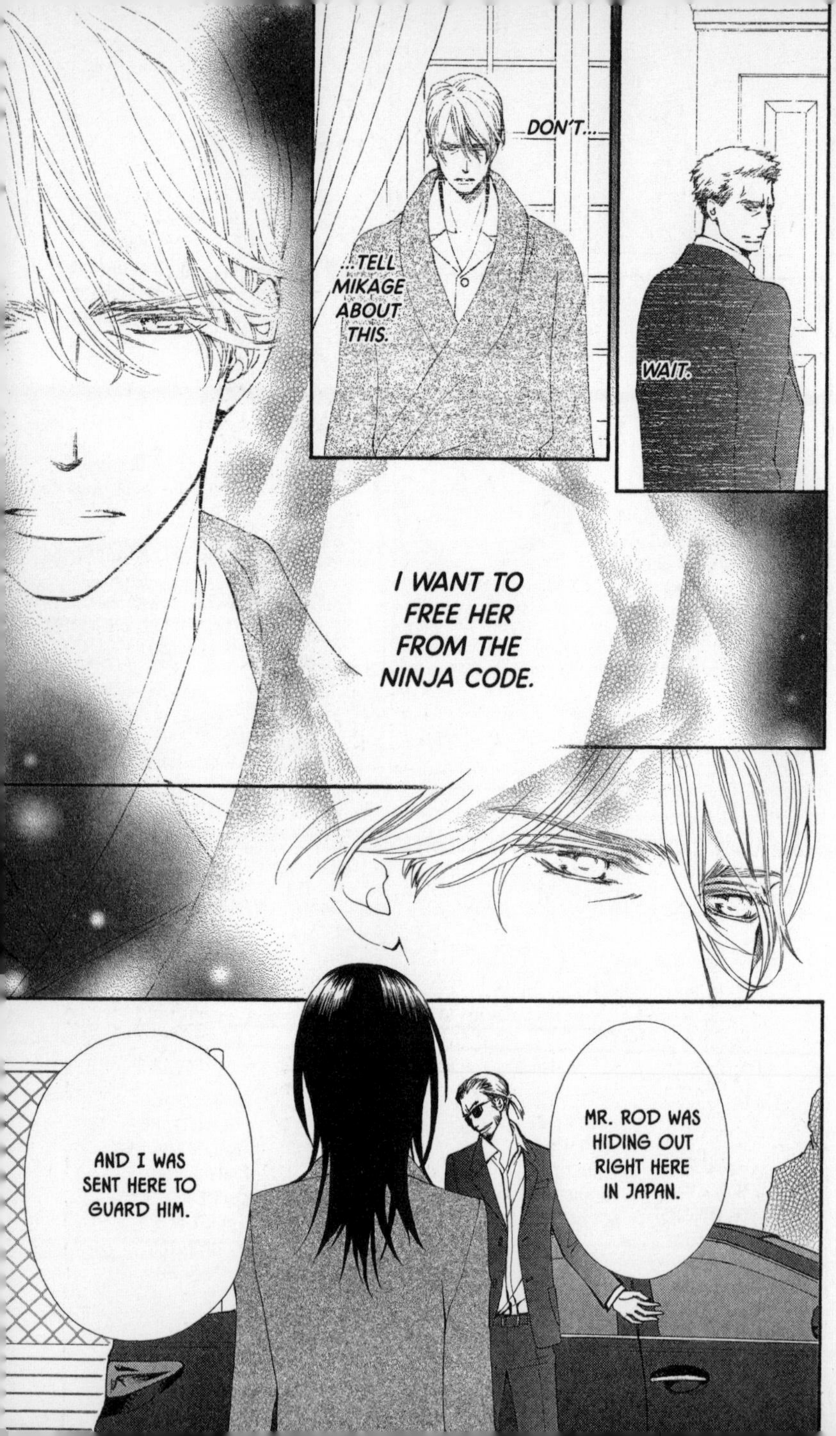
WAIT.
DON'T...
...TELL MIKAGE ABOUT THIS.
I WANT TO FREE HER FROM THE NINJA CODE.
MR. ROD WAS HIDING OUT RIGHT HERE IN JAPAN.
AND I WAS SENT HERE TO GUARD HIM.

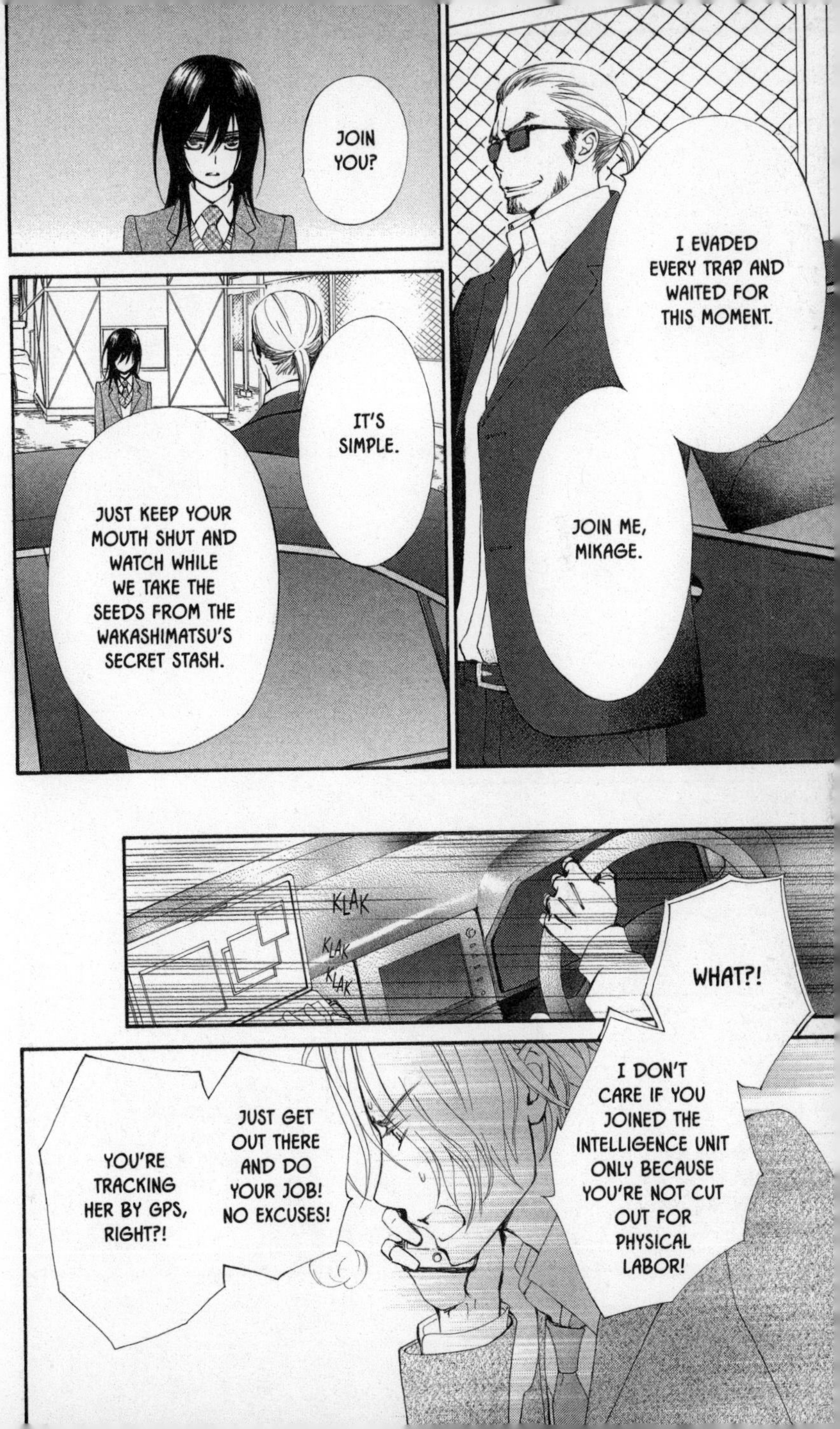
I EVADED EVERY TRAP AND WAITED FOR THIS MOMENT.
JOIN ME, MIKAGE.
JOIN YOU?
IT'S SIMPLE.
JUST KEEP YOUR MOUTH SHUT AND WATCH WHILE WE TAKE THE SEEDS FROM THE WAKASHIMATSU'S SECRET STASH.
WHAT?!
KLAK
KLAK
KLAK
I DON'T CARE IF YOU JOINED THE INTELLIGENCE UNIT ONLY BECAUSE YOU'RE NOT CUT OUT FOR PHYSICAL LABOR!
JUST GET OUT THERE AND DO YOUR JOB! NO EXCUSES!
YOU'RE TRACKING HER BY GPS, RIGHT?!

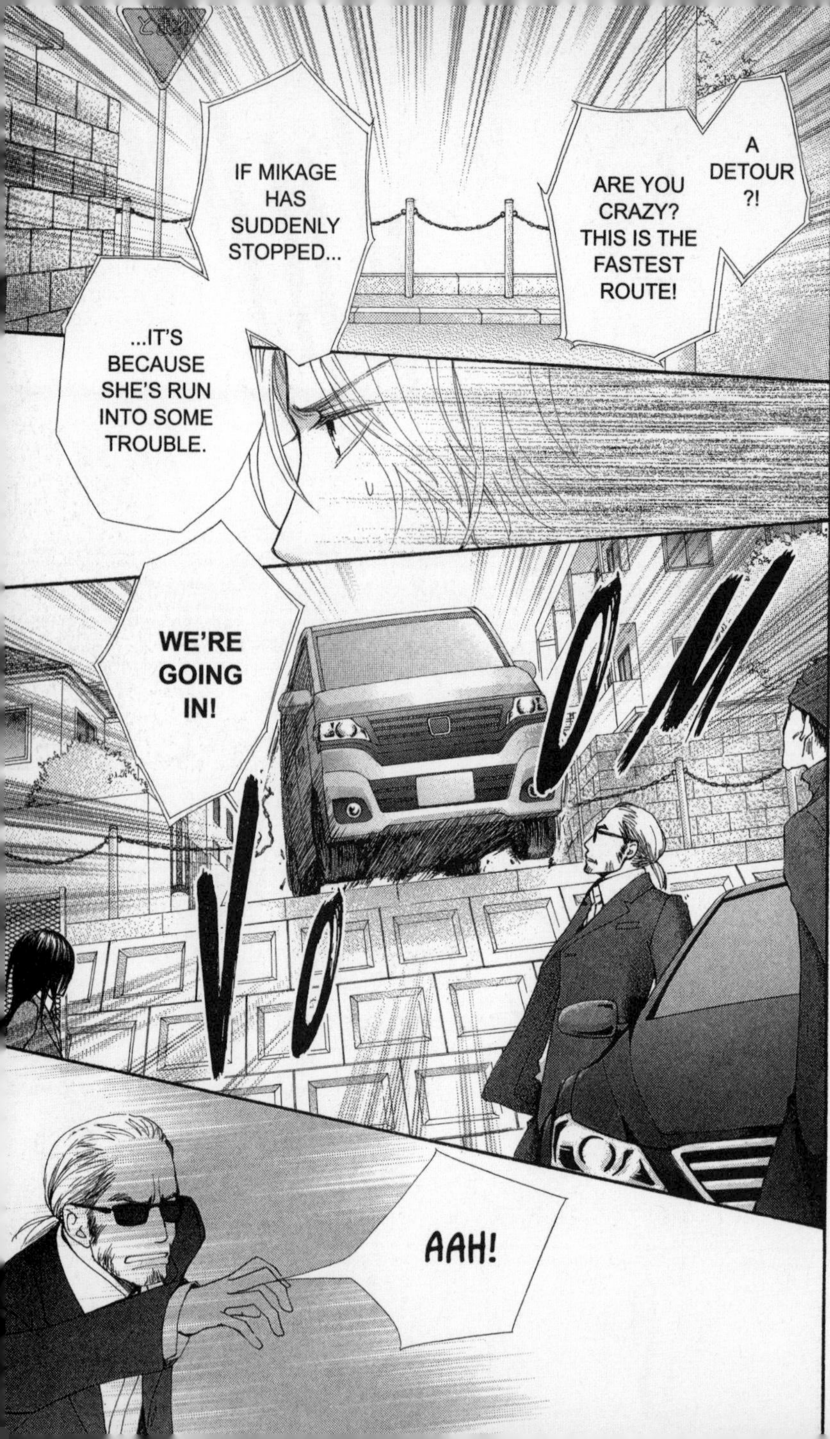
A DETOUR?!
ARE YOU CRAZY? THIS IS THE FASTEST ROUTE!
IF MIKAGE HAS SUDDENLY STOPPED...
...IT'S BECAUSE SHE'S RUN INTO SOME TROUBLE.
WE'RE GOING IN!
VOOM
AAH!

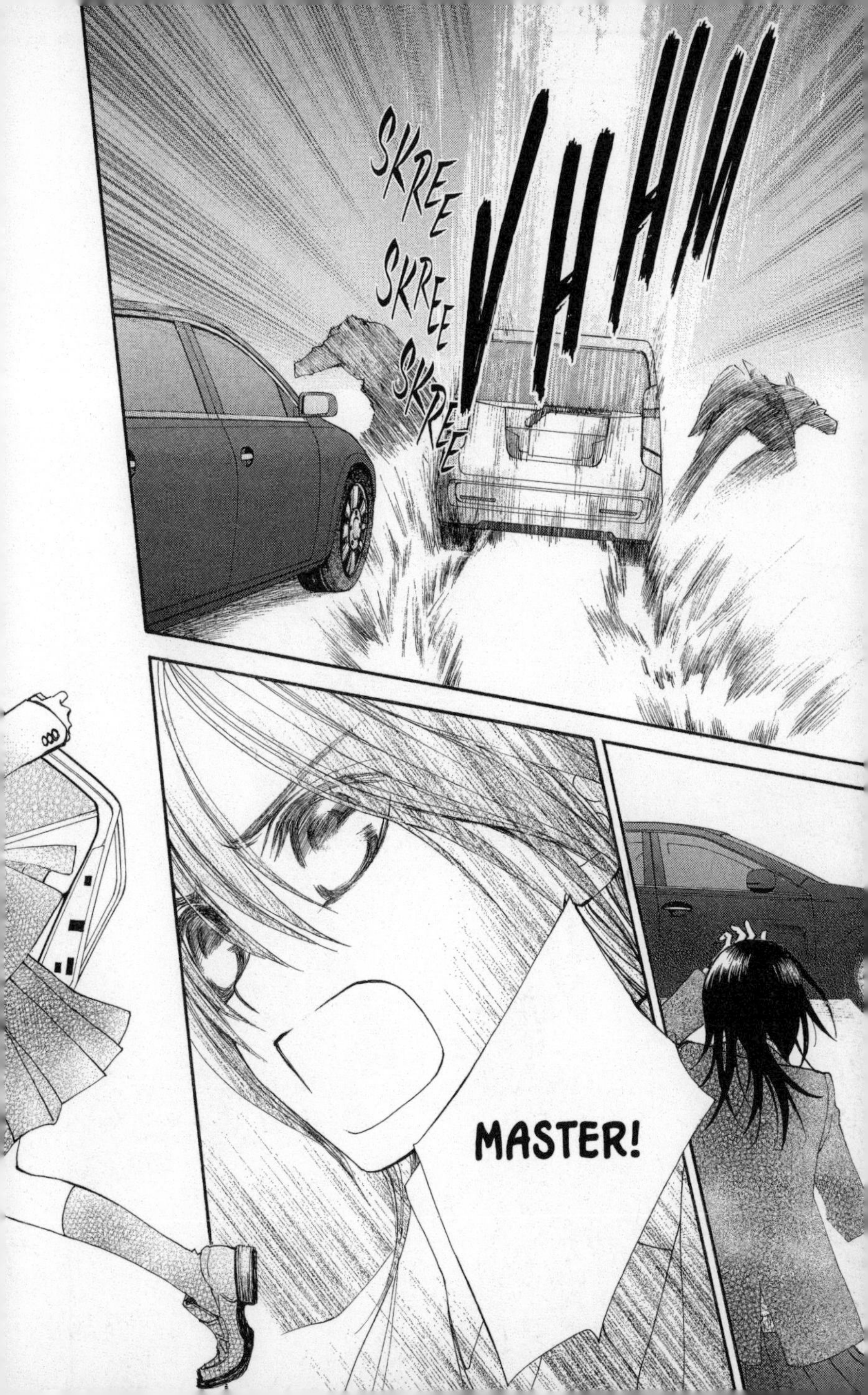
VMMM
SKREE SKREE SKREE
MASTER!

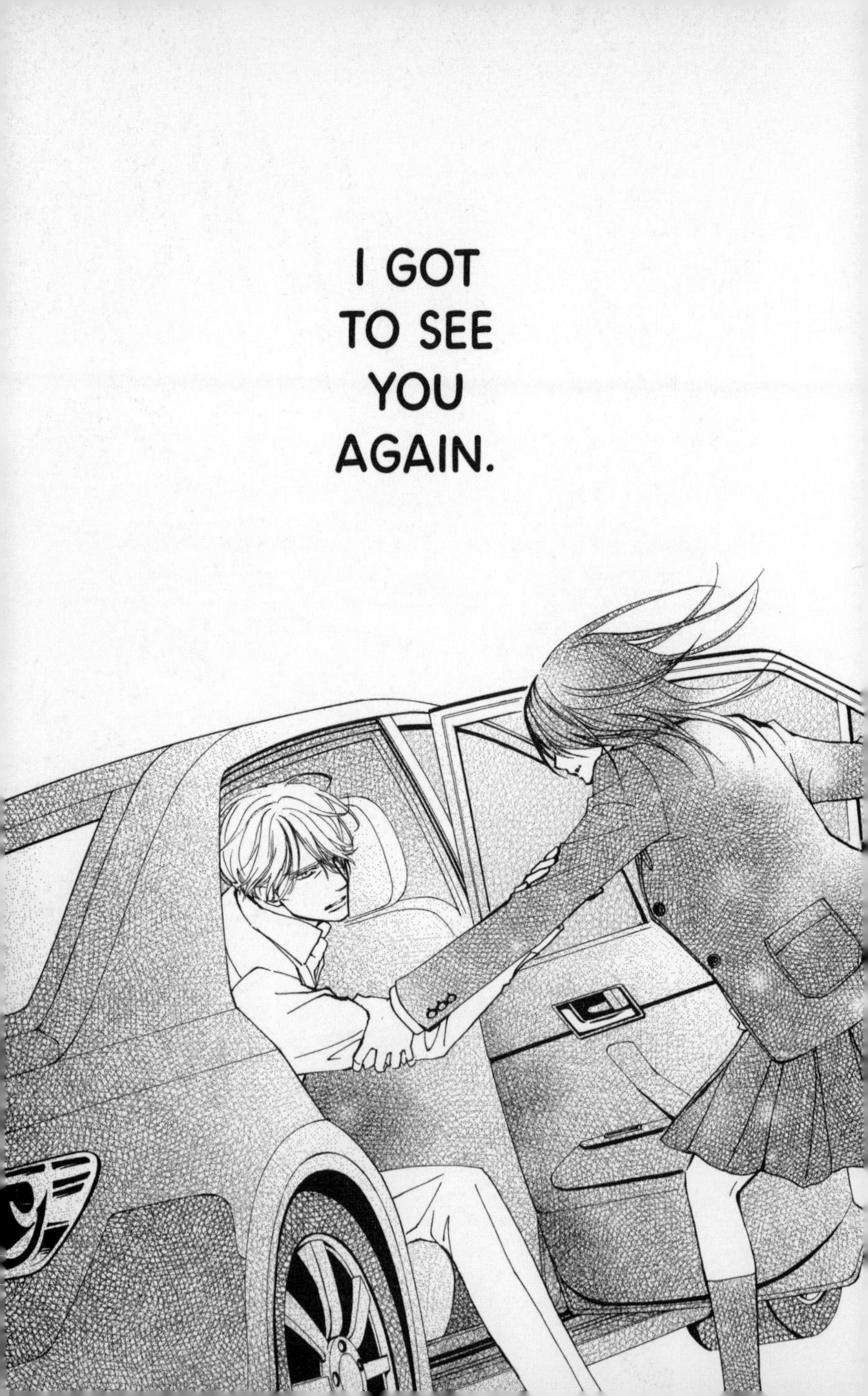
I GOT TO SEE YOU AGAIN.

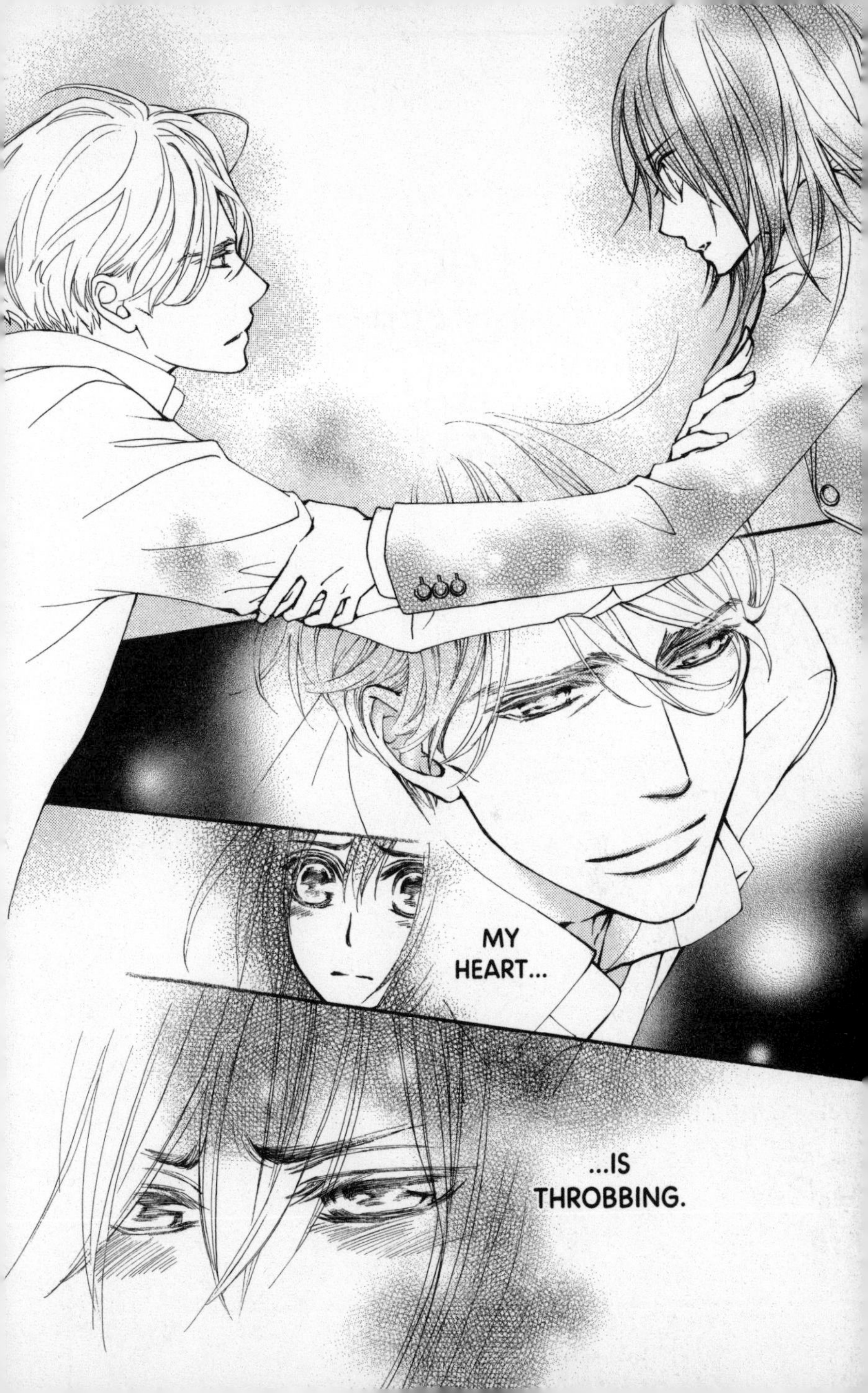
MY HEART...
...IS THROBBING.

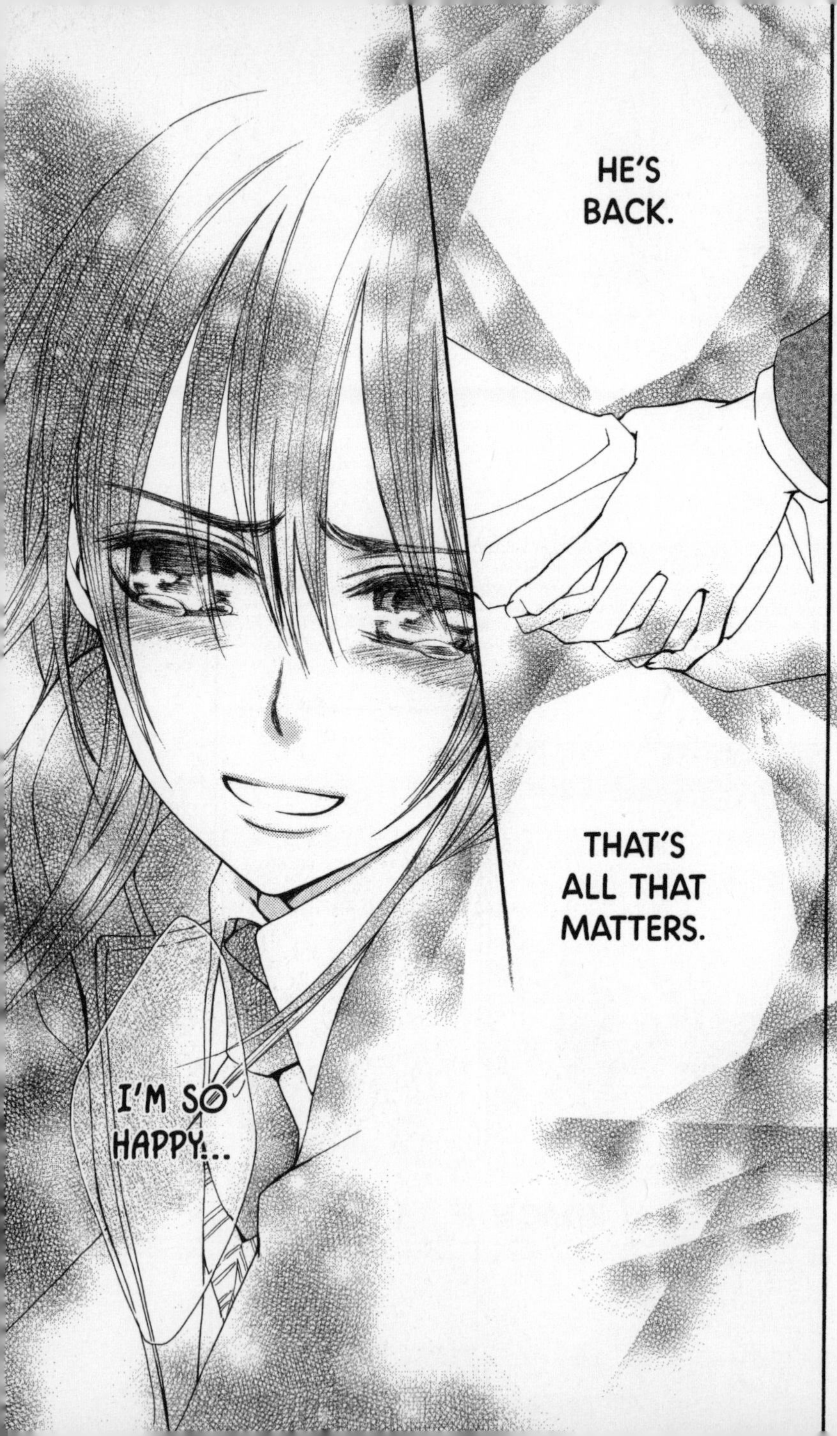
HE'S BACK.
THAT'S ALL THAT MATTERS.
I'M SO HAPPY...

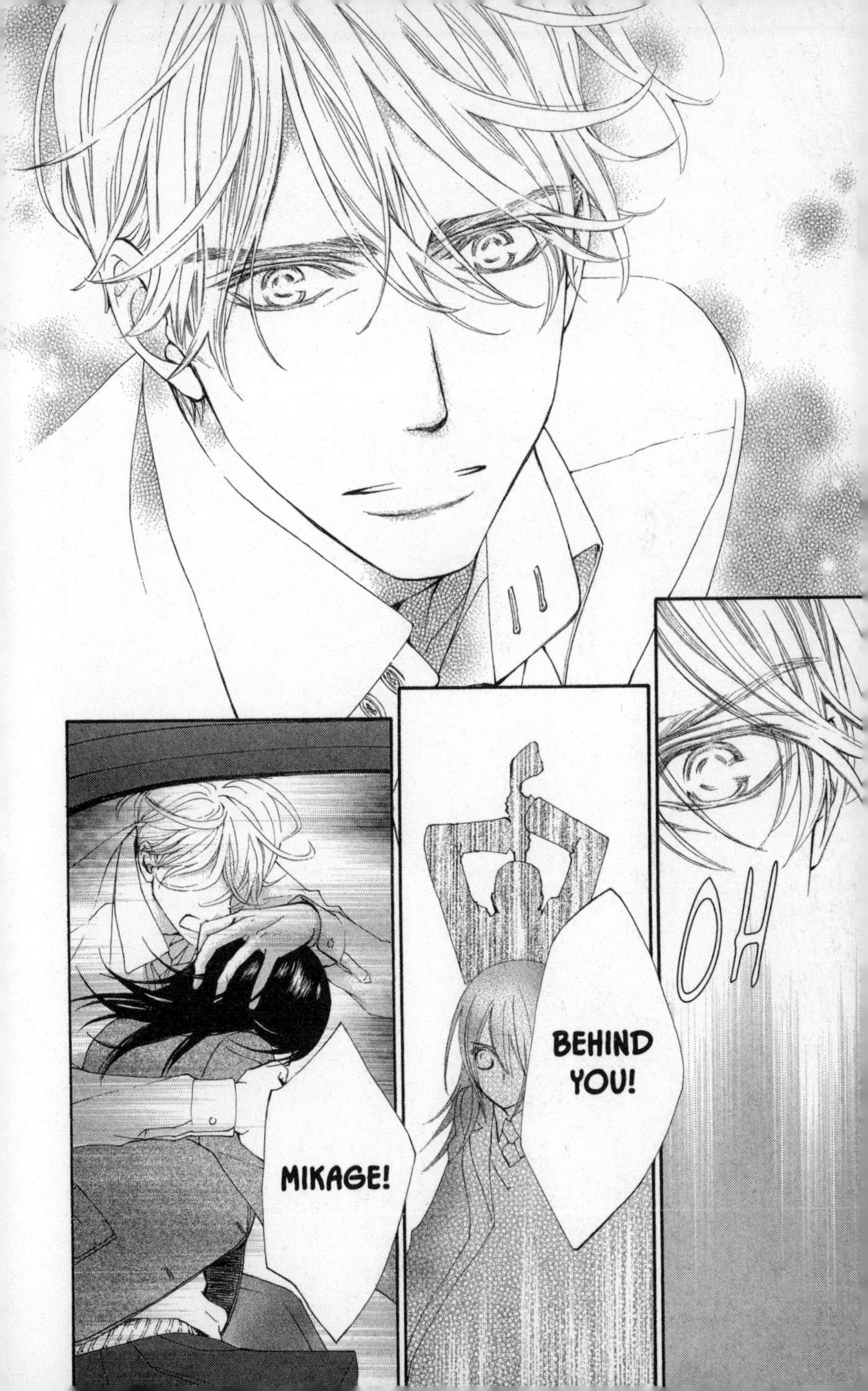
OH
BEHIND YOU!
MIKAGE!

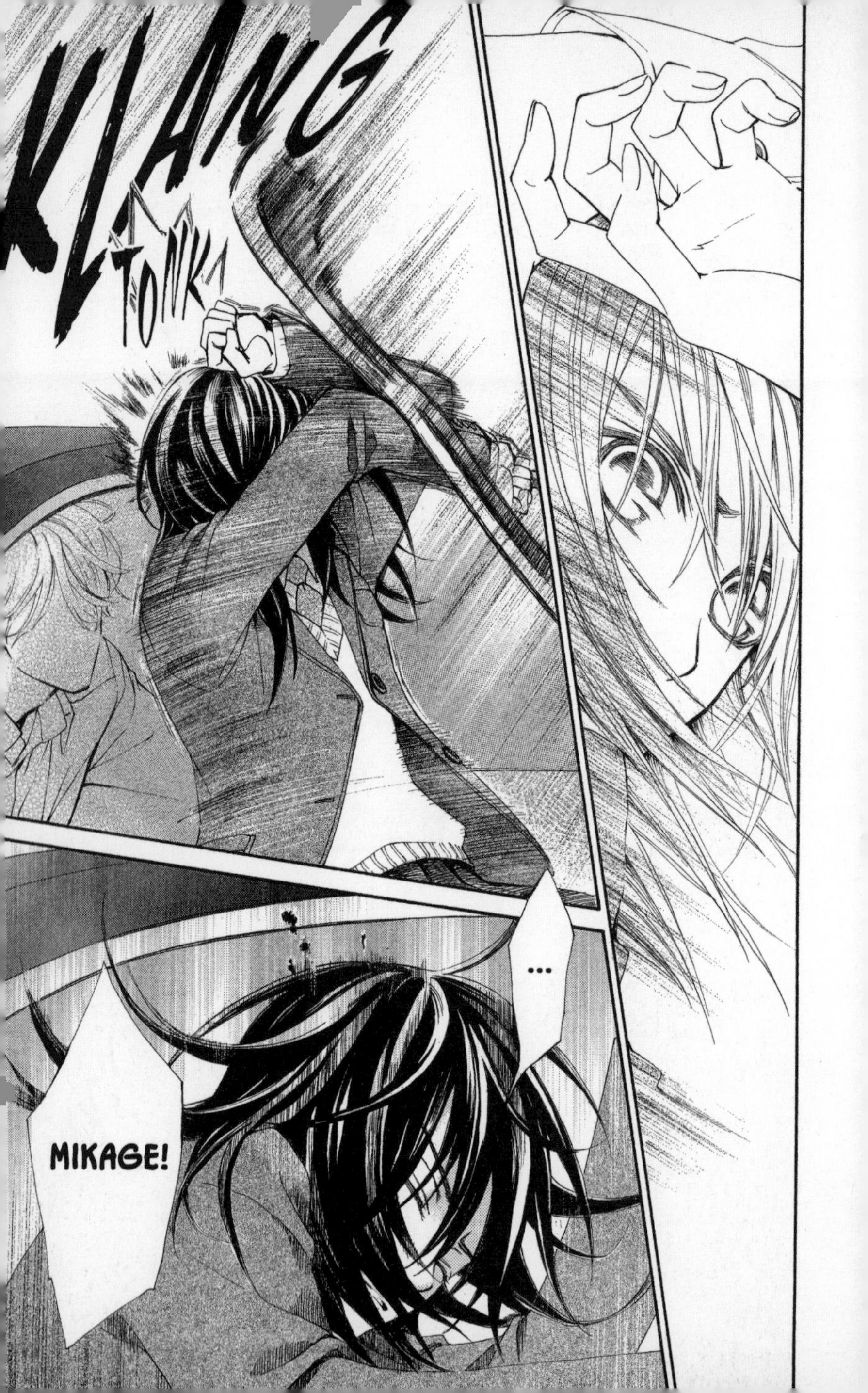
KLANG
TONKA
...
MIKAGE!

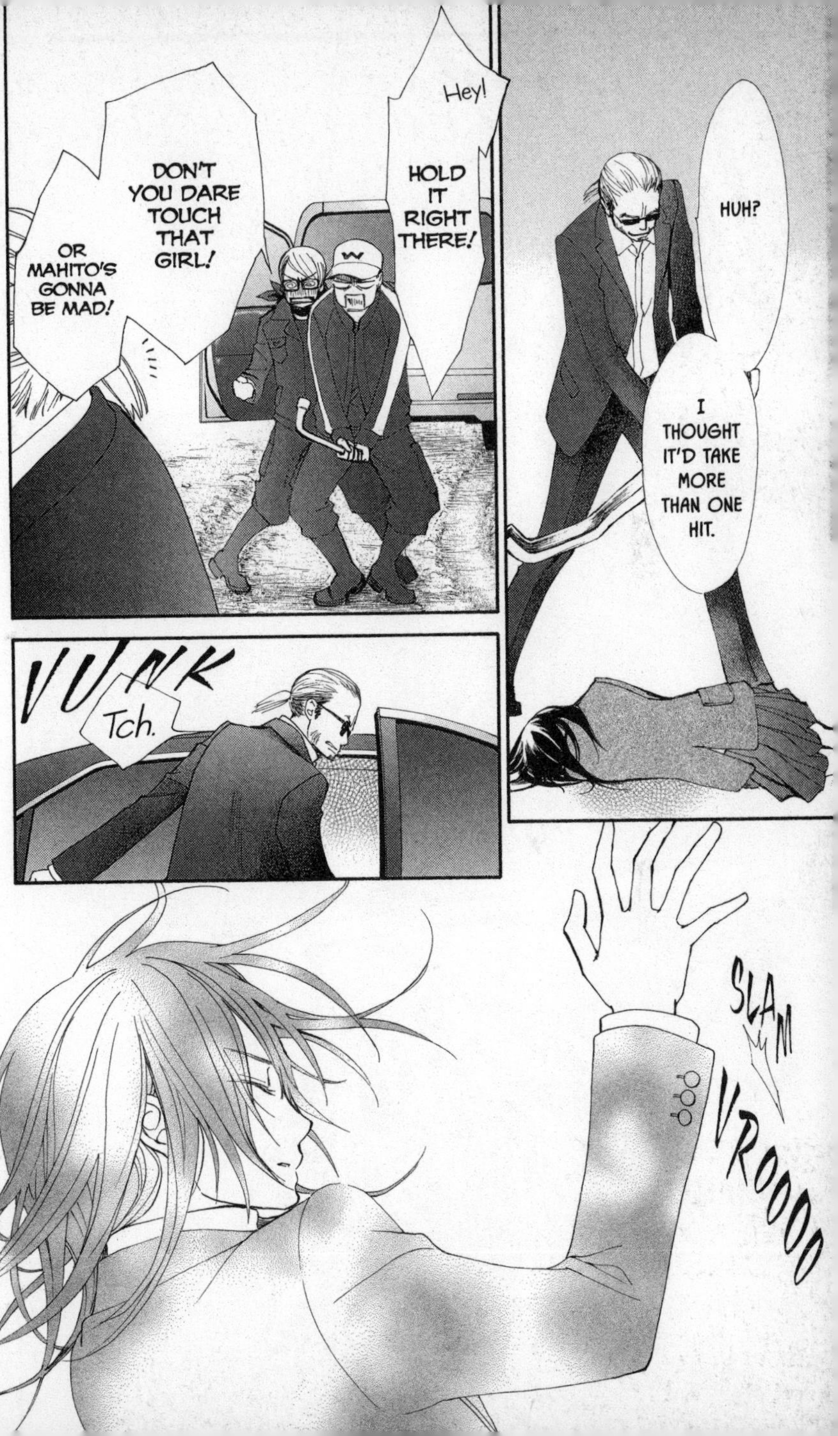
HUH?
I THOUGHT IT'D TAKE MORE THAN ONE HIT.
Hey!
HOLD IT RIGHT THERE!
DON'T YOU DARE TOUCH THAT GIRL!
OR MAHITO'S GONNA BE MAD!
VUNK
Tch.
SLAM
VROOOOO

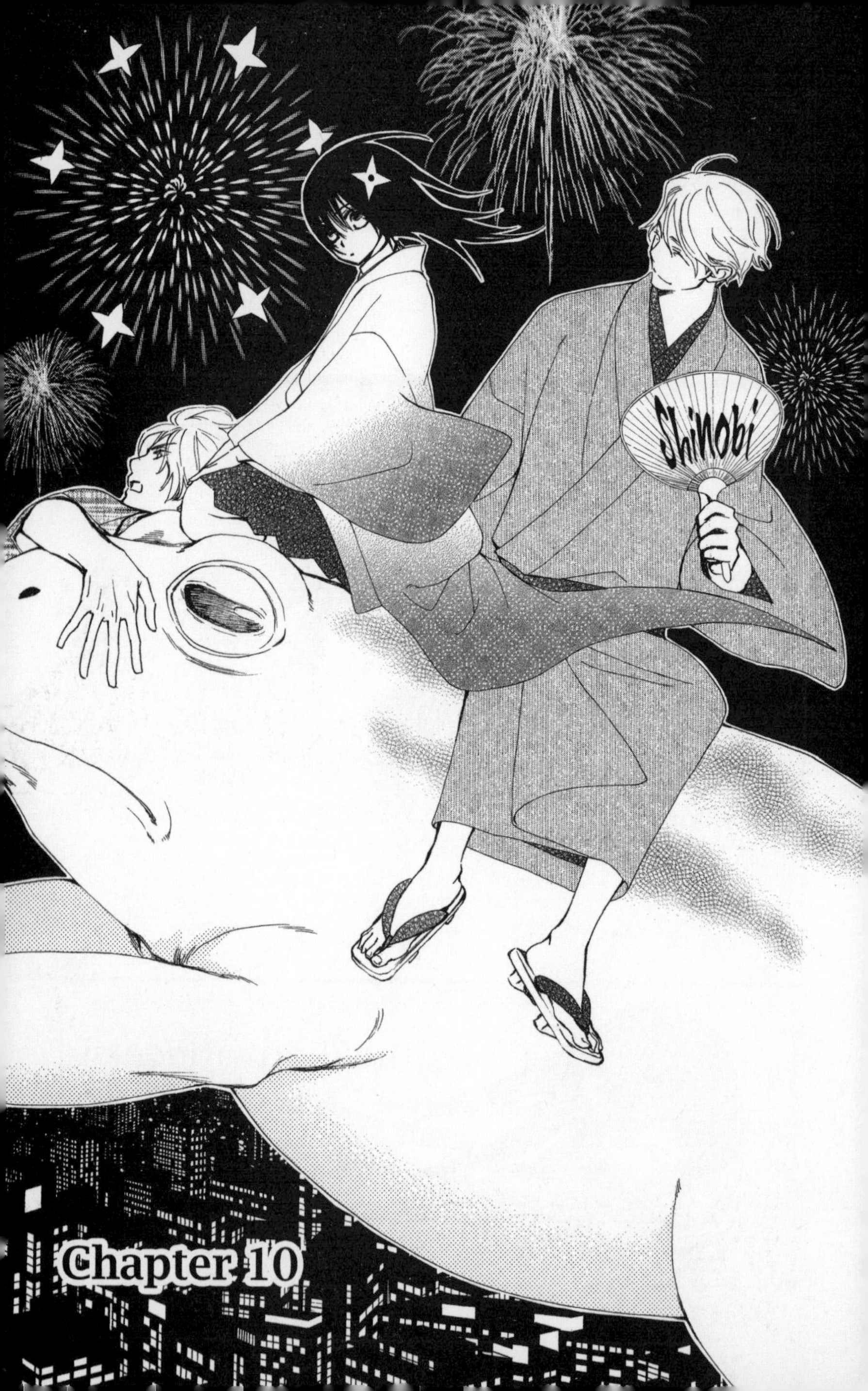
SHINOBI
Chapter 10

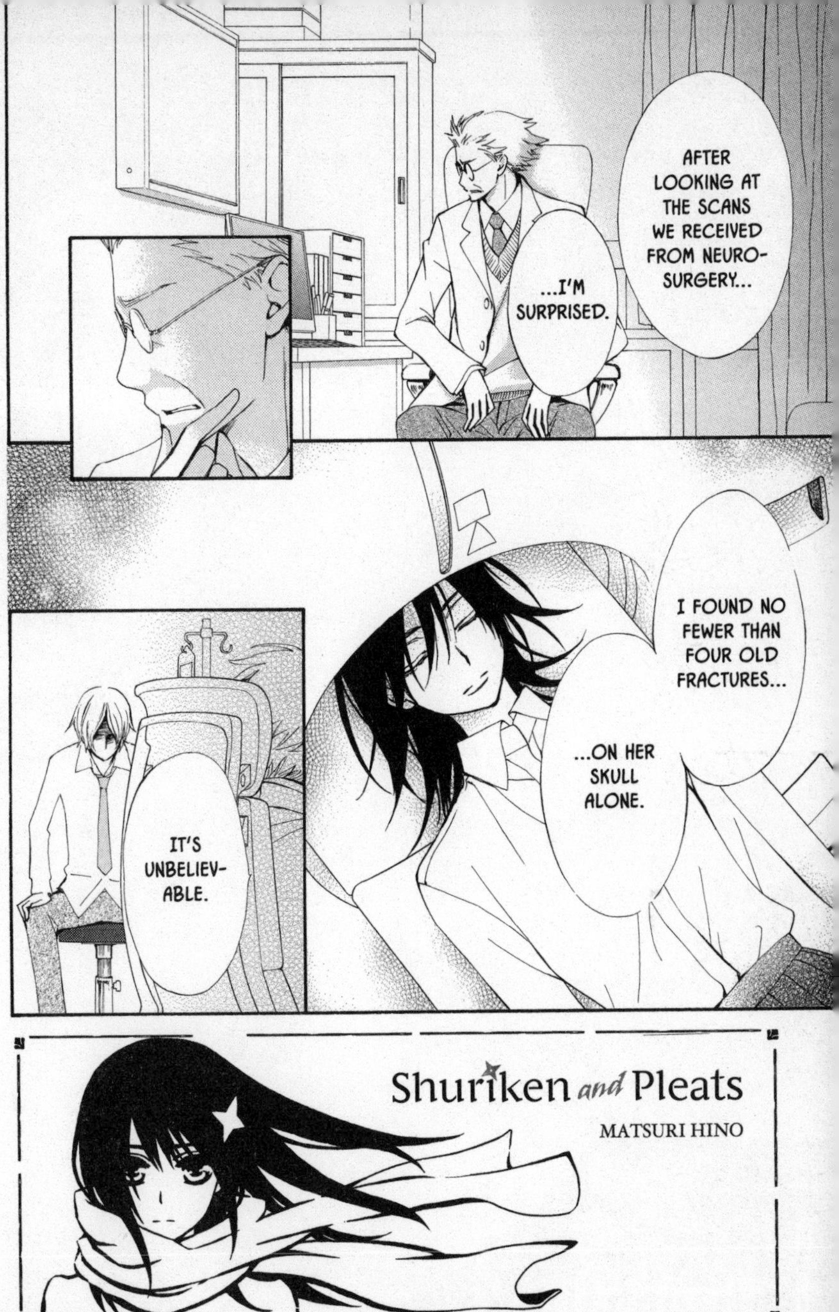
AFTER LOOKING AT THE SCANS WE RECEIVED FROM NEURO-SURGERY...
...I'M SURPRISED.
I FOUND NO FEWER THAN FOUR OLD FRACTURES...
...ON HER SKULL ALONE.
IT'S UNBELIEV-ABLE.
Shuriken and Pleats
MATSURI HINO

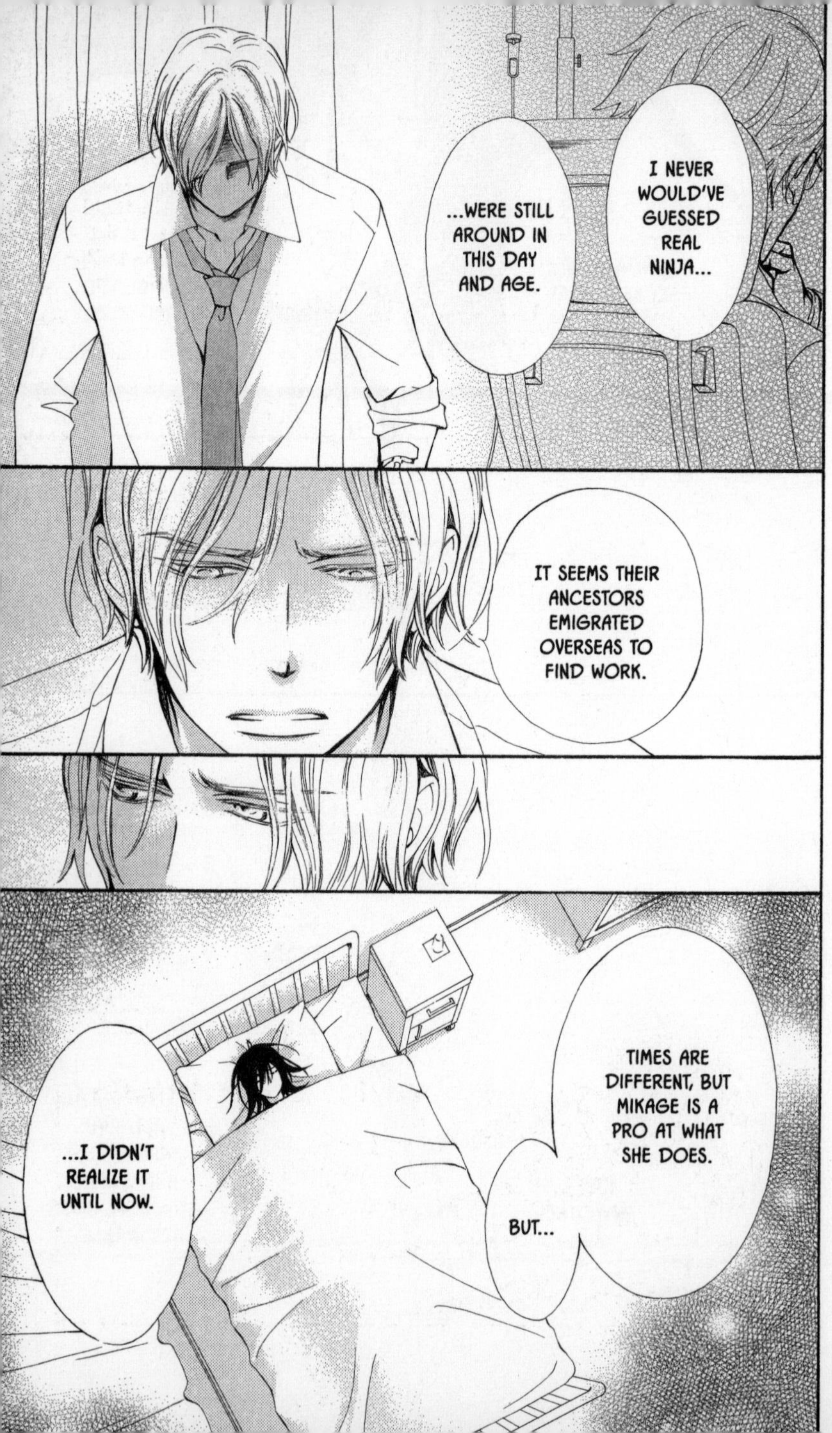
I NEVER WOULD'VE GUESSED REAL NINJA...
...WERE STILL AROUND IN THIS DAY AND AGE.
IT SEEMS THEIR ANCESTORS EMIGRATED OVERSEAS TO FIND WORK.
TIMES ARE DIFFERENT, BUT MIKAGE IS A PRO AT WHAT SHE DOES.
BUT...
...I DIDN'T REALIZE IT UNTIL NOW.

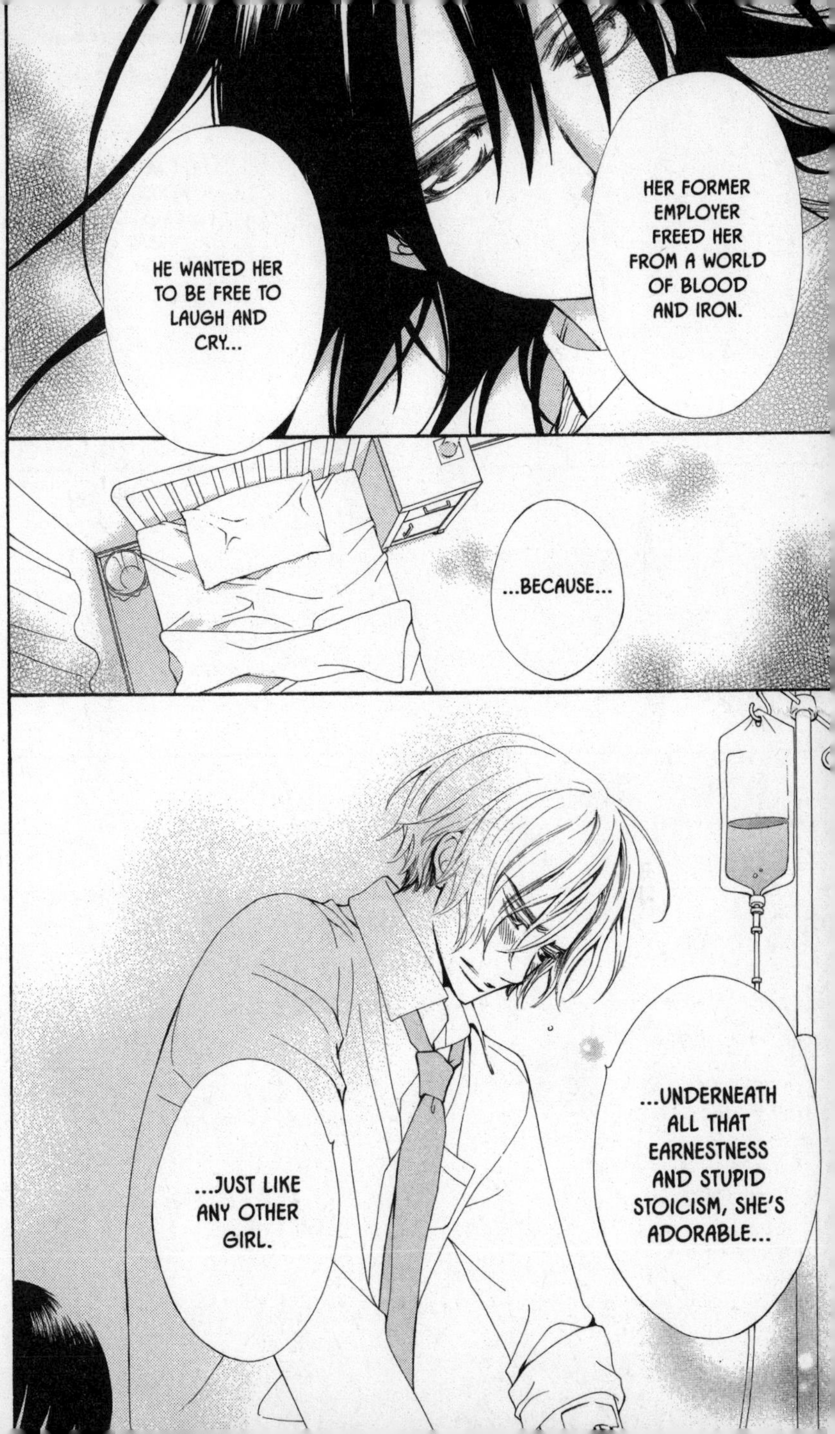
HER FORMER EMPLOYER FREED HER FROM A WORLD OF BLOOD AND IRON.
HE WANTED HER TO BE FREE TO LAUGH AND CRY...
...BECAUSE...
...UNDERNEATH ALL THAT EARNESTNESS AND STUPID STOICISM, SHE'S ADORABLE...
...JUST LIKE ANY OTHER GIRL.

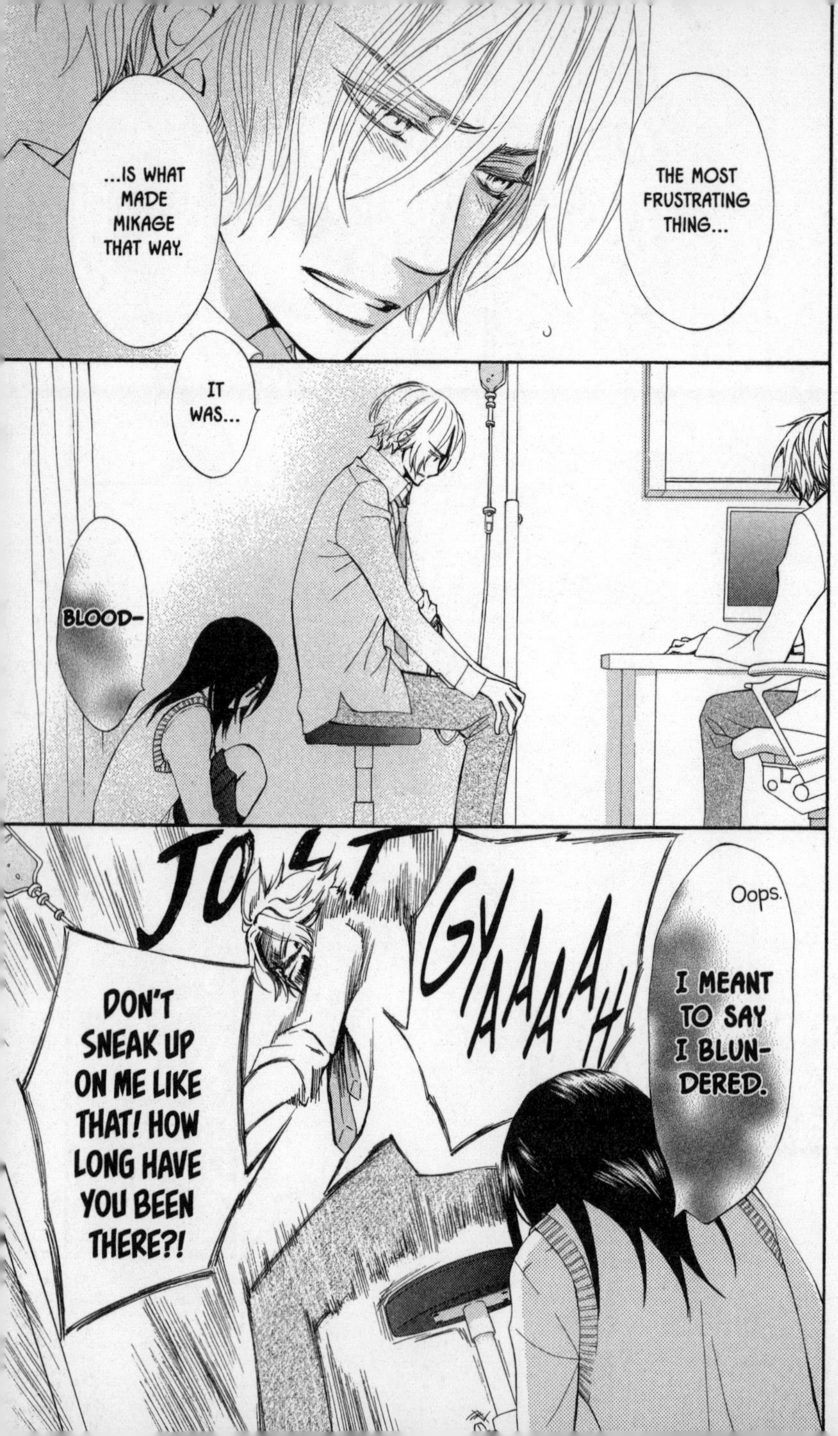
THE MOST FRUSTRATING THING...
...IS WHAT MADE MIKAGE THAT WAY.
IT WAS...
BLOOD-
Oops.
I MEANT TO SAY I BLUNDERED.
JOLT
GYAAAAH
DON'T SNEAK UP ON ME LIKE THAT! HOW LONG HAVE YOU BEEN THERE?!

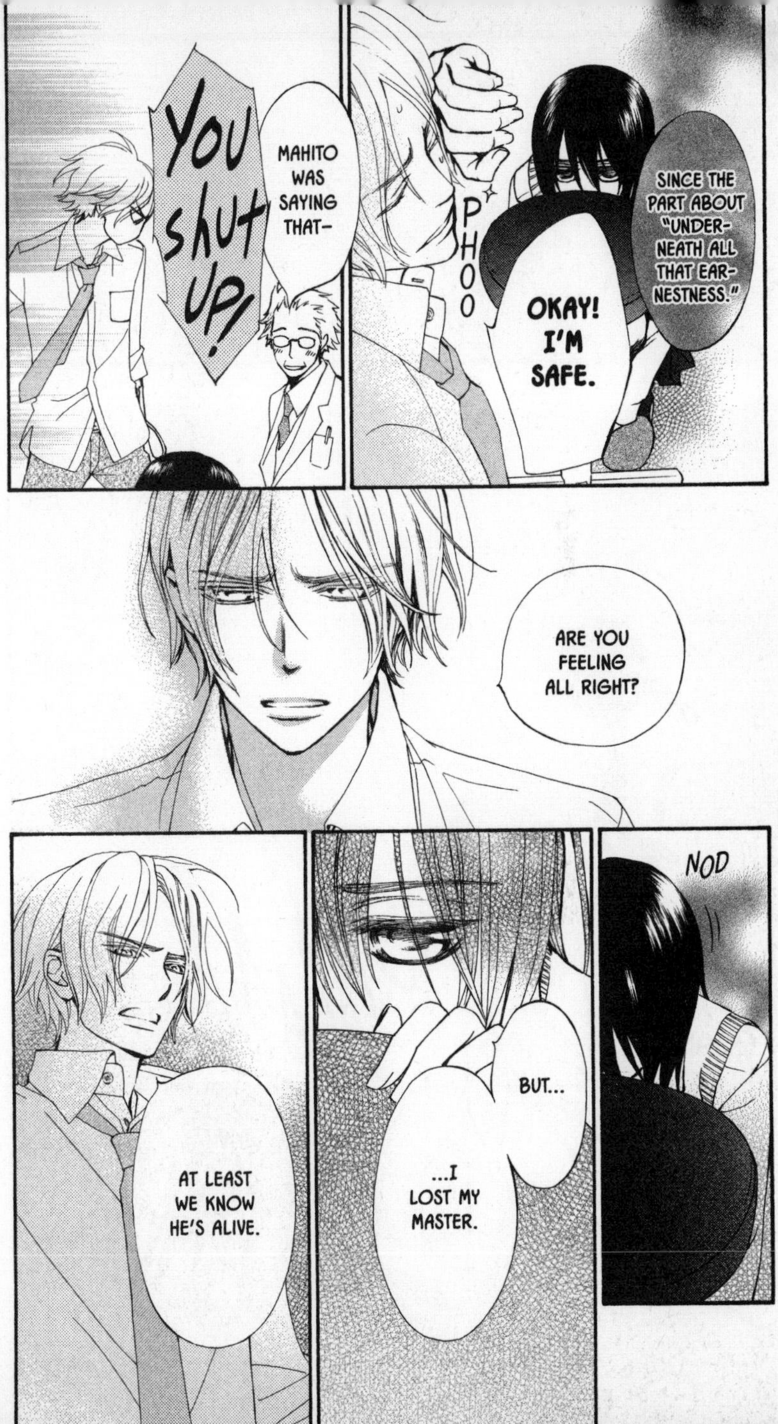
SINCE THE PART ABOUT "UNDERNEATH ALL THAT EARNESTNESS."
PHOO
OKAY! I'M SAFE.
MAHITO WAS SAYING THAT-
YOU SHUT UP!
ARE YOU FEELING ALL RIGHT?
NOD
BUT...
...I LOST MY MASTER.
AT LEAST WE KNOW HE'S ALIVE.

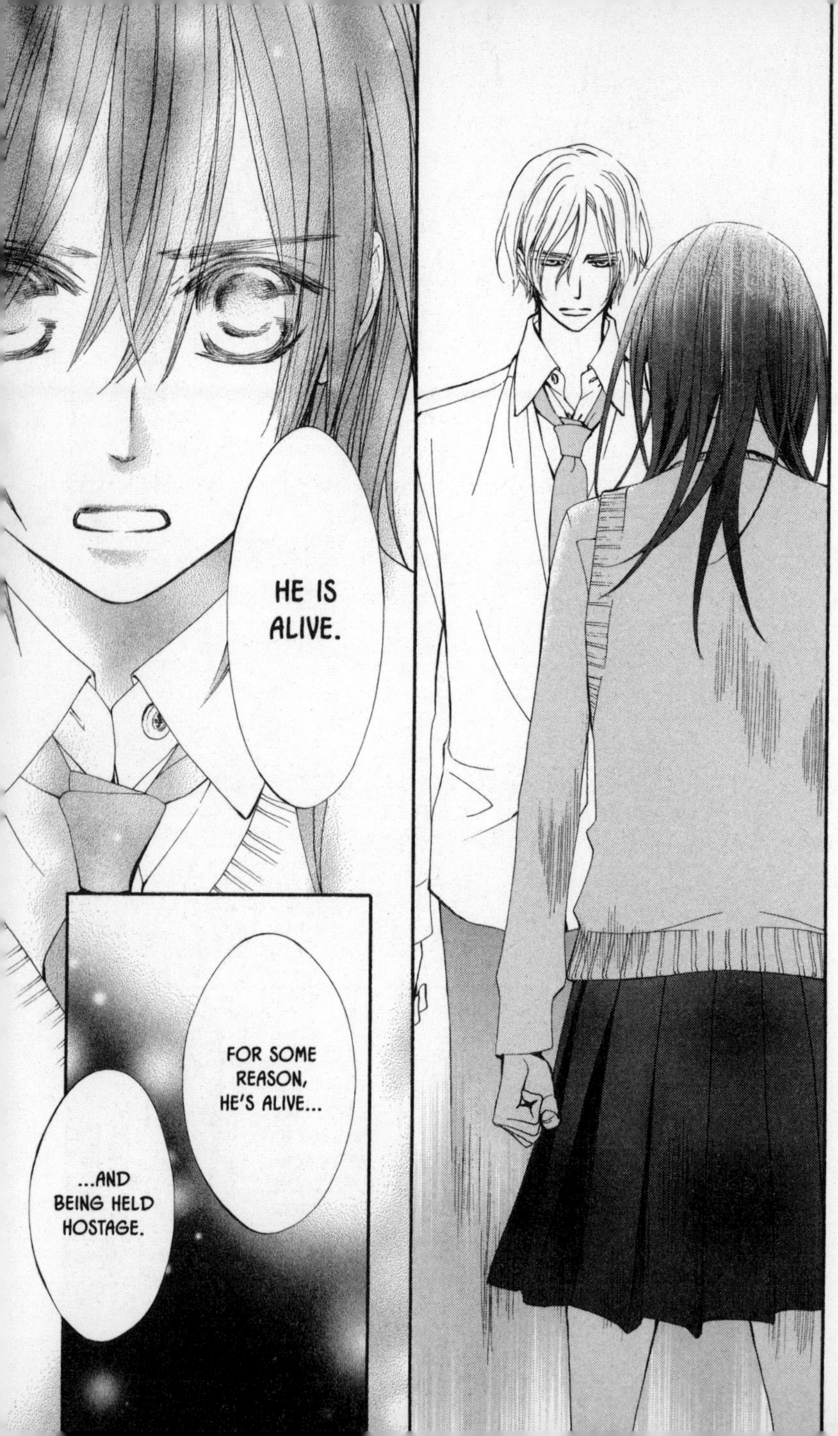
HE IS ALIVE.
FOR SOME REASON, HE'S ALIVE...
...AND BEING HELD HOSTAGE.

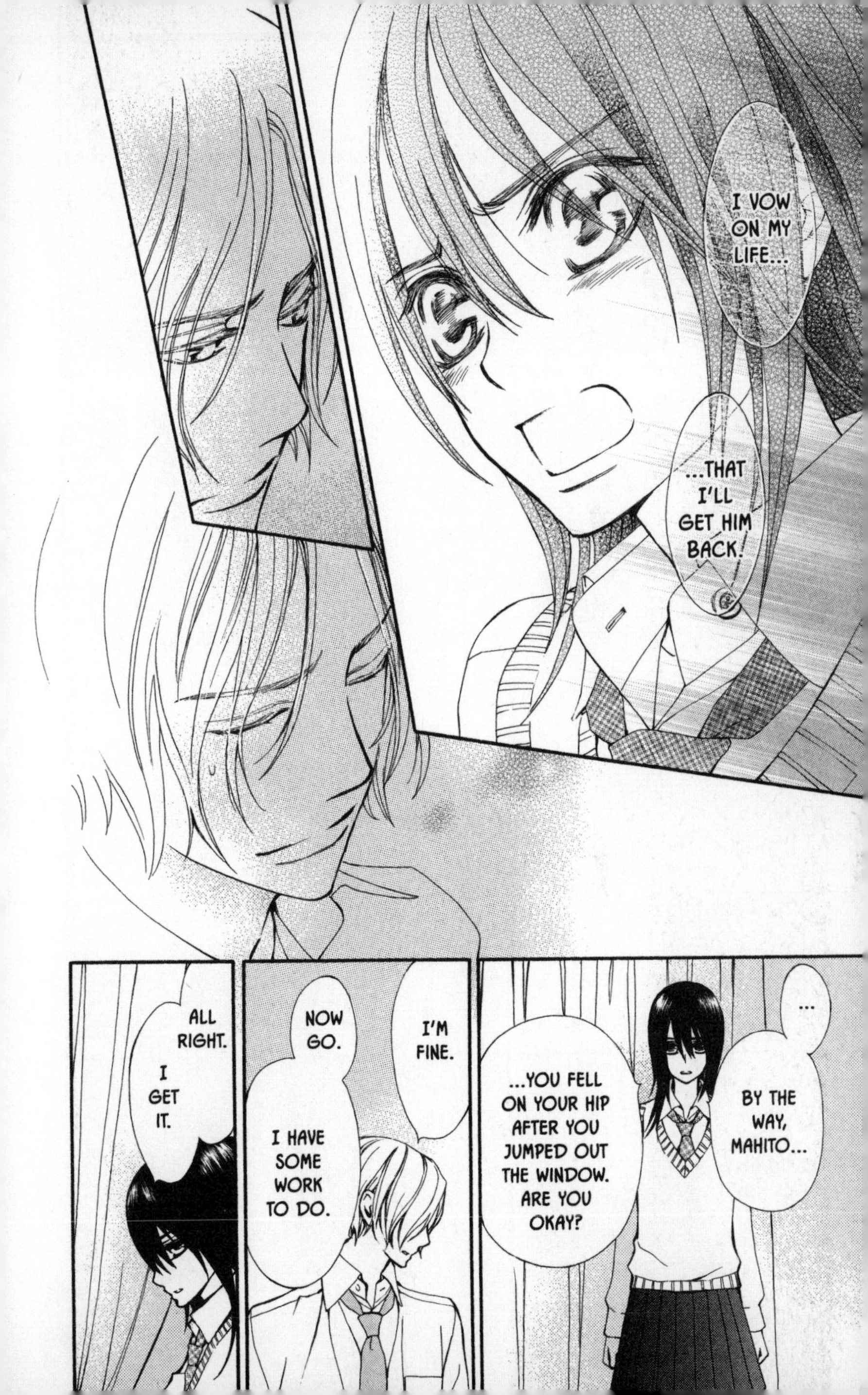
I VOW ON MY LIFE...
...THAT I'LL GET HIM BACK.
...
BY THE WAY, MAHITO...
...YOU FELL ON YOUR HIP AFTER YOU JUMPED OUT THE WINDOW. ARE YOU OKAY?
I'M FINE.
NOW GO.
I HAVE SOME WORK TO DO.
ALL RIGHT.
I GET IT.

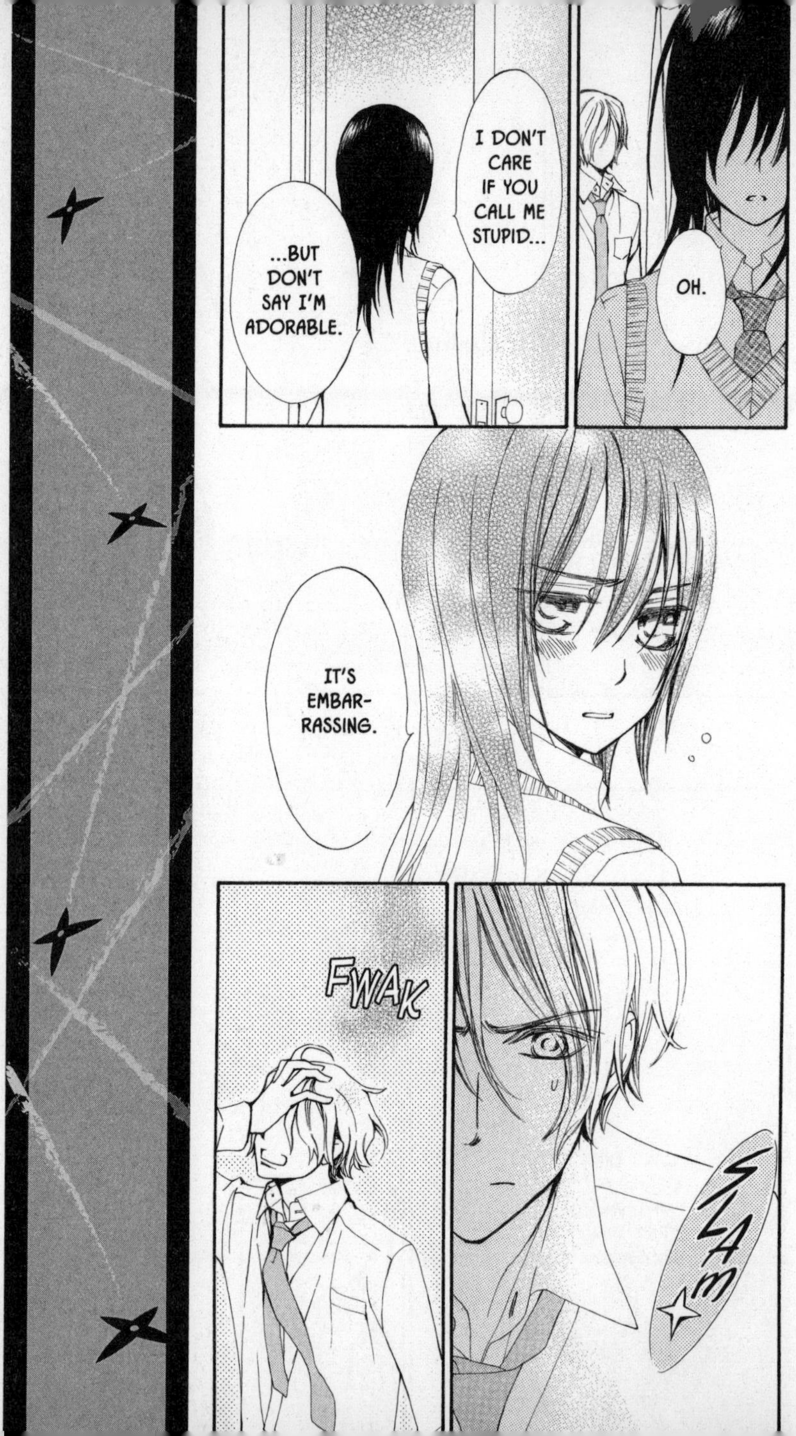
OH.
I DON'T CARE IF YOU CALL ME STUPID...
...BUT DON'T SAY I'M ADORABLE.
IT'S EMBAR-RASSING.
SLAM
FWAK

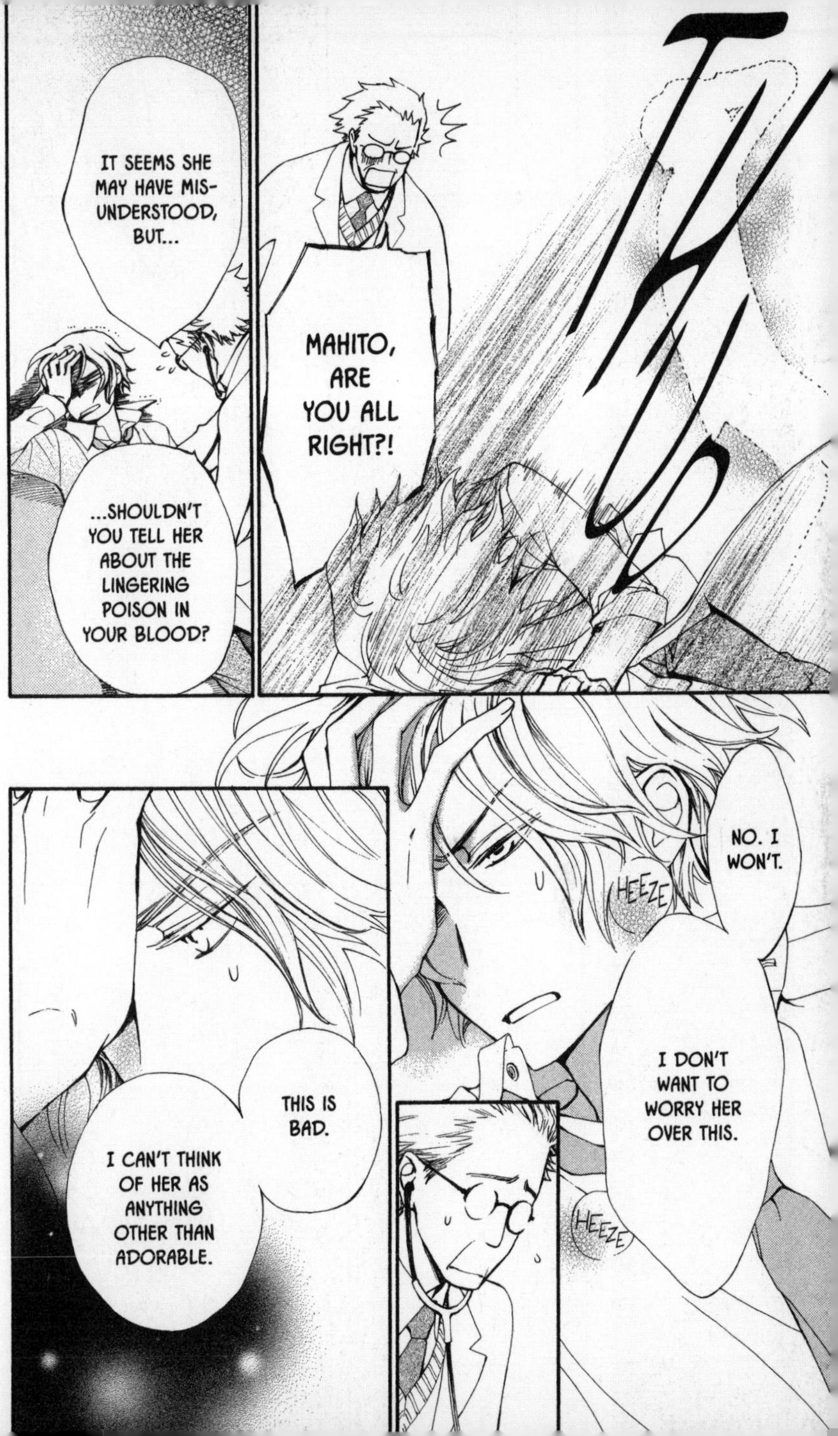
THUD
MAHITO, ARE YOU ALL RIGHT?!
IT SEEMS SHE MAY HAVE MIS-UNDERSTOOD, BUT...
...SHOULDN'T YOU TELL HER ABOUT THE LINGERING POISON IN YOUR BLOOD?
NO. I WON'T.
HEEZE
I DON'T WANT TO WORRY HER OVER THIS.
HEEZE
THIS IS BAD.
I CAN'T THINK OF HER AS ANYTHING OTHER THAN ADORABLE.

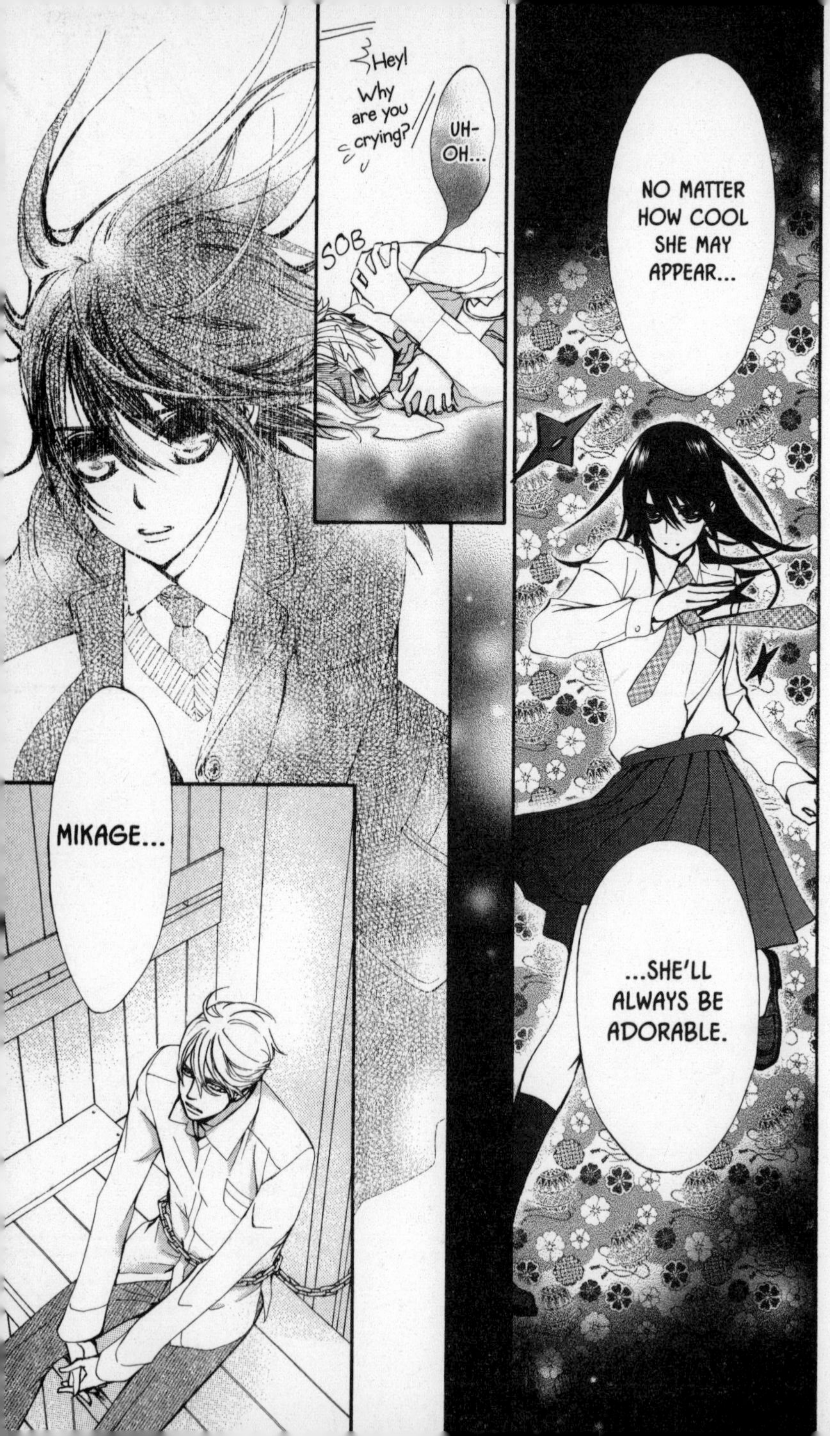
NO MATTER HOW COOL SHE MAY APPEAR...
...SHE'LL ALWAYS BE ADORABLE.
UH-OH...
SOB
Hey! Why are you crying?
MIKAGE...

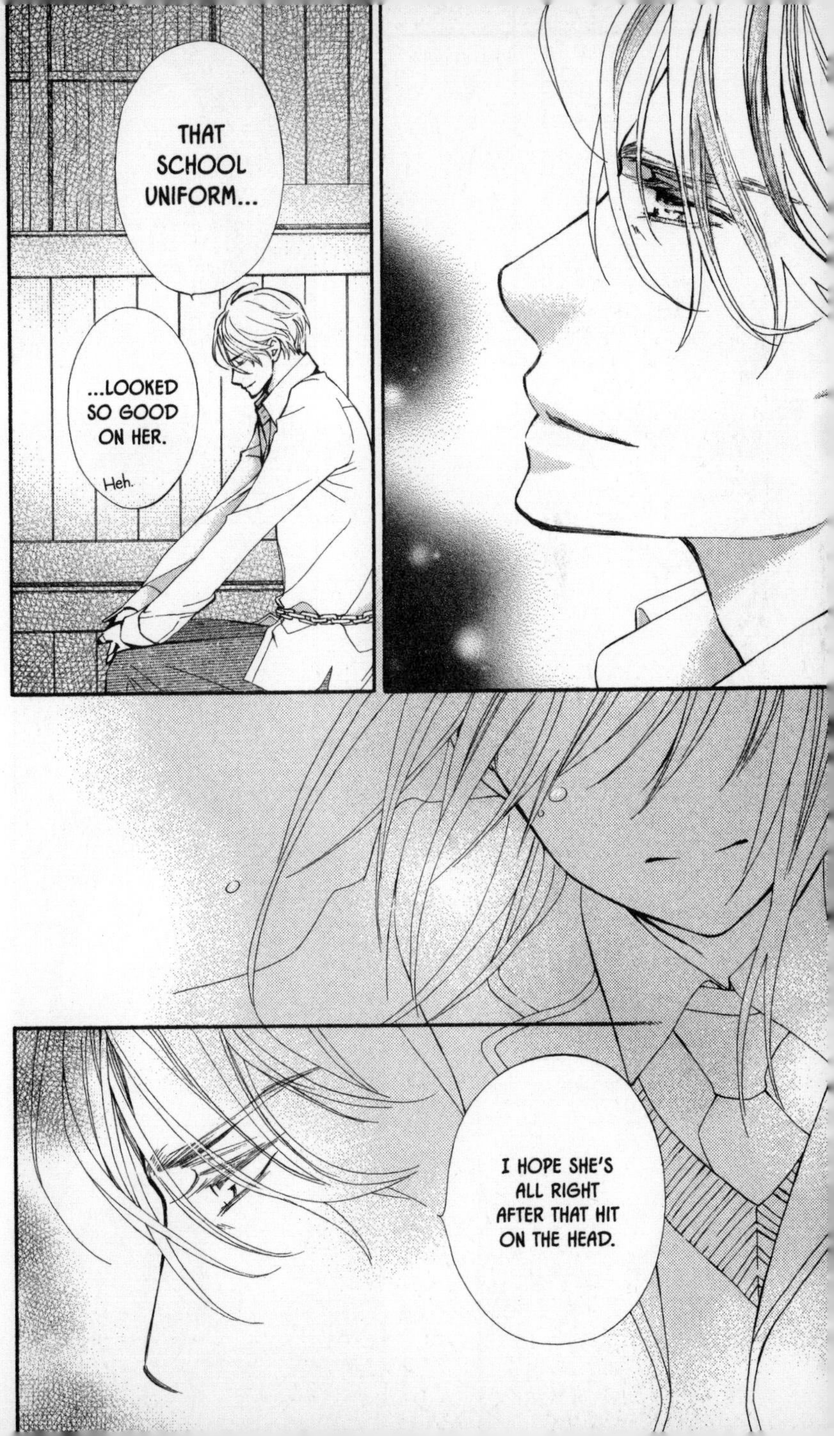
THAT SCHOOL UNIFORM...
...LOOKED SO GOOD ON HER.
Heh.
I HOPE SHE'S ALL RIGHT AFTER THAT HIT ON THE HEAD.

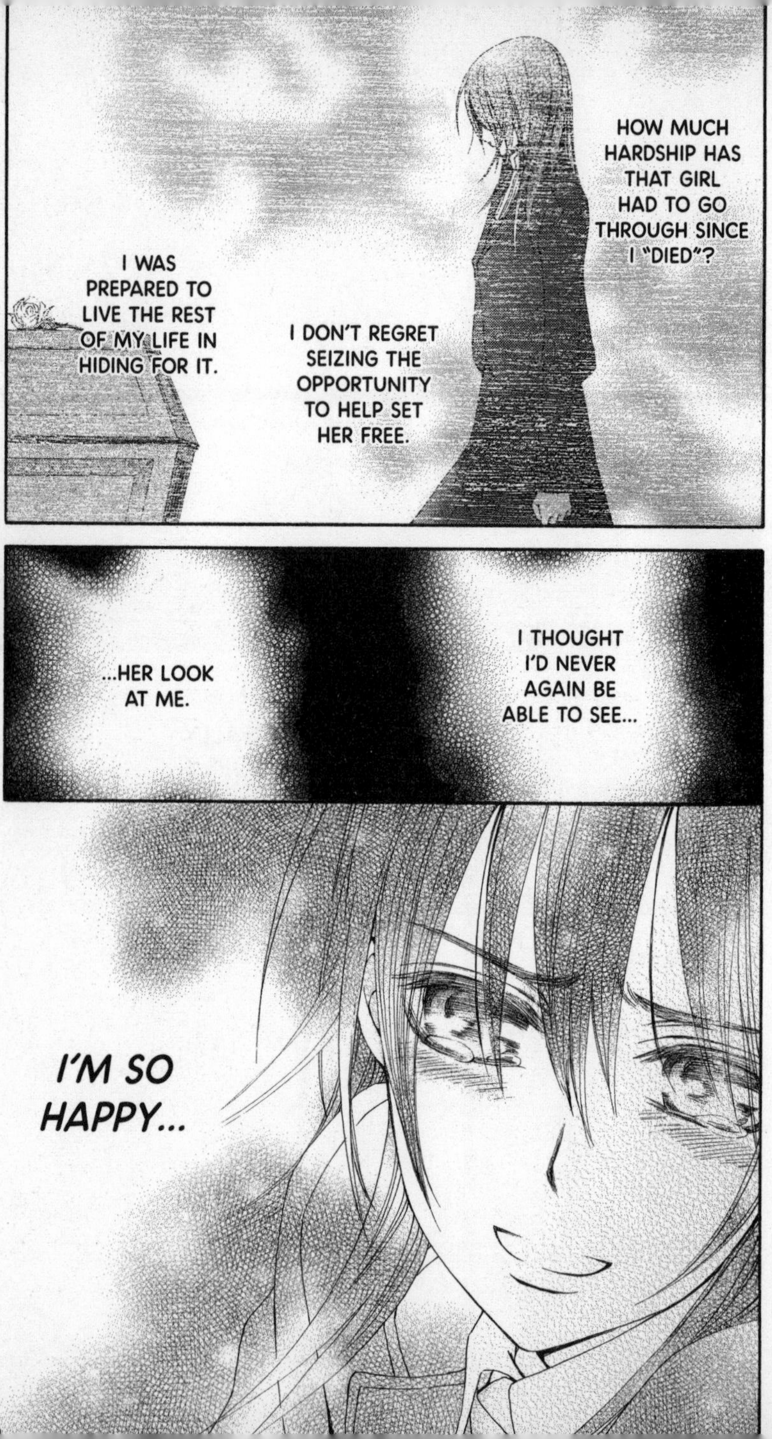
HOW MUCH HARDSHIP HAS THAT GIRL HAD TO GO THROUGH SINCE I "DIED"?
I DON'T REGRET SEIZING THE OPPORTUNITY TO HELP SET HER FREE.
I WAS PREPARED TO LIVE THE REST OF MY LIFE IN HIDING FOR IT.
I THOUGHT I'D NEVER AGAIN BE ABLE TO SEE...
...HER LOOK AT ME.
I'M SO HAPPY...

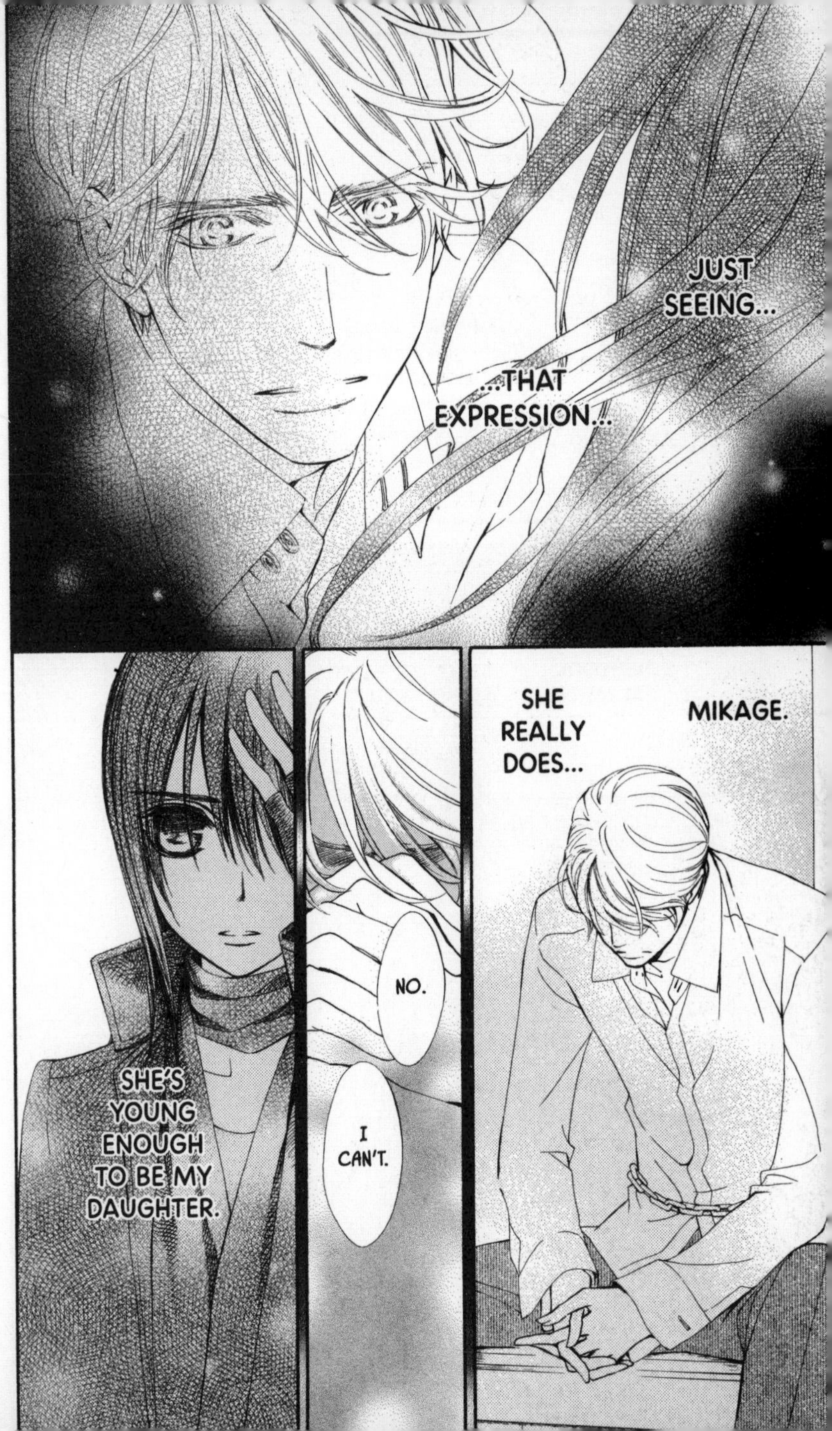
JUST SEEING...
...THAT EXPRESSION...
MIKAGE.
SHE REALLY DOES...
NO.
I CAN'T.
SHE'S YOUNG ENOUGH TO BE MY DAUGHTER.

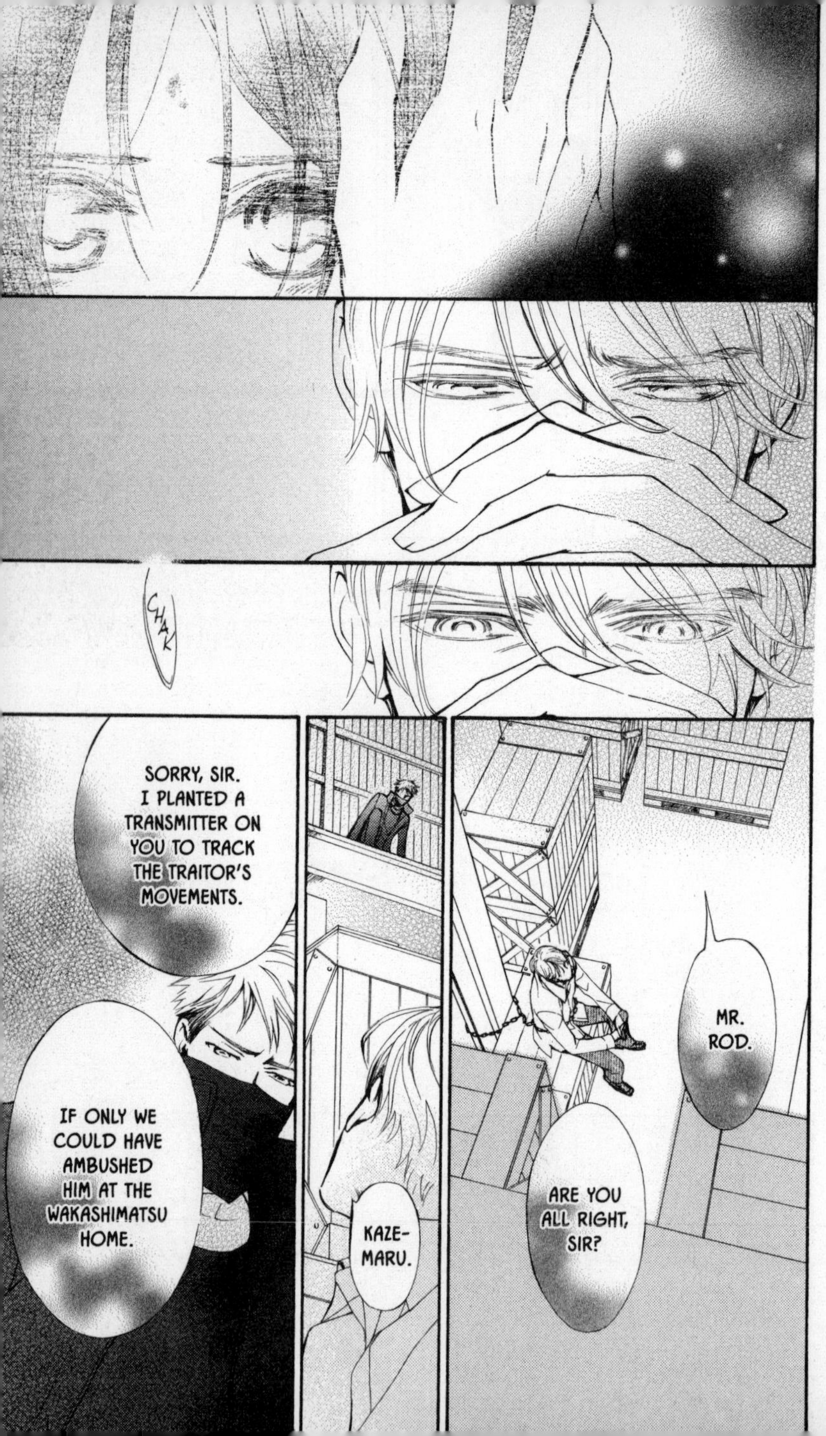
CHAK
MR. ROD.
ARE YOU ALL RIGHT, SIR?
KAZE-MARU.
SORRY, SIR. I PLANTED A TRANSMITTER ON YOU TO TRACK THE TRAITOR'S MOVEMENTS.
IF ONLY WE COULD HAVE AMBUSHED HIM AT THE WAKASHIMATSU HOME.

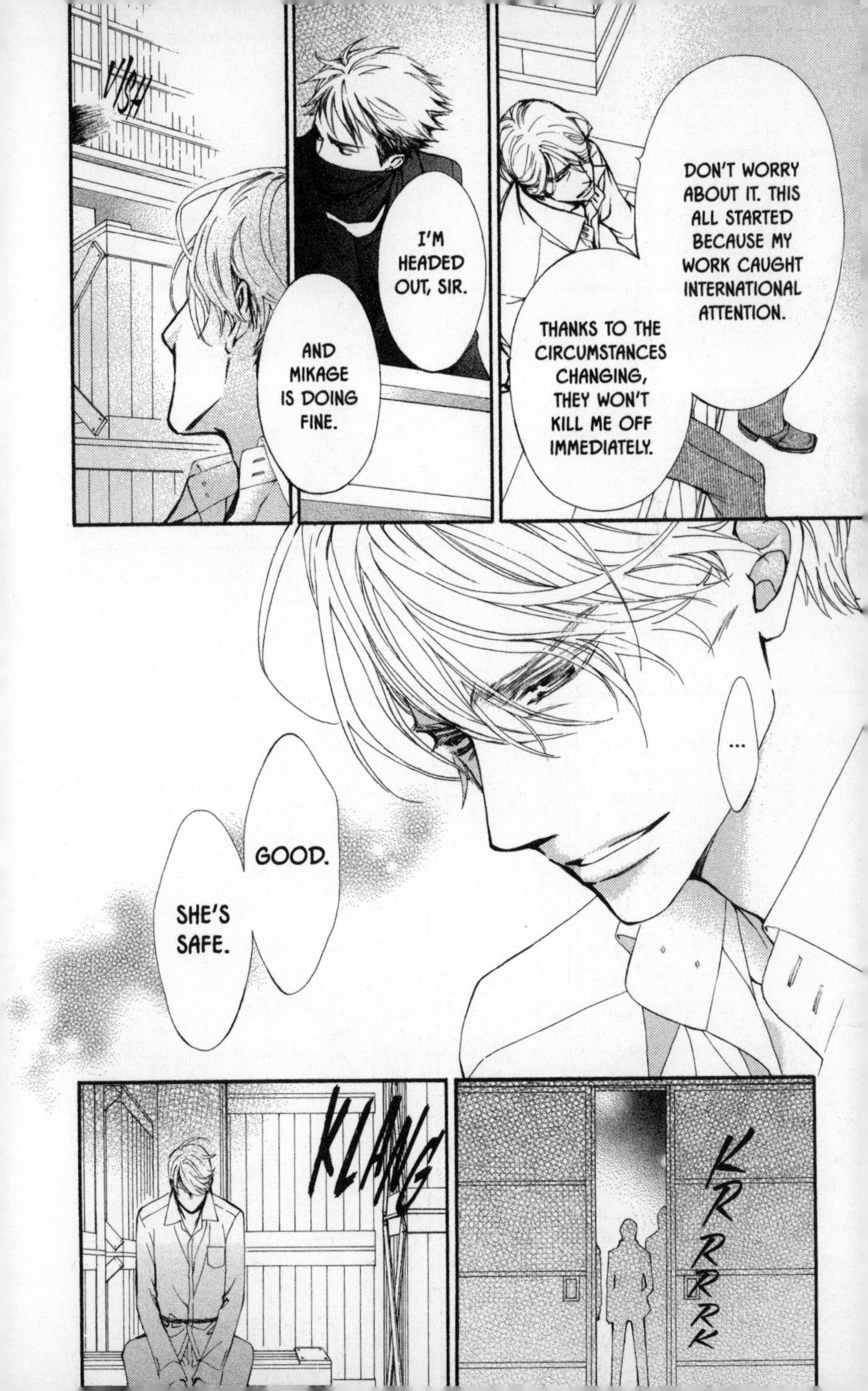
DON'T WORRY ABOUT IT. THIS ALL STARTED BECAUSE MY WORK CAUGHT INTERNATIONAL ATTENTION.
THANKS TO THE CIRCUMSTANCES CHANGING, THEY WON'T KILL ME OFF IMMEDIATELY.
I'M HEADED OUT, SIR.
VISH
AND MIKAGE IS DOING FINE.
...
GOOD.
SHE'S SAFE.
KRRRRK
KLANG

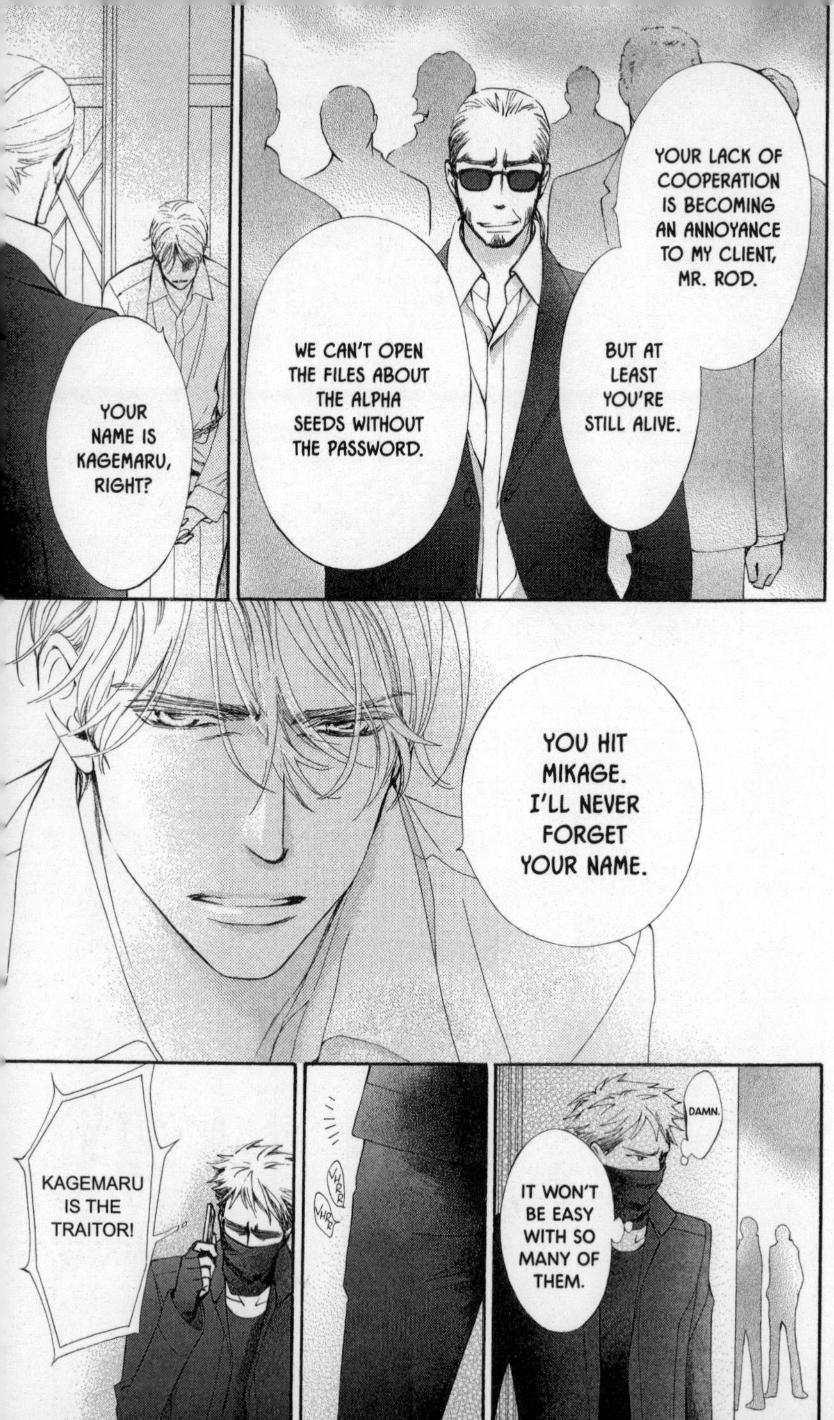
YOUR LACK OF COOPERATION IS BECOMING AN ANNOYANCE TO MY CLIENT, MR. ROD.
BUT AT LEAST YOU'RE STILL ALIVE.
WE CAN'T OPEN THE FILES ABOUT THE ALPHA SEEDS WITHOUT THE PASSWORD.
YOUR NAME IS KAGEMARU, RIGHT?
YOU HIT MIKAGE. I'LL NEVER FORGET YOUR NAME.
DAMN.
IT WON'T BE EASY WITH SO MANY OF THEM.
VHRR
VHRR
KAGEMARU IS THE TRAITOR!

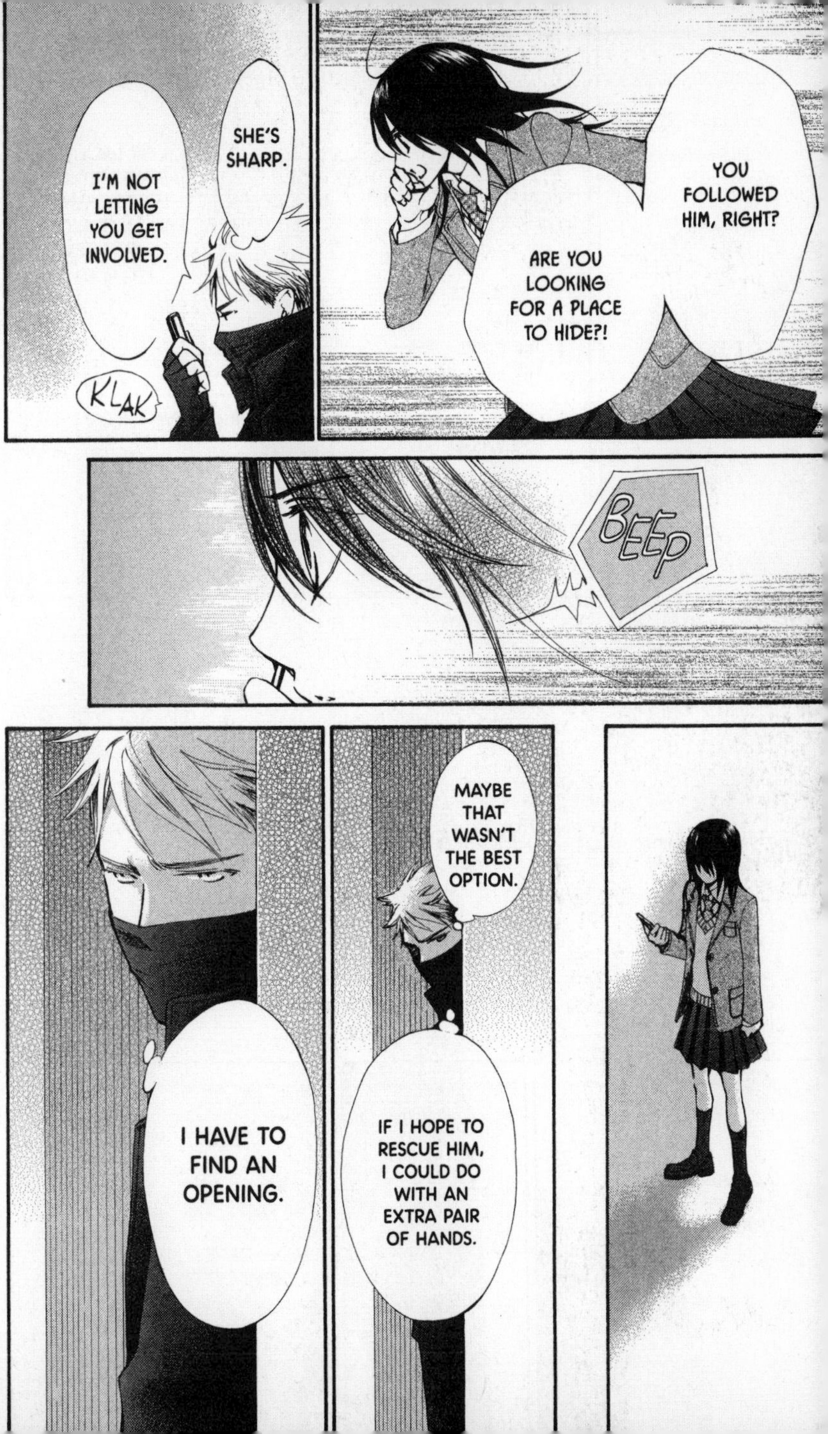
YOU FOLLOWED HIM, RIGHT?
ARE YOU LOOKING FOR A PLACE TO HIDE?!
SHE'S SHARP.
I'M NOT LETTING YOU GET INVOLVED.
KLAK
BEEP
MAYBE THAT WASN'T THE BEST OPTION.
IF I HOPE TO RESCUE HIM, I COULD DO WITH AN EXTRA PAIR OF HANDS.
I HAVE TO FIND AN OPENING.

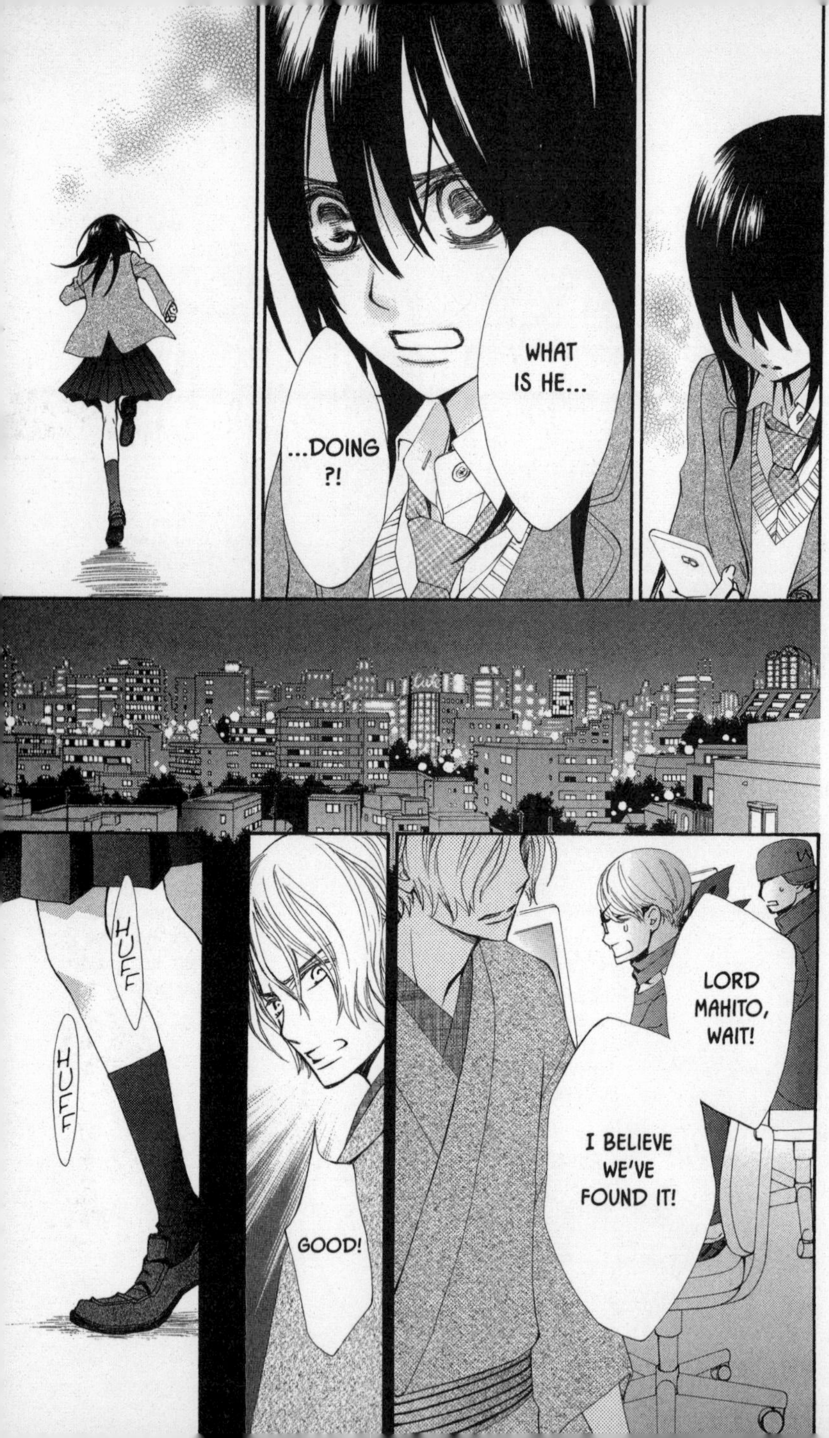
WHAT IS HE...
...DOING ?!
LORD MAHITO, WAIT!
I BELIEVE WE'VE FOUND IT!
GOOD!
HUFF
HUFF

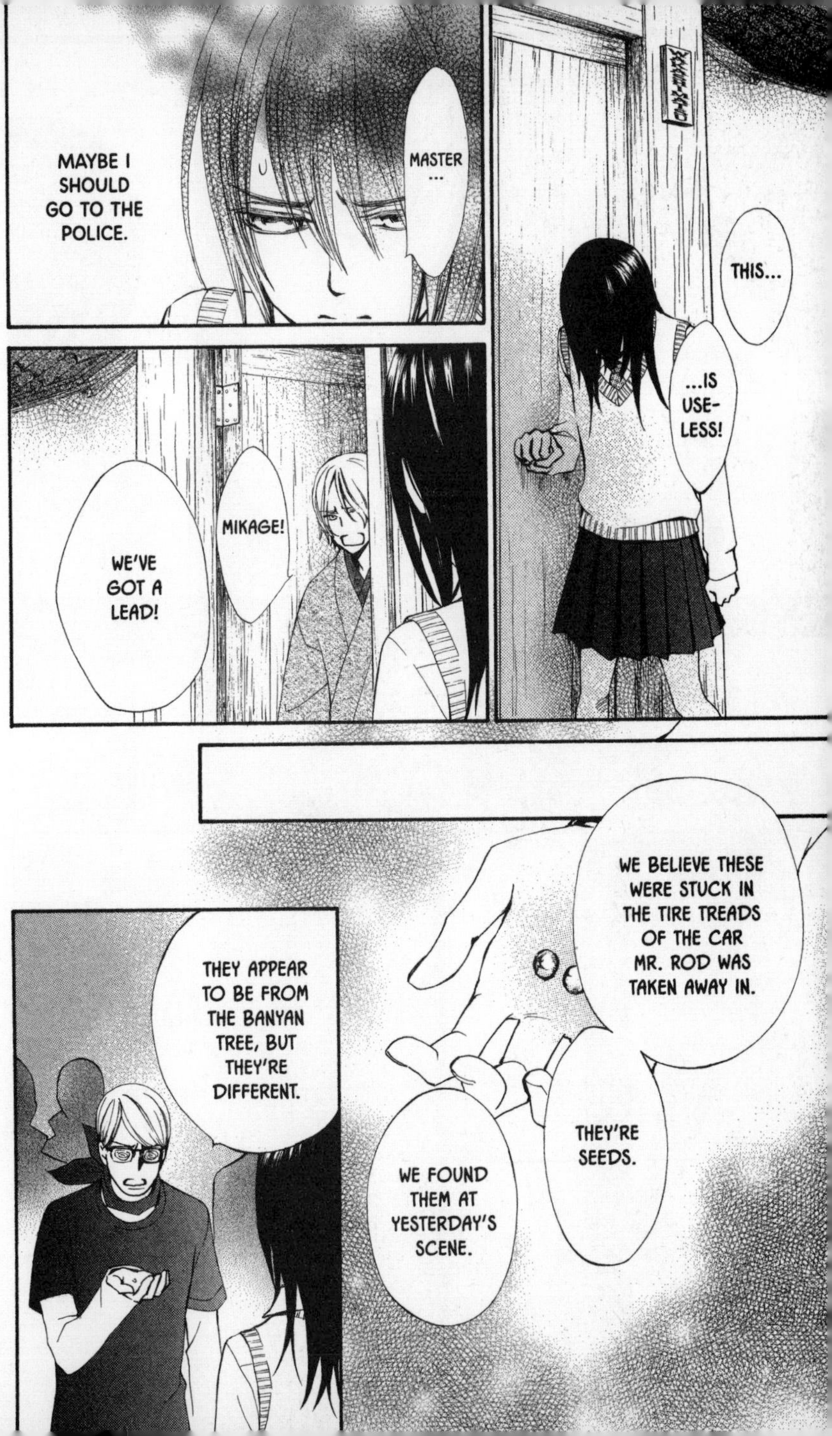
THIS...
...IS USE-LESS!
MASTER...
MAYBE I SHOULD GO TO THE POLICE.
MIKAGE!
WE'VE GOT A LEAD!
WE BELIEVE THESE WERE STUCK IN THE TIRE TREADS OF THE CAR MR. ROD WAS TAKEN AWAY IN.
THEY'RE SEEDS.
WE FOUND THEM AT YESTERDAY'S SCENE.
THEY APPEAR TO BE FROM THE BANYAN TREE, BUT THEY'RE DIFFERENT.

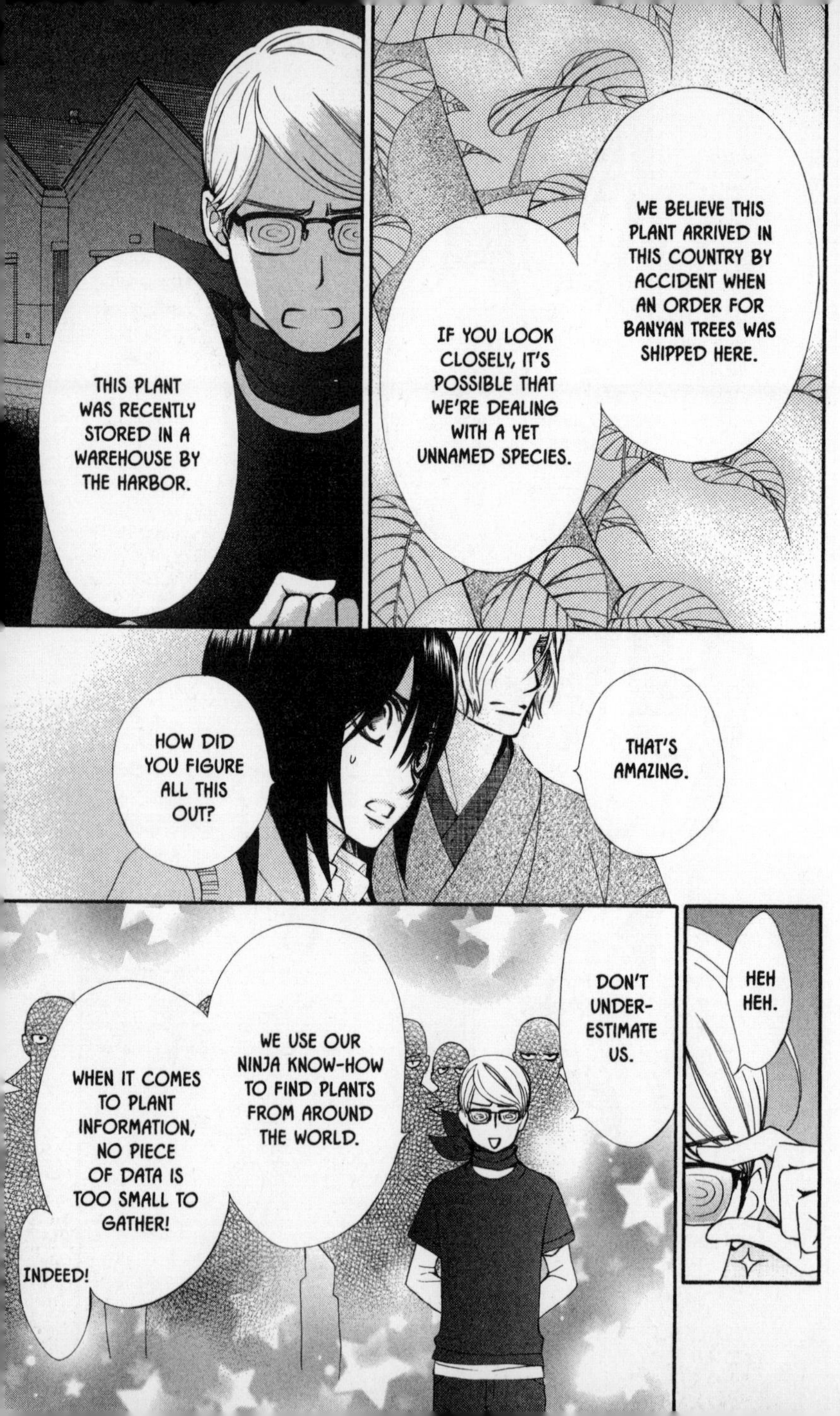
WE BELIEVE THIS PLANT ARRIVED IN THIS COUNTRY BY ACCIDENT WHEN AN ORDER FOR BANYAN TREES WAS SHIPPED HERE.
IF YOU LOOK CLOSELY, IT'S POSSIBLE THAT WE'RE DEALING WITH A YET UNNAMED SPECIES.
THIS PLANT WAS RECENTLY STORED IN A WAREHOUSE BY THE HARBOR.
THAT'S AMAZING.
HOW DID YOU FIGURE ALL THIS OUT?
HEH HEH.
DON'T UNDER-ESTIMATE US.
WE USE OUR NINJA KNOW-HOW TO FIND PLANTS FROM AROUND THE WORLD.
WHEN IT COMES TO PLANT INFORMATION, NO PIECE OF DATA IS TOO SMALL TO GATHER!
INDEED!

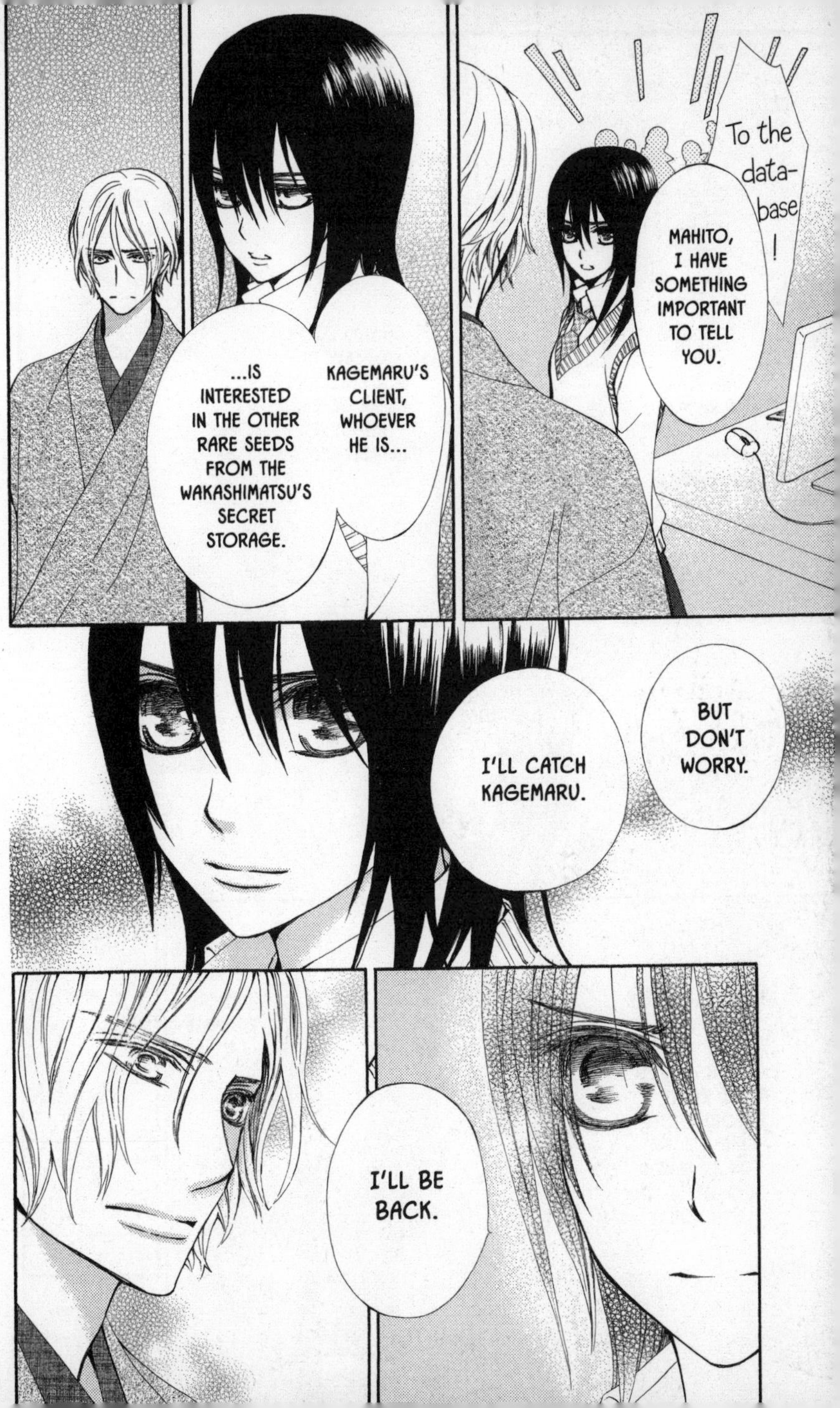
To the data-base!
MAHITO, I HAVE SOMETHING IMPORTANT TO TELL YOU.
KAGEMARU'S CLIENT, WHOEVER HE IS...
...IS INTERESTED IN THE OTHER RARE SEEDS FROM THE WAKASHIMATSU'S SECRET STORAGE.
BUT DON'T WORRY.
I'LL CATCH KAGEMARU.
I'LL BE BACK.

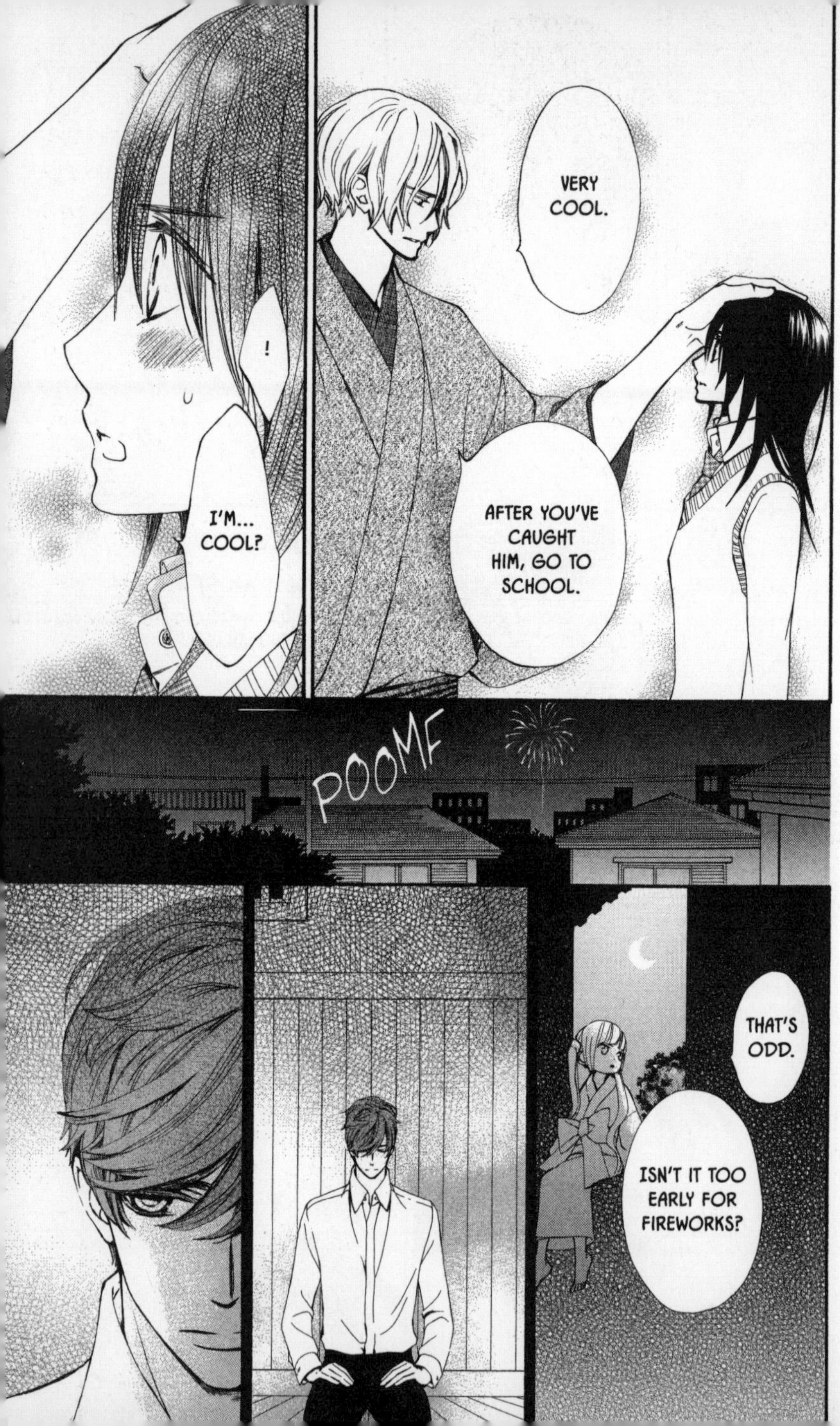
VERY COOL.
AFTER YOU'VE CAUGHT HIM, GO TO SCHOOL.
!
I'M... COOL?
POOMF
THAT'S ODD.
ISN'T IT TOO EARLY FOR FIREWORKS?

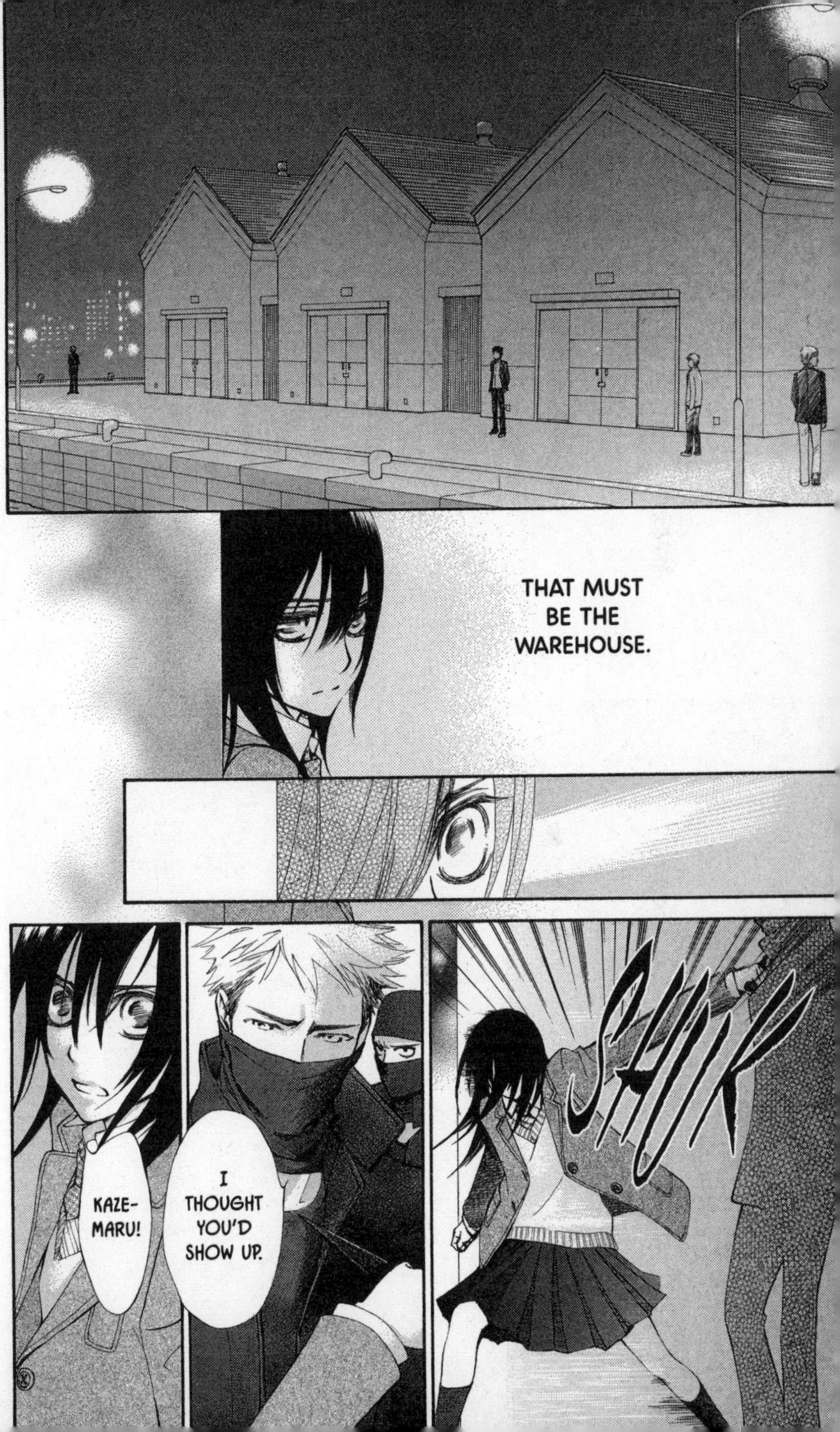
THAT MUST BE THE WAREHOUSE.
SHIK
I THOUGHT YOU'D SHOW UP.
KAZE-MARU!

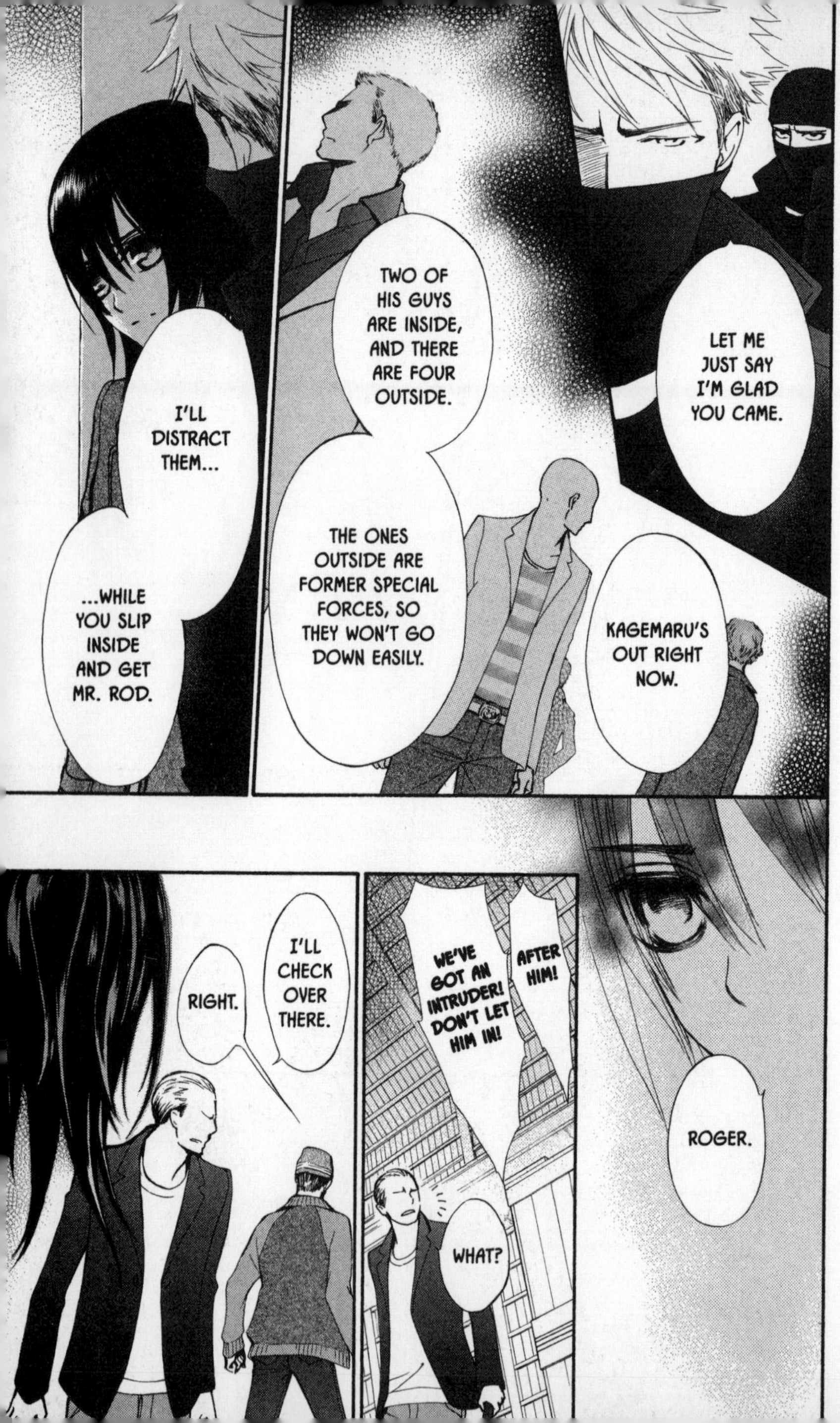
LET ME JUST SAY I'M GLAD YOU CAME.
KAGEMARU'S OUT RIGHT NOW.
TWO OF HIS GUYS ARE INSIDE, AND THERE ARE FOUR OUTSIDE.
THE ONES OUTSIDE ARE FORMER SPECIAL FORCES, SO THEY WON'T GO DOWN EASILY.
I'LL DISTRACT THEM...
...WHILE YOU SLIP INSIDE AND GET MR. ROD.
ROGER.
AFTER HIM!
WE'VE GOT AN INTRUDER! DON'T LET HIM IN!
WHAT?
I'LL CHECK OVER THERE.
RIGHT.

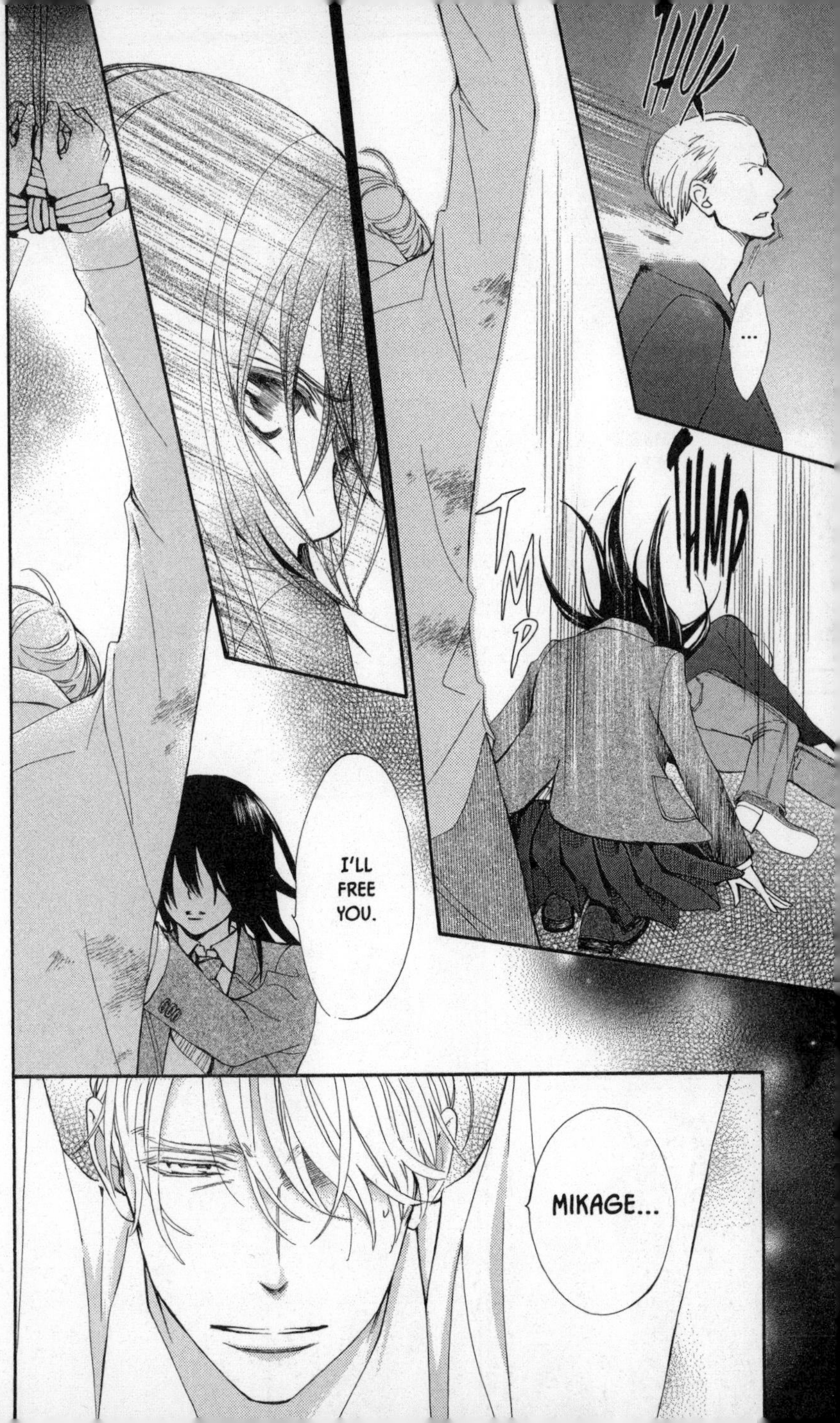
THUK
...
THMP
TMP
I'LL FREE YOU.
MIKAGE...

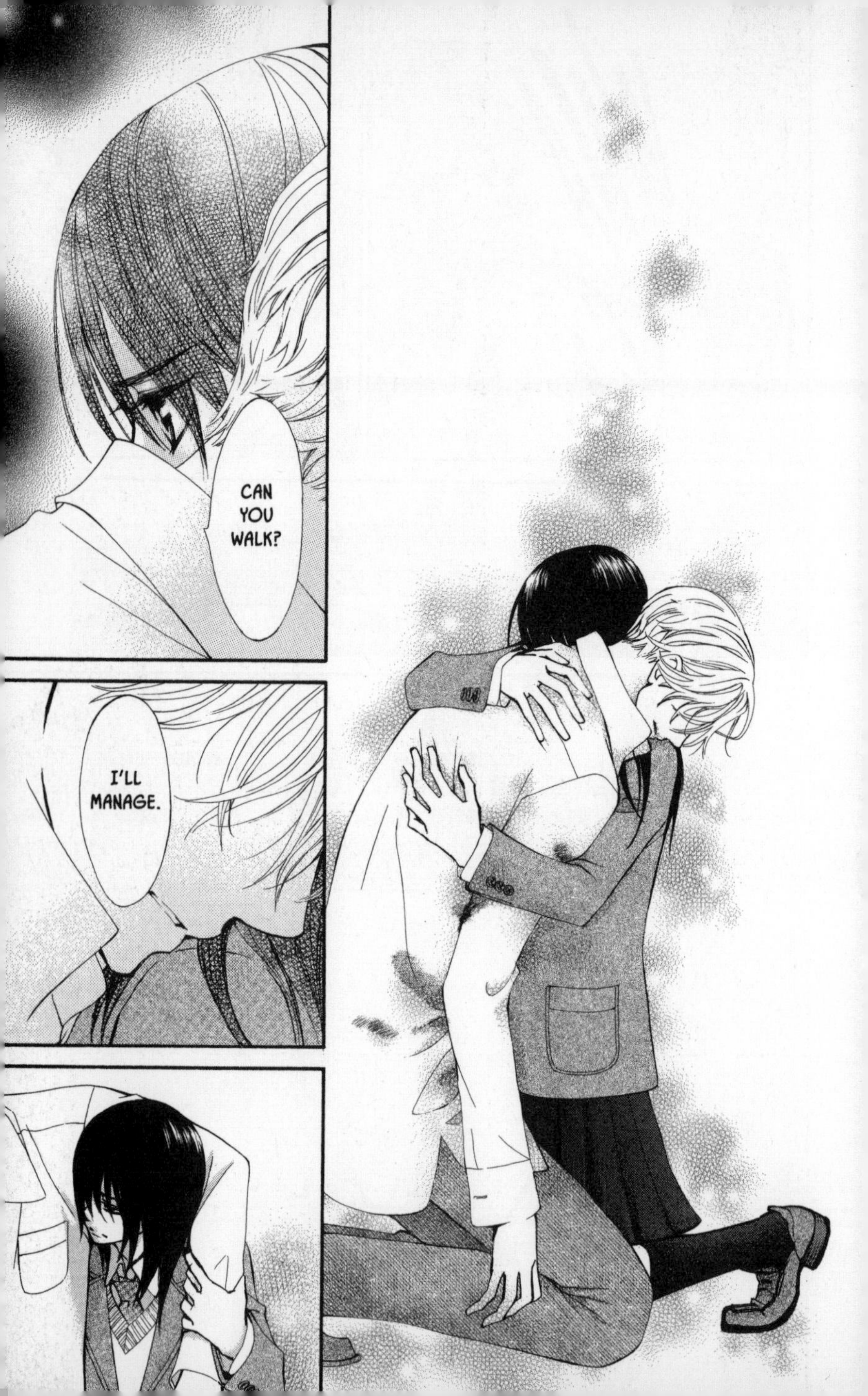
CAN YOU WALK?
I'LL MANAGE.

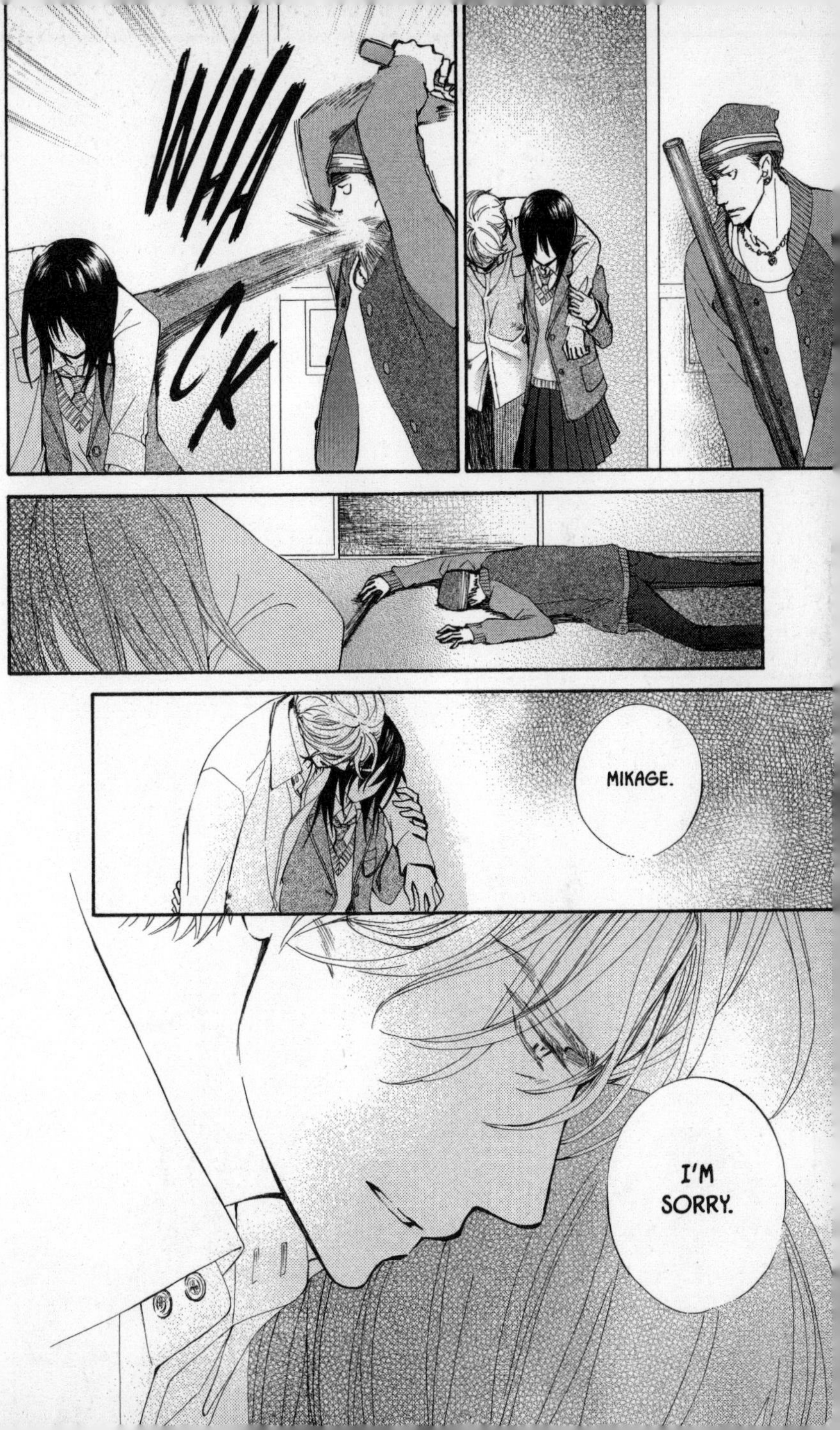
WHACK
MIKAGE.
I'M SORRY.

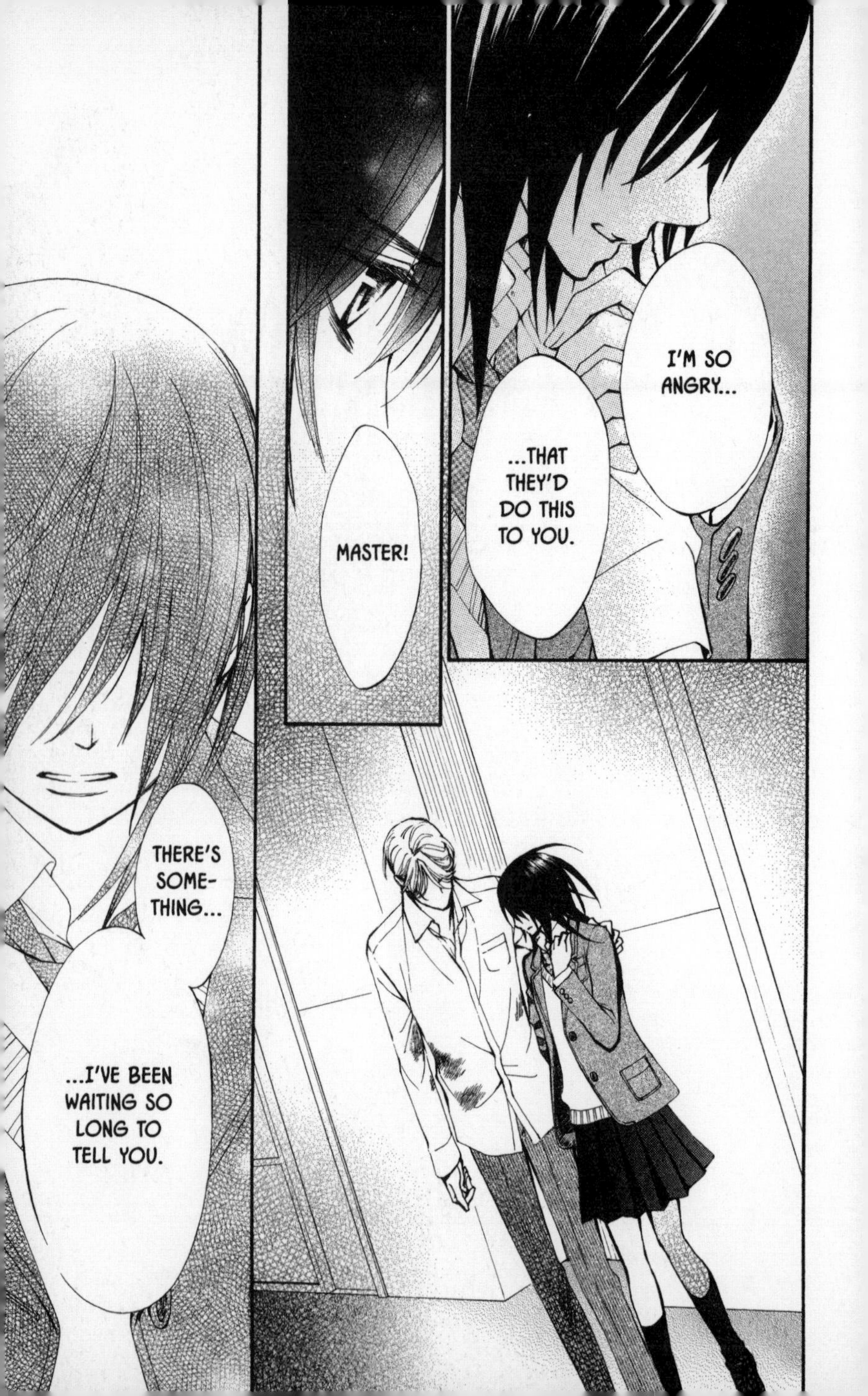
I'M SO ANGRY...
...THAT THEY'D DO THIS TO YOU.
MASTER!
THERE'S SOME-THING...
...I'VE BEEN WAITING SO LONG TO TELL YOU.

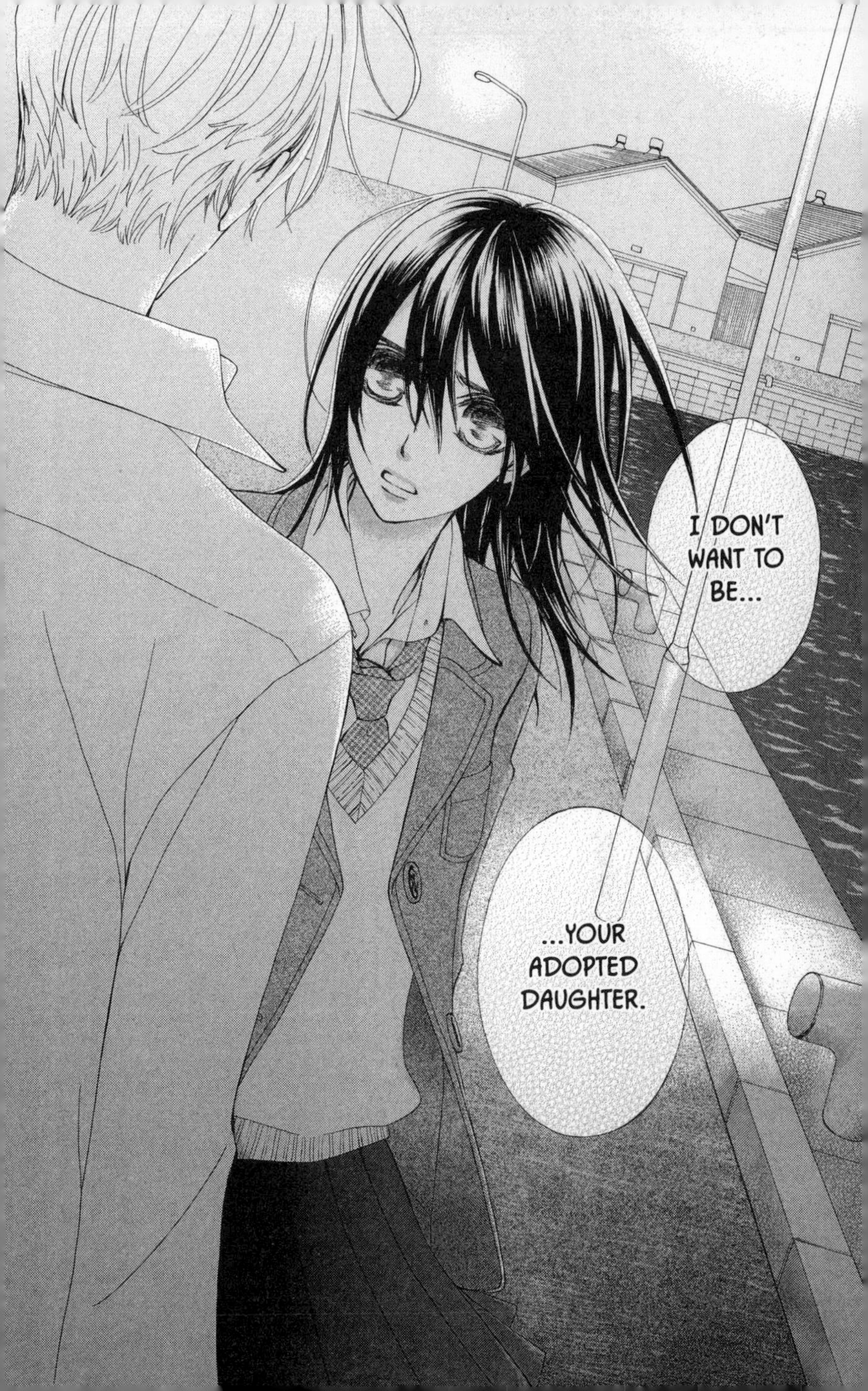
I DON'T WANT TO BE...
...YOUR ADOPTED DAUGHTER.

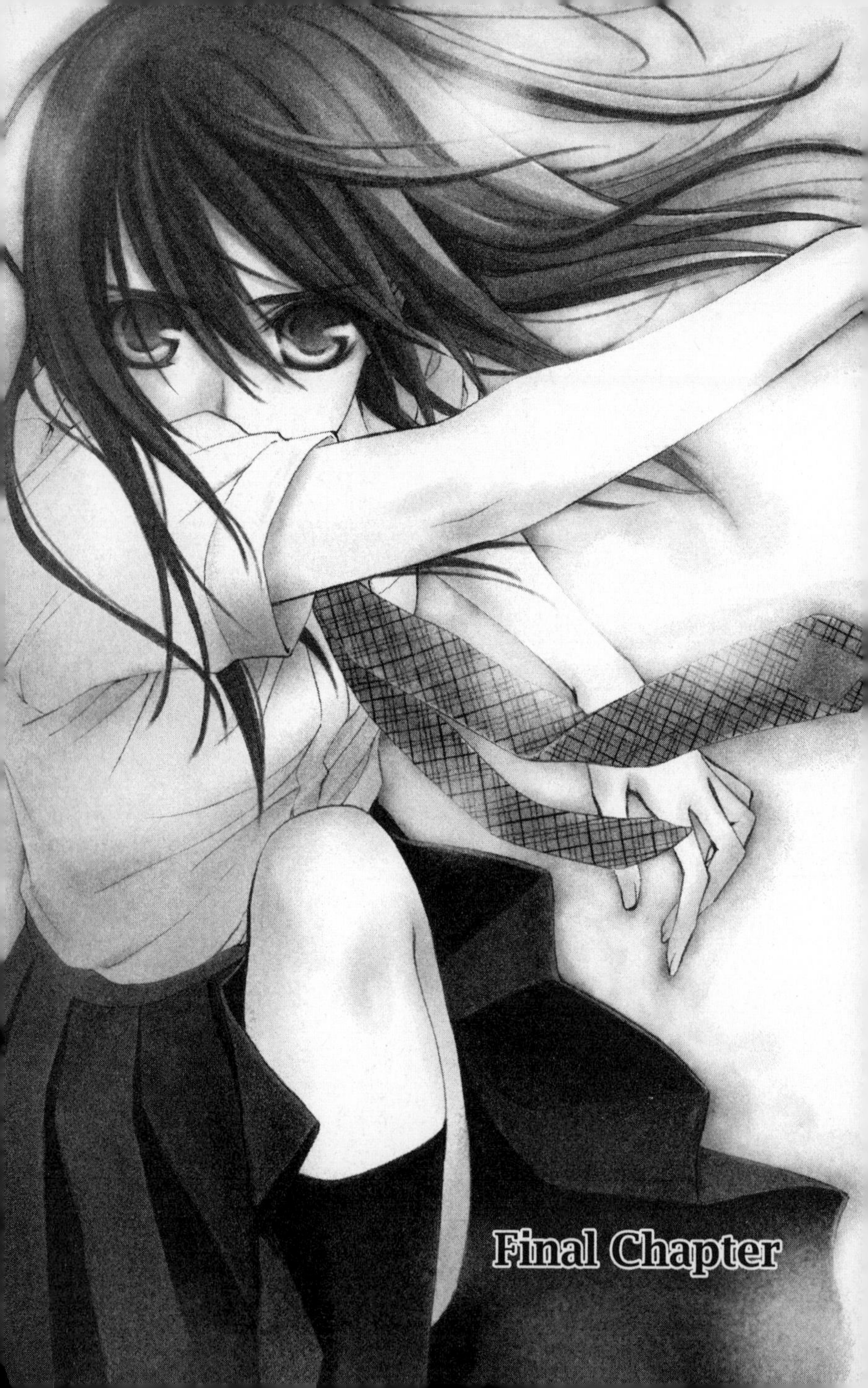
Final Chapter

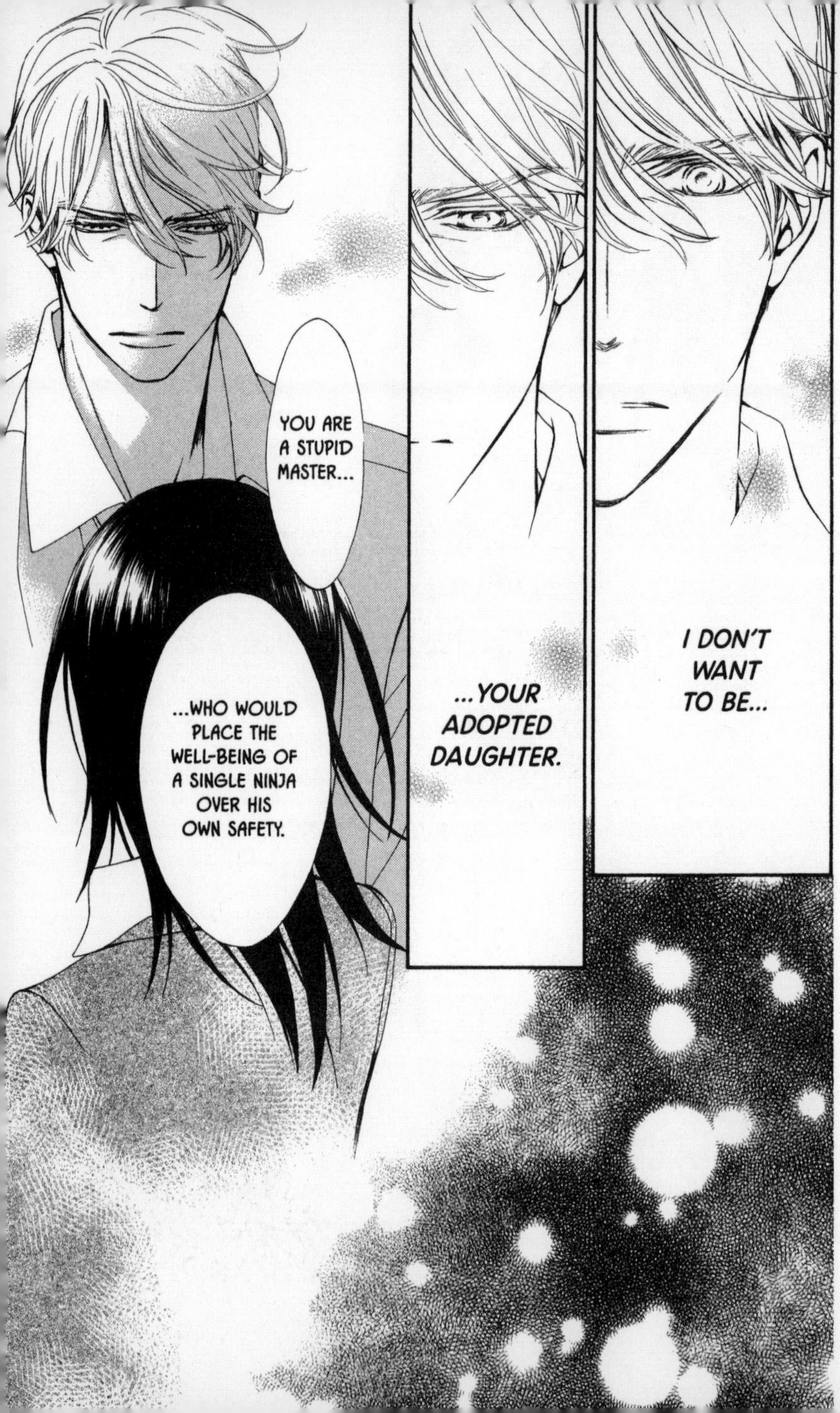
I DON'T WANT TO BE...
...YOUR ADOPTED DAUGHTER.
YOU ARE A STUPID MASTER...
...WHO WOULD PLACE THE WELL-BEING OF A SINGLE NINJA OVER HIS OWN SAFETY.

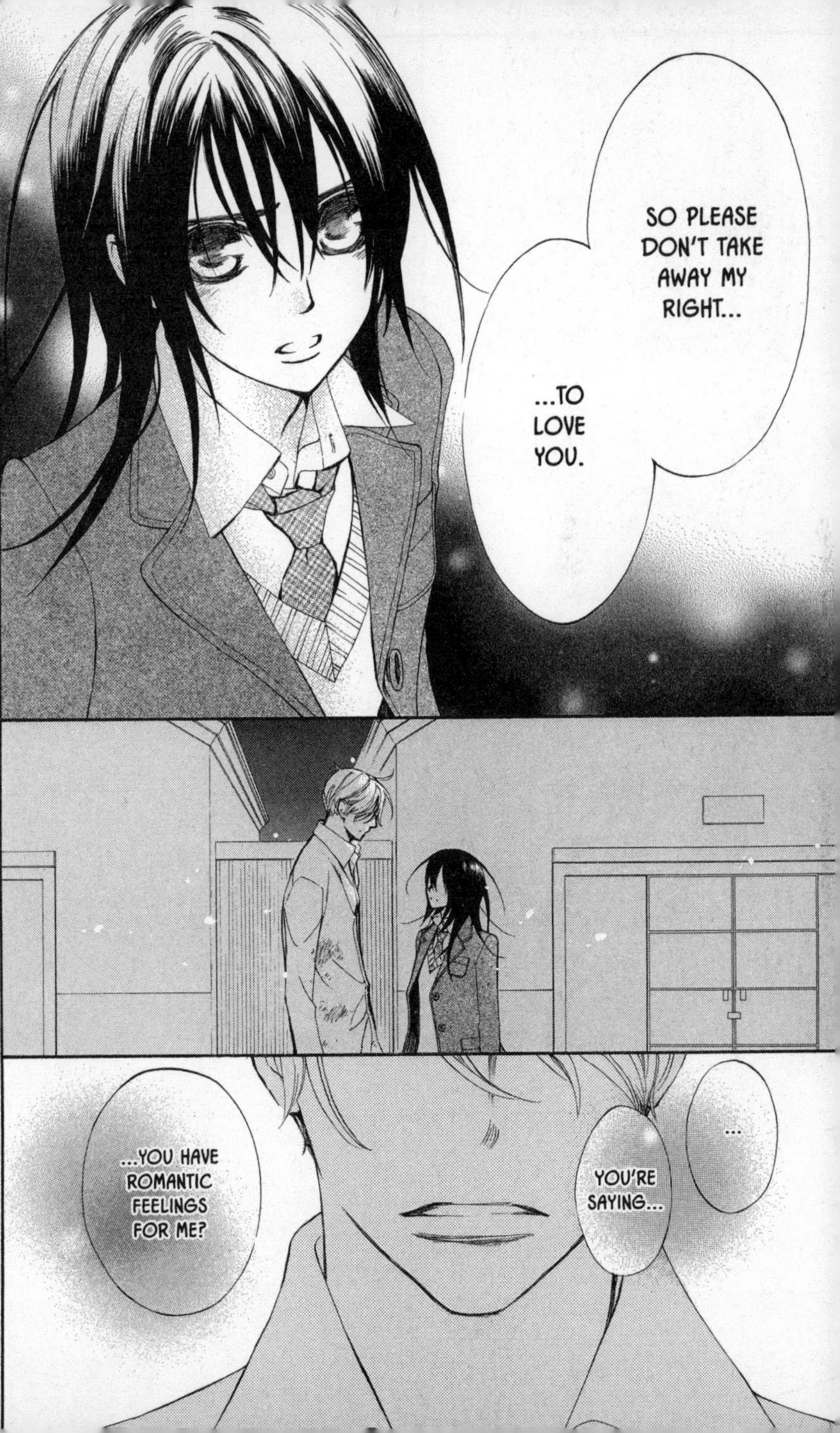
SO PLEASE DON'T TAKE AWAY MY RIGHT...
...TO LOVE YOU.
...
YOU'RE SAYING...
...YOU HAVE ROMANTIC FEELINGS FOR ME?

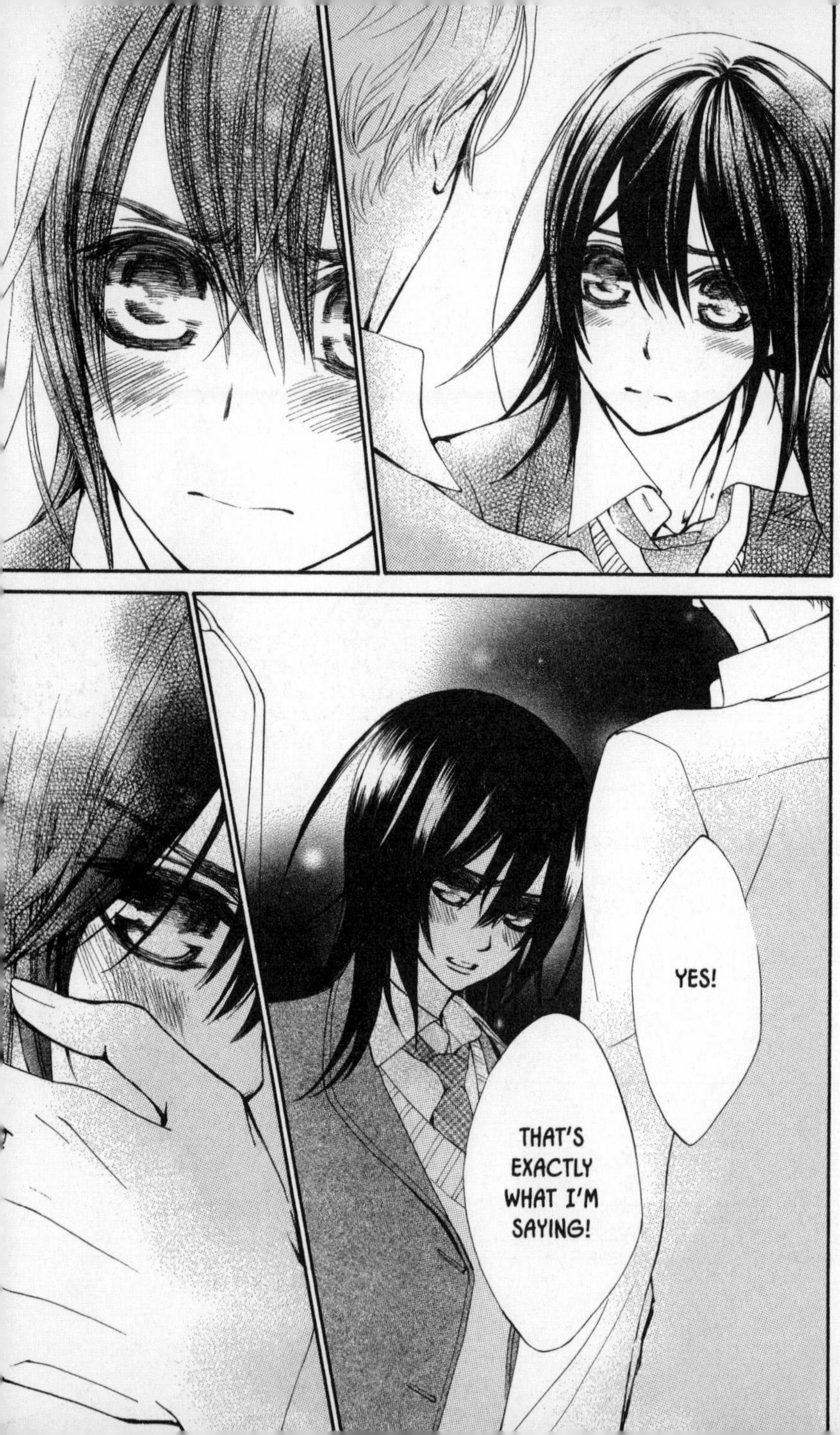
YES!
THAT'S EXACTLY WHAT I'M SAYING!

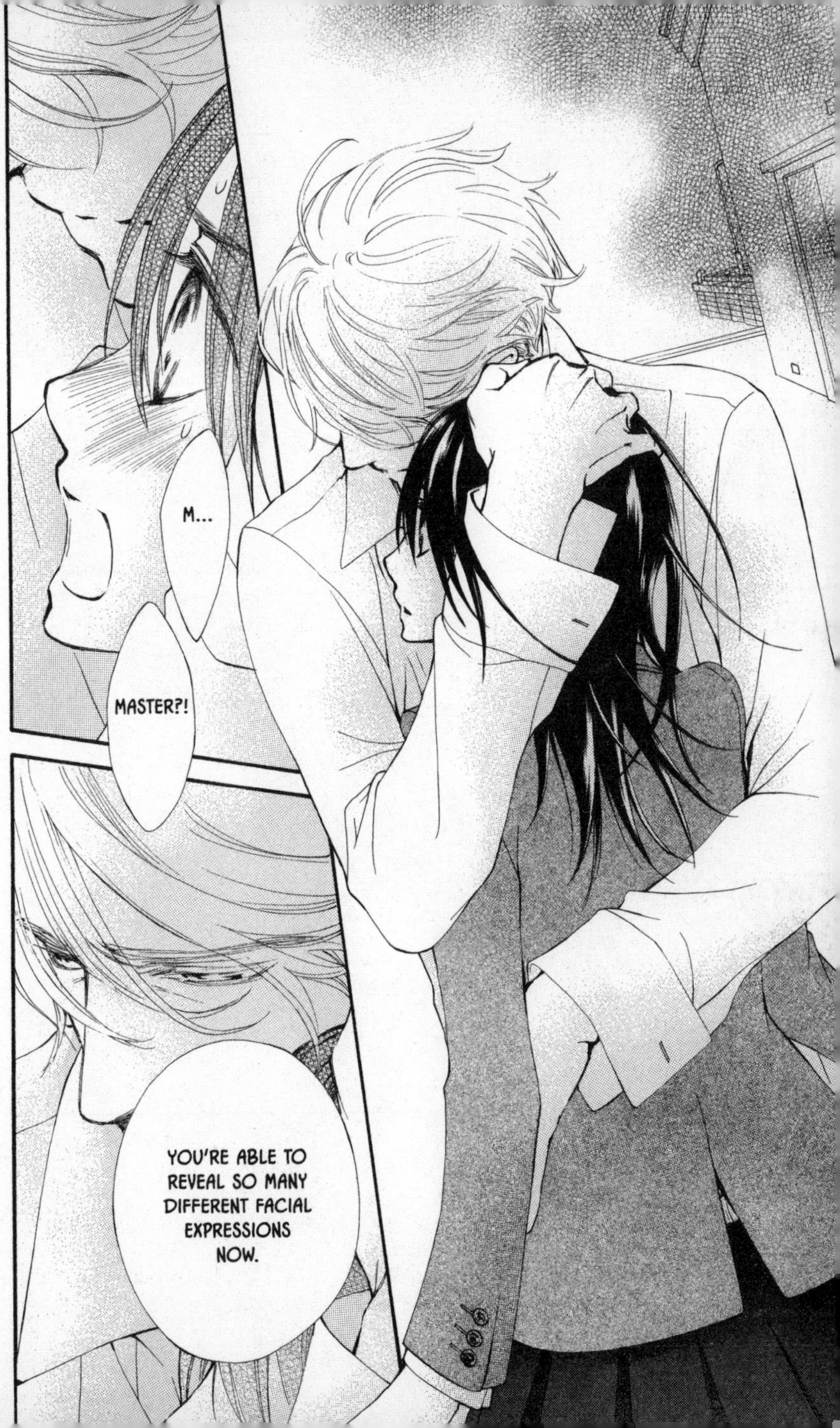
M...
MASTER?!
YOU'RE ABLE TO REVEAL SO MANY DIFFERENT FACIAL EXPRESSIONS NOW.

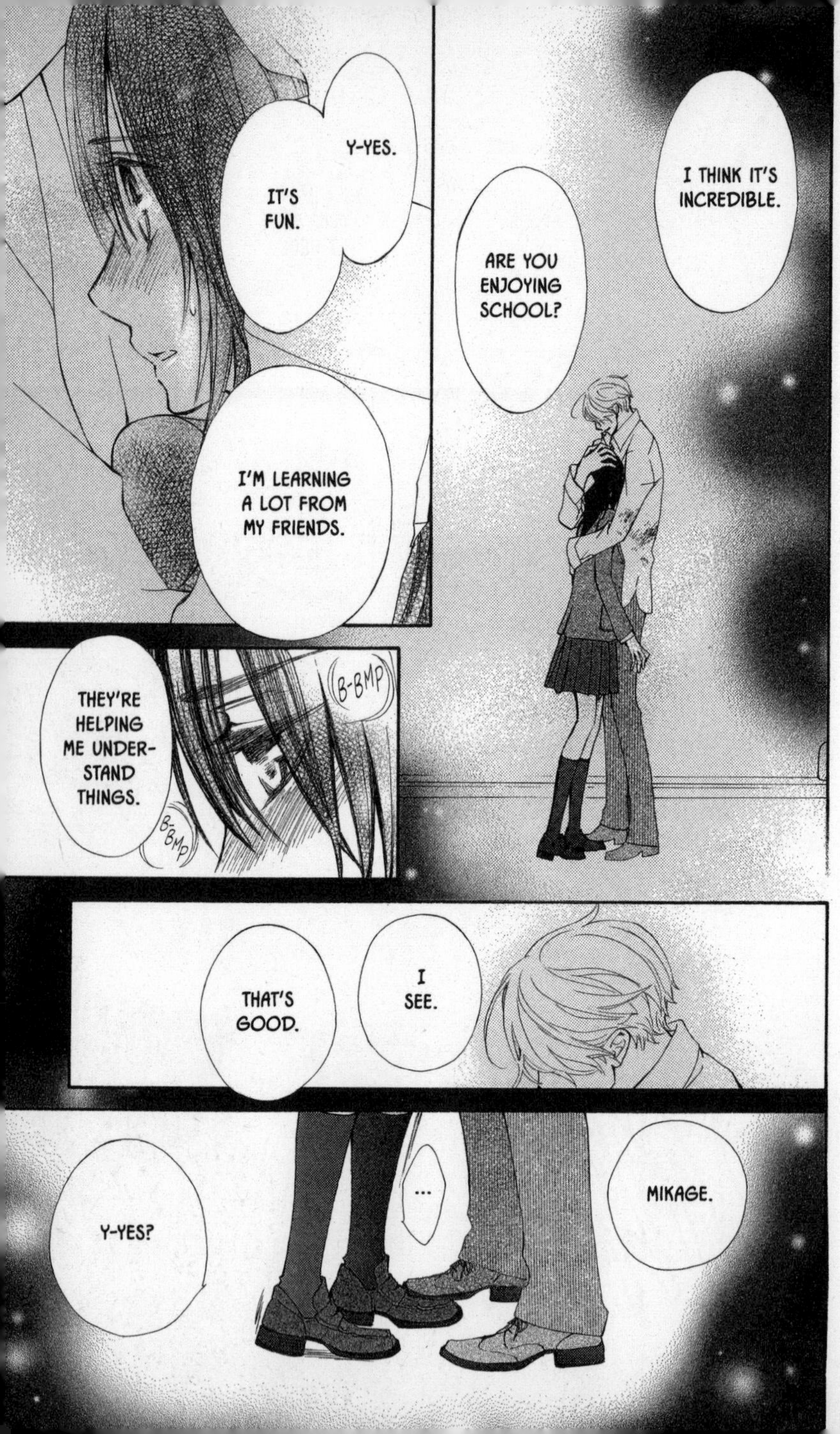
I THINK IT'S INCREDIBLE.
ARE YOU ENJOYING SCHOOL?
Y-YES.
IT'S FUN.
I'M LEARNING A LOT FROM MY FRIENDS.
B-BMP
THEY'RE HELPING ME UNDER-STAND THINGS.
B-BMP
I SEE.
THAT'S GOOD.
MIKAGE.
...
Y-YES?

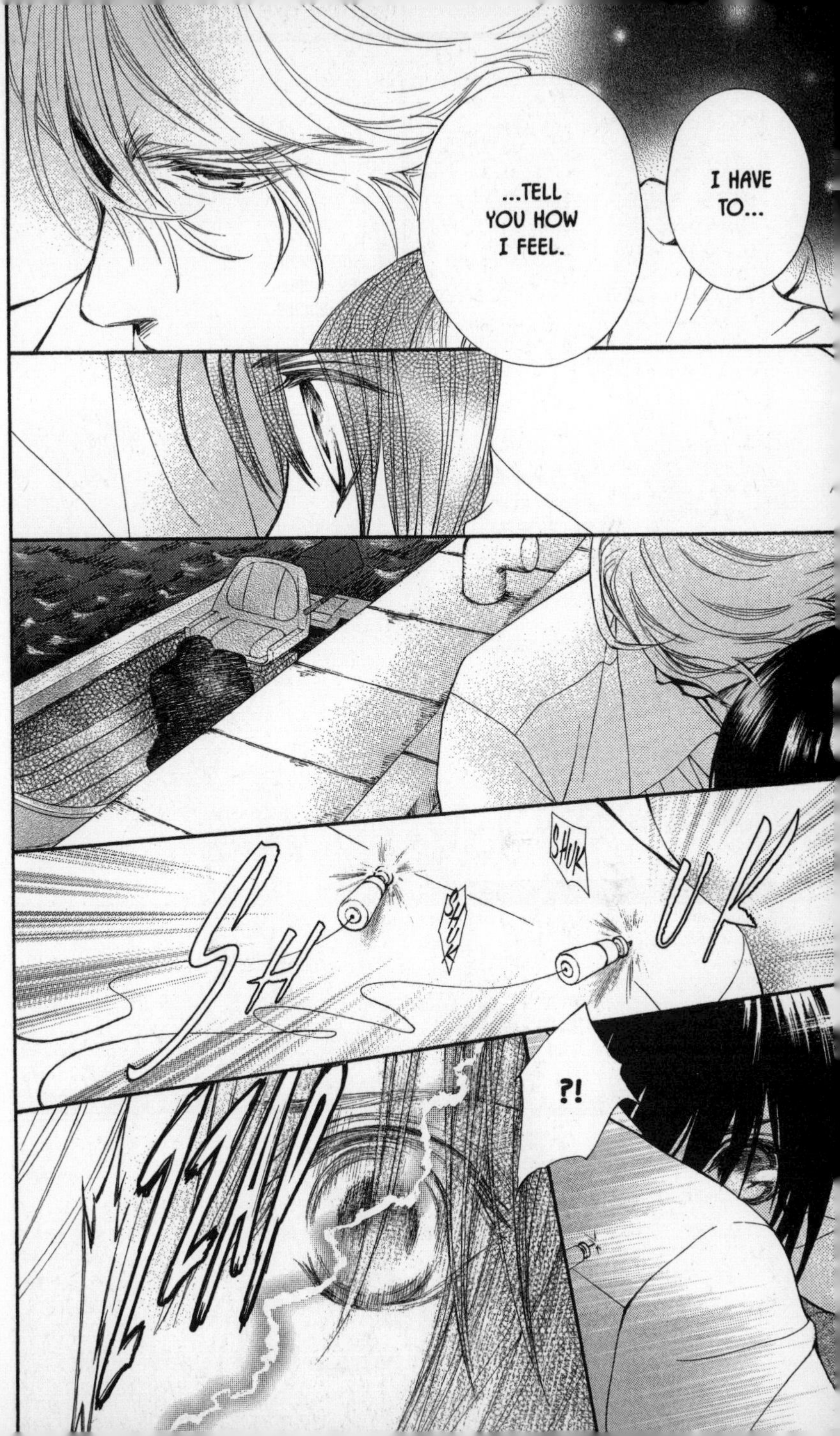
I HAVE TO...
...TELL YOU HOW I FEEL.
SHUK
SHUK
SHUK
?!
ZZAP

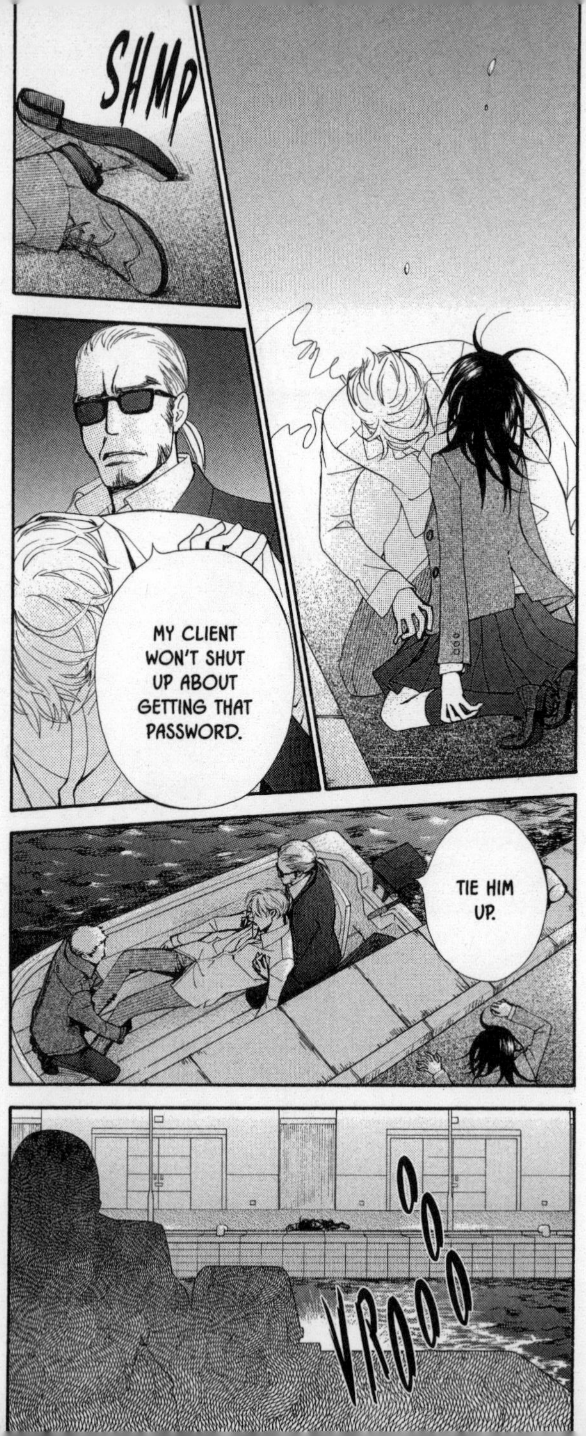
SHMP
MY CLIENT WON'T SHUT UP ABOUT GETTING THAT PASSWORD.
TIE HIM UP.
VROOOOO

I love how Mikage looks at every situation so simply. I don't think I could deny that the reason I made Mahito so pure and simple was to counterbalance someone in a previous series I did. (laugh) (Just to set the record straight, I still adore him. I really do. I love him so much.) ← I'm talking about *Vampire Knight*.

As for Mr. Rod... Yes. I can't hide the truth that I've just laid bare all my preferences. (laugh)

I'm sad to have to say goodbye to *Shuriken and Pleats*. It was fun writing it. Thanks for staying with me through it. I'll work hard so that you come back to read my next manga!!

Thank you to
Mio O.-sama
Midori K.-sama
Ichiya A.-sama
and to my editor, everyone who supported me, my friends, and my mom!!

樋野まつり
Matsuri Hino

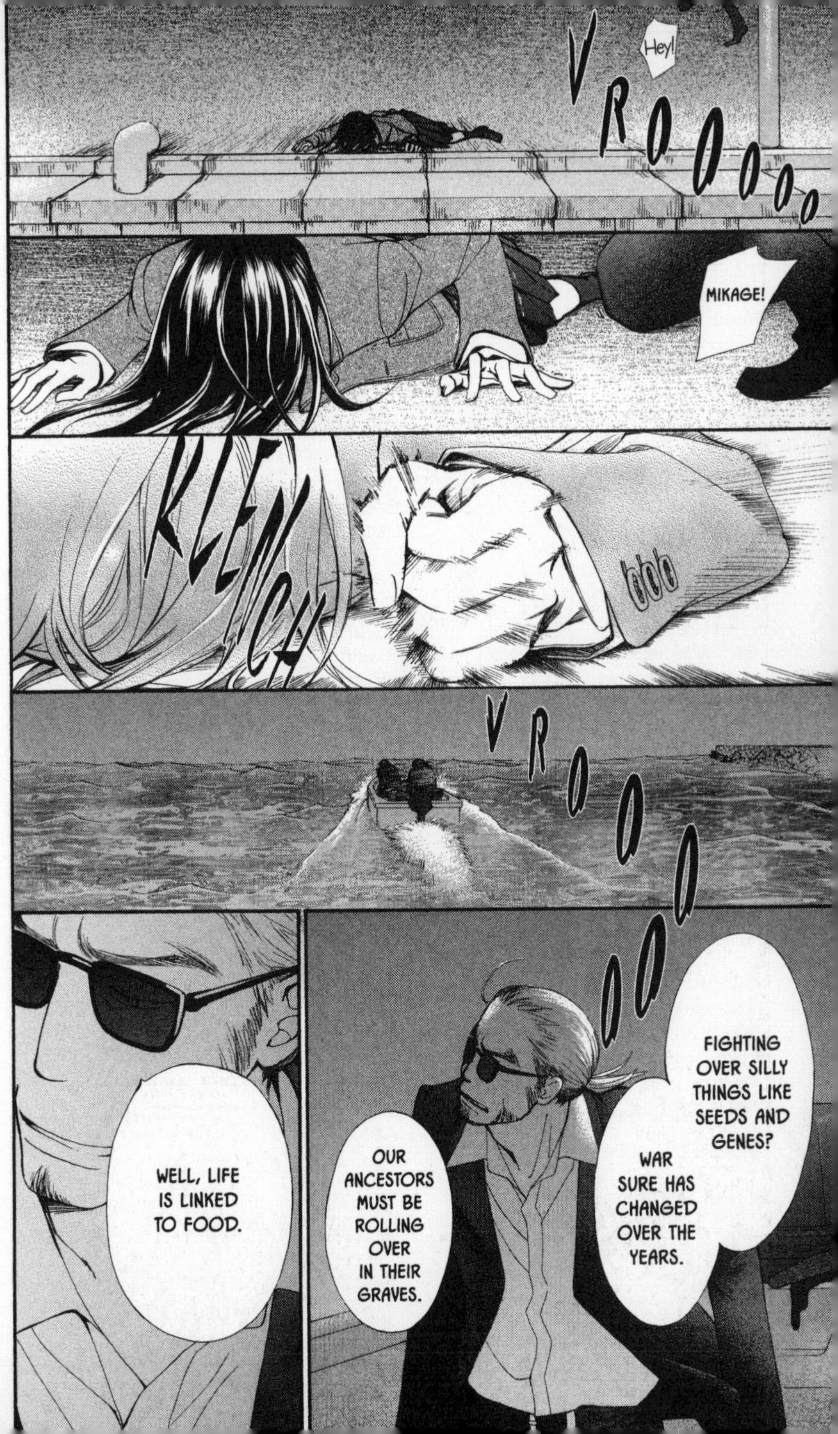
VROOOOO
Hey!
MIKAGE!
KLENCH
VROOOOOOO
FIGHTING OVER SILLY THINGS LIKE SEEDS AND GENES?
WAR SURE HAS CHANGED OVER THE YEARS.
OUR ANCESTORS MUST BE ROLLING OVER IN THEIR GRAVES.
WELL, LIFE IS LINKED TO FOOD.

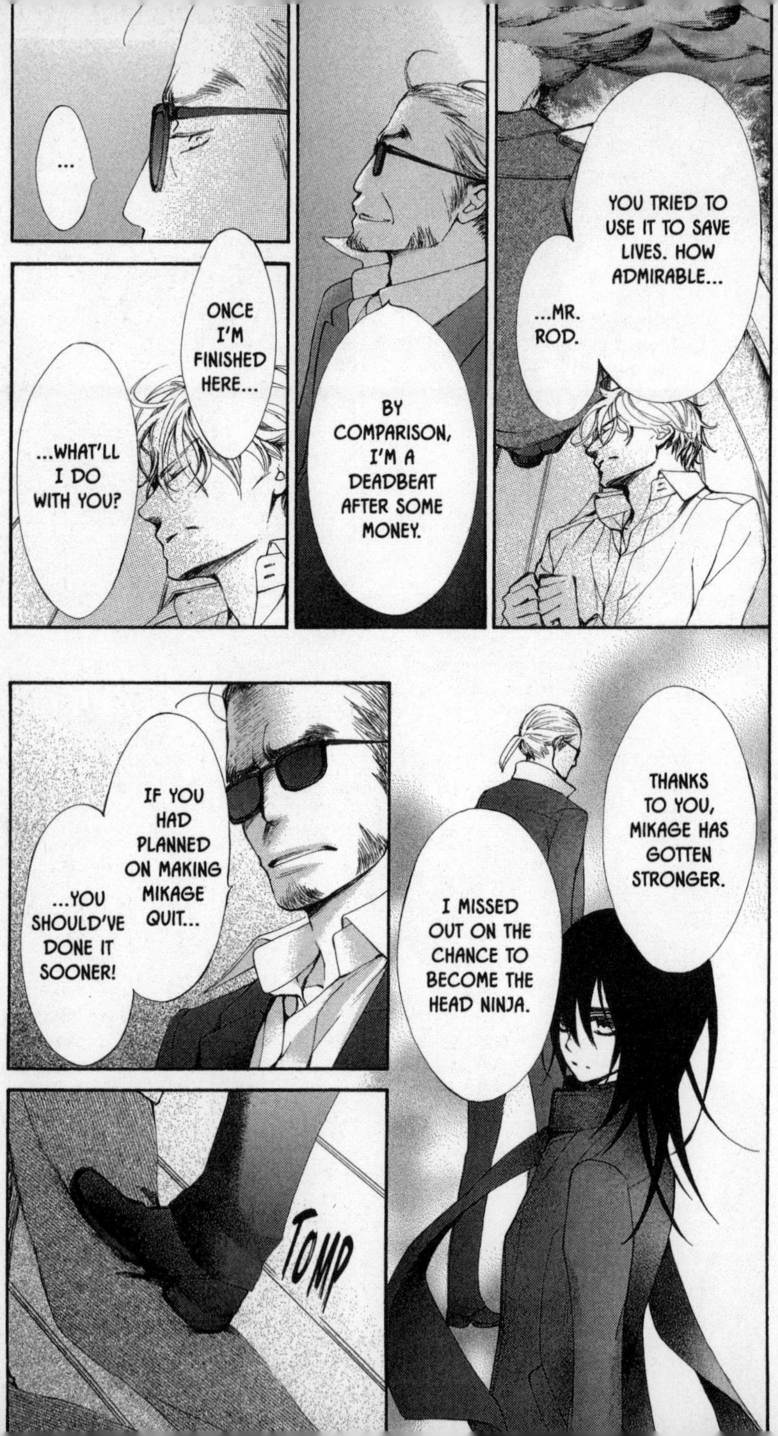
YOU TRIED TO USE IT TO SAVE LIVES. HOW ADMIRABLE...
...MR. ROD.
BY COMPARISON, I'M A DEADBEAT AFTER SOME MONEY.
...
ONCE I'M FINISHED HERE...
...WHAT'LL I DO WITH YOU?
THANKS TO YOU, MIKAGE HAS GOTTEN STRONGER.
I MISSED OUT ON THE CHANCE TO BECOME THE HEAD NINJA.
IF YOU HAD PLANNED ON MAKING MIKAGE QUIT...
...YOU SHOULD'VE DONE IT SOONER!
TOMP

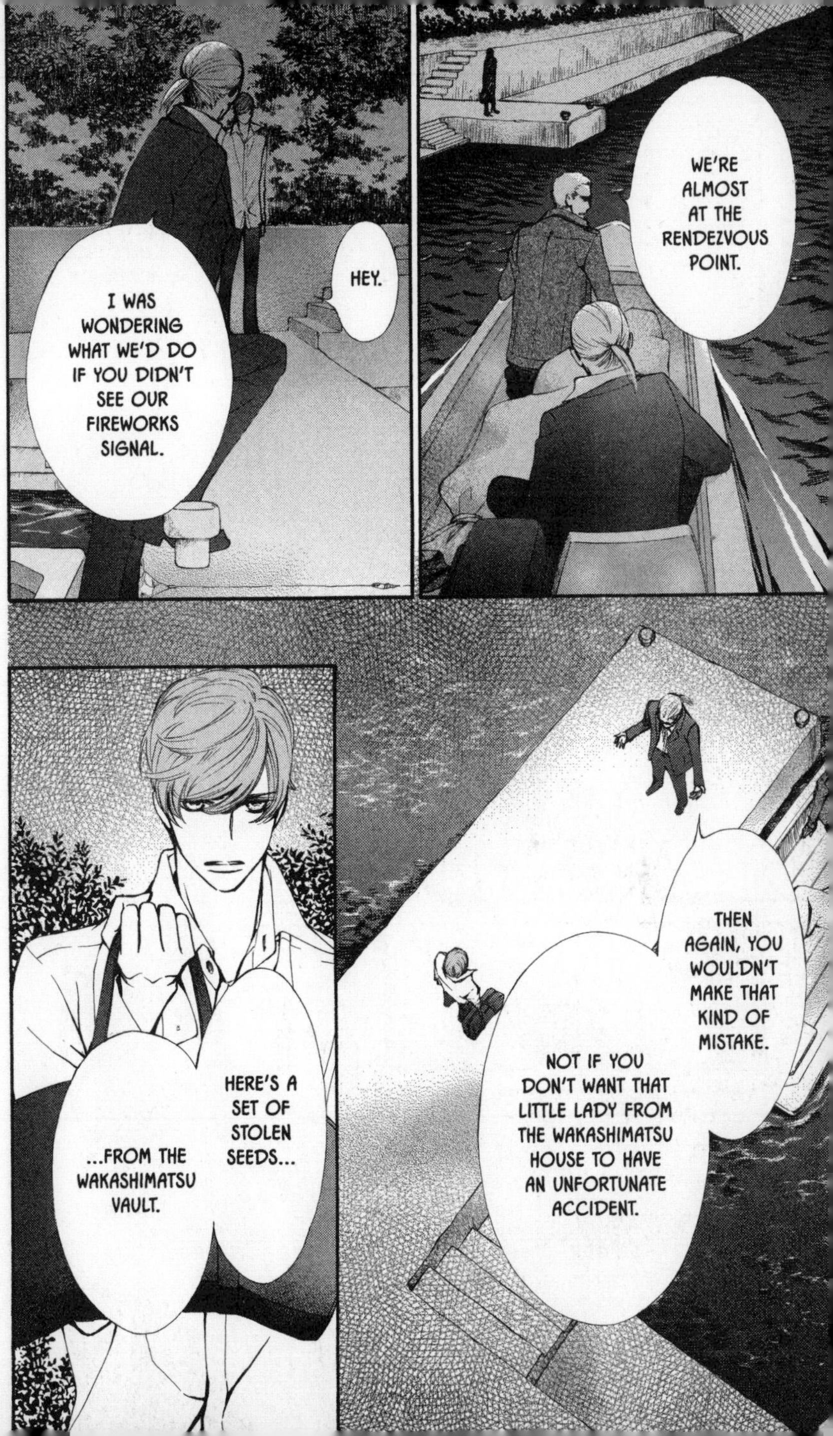
WE'RE ALMOST AT THE RENDEZVOUS POINT.
HEY.
I WAS WONDERING WHAT WE'D DO IF YOU DIDN'T SEE OUR FIREWORKS SIGNAL.
THEN AGAIN, YOU WOULDN'T MAKE THAT KIND OF MISTAKE.
NOT IF YOU DON'T WANT THAT LITTLE LADY FROM THE WAKASHIMATSU HOUSE TO HAVE AN UNFORTUNATE ACCIDENT.
HERE'S A SET OF STOLEN SEEDS...
...FROM THE WAKASHIMATSU VAULT.

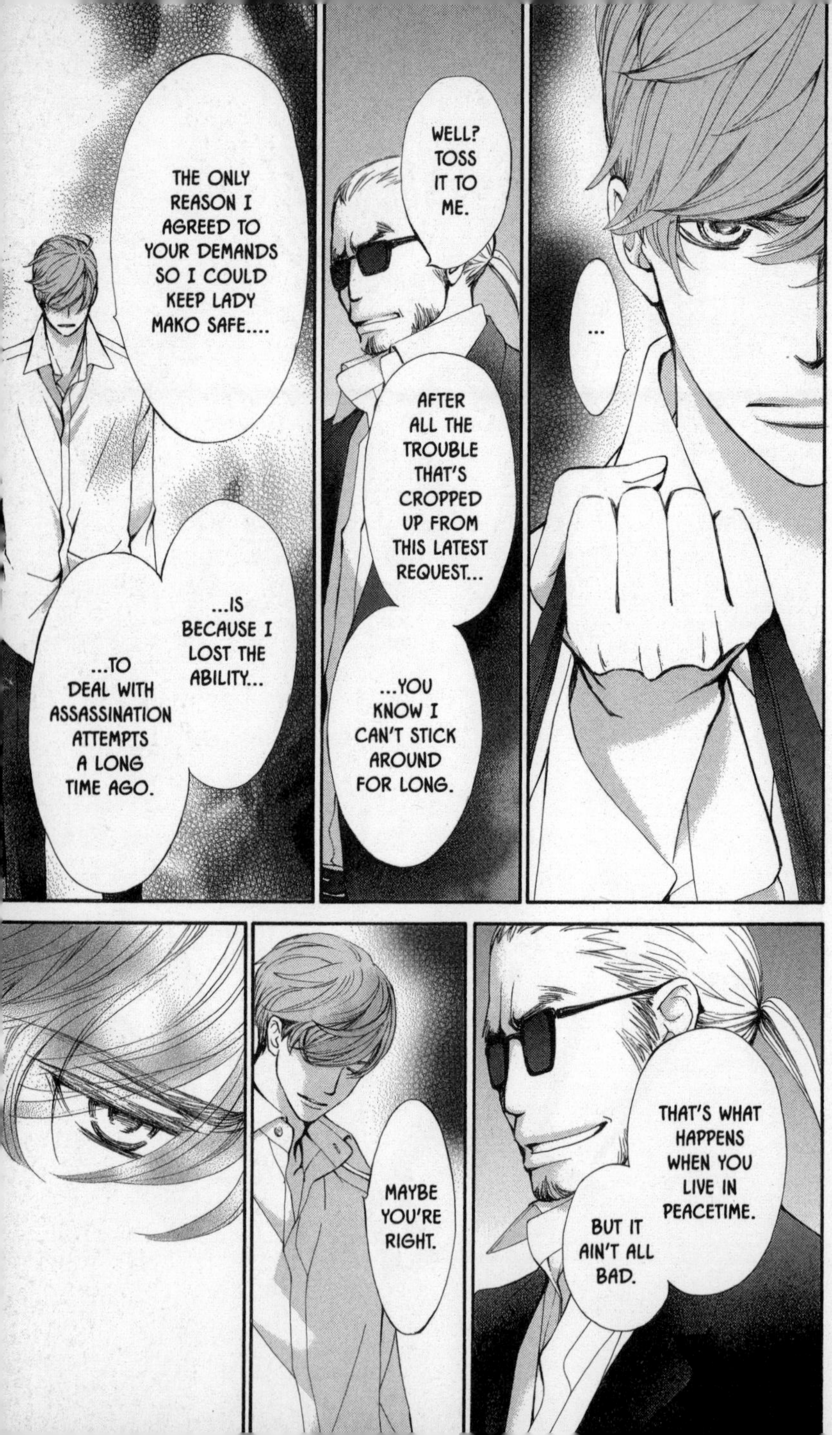
...
WELL? TOSS IT TO ME.
AFTER ALL THE TROUBLE THAT'S CROPPED UP FROM THIS LATEST REQUEST...
...YOU KNOW I CAN'T STICK AROUND FOR LONG.
THE ONLY REASON I AGREED TO YOUR DEMANDS SO I COULD KEEP LADY MAKO SAFE....
...IS BECAUSE I LOST THE ABILITY...
...TO DEAL WITH ASSASSINATION ATTEMPTS A LONG TIME AGO.
THAT'S WHAT HAPPENS WHEN YOU LIVE IN PEACETIME.
BUT IT AIN'T ALL BAD.
MAYBE YOU'RE RIGHT.

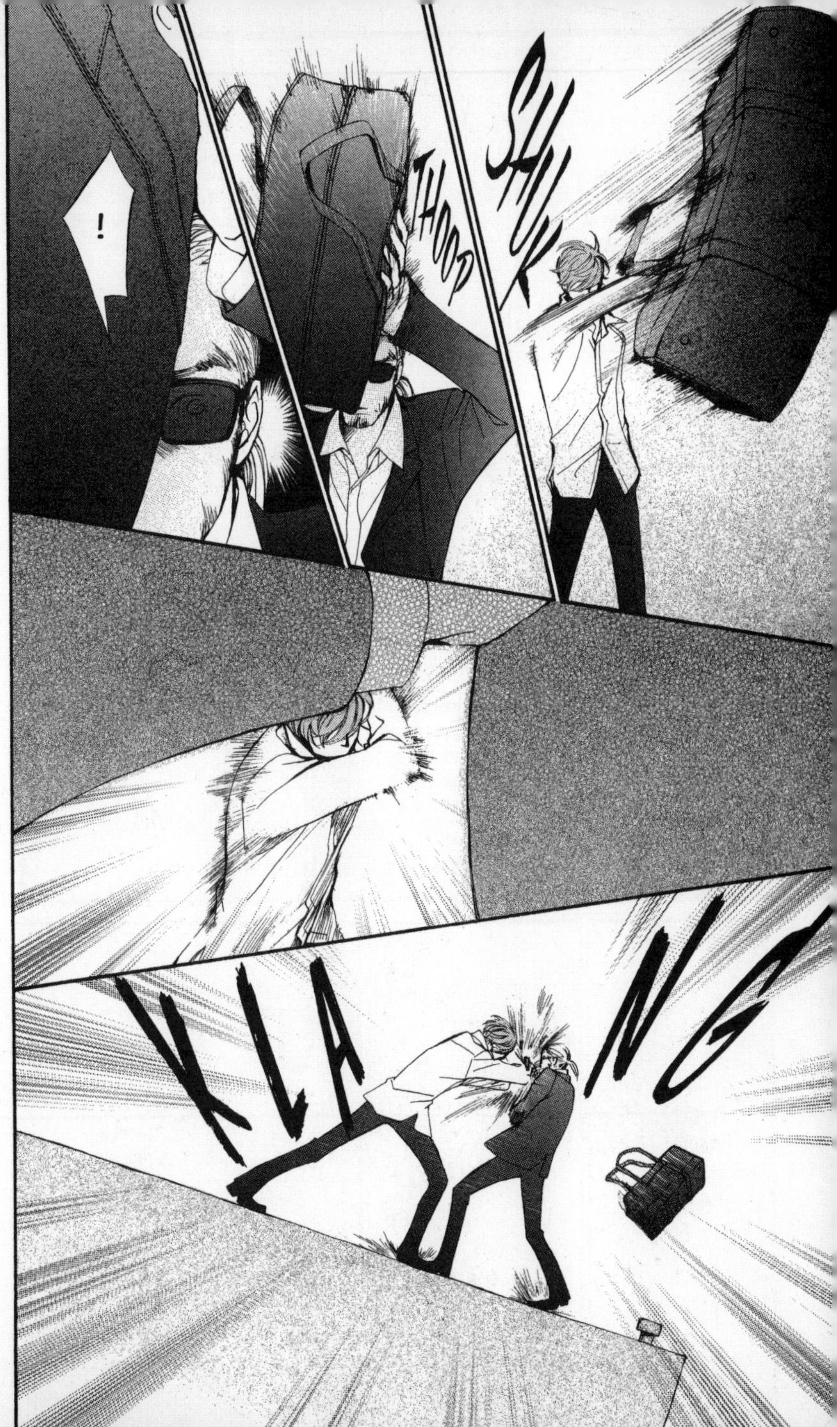
SHUK
THOOD
!
KLANG

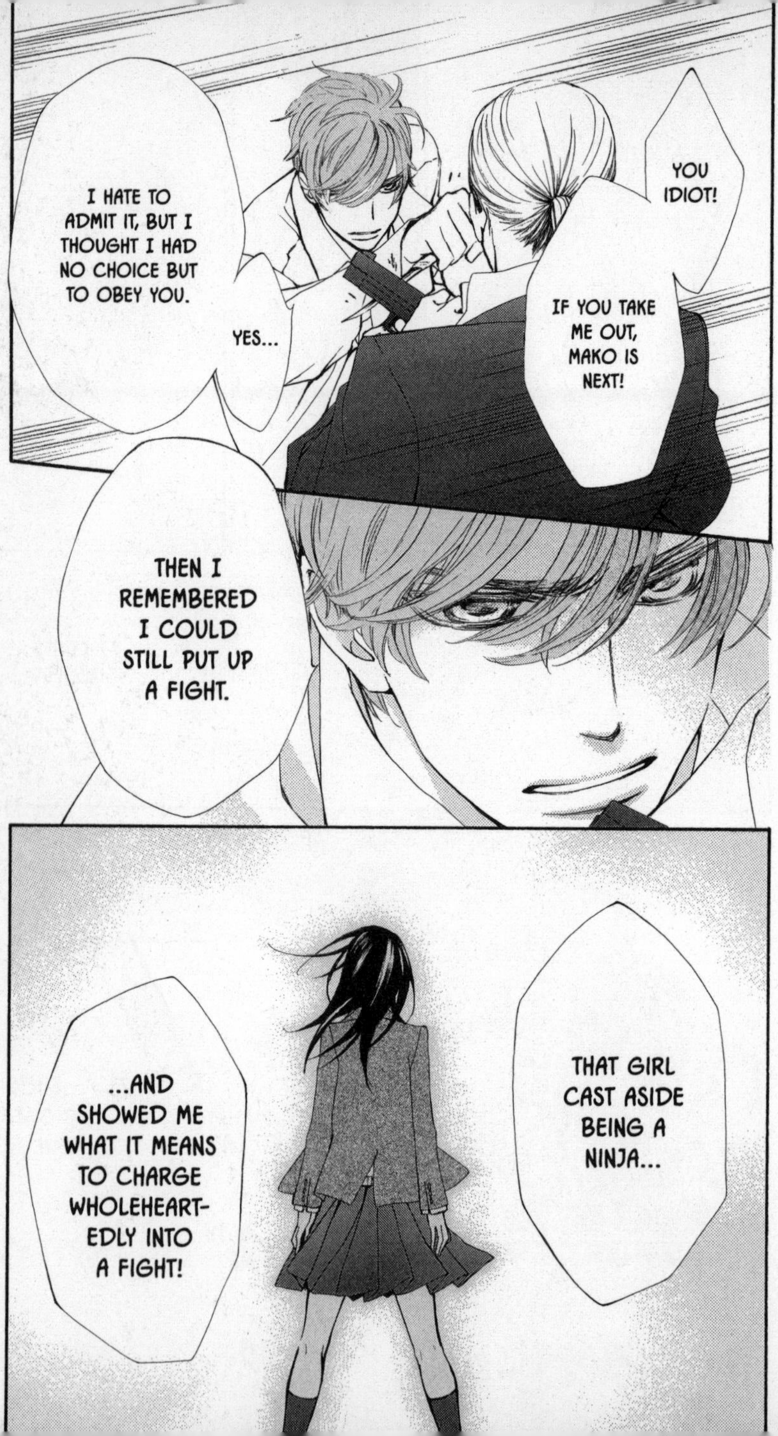
YOU IDIOT!
IF YOU TAKE ME OUT, MAKO IS NEXT!
YES...
I HATE TO ADMIT IT, BUT I THOUGHT I HAD NO CHOICE BUT TO OBEY YOU.
THEN I REMEMBERED I COULD STILL PUT UP A FIGHT.
THAT GIRL CAST ASIDE BEING A NINJA...
...AND SHOWED ME WHAT IT MEANS TO CHARGE WHOLEHEART-EDLY INTO A FIGHT!

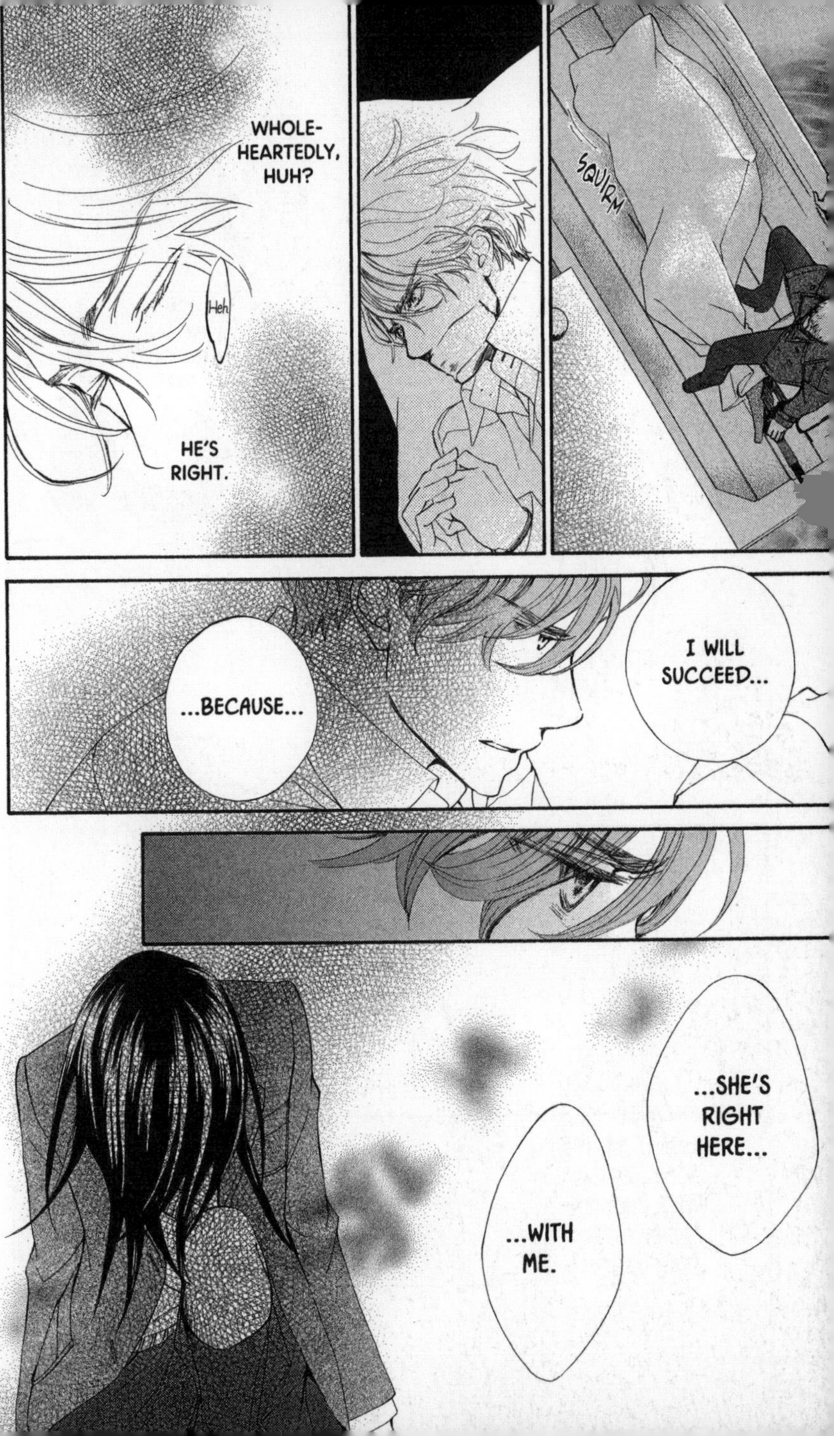
SQUIRM
WHOLE-HEARTEDLY, HUH?
Heh
HE'S RIGHT.
I WILL SUCCEED...
...BECAUSE...
...SHE'S RIGHT HERE...
...WITH ME.

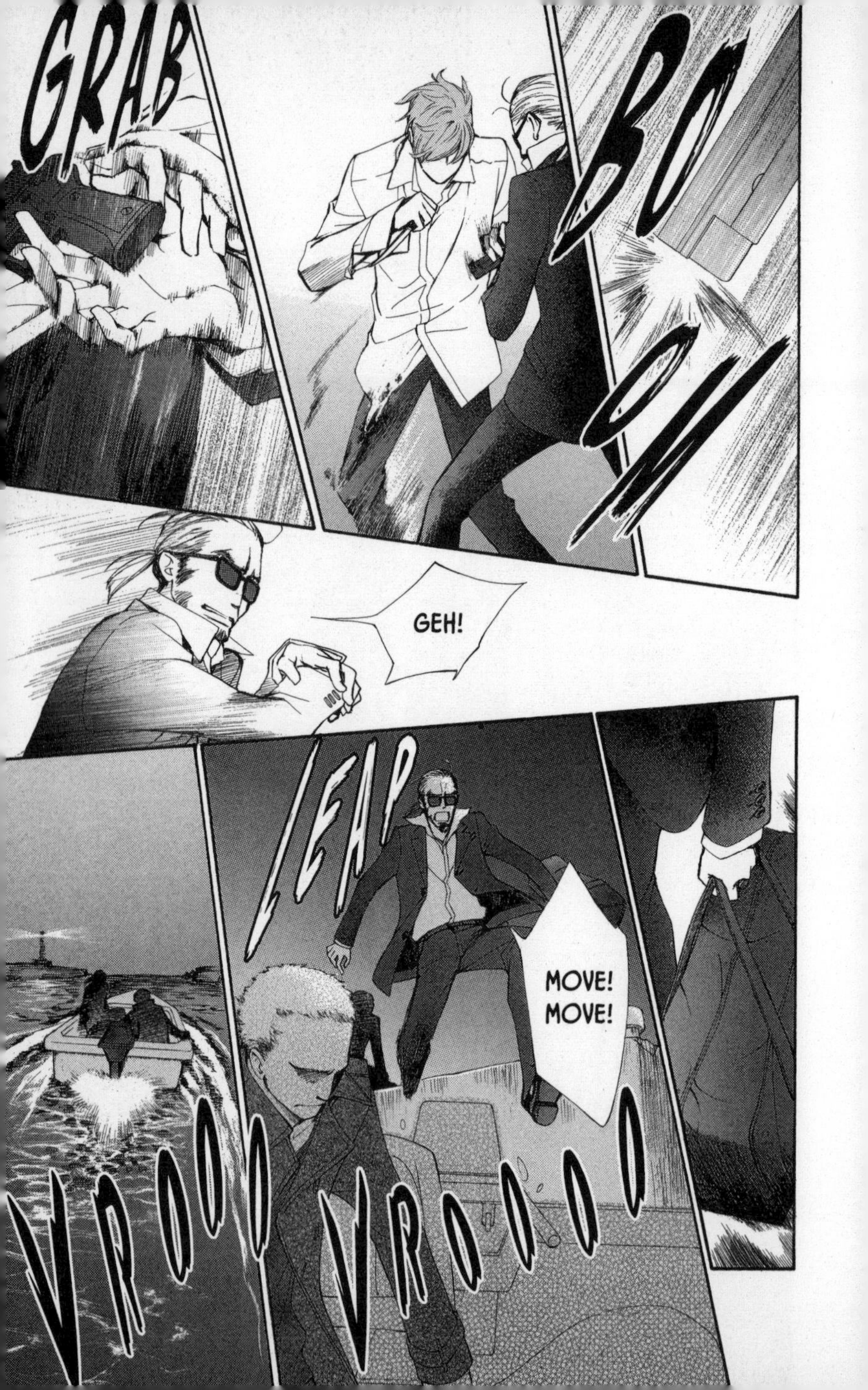
BOOM
GRAB
GEH!
LEAP
MOVE! MOVE!
VROOOOO
VROOO

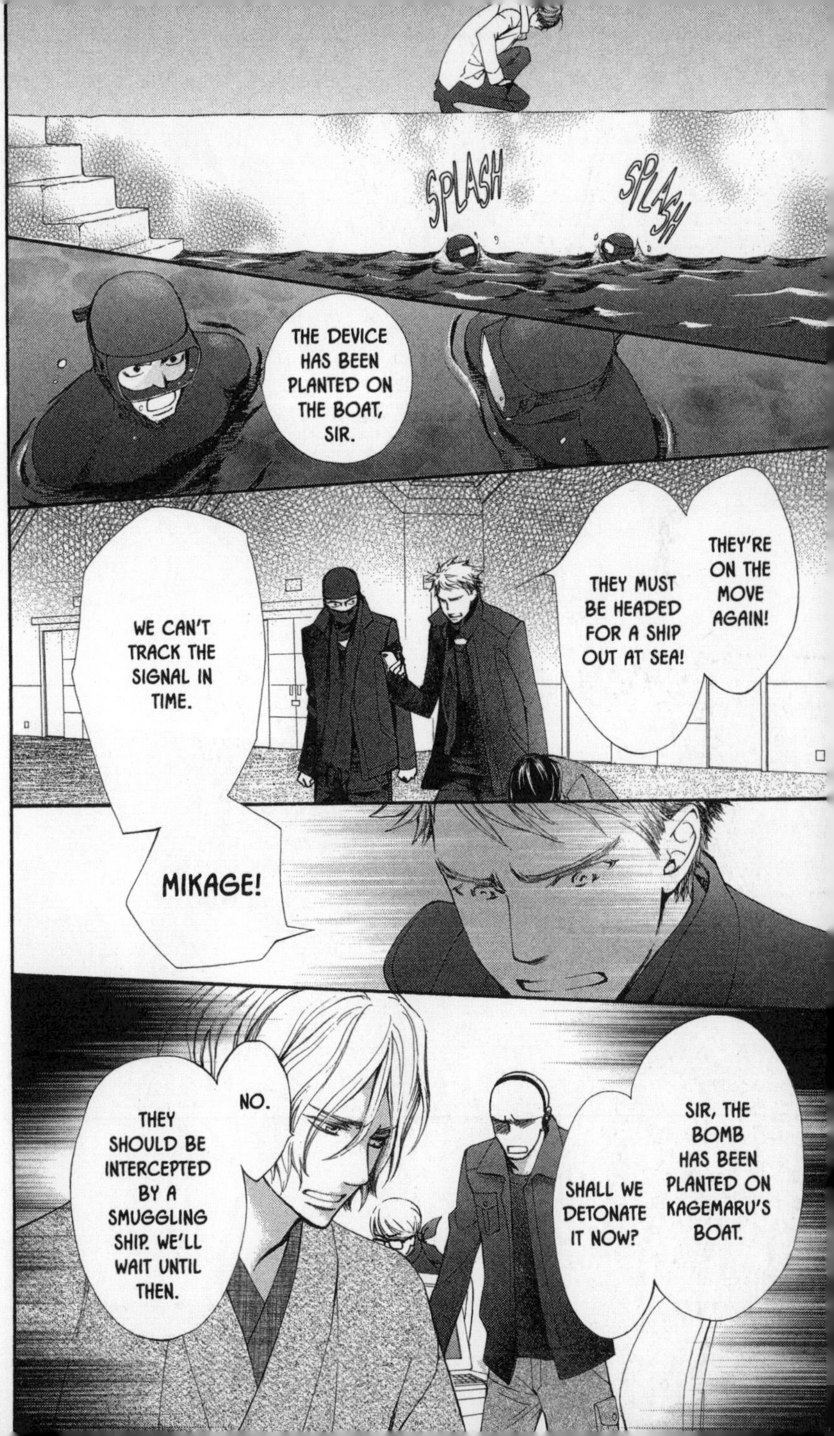
SPLASH
SPLASH
THE DEVICE HAS BEEN PLANTED ON THE BOAT, SIR.
THEY'RE ON THE MOVE AGAIN!
THEY MUST BE HEADED FOR A SHIP OUT AT SEA!
WE CAN'T TRACK THE SIGNAL IN TIME.
MIKAGE!
SIR, THE BOMB HAS BEEN PLANTED ON KAGEMARU'S BOAT.
SHALL WE DETONATE IT NOW?
NO.
THEY SHOULD BE INTERCEPTED BY A SMUGGLING SHIP. WE'LL WAIT UNTIL THEN.

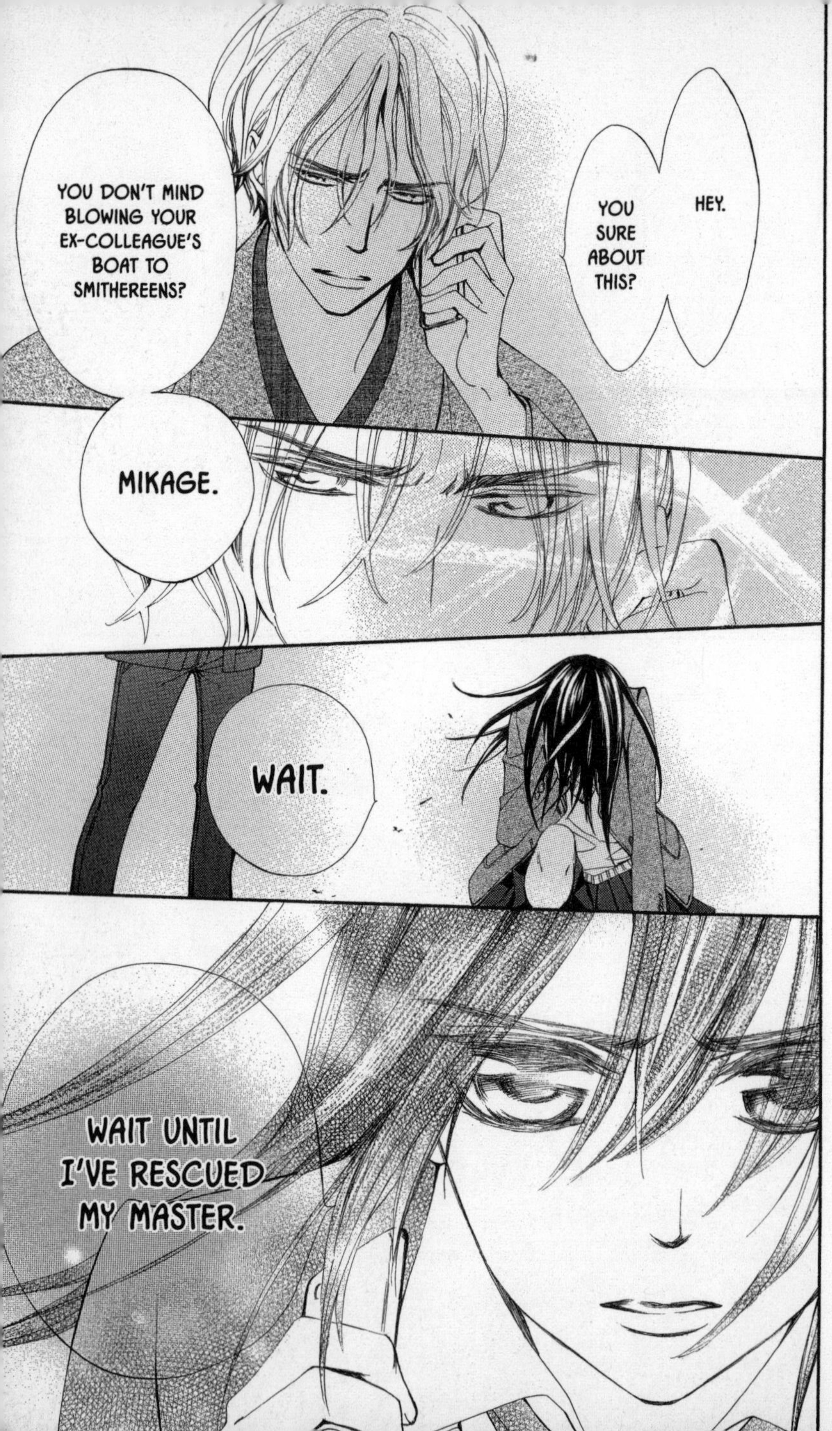
HEY.
YOU SURE ABOUT THIS?
YOU DON'T MIND BLOWING YOUR EX-COLLEAGUE'S BOAT TO SMITHEREENS?
MIKAGE.
WAIT.
WAIT UNTIL I'VE RESCUED MY MASTER.

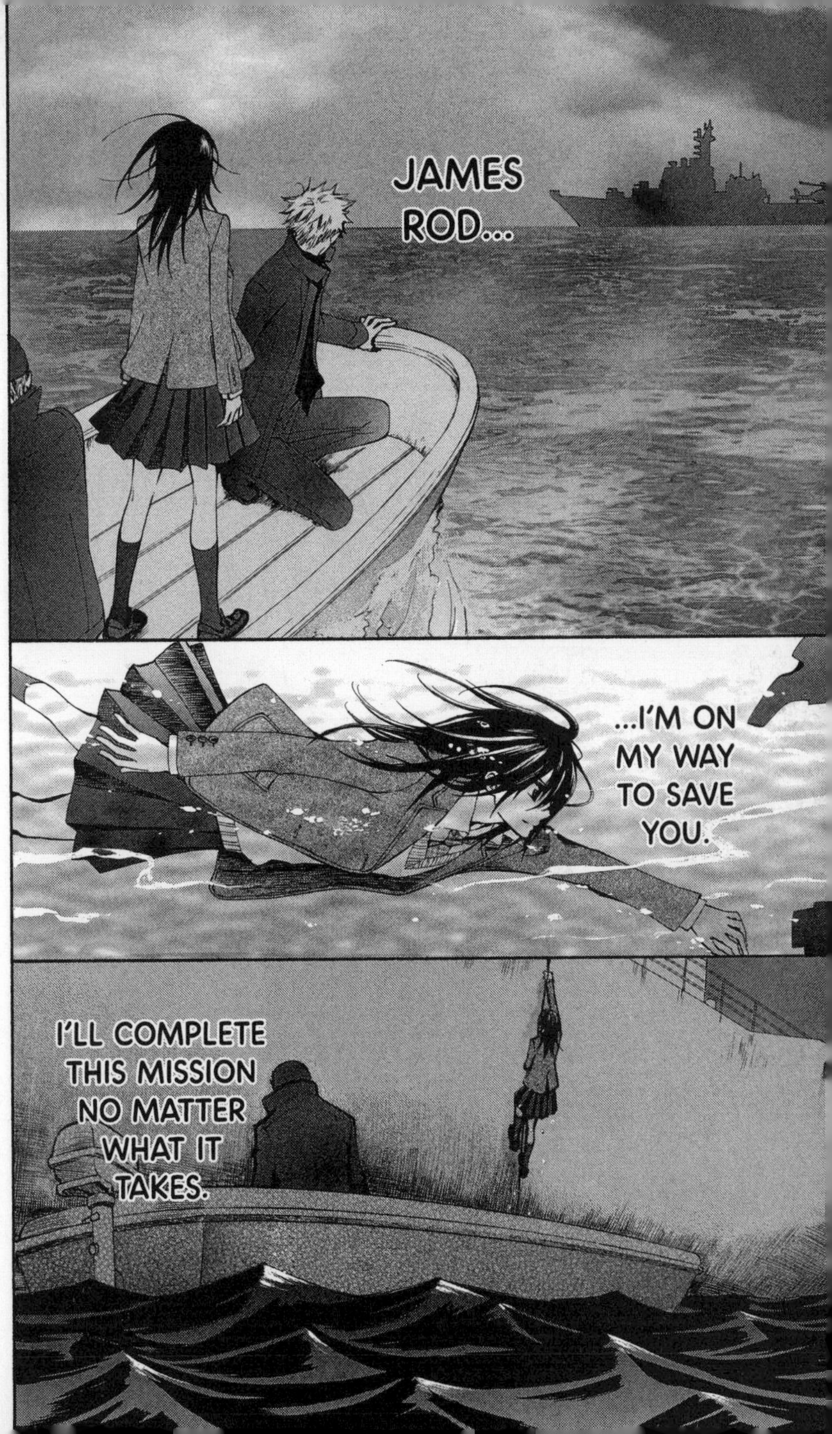
JAMES ROD...
...I'M ON MY WAY TO SAVE YOU.
I'LL COMPLETE THIS MISSION NO MATTER WHAT IT TAKES.

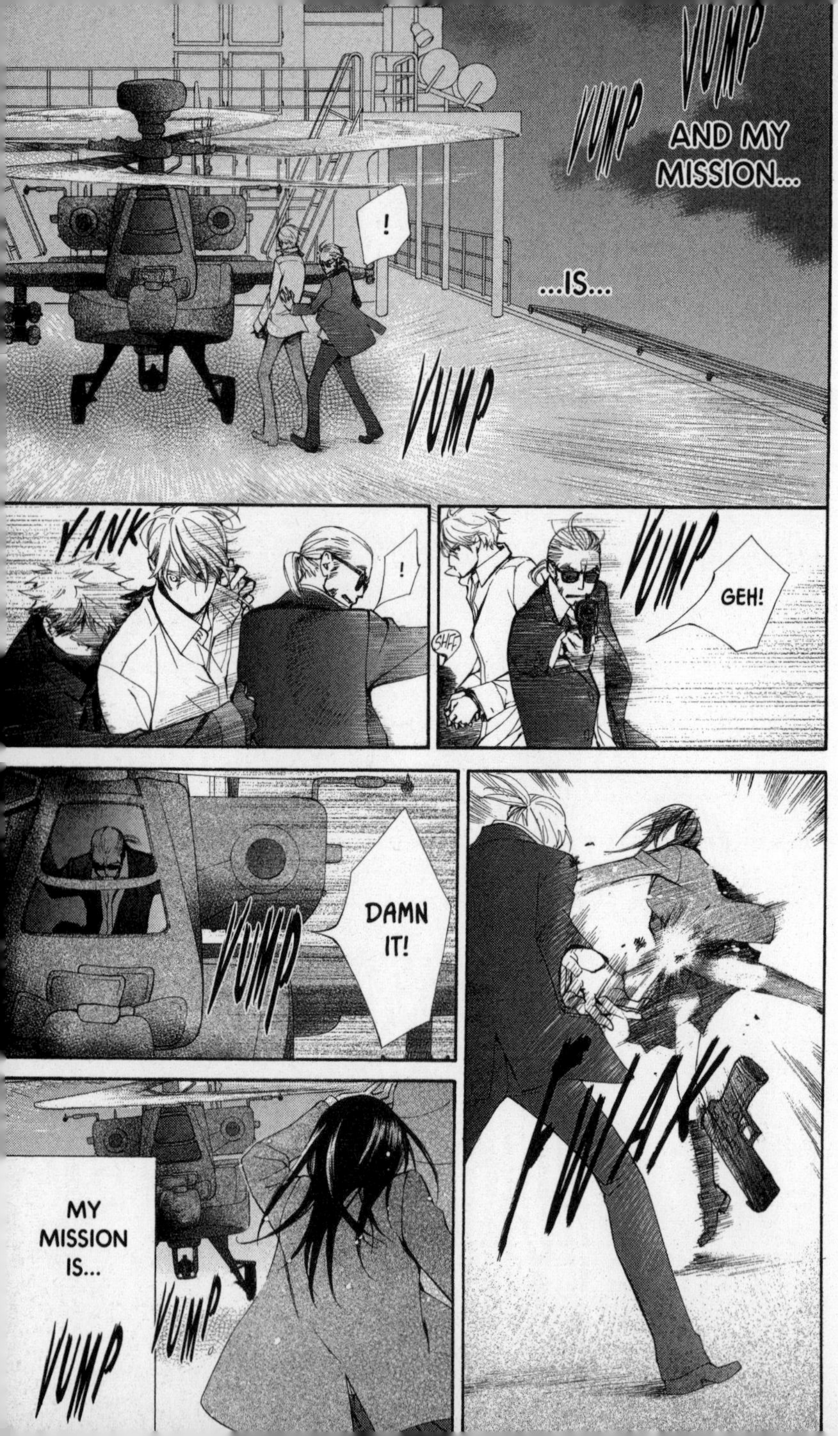
VUMP
VUMP
AND MY MISSION...
...IS...
!
VUMP
VUMP
GEH!
SHFF
YANK
!
FWAK
DAMN IT!
VUMP
MY MISSION IS...
VUMP
VUMP

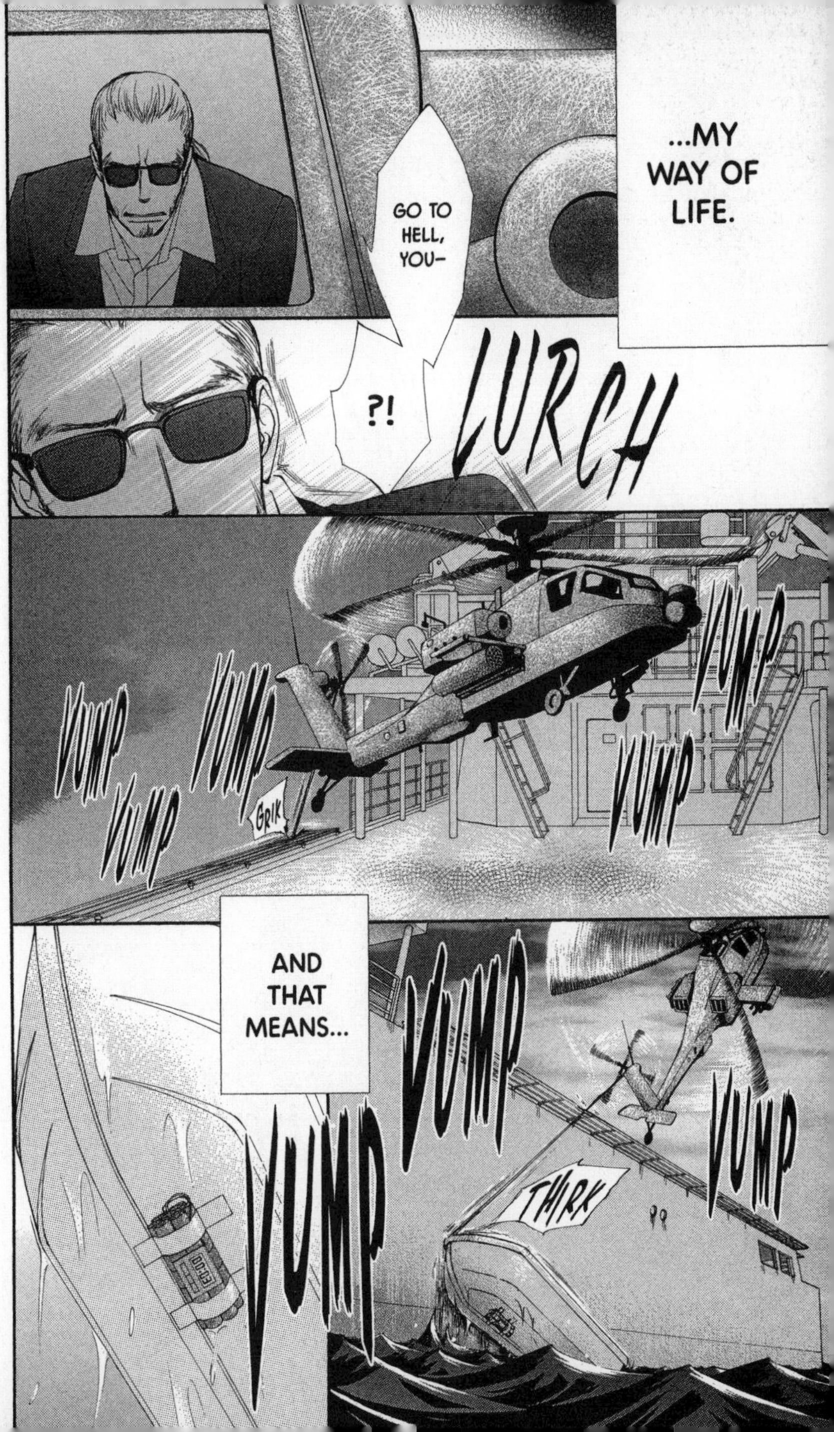
...MY WAY OF LIFE.
GO TO HELL, YOU–
LURCH
?!
VUMP
VUMP
VUMP
VUMP
VUMP
GRIK
AND THAT MEANS...
VUMP
VUMP
THIRK
VUMP
VUMP

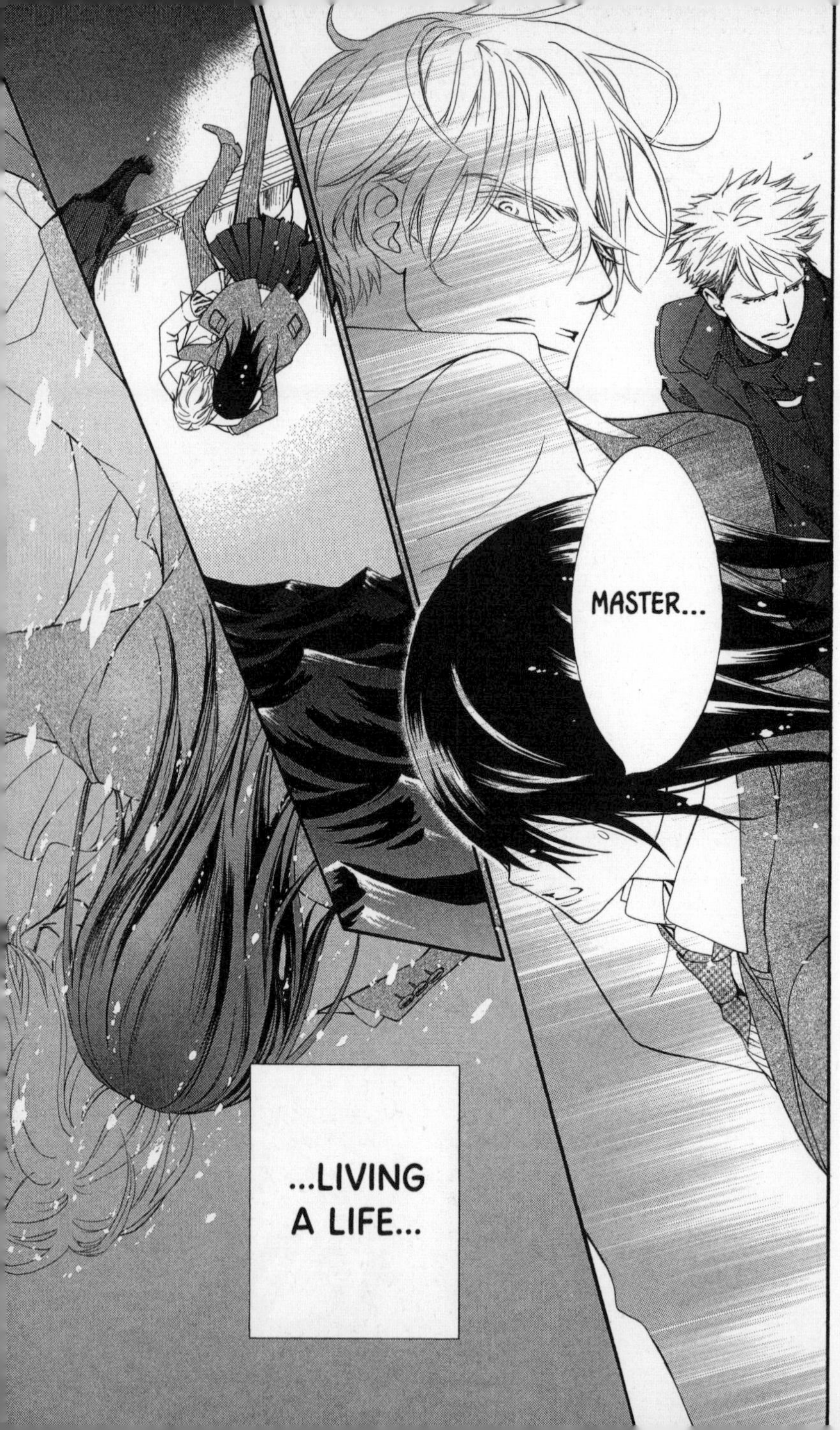
MASTER...
...LIVING A LIFE...

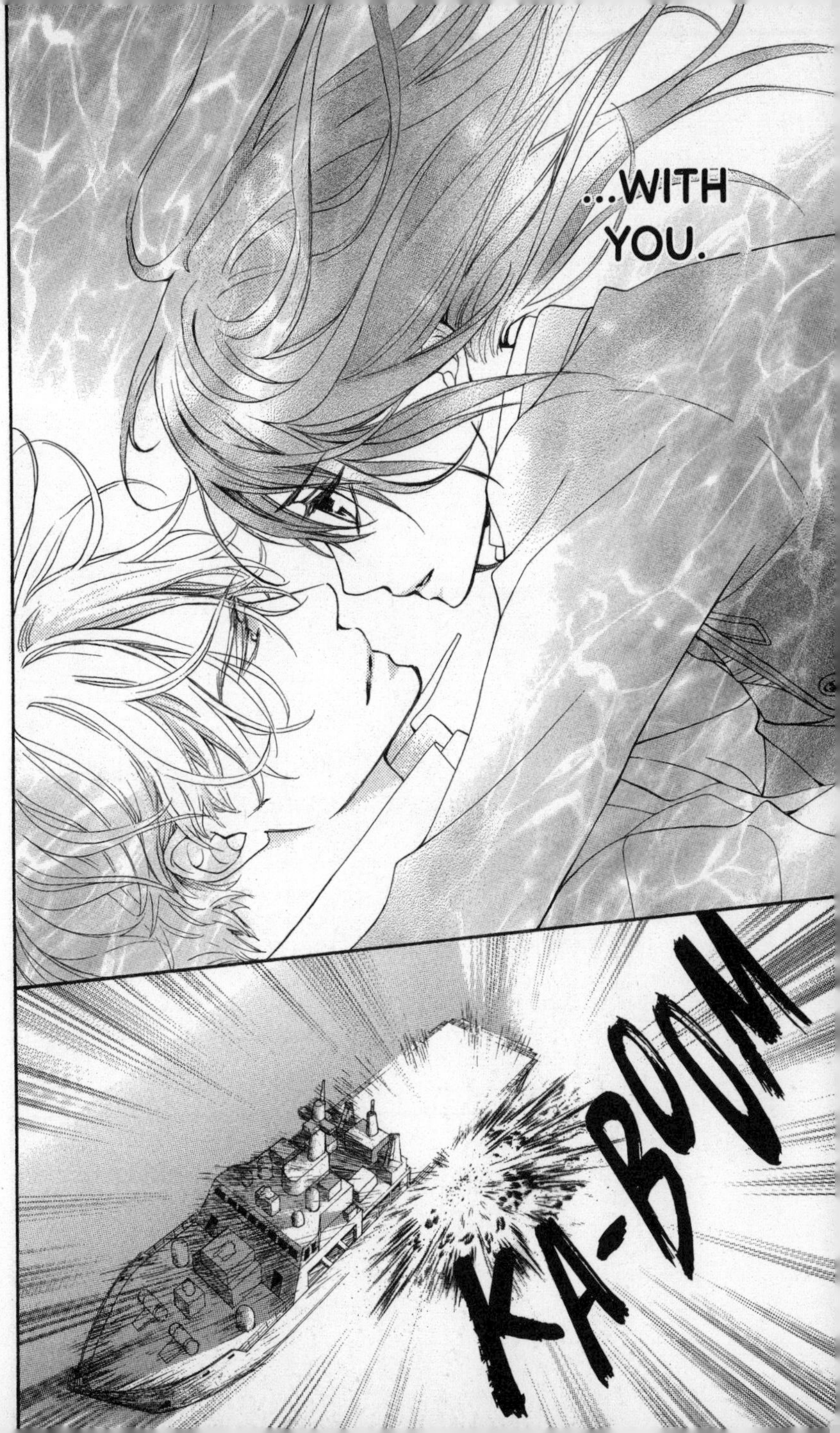
...WITH YOU.
KA-BOOM

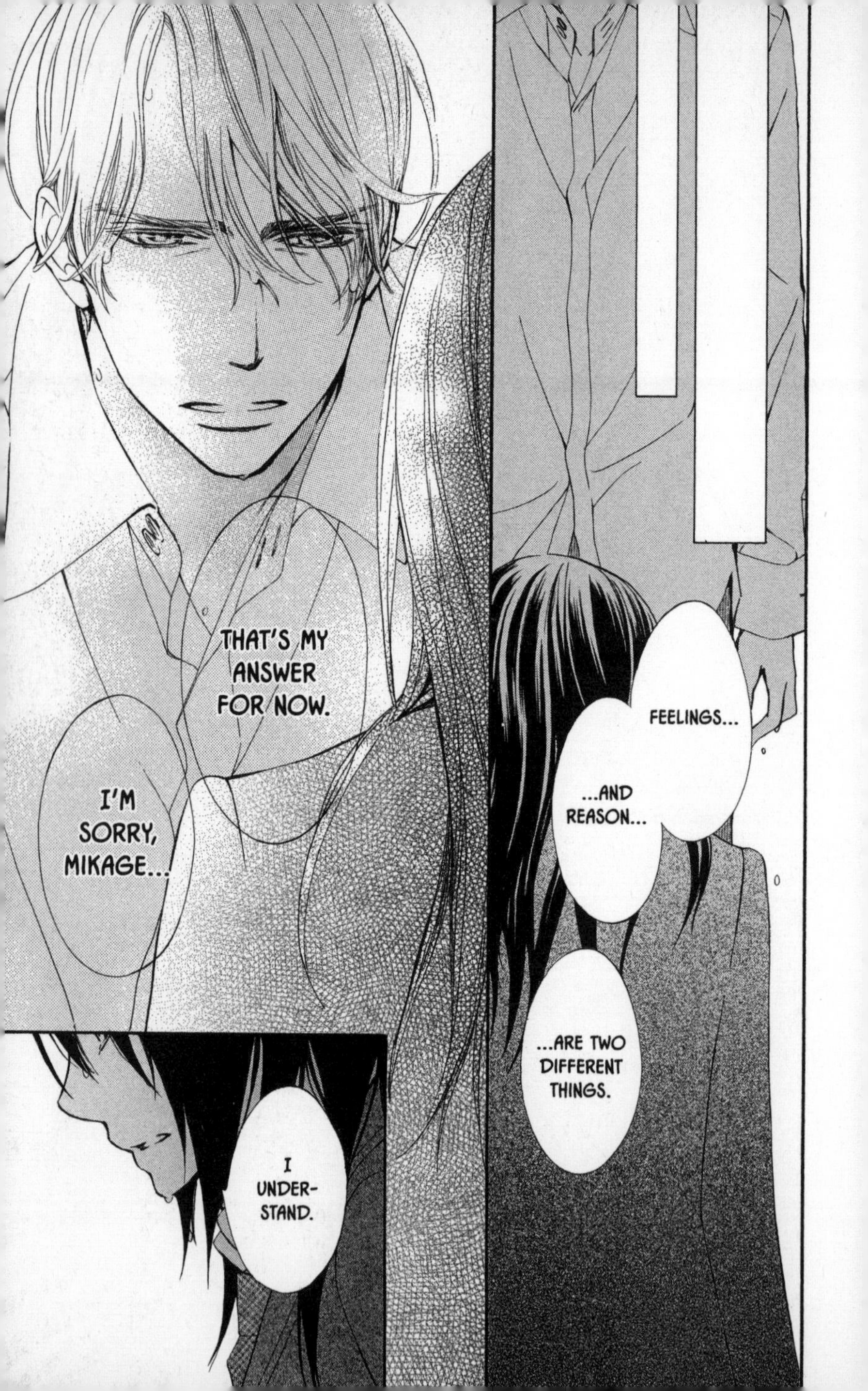
FEELINGS...
...AND REASON...
...ARE TWO DIFFERENT THINGS.
THAT'S MY ANSWER FOR NOW.
I'M SORRY, MIKAGE...
I UNDERSTAND.

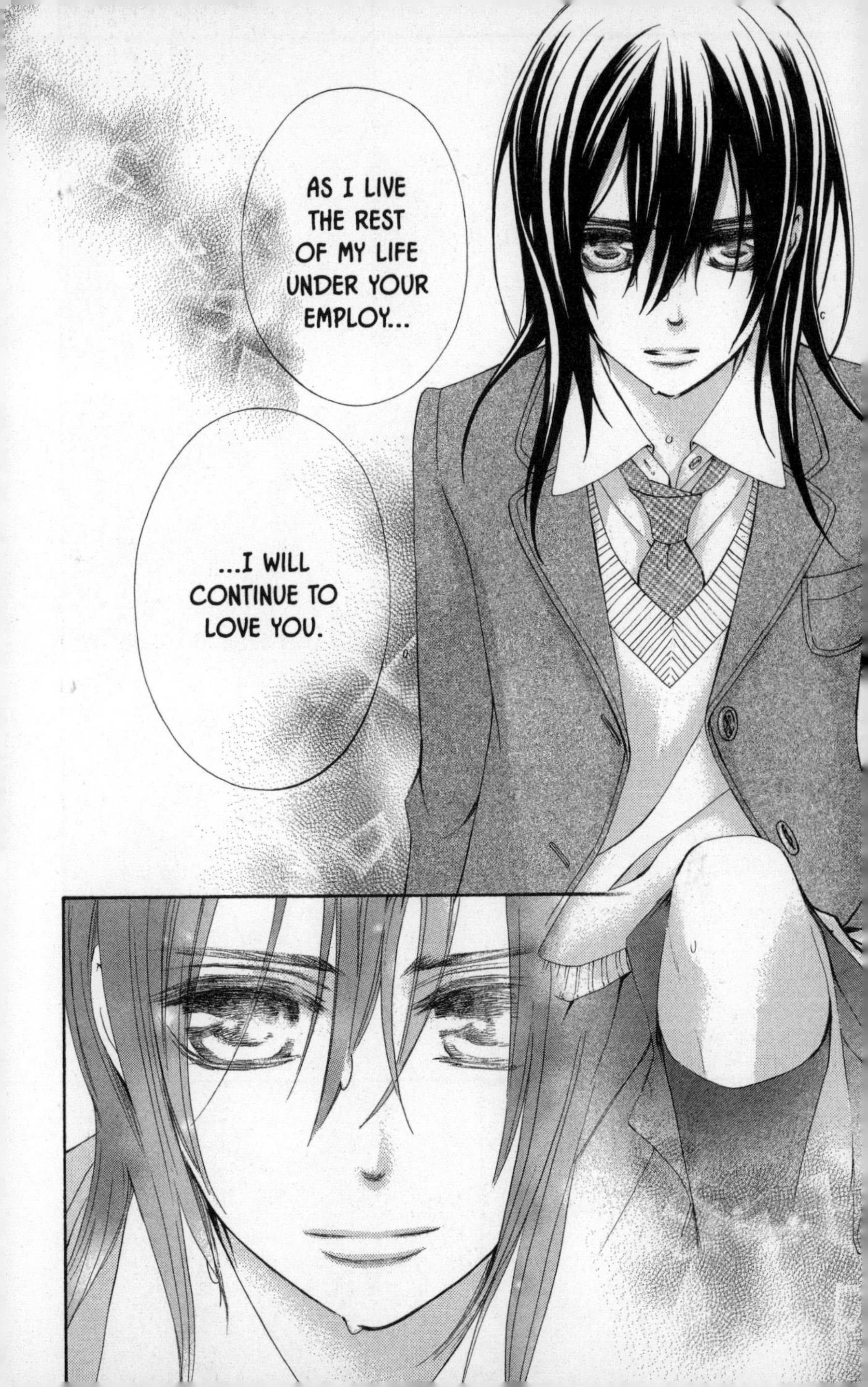
AS I LIVE THE REST OF MY LIFE UNDER YOUR EMPLOY...
...I WILL CONTINUE TO LOVE YOU.

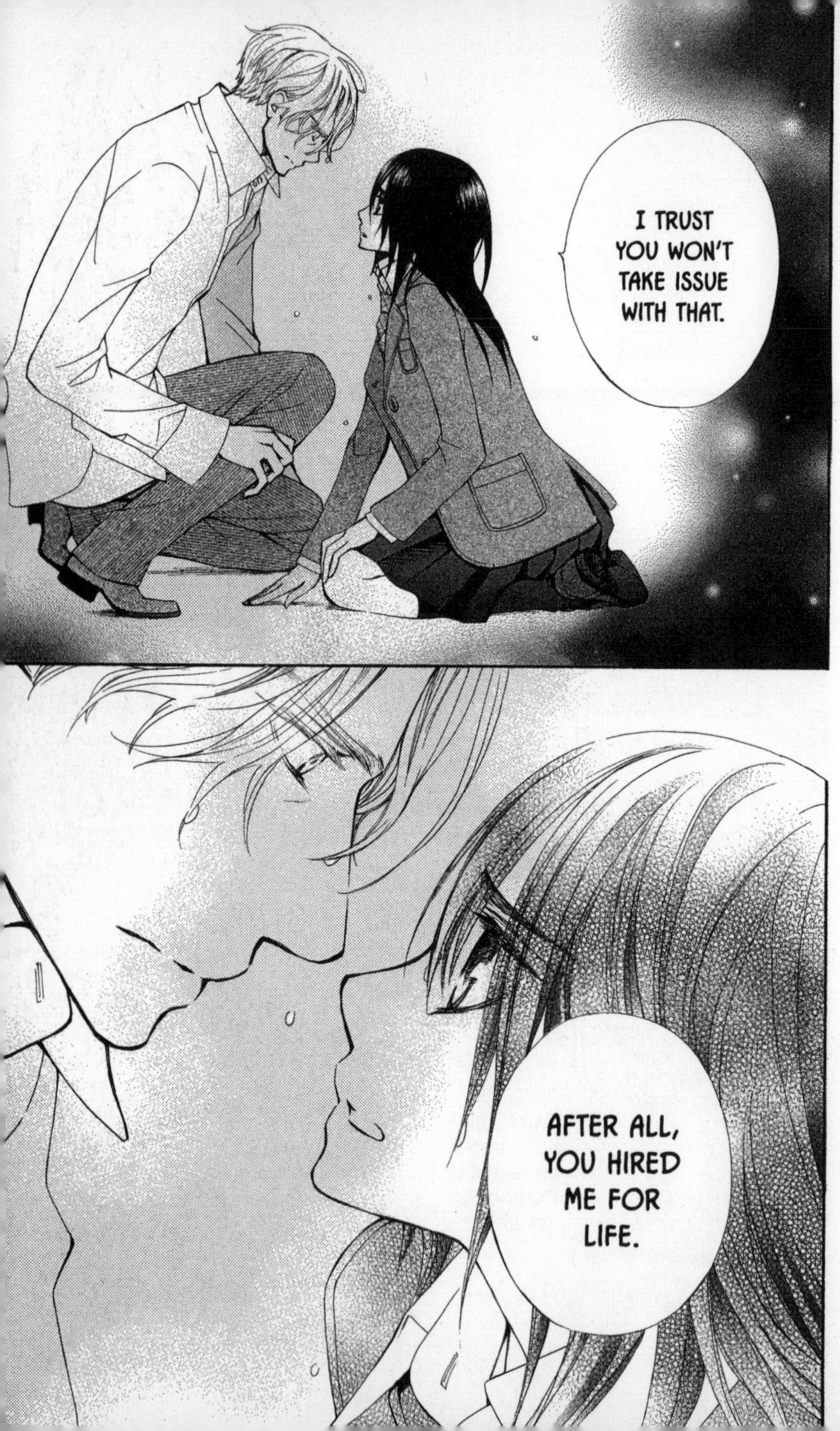
I TRUST YOU WON'T TAKE ISSUE WITH THAT.
AFTER ALL, YOU HIRED ME FOR LIFE.

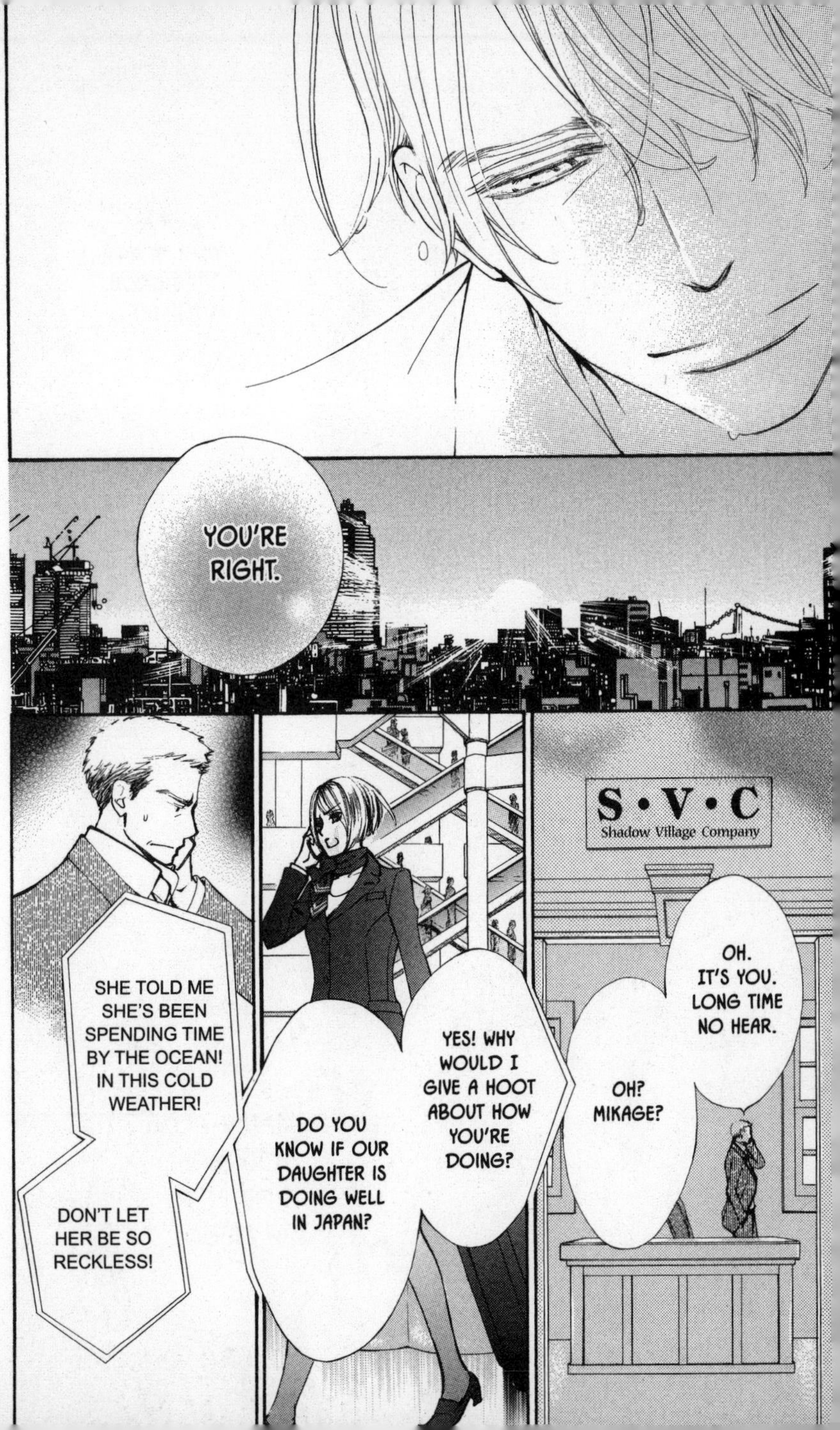
YOU'RE RIGHT.
S•V•C
Shadow Village Company
OH. IT'S YOU. LONG TIME NO HEAR.
OH? MIKAGE?
YES! WHY WOULD I GIVE A HOOT ABOUT HOW YOU'RE DOING?
DO YOU KNOW IF OUR DAUGHTER IS DOING WELL IN JAPAN?
SHE TOLD ME SHE'S BEEN SPENDING TIME BY THE OCEAN! IN THIS COLD WEATHER!
DON'T LET HER BE SO RECKLESS!

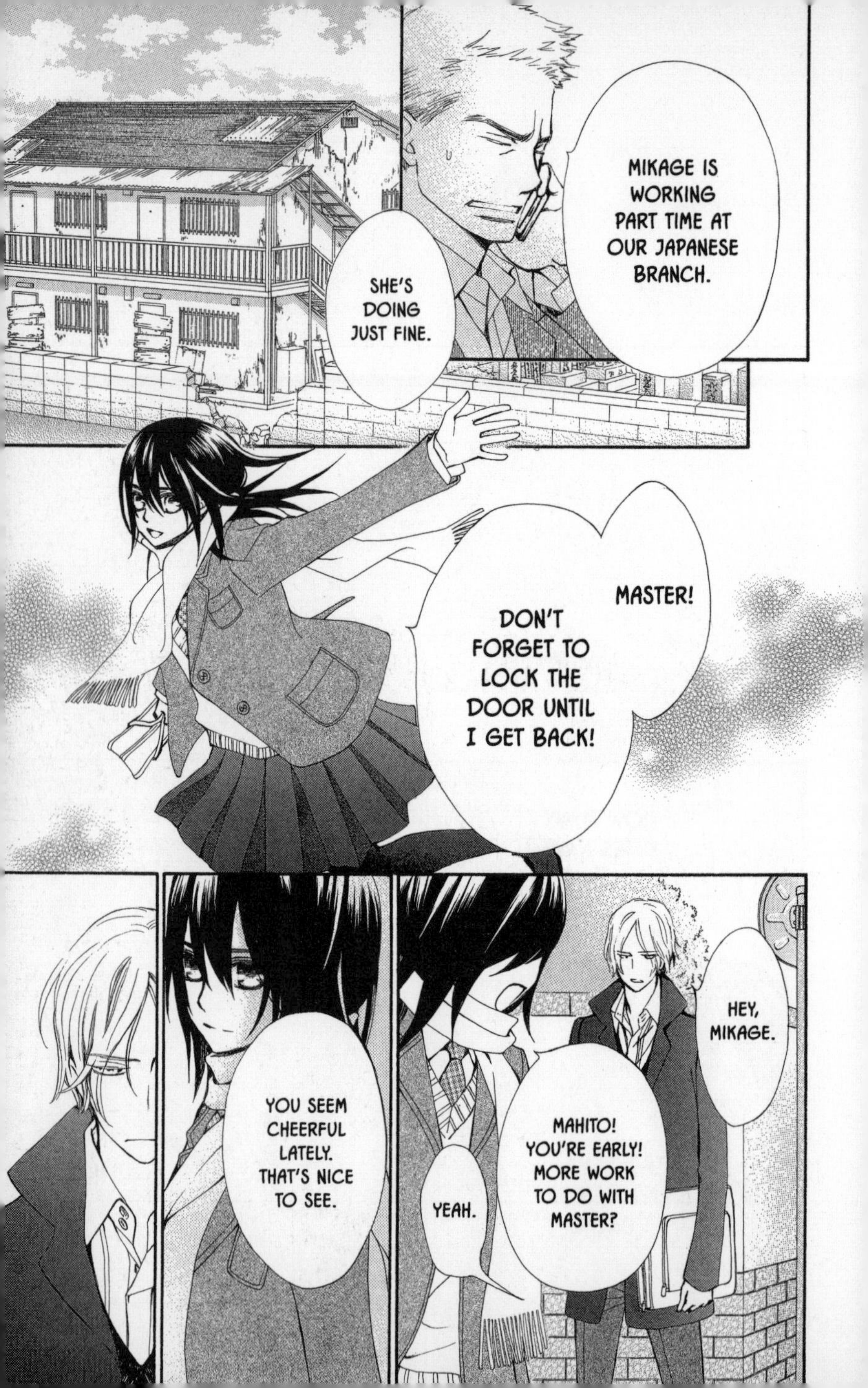
MIKAGE IS WORKING PART TIME AT OUR JAPANESE BRANCH.
SHE'S DOING JUST FINE.
MASTER!
DON'T FORGET TO LOCK THE DOOR UNTIL I GET BACK!
HEY, MIKAGE.
MAHITO! YOU'RE EARLY! MORE WORK TO DO WITH MASTER?
YEAH.
YOU SEEM CHEERFUL LATELY. THAT'S NICE TO SEE.

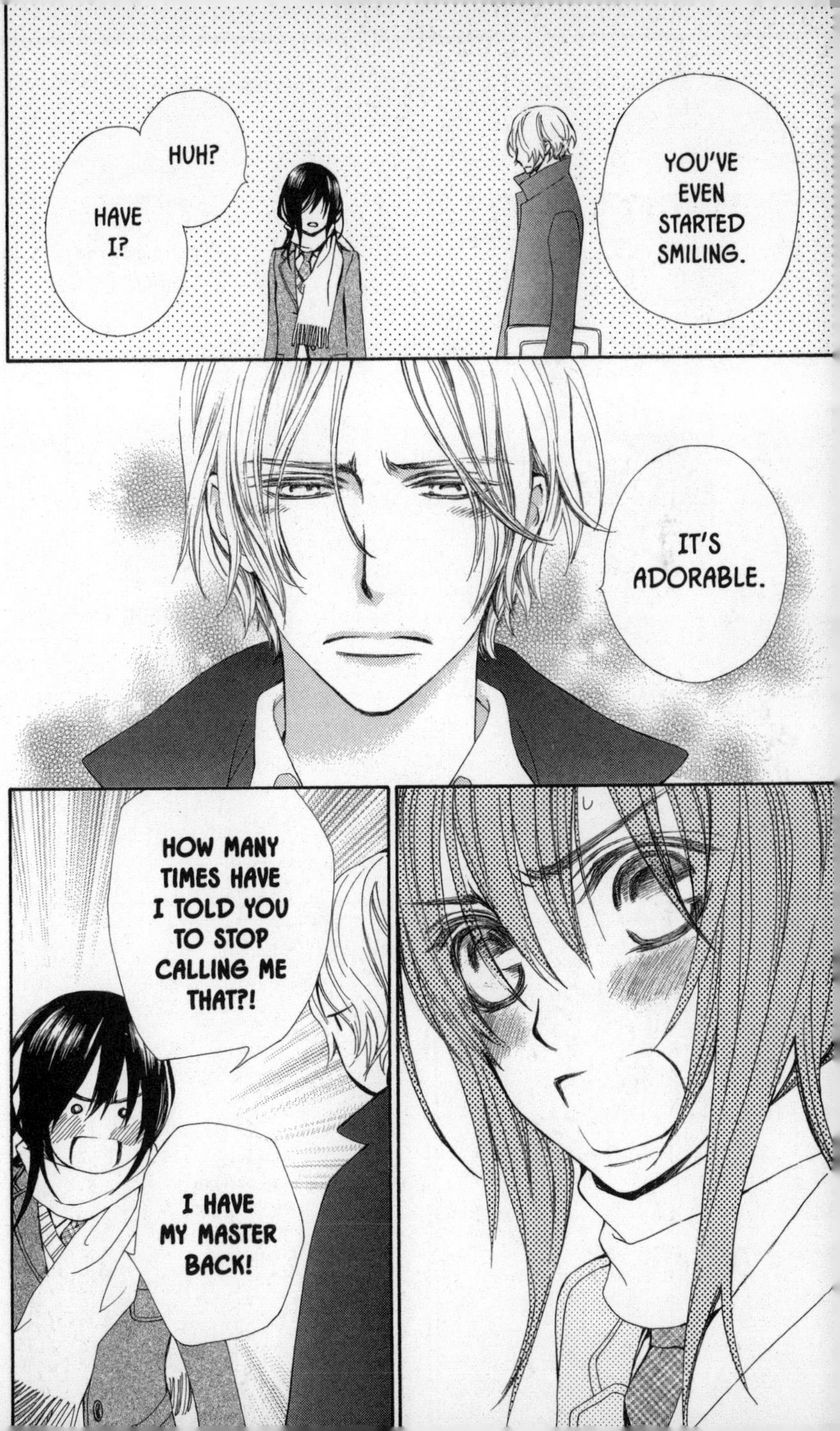
YOU'VE EVEN STARTED SMILING.
HUH? HAVE I?
IT'S ADORABLE.
HOW MANY TIMES HAVE I TOLD YOU TO STOP CALLING ME THAT?!
I HAVE MY MASTER BACK!

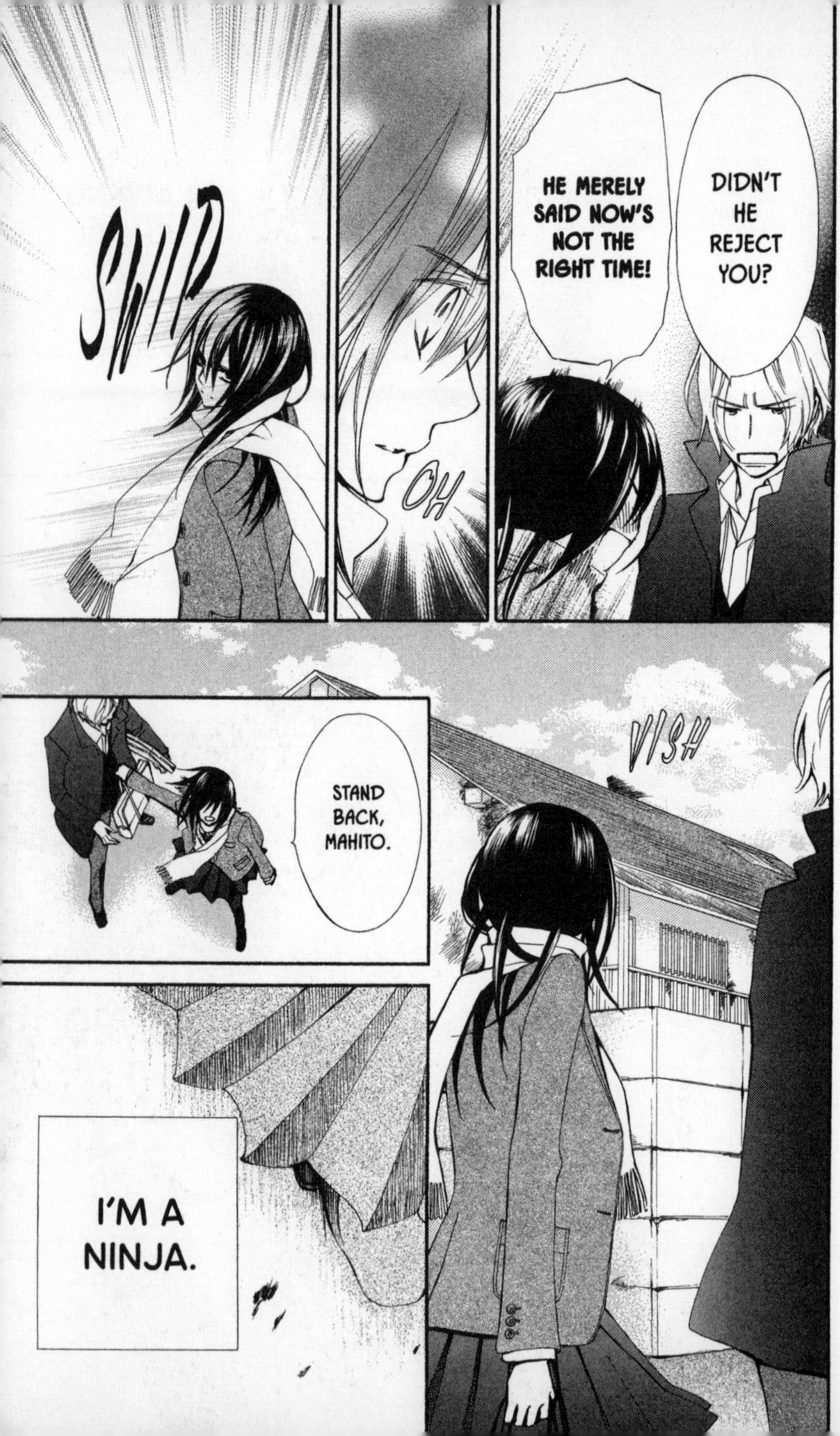
DIDN'T HE REJECT YOU?
HE MERELY SAID NOW'S NOT THE RIGHT TIME!
OH
SWIP
VISH
STAND BACK, MAHITO.
I'M A NINJA.

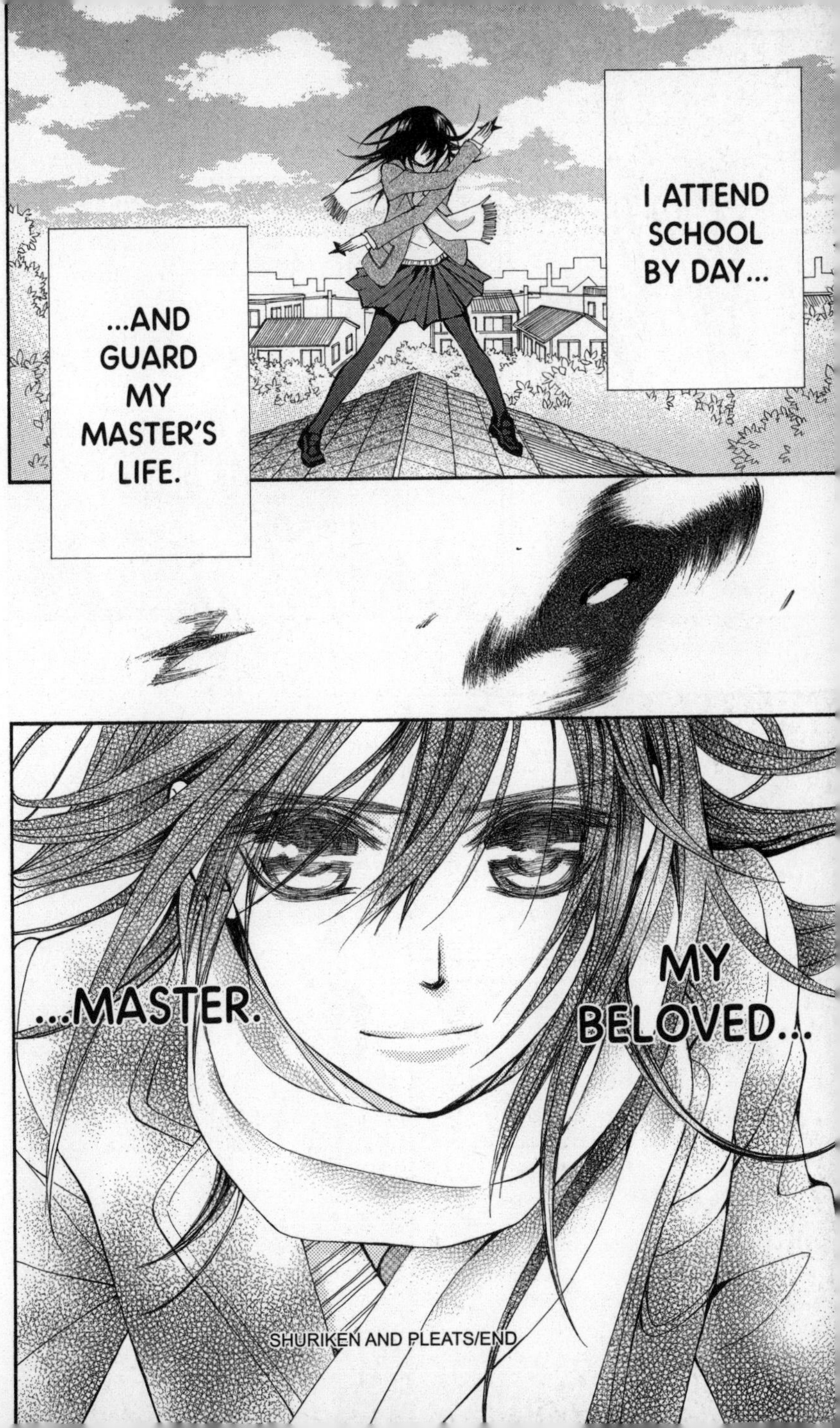
I ATTEND SCHOOL BY DAY...
...AND GUARD MY MASTER'S LIFE.
MY BELOVED...
...MASTER.
SHURIKEN AND PLEATS/END

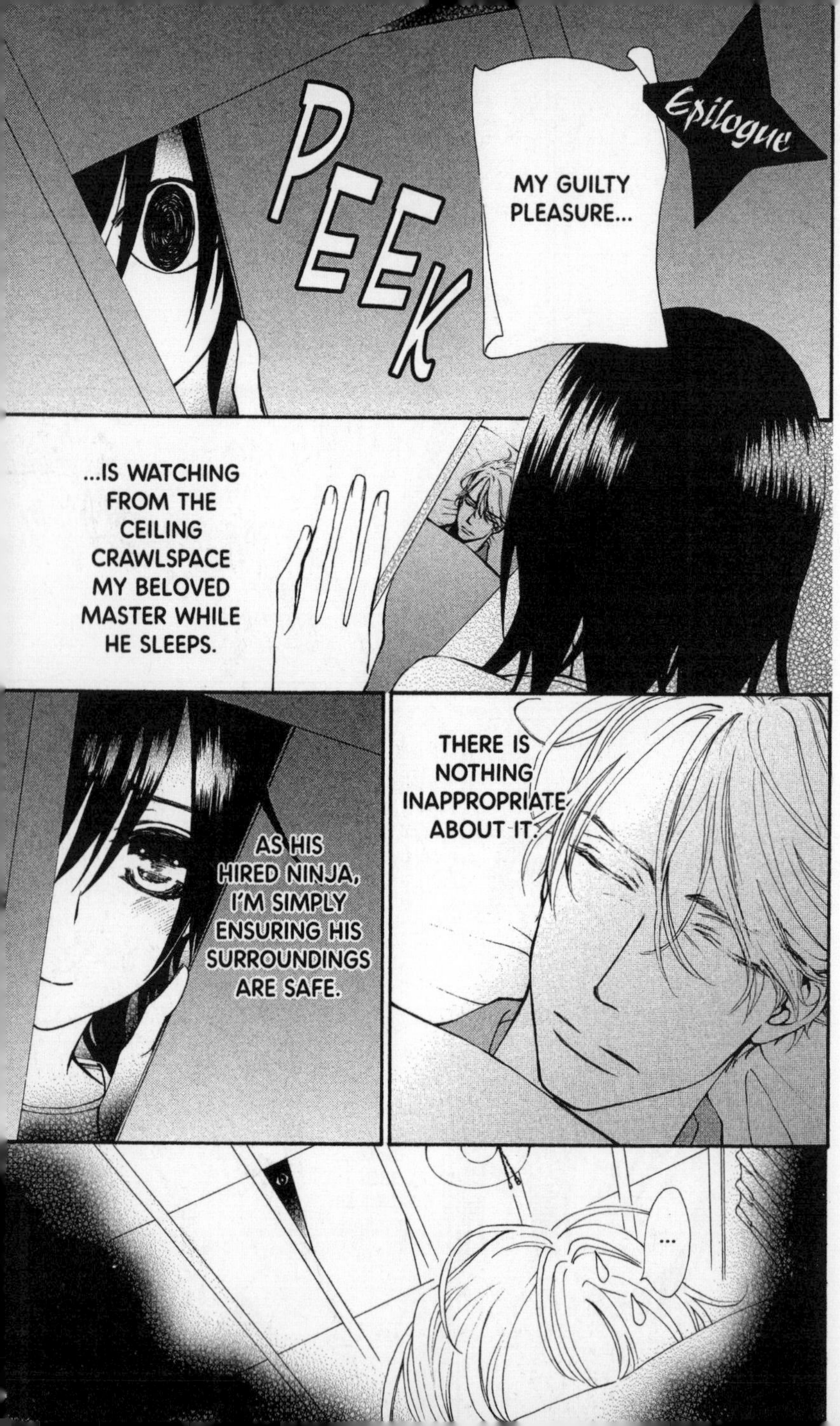
Epilogue
MY GUILTY PLEASURE...
PEEK
...IS WATCHING FROM THE CEILING CRAWLSPACE MY BELOVED MASTER WHILE HE SLEEPS.
THERE IS NOTHING INAPPROPRIATE ABOUT IT.
AS HIS HIRED NINJA, I'M SIMPLY ENSURING HIS SURROUNDINGS ARE SAFE.
...

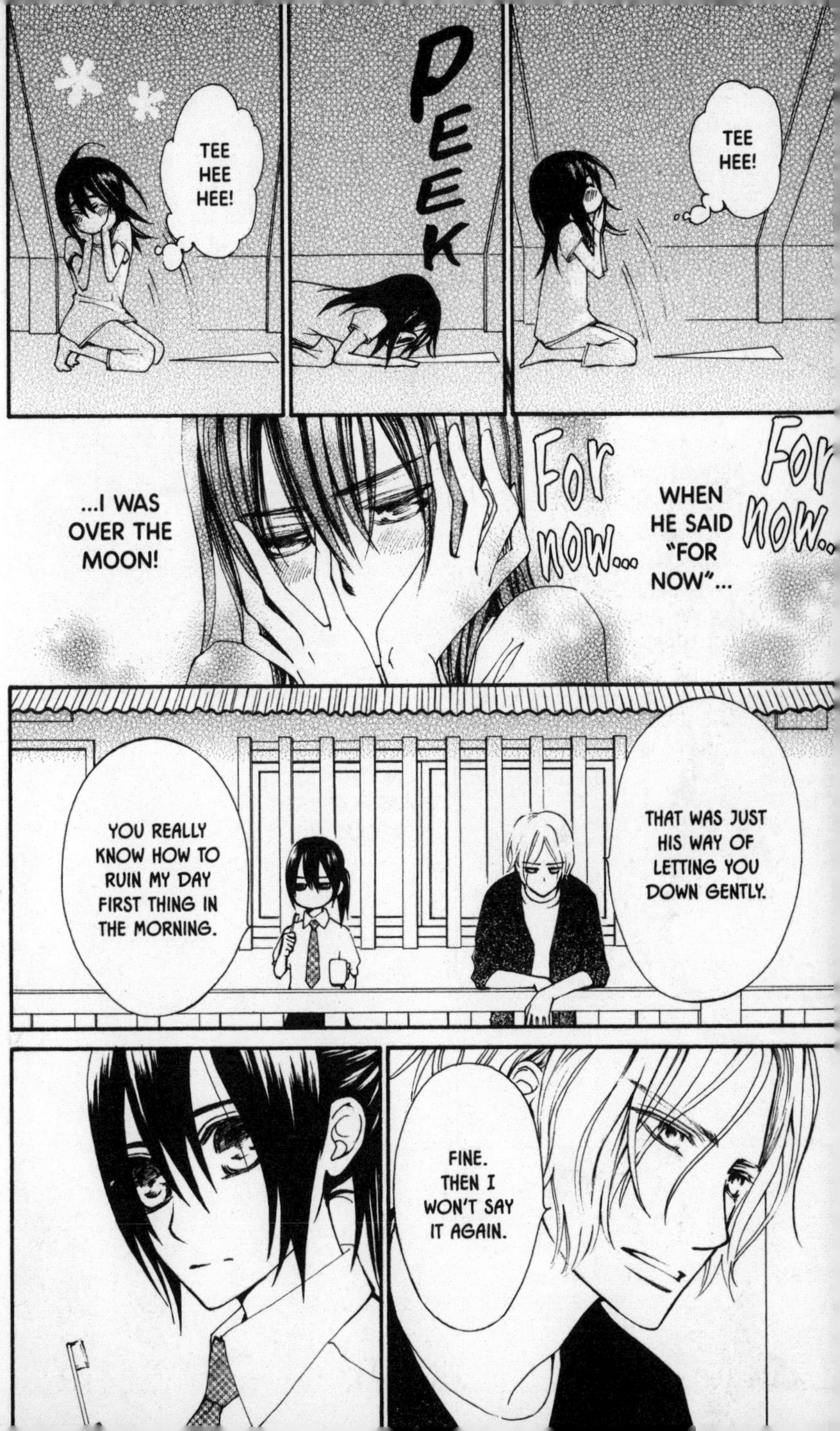
TEE HEE!
PEEK
TEE HEE HEE!
For now...
WHEN HE SAID "FOR NOW"...
For now...
...I WAS OVER THE MOON!
THAT WAS JUST HIS WAY OF LETTING YOU DOWN GENTLY.
YOU REALLY KNOW HOW TO RUIN MY DAY FIRST THING IN THE MORNING.
FINE. THEN I WON'T SAY IT AGAIN.

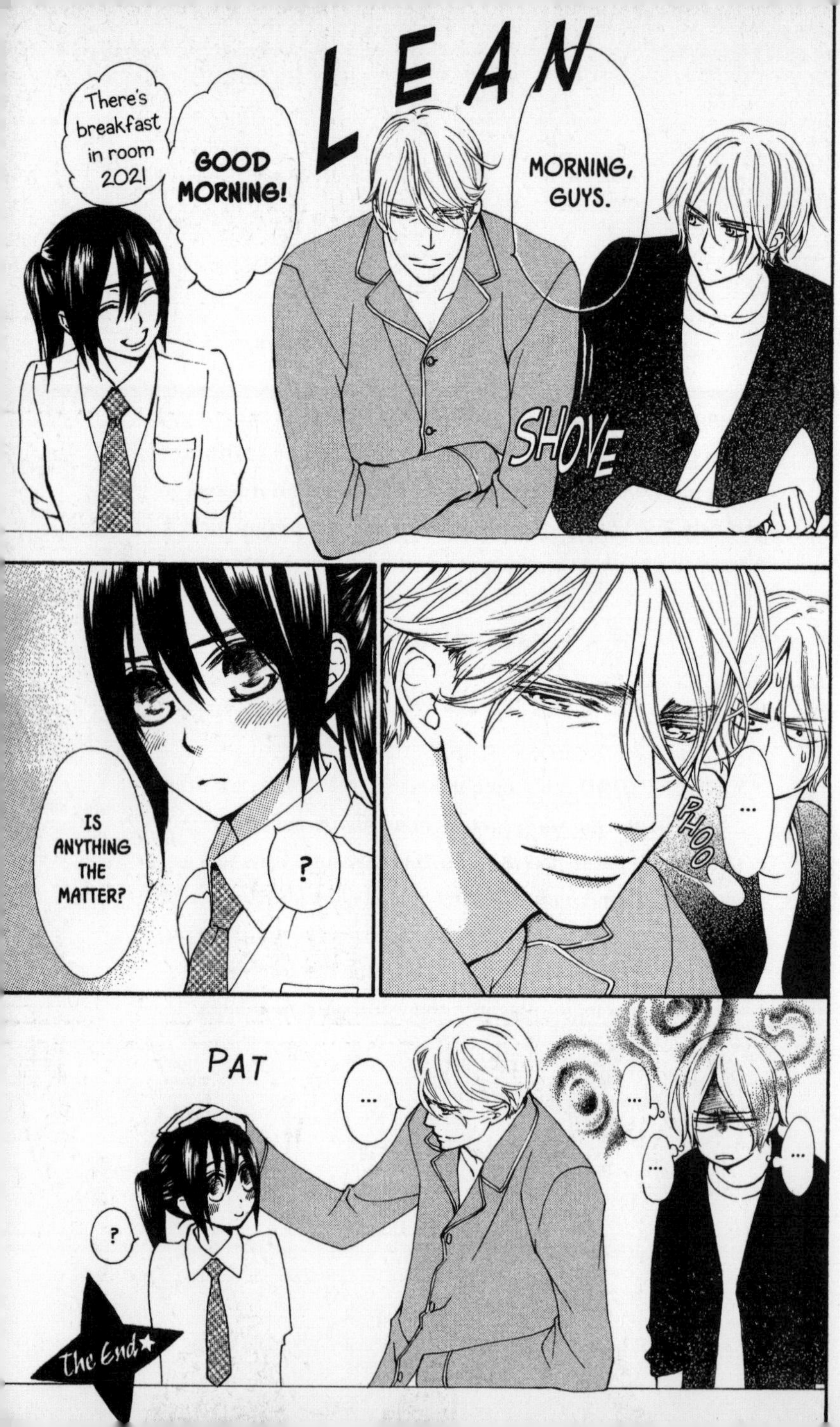
MORNING, GUYS.
LEAN
GOOD MORNING!
There's breakfast in room 2021
SHOVE
...
PHOO
?
IS ANYTHING THE MATTER?
...
...
...
...
PAT
?
The End★

# ST

## You may be reading the wrong way!

In keeping with the original Japanese comic format, this book reads from right to left—so action, sound effects and word balloons are completely reversed to preserve the orientation of the original artwork.

Check out the diagram shown here to get the hang of things, and then turn to the other side of the book to get started!

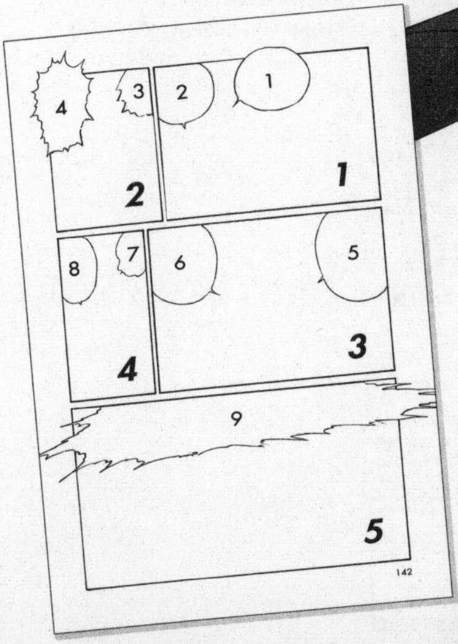
1
2
3
4
1
2
5
6
7
8
3
4
9
5
142

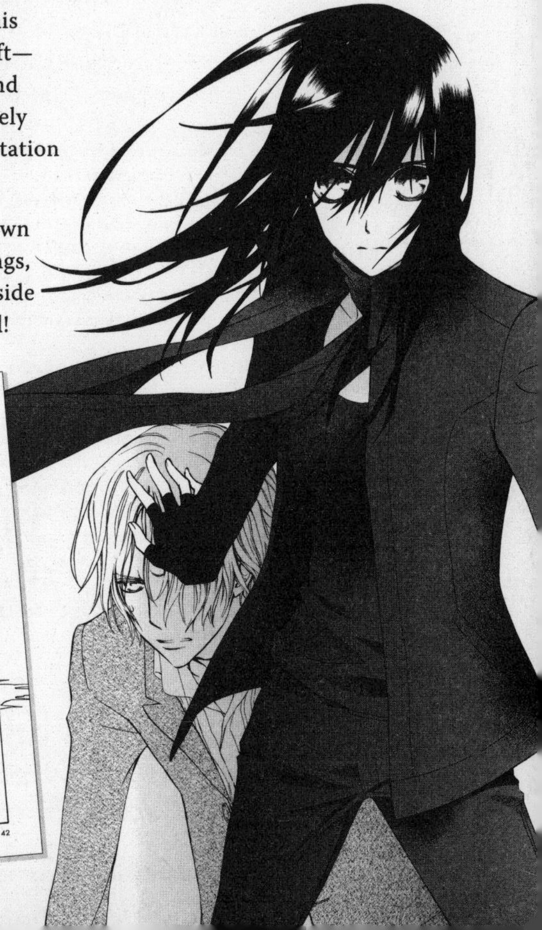